themelios

DESCRIPTION

Themelios is an international, evangelical, peer-reviewed theological journal that expounds and defends the historic Christian faith. Its primary audience is theological students and pastors, though scholars read it as well. Themelios began in 1975 and was operated by RTSF/UCCF in the UK, and it became a digital journal operated by The Gospel Coalition in 2008. The editorial team draws participants from across the globe as editors, essayists, and reviewers. *Themelios* is published three times a year online at The Gospel Coalition website in PDF and HTML, and may be purchased in digital format with Logos Bible Software and in print with Wipf and Stock. *Themelios* is copyrighted by The Gospel Coalition. Readers are free to use it and circulate it in digital form without further permission, but they must acknowledge the source and may not change the content.

EDITORS

General Editor: Brian Tabb
Bethlehem College & Seminary
720 13th Avenue South
Minneapolis, MN 55415, USA
brian.tabb@thegospelcoalition.org

Contributing Editor: D. A. Carson
Trinity Evangelical Divinity School
2065 Half Day Road
Deerfield, IL 60015, USA
themelios@thegospelcoalition.org

Contributing Editor: Daniel Strange
Crosslands Forum
MEA House, Ellison Place
Newcastle-upon-Tyne NE1 8XS UK
dan.strange@crosslands.training

Administrator: Andy Naselli
Bethlehem College & Seminary
720 13th Avenue South
Minneapolis, MN 55415, USA
themelios@thegospelcoalition.org

BOOK REVIEW EDITORS

Old Testament: Peter Lau
OMF International
18-20 Oxford St
Epping, NSW 1710, Australia
peter.lau@thegospelcoalition.org

New Testament: David Starling
Morling College
120 Herring Road
Macquarie Park, NSW 2113, Australia
david.starling@thegospelcoalition.org

History and Historical Theology:
Geoff Chang
Midwestern Baptist Theological Seminary
5001 N Oak Trafficway
Kansas City, MO 64118
geoff.chang@thegospelcoalition.org

Systematic Theology: Julián Gutiérrez
United Church of Bogotá
Carrera 4 # 69-06
Bogotá D.C., Colombia
julian.gutierrez@thegospelcoalition.org

Ethics and Pastoralia: Rob Smith
Sydney Missionary & Bible College
43 Badminton Road
Croydon, NSW 2132, Australia
rob.smith@thegospelcoalition.org

Mission and Culture:
Matthew Bennett
Cedarville University
251 N. Main St.
Cedarville, OH 45314 USA
matt.bennett@thegospelcoalition.org

EDITORIAL BOARD

Gerald Bray, *Beeson Divinity School*; Hassell Bullock, *Wheaton College*; David Garner, *Westminster Seminary*; Benjamin Gladd, *Reformed Theological Seminary*; Paul Helseth, *University of Northwestern, St. Paul*; Paul House, *Beeson Divinity School*; Andreas Köstenberger, *Midwestern Baptist Theological Seminary*; Hans Madueme, *Covenant College*; Ken Magnuson, *The Evangelical Theological Society*; Ken Stewart, *Covenant College*; Sam Storms, *Bridgeway Church*; Mark D. Thompson, *Moore Theological College*; Paul Williamson, *Moore Theological College*; Mary Willson, *Second Presbyterian Church*; Stephen Witmer, *Pepperell Christian Fellowship*; Robert Yarbrough, *Covenant Seminary*.

ARTICLES

Themelios typically publishes articles that are 4,000 to 9,000 words (including footnotes). Prospective contributors should submit articles by email to the managing editor in Microsoft Word (.doc or .docx) or Rich Text Format (.rtf). Submissions should not include the author's name or institutional affiliation for blind peer-review. Articles should use clear, concise English and should consistently adopt either UK or USA spelling and punctuation conventions. Special characters (such as Greek and Hebrew) require a Unicode font. Abbreviations and bibliographic references should conform to *The SBL Handbook of Style* (2nd ed.), supplemented by *The Chicago Manual of Style* (17th ed.). For examples of the the journal's style, consult the most recent issues and the contributor guidelines.

REVIEWS

The book review editors generally select individuals for book reviews, but potential reviewers may contact them about reviewing specific books. As part of arranging book reviews, the book review editors will supply book review guidelines to reviewers.

Printed by Wipf and Stock Publishers, 199 W. 8th Ave., Eugene, OR 97401. www.wipfandstock.com. ISBN:

EDITORIAL

The Pastor as Biblical Theologian

— Brian J. Tabb —

Brian Tabb is academic dean and professor of biblical studies at Bethlehem College & Seminary in Minneapolis and general editor of Themelios.

"For I did not shrink from declaring to you the whole counsel of God." (Acts 20:27)[1]

I've heard pastors say many times in the past few years, "I never had a class on *this* in seminary."[2] Pastors and churches have adapted to the ever-changing public health crisis of COVID-19. We have weathered significant political divisions and social unrest—particularly here in the Twin Cities. We have also faced the difficult task of discipling church members who are being constantly formed by social media exposure. Who is sufficient for these things?

In recent years, there have been calls for local church pastors to promote and produce careful theological reflection (see, for example, the work of the Center for Pastor Theologians). This column considers the pastor's vocation as a biblical theologian. My thesis is that careful, Christ-centered biblical theology offers pastors rich resources for teaching and shepherding the people of God in our fraught, fractured, and fearful world.

I'll begin with some preliminary definitions of "pastor" and "biblical theology," offer a sketch of "the pastor as biblical theologian," and conclude with three proposals.

1. Who Is a Pastor?

I recognize that for many *Themelios* readers, it may seem rather unnecessary to spend precious time defining the term "pastor," but here we go. By *pastor*, I mean a spiritually mature man who teaches, oversees, and shepherds a local congregation of believers. The NT uses various complementary terms to refer to the same church office: elders (Acts 14:23; 1 Tim 5:17; Tit 1:5), overseers (Acts 20:28; Phil 1:1; 1 Tim 3:1–2), leaders (Heb 13:7, 17, 24), and pastors and teachers (Eph 4:11).[3] Pastors may be paid church employees or volunteers. They may be called pastors, elders, ministers, or rectors, depending on their church tradition. They may preach regularly or rarely. They may have general ministerial responsibilities in a smaller church or specialized duties in a larger congregation (senior pastor, executive pastor, pastor for small groups, etc.). Regardless, I understand "pastors" to be godly, faithful men who are called by a

---

[1] Unless otherwise noted, Scripture citations come from the ESV.

[2] For thoughtful reflections along these lines, see Collin Hansen and Jeff Robinson Sr., eds., *15 Things Seminary Couldn't Teach Me* (Wheaton, IL: Crossway, 2018).

[3] For further discussion and analysis, see Benjamin L. Merkle, *40 Questions about Elders and Deacons* (Grand Rapids: Kregel, 2008), 61–100.

local church to teach God's word and exercise spiritual oversight for the spiritual good of the saints in their care. Their lives reflect the character qualifications in 1 Timothy 3 and Titus 1. As Bobby Jamieson writes, "Elders walk in the ways of Christ, instruct Christ's people in those ways, and exhort others to follow."[4]

2. What Is Biblical Theology?

Now for our second definition: *biblical theology*. Specialists disagree about *what* biblical theology is and *how* to pursue it.[5] By "biblical theology," I mean more than just theology that is *biblical* rather than *unbiblical*. I have in mind the discipline of biblical theology, which is distinct from yet complementary to systematic theology or dogmatics. While biblical theology and systematics draw upon the canonical Scriptures as their ultimate authority, these disciplines are organized differently and employ their own grammars.[6] Systematic theology is a synthesizing discipline that logically orders key doctrines following a redemptive-historical or creedal arrangement.[7] Systematics texts often begin with some combination of the doctrine of the Triune God, the doctrine of revelation, and a discussion of how we know God.[8] Biblical theology is typically organized around the unfolding storyline of the biblical canon,[9] moving from creation in Genesis 1 to the new creation and consummation of history in Revelation 22.

For the purposes of this column let's start with two definitions of biblical theology that complement each other yet approach the question in rather different ways. First, Jason DeRouchie, Oren Martin, and Andy Naselli propose the following definition:

> Biblical theology is a way of analyzing and synthesizing the Bible that makes organic, salvation-historical connections with the whole canon on its own terms, especially regarding how the Old and New Testaments progress, integrate, and climax in Christ.[10]

---

[4] Bobby Jamieson, *The Path to Being a Pastor: A Guide for the Aspiring*, 9Marks (Wheaton, IL: Crossway, 2021), 51.

[5] See the exchange between Gerald Bray and Thomas R. Schreiner in *Themelios* 39 (2014): 9–28, as well as the taxonomy of approaches in Edward Klink, III and Darian R. Lockett, *Understanding Biblical Theology: A Comparison of Theory and Practice* (Grand Rapids: Zondervan, 2012). A thorough overview of the discipline is provided by Eckhard J. Schnabel, "Biblical Theology from a New Testament Perspective," *JETS* 62 (2019): 225–49.

[6] See, for example, D. A. Carson, "Systematic Theology and Biblical Theology," in *New Dictionary of Biblical Theology*, ed. T. Desmond Alexander and Brian S. Rosner (Downers Grove, IL: InterVarsity Press, 2000), 89–104.

[7] Michael. Allen, "Systematic Theology and Biblical Theology—Part Two," *Journal of Reformed Theology* 14 (2020): 356.

[8] Consider the approach of two recently published volumes. Christopher W. Morgan and Robert A. Peterson's *Christian Theology: The Biblical Story and Our Faith* (Nashville: Broadman & Holman, 2020) opens with chapters on (1) Knowing God, (2) God's Revelation, (3) God the Trinity, and (4) God's Attributes and Works. Letham's *Systematic Theology* (Wheaton, IL: Crossway, 2019) addresses the Triune God in part 1, the Word of God in part 2, and the Works of God in part 3.

[9] Cf. Thomas R. Schreiner, *The King in His Beauty: A Biblical Theology of the Old and New Testaments* (Grand Rapids: Baker, 2013), xii.

[10] Jason S. DeRouchie, Oren R. Martin, and Andrew David Naselli, *40 Questions about Biblical Theology*, 40 Questions (Grand Rapids: Kregel, 2020), 20.

This definition recognizes that we should grapple with the diversity of genres and historical circumstances of the Scriptures while stressing their fundamental unity and coherence in an unfolding narrative of redemption with Christ at the center.

Second, James Hamilton calls biblical theology "the attempt to understand and embrace the interpretive perspective of the biblical authors."[11] In other words, biblical theology entails sharing the apostles' assumptions and presuppositions about the Scriptures and following their hermeneutical lead.

3. What Does a Pastor Do as a Biblical Theologian?

So, having explained what I mean by "pastor" and "biblical theology," let's consider *the pastor as biblical theologian*. Peter Leithart, in a learned and eclectic essay on this topic, calls for the "development of a biblical theology from the church for the church."[12] Leithart insists that "ecclesial theology must orient its hermeneutics towards homiletics" in the context of the church's liturgy, which is about as close as he comes to a summary of pastoral biblical theology.[13] I commend his call for pastors to teach biblical texts "to equip the people of God for the work of ministry and for the mission of God."[14] But I disagree with Leithart's claims that preachers must incorporate "Christological allegory and tropological exhortation" and that "detached from eucharistic liturgy, preaching is at sea."[15]

I understand the pastor-biblical theologian to be a godly man called by the church whose teaching and shepherding ministry is marked by careful, Christ-centered exposition of the whole Bible to edify the people of God. Let's unpack this definition in four steps.

3.1. Carefully Expound God's Word

First, the pastor-biblical theologian *carefully* expounds God's word—whenever possible in the original languages.[16] He assiduously attends to the details of a given biblical text—its genre, syntax, choice of words, flow of thought, literary context, etc.—while reading each part of Scripture in light of the whole canon.[17] He cares what the biblical text actually says, not just what commentators say about the text. He is also aware of how a given text relates to earlier and later biblical texts, regularly looking up cross-references in the margins of his Study Bible and NA28 Greek New Testament and evaluating

---

[11] James M. Hamilton, Jr., *Typology: Understanding the Bible's Promise-Shaped Patterns; How Old Testament Expectations Are Fulfilled in Christ* (Grand Rapids Zondervan, 2022), 30; cf. James M. Hamilton, *What Is Biblical Theology? A Guide to the Bible's Story, Symbolism, and Patterns* (Wheaton, IL: Crossway, 2013), 15–16.

[12] Peter J. Leithart, "The Pastor Theologian as Biblical Theologian: From the Church for the Church," in *Becoming a Pastor Theologian: New Possibilities for Church Leadership*, ed. Todd Wilson and Gerald Hiestand (Downers Grove, IL: InterVarsity Press, 2016), 7.

[13] Leithart, "The Pastor Theologian as Biblical Theologian," 16, 19.

[14] Leithart, "The Pastor Theologian as Biblical Theologian," 16.

[15] Leithart, "The Pastor Theologian as Biblical Theologian," 16, 21.

[16] See Jason S. DeRouchie, "The Profit of Employing the Biblical Languages: Scriptural and Historical Reflections," *Themelios* 37 (2012): 32–50.

[17] Cf. James M. Hamilton, Jr., "Biblical Theology and Preaching," in *Text-Driven Preaching: God's Word at the Heart of Every Sermon*, ed. Daniel L. Akin, et al. (Nashville: B&H Academic, 2010), 198.

potential allusions and parallels.[18] He is willing to invest the time needed in the study to understand the God-breathed text that he "may be thoroughly equipped for every good work" (2 Tim 3:17 NIV).

3.2. Be Thoroughly Christ-Centered

Second, the pastor-biblical theologian's ministry of the word is thoroughly *Christ-centered*. He reflects the interpretive perspective of the risen Lord Jesus, who explains "in all the Scriptures the things concerning himself" (Luke 24:27). In Luke 24, Jesus summarizes the Bible's central *message* concerning the Messiah's suffering, resurrection, and mission among all nations (vv. 44–47), and he offers a hermeneutical *model* for his disciples.[19] Thus, Peter appeals to the prophets and Psalms to demonstrate that everyone who calls on the name of the crucified and risen Lord Jesus shall be saved (Acts 2:21–36). Paul reasons from the Scriptures with those in the synagogue, "explaining and proving that it was necessary for the Christ to suffer and to rise from the dead" (17:2–3). Later Paul declares "nothing but what the prophets and Moses said would come to pass: that the Christ must suffer and that, by being the first to rise from the dead, he would proclaim light both to our people and to the Gentiles" (26:22–23). The pastor-biblical theologian likewise explains how the promises and patterns of the Scriptures progress, integrate, and culminate in the Lord Jesus. He shows how Christ is the last Adam (1 Cor 15:45), the prophet like Moses (Acts 3:22), the great high priest (Heb 7:26–28), the messianic king (Luke 1:32–33), the incarnate Word (John 1:14), the better temple (John 2:21), the true Israel (Matt 2:15), the suffering servant (Acts 8:32–35), the sacrificial lamb (1 Cor 5:7), and the coming bride groom (Matt 9:15).[20]

3.3. Be Committed to Teaching the Whole Bible

Third, as a biblical theologian the pastor is committed to expounding *the whole Bible*. If "*all Scripture* is breathed out by God and profitable" for teaching, correcting, and training God's people (2 Tim 3:16), and if "*whatever* was written in former days was written for our instruction" (Rom 15:4), then the whole counsel of God should shape the pastor's ministry from the pulpit to the living room. To be sure, "there are some things … that are hard to understand" in Paul's letters (2 Pet 3:16)—the man of lawlessness comes to mind (2 Thess 2:3)! And many preachers studying apocalyptic prophecies may say with Daniel, "my spirit within me was anxious, and the visions … alarmed me" (Dan 7:15). But God has called us to devote ourselves to *these* sacred writings, which are perfect, sure, right, pure, true, and desirable (Ps 19:7–11). Of course, there's no one-size-fits-all rule for planning sermon series, worship services, and Sunday school classes. But over the course of five, ten, twenty, or more years, church members would benefit from regular exposure to and teaching from the Old and New Testaments.

Consider, for example, Paul's exemplary exposition of the Scriptures in Acts 13. After the reading of the Law and the Prophets, Paul offers this "word of encouragement" to those gathered in the synagogue:

> The God of this people Israel chose our fathers and made the people great during their
> stay in the land of Egypt, and with uplifted arm he led them out of it. And for about

---

[18] See also the Scripture index in G. K. Beale and D. A. Carson, eds., *Commentary on the New Testament Use of the Old Testament* (Grand Rapids: Baker Academic, 2007).

[19] This summarizes the thesis of Brian J. Tabb, *After Emmaus: How the Church Fulfills the Mission of Christ* (Wheaton, IL: Crossway, 2021).

[20] For expositions of these and other "promise-shaped patterns" fulfilled by Christ, see Hamilton, *Typology*.

forty years he put up with them in the wilderness. And after destroying seven nations in the land of Canaan, he gave them their land as an inheritance. All this took about 450 years. And after that he gave them judges until Samuel the prophet. Then they asked for a king, and God gave them Saul the son of Kish, a man of the tribe of Benjamin, for forty years. And when he had removed him, he raised up David to be their king, of whom he testified and said, "I have found in David the son of Jesse a man after my heart, who will do all my will." Of this man's offspring God has brought to Israel a Savior, Jesus, as he promised. (vv. 17–23)

This sweeping scriptural summary, which strikingly parallels 2 Samuel 7, surveys about a thousand years of OT history.[21] Paul recounts God's promises to the patriarchs (Genesis), Israel's rescue from Egypt (Exodus), the wilderness wanderings (Numbers), the conquest and inheritance of the land (Joshua), the time of the judges (Judges), and the establishment of the monarchy (1–2 Samuel). He then announces that Jesus is the promised Savior descended from David (2 Sam 7:12–16; Ps 132:11). Later in this address, Paul cites texts from the Psalms and Isaiah as proofs for Christ's resurrection (vv. 33–35)[22] before closing with a warning from the prophet Habakkuk (vv. 40–41). Thus, Acts 13 illustrates powerful Christ-centered preaching from the Law, Prophets, and Psalms.

3.4. Edify the People of God

Fourth, the pastor-biblical theologian expounds the Scriptures *to edify the people of God.* We should not think of biblical theology as merely an academic discipline; biblical theology is a practical, pastoral treasure trove for the church. Christians face challenges of all sorts in this life—sickness and chronic pain, the death of loved ones, fractured relationships, financial troubles, fears about the future, pressures at work, difficulties at home, natural disasters, social unrest, wars and rumors of war, and the daunting daily call to deny ourselves and follow Christ. Many if not most of the saints are discouraged by hardships and distracted by the world, and they desperately need "the encouragement of the Scriptures" (Rom 15:4). Do your church members deal with partiality or resentment or a lack of affection for one another? Following the example of Jesus and the apostles, we could appeal to the Law: "You shall love your neighbor as yourself" (Lev 19:18; cf. Matt 19:19; Mark 12:31; Rom 13:9; Gal 5:14; Jas 2:8). Are your people enticed by sexual sin or substitute saviors? Warn them of the folly of the golden calf and the disastrous consequences of Israel's rebellions in the wilderness: "Now these things took place as examples for us, that we might not desire evil as they did" (1 Cor 10:6; cf. 10:1–13; Heb 3:7–19). Do your people need patience in times of suffering? James advises that you consider Jeremiah's ministry of tears, Job's steadfastness, and God's compassionate and merciful character as revealed to Moses (Jas 5:10–11; cf. Exod 34:6). Does your congregation struggle to believe that God hears their prayers? Remember the example of Elijah, who fervently prayed and God shut the sky for three years and six months (Jas 5:17–18; cf. 1 Kgs 17:1). Are your people experiencing unjust suffering or slander? Look to Jesus Christ, the Suffering Servant, who "also suffered for you, leaving you an example, so that you might follow in his steps" (1 Pet 2:21; cf. 2:18–25; Isa 53:4–12). What about believers who lack contentment and are tempted by the love of money? Remember God's promise to Joshua: "I will never leave you nor forsake

---

[21] See Table 5.1 in Tabb, *After Emmaus*, 129; cf. Chris Bruno, Jared Compton, and Kevin McFadden, *Biblical Theology According to the Apostles: How the Earliest Christians Told the Story of Israel*, NSBT 52 (Downers Grove, IL: InterVarsity Press, 2020), 67–80.

[22] For discussion, see Tabb, *After Emmaus*, 128–33.

you" (Heb 13:5; cf. Josh 1:5). Do the saints need encouragement to give generously and support the ministry of the church? Consider the righteous person of Psalm 112 who "has distributed freely" (2 Cor 9:9) or reflect on the Law's teaching about the unmuzzled ox and our Lord's instruction: "The laborer deserves his wages" (1 Tim 5:18; cf. Deut 25:4; Luke 10:7; 1 Cor 9:9). We could multiply examples, but my point is that careful, Christ-centered, biblical theological exposition of the God-breathed Scriptures offers rich resources for teaching, warning, and training God's people that they may abound in love, approve what is excellent, and be ready for the day of Christ (cf. Phil 1:9–11).

4. Three Proposals

So what does it look like for a pastor to edify God's people with careful, Christ-centered expositions of the whole counsel of God? In my view, the pastor as biblical theologian shares the *presuppositions* of the apostles, cultivates personal and corporate *practices* for whole-Bible intake, and embraces the glorious *purpose* of magnifying Christ in all areas of life. Presuppositions, practices, and purpose—three Ps for those readers who appreciate alliteration.

4.1. Share the Apostles' Presuppositions

First, the pastor as biblical theologian shares the apostles' *presuppositions* about the authority, unity, and fulfillment of the Scriptures. The first Christians "devoted themselves to the apostles' teaching" (Acts 2:42), which has served as the doctrinal bedrock of the church in every generation and in every place. But there is a longstanding debate about whether believers today can and should follow the apostles' presuppositions and practices as well as their conclusions.[23] Some scholars are cautious, citing the apostles' unique revelatory stance and their use of Jewish exegetical practices that were appropriate to explain the gospel for their first-century audience but not for contemporary readers. Thus, Richard Longenecker contends that "unless we are 'restorationists' in our attitude toward hermeneutics, Christians today are committed to the apostolic faith and doctrine of the NT, but not necessarily to the apostolic exegetical practices as detailed for us in the NT."[24] Others contend that following apostles' authoritative teaching entails embracing their hermeneutics and presuppositions about the unity of the Scriptures and the centrality of Christ in salvation history. Thus, G. K. Beale reasons that while we cannot replicate the biblical authors' "inspired *certainty*," their interpretive practices remain "viable … for all saints to employ today."[25]

The "task of biblical theology," according to Hamilton, is to recognize the biblical authors' "interpretive perspective" as "both *valid* and *normative*" and then embrace it for ourselves.[26] In this

---

[23] The next few sentences adapt material in Brian J. Tabb and Andrew M. King, eds., *Five Views on Christ in the Old Testament: Genre, Authorial Intent, and the Nature of Scripture*, Counterpoints (Grand Rapids: Zondervan, 2022).

[24] Richard N. Longenecker, "'Who is the Prophet Talking About?' Some Reflections on the New Testament's Use of the Old," *Themelios* 13 (1987): 8. This argument is developed further in Richard N. Longenecker, *Biblical Exegesis in the Apostolic Period*, 2nd ed. (Grand Rapids: Eerdmans, 1999), xxxiv–xxxix.

[25] G. K. Beale, *Handbook on the New Testament Use of the Old Testament: Exegesis and Interpretation* (Grand Rapids: Baker Academic, 2012), 25, emphasis original.

[26] Hamilton, *Typology*, 27–28.

regard, I find the risen Lord's climactic exposition of the Scriptures in Luke 24:44–47 to be incredibly important as a model and guide for his followers (I unpack this in *After Emmaus*).

Here are five fundamental beliefs or presuppositions that, in my view, guide how Jesus and his followers read the Bible.[27]

1. They believe the Scriptures—the Law, Prophets, and Writings—to be the holy, inspired word of God, supremely truthful and authoritative in every way. "As it is written" invokes the sacred, binding authority of the God who has spoken.

2. Jesus and the apostles presuppose that the God-breathed Scriptures reflect consistent patterns or correspondences between God's work in the past, present, and future. This is the conviction that underlies "typology," the study of people, events, or institutions (types) that correspond to and prophetically prefigure later and greater fulfillments (antitypes) within biblical history.

3. They affirm the biblical principle of corporate solidarity, in which one individual represents the many. As high priests, prophets, and kings represent the nation of Israel, the NT authors claim that Jesus the Messiah is the true representative of his people.

4. They believe that Christ's death, resurrection, ascension, and gift of the Holy Spirit ushered in "the last days" that were foretold by the prophets long ago. "In these last days he has spoken to us by his Son" (Heb 1:2), and we await Christ's return to consummate God's purposes to judge his foes, deliver his people, and restore all things. Scholars typically refer to this reality as "inaugurated eschatology."

5. The NT authors recognize Jesus as the focus and fulfillment of the Scriptures, following the Lord's own claims in texts like Luke 24:44—"Everything written *about me* in the Law of Moses and the Prophets and the Psalms must be fulfilled"—and John 5:39—"the Scriptures … bear witness *about me*." Said another way, the NT writers "all share the fundamental premise that the story of Israel culminates in the Messiah" and then "continues with the life and mission of the church."[28]

The pastor as biblical theologian embraces these apostolic convictions about the nature, unity, and fulfillment of the sacred Scriptures and models them in his word-based ministry in the pulpit, the classroom, and the living room.

4.2. Cultivate Personal and Corporate Practices for Whole-Bible Intake

This leads to my second proposal: the pastor as biblical theologian cultivates personal and corporate *practices* for whole Bible intake. Let's begin with personal practices and then move to public ministry considerations, following the example of Ezra the scribe, who "set his heart to study the Law of the LORD, and to do it and to teach his statutes and rules in Israel" (Ezra 7:10).

First, the pastor as biblical theologian should consistently, systematically, prayerfully read through the whole Bible. The blessed man of Psalm 1 delights in the instruction of the Lord and meditates on it day and night. There are numerous reading plans available to help you plan your route through

---

[27] Here I adapt material published in Tabb, *After Emmaus*, 35–36. For a complementary summary with extended explanations of the biblical authors' presuppositions, see Beale, *Handbook on the New Testament Use of the Old Testament*, 95–102.

[28] Bruno, Compton, and McFadden, *Biblical Theology According to the Apostles*, 184.

the 929 chapters of the Old Testament and 260 chapters of the New. You can read in canonical or chronological or casual order. *The Listener's Bible* narrated by Max McLean covers both testaments in just over seventy-five hours (in NIV or ESV). Romans takes under an hour to read, Jeremiah (the longest of the prophetic books) takes under four hours, while Obadiah and Jude each take about four minutes.[29] By comparison, one report estimates that the average American spent more than 1,300 hours on social media in 2020.[30] Pastors and parishioners alike would likely benefit from a renovation of our daily and weekly habits so that we might consume substantially more of the life-giving word of God and substantially reduce our time spent on Facebook and Netflix. "Let the word of Christ dwell in you richly" (Col 3:16).

Further, the pastor as biblical theologian should endeavor to study the Scriptures in their original languages. Consider these bold words from Martin Luther:

> And let us be sure of this: we will not long preserve the gospel without the languages. The languages are the sheath in which this sword of the Spirit [Eph. 6:17] is contained; they are the casket in which this jewel is enshrined; they are the vessel in which this wine is held; they are the larder in which this food is stored.[31]

I realize that I'm a professor of biblical studies addressing readers with varying situations. Many of you have attended seminary and are paid full-time pastors or academics; some are businessmen, doctors, and craftsmen who serve as lay elders or bi-vocational ministers; and others are students preparing for vocational ministry. Let me be clear: you don't need to read Greek and Hebrew to be a faithful Christian or a faithful pastor. But for those who regularly preach and teach God's word, I highly recommend gaining—and maintaining—facility in Greek and Hebrew. Reading biblical texts in the original languages moves you beyond cursory familiarity and forces you to slow down and become more deliberate in your study. Working through a sermon text in Greek or Hebrew also gives you greater clarity about its structure and style and greater precision and confidence in your interpretations. Here's what Jason DeRouchie says in his excellent article on the profit of employing the biblical languages:

> For the Christian minister who is charged to proclaim God's truth with accuracy and to preserve the gospel's purity with integrity, the biblical languages help in one's study, practice, and teaching of the Word. Properly using the languages opens doors of biblical discovery that would otherwise remain locked and provides interpreters with accountability that they would not otherwise have. The minister who knows Hebrew and Greek will not only feed himself but will also be able to gain a level of biblical discernment that will allow him to respond in an informed way to new translations, new theological perspectives, and other changing trends in Church and culture. With the languages, the interpreter's observations can be more accurate and thorough,

---

[29] "Infographic: You Have More Time for Bible Reading than You Think," *Crossway*, 19 November 2018, https://www.crossway.org/articles/infographic-you-can-read-more-of-the-bible-than-you-think/.

[30] Peter Suciu, "Americans Spent on Average more than 1,300 Hours on Social Media Last Year," *Forbes*, 24 June 2021, https://tinyurl.com/ym56awje.

[31] Martin Luther, "To the Councilmen of All Cities in Germany That They Establish and Maintain Christian Schools (1524)," in *Martin Luther's Basic Theological Writings*, ed. William R. Russell and Timothy F. Lull, 3rd ed. (Minneapolis: Fortress, 2012), 463.

understanding more clear, evaluation more fair, feelings more aligned with truth, application more wise and helpful, and expression more compelling.[32]

So pick up a reader's edition of the Tyndale House *Greek New Testament*, open up your Logos Bible Software, and experience the joy of studying the Scriptures in the original languages. For practical strategies and additional motivation for acquiring and maintaining facility in the languages, consider reading helpful resources like *Greek for Life* and *Hebrew for Life*.[33]

Third, the pastor as biblical theologian should make a practice of reading serious works of biblical theology. We are living in something of a golden age of biblical theology. There are multiple well-regarded series of books addressing various biblical theological themes, such as New Studies in Biblical Theology (IVP Academic, edited by D. A. Carson), Essential Studies in Biblical Theology (IVP Academic, edited by Benjamin L. Gladd), Short Studies in Biblical Theology (Crossway, edited by Dane Ortlund and Miles Van Pelt), and Biblical Theology for Life (Zondervan, edited by Jonathan Lunde). There are numerous reference works available, such as the *NIV Biblical Theology Study Bible* and *New Dictionary of Biblical Theology*.[34] Well-known scholars have published massive whole-Bible theologies,[35] and there are multiple popular-level entrees into biblical theology for non-specialists and even children, such as Kevin DeYoung's *The Biggest Story*.[36] I realize that pastors have sermons to prepare, couples to counsel, programs to plan, and ministry crises to address. But I commend carving out regular time to read books that offer fresh insights and compelling biblical-theological expositions that will edify your own faith and enrich your own teaching.

Moving from personal habits to public ministry, pastors as biblical theologians should endeavor to preach and teach the whole counsel of God. Mark Dever and Greg Gilbert write, "We as preachers are called to preach the whole Bible to our people. If people sit under our preaching for any length of time, they should eventually hear us preach from a good cross-section of the entire Bible."[37] There are various ways to faithfully expound the whole counsel of God, and I offer three possibilities. First, Dever and Gilbert suggest planning a preaching schedule that exposes the congregation to the major genres and sections of the OT and NT: a book of Law, then one of the Gospels, an OT historical book, a NT letter, some psalms, etc.[38] Second, pastors may teach a class or devote a sermon series to the storyline of Scripture. D. A. Carson's *The God Who Is There* or Chris Bruno's *The Whole Story of the Bible in 16 Verses* could serve as helpful guides for such an effort.[39] Third, pastors may preach or teach through

---

[32] DeRouchie, "The Profit of Employing the Biblical Languages," 50.

[33] Benjamin L. Merkle and Robert L. Plummer, *Greek for Life: Strategies for Learning, Retaining, and Using New Testament Greek in Ministry* (Grand Rapids: Baker Academic, 2017); Adam J. Howell, Benjamin L. Merkle, and Robert L. Plummer, *Hebrew for Life: Strategies for Learning, Retaining, and Reviving Biblical Hebrew* (Grand Rapids: Baker Academic, 2020).

[34] D. A. Carson, ed., *NIV Biblical Theology Study Bible* (Grand Rapids: Zondervan, 2018); T. Desmond Alexander and Brian S. Rosner, eds., *New Dictionary of Biblical Theology* (Downers Grove, IL: InterVarsity Press, 2000).

[35] For example, Schreiner, *The King in His Beauty*.

[36] Kevin DeYoung, *The Biggest Story: How the Snake Crusher Brings Us Back to the Garden* (Wheaton, IL: Crossway, 2015).

[37] Mark Dever and Greg Gilbert, *Preach: Theology Meets Practice* (Wheaton, IL: Crossway, 2012), 68.

[38] Dever and Gilbert, *Preach*, 69.

[39] D. A. Carson, *The God Who Is There: Finding Your Place in God's Story* (Grand Rapids: Baker Books, 2010); Chris Bruno, *The Whole Message of the Bible in 16 Verses*, Wheaton, IL (Crossway: 2015).

a NT book like Hebrews as a sort of biblical-theological primer for the congregation. Hebrews 13:22 identifies the book as "a word of exhortation," the same phrase used in Acts 13:15 for a sermon to a gathered congregation. Hebrews begins by crisply comparing God's revelation in former times "by the prophets" with his message to us "in these last days … by his Son" (1:1–2). The remainder of the first chapter marshals seven OT citations to demonstrate the Son's superiority. And chapter 11 offers the NT's most extensive summary of the OT story.[40] Dennis Johnson with good reason calls Hebrews "an apostolic preaching paradigm."[41]

4.3. Embrace the Glorious Purpose to Magnify Christ

Thus far, I've argued that the pastor as biblical theologian embraces the apostles' convictions about the Scriptures' authority, unity, and fulfillment in Christ and that he cultivates personal and corporate habits to study and teach the whole counsel of God. My final appeal is that ministers make it their ambition to magnify Jesus Christ and present their church members mature in Christ. Paul sums up his ministry outlook this way in Colossians 1:28: "Him we proclaim, warning everyone and teaching everyone with all wisdom, that we may present everyone mature in Christ." In the context, he explains that God has revealed a mystery previously hidden: "Christ in you, the hope of glory" (Χριστὸς ἐν ὑμῖν, ἡ ἐλπὶς τῆς δόξης)—note that "you" (ὑμῖν) refers particularly to Gentile believers who were previously God's enemies before Christ's saving intervention (1:27; cf. 1:21–22). The apostle labors to present believers "mature" or "complete" (τέλειος), reaching their τέλος in Christ. His friend Epaphras likewise struggles in prayer "that you may stand mature [τέλειοι] and fully assured in all the will of God" (4:12). Their aims align with Christ's own saving purpose: "in order to present you holy and blameless and above reproach before him, if indeed you continue in the faith, stable and steadfast, not shifting from the hope of the gospel that you heard (1:22–23).

Our email inboxes, calendars, and to-do lists are chock-full of requests and tasks calling for our immediate attention. We're also distracted by social media, sports, political commentary, and the daily news cycle. As a result, we rarely fixate on the interrelated ultimate goals that consumed the apostle: the glory of Jesus and the maturity of his people. A healthy dose of biblical theology can guide pastors— and church members—to focus our efforts on the apostles' priorities of magnifying the Lord Jesus and building up his people unto maturity. A strong grasp of biblical theology also guards pastors against proof-texting and moralistic preaching.[42] For example, rather than calling the church to be courageous like David the giant slayer, we see in 1 Samuel 17 a picture of Yahweh's saving strength alongside his servant's weakness and zeal for God's glory (see 17:45, 47).[43] We see an outworking of the Lord's commitment to break the bows of the mighty, to lift up the needy, to "give strength to his king and exalt the horn of his anointed," just as Hannah declares (2:10; cf. 2:4, 8) and just as God does in the fullness of time when he sends David's greater son.

---

[40] See Bruno, Compton, and McFadden, *Biblical Theology According to the Apostles*, 149–82.

[41] Dennis E. Johnson, *Him We Proclaim: Preaching Christ from All the Scriptures* (Phillipsburg, NJ: P&R Publishing, 2007), ch. 6.

[42] Nick Roark and Robert Cline, *Biblical Theology: How the Church Faithfully Teaches the Gospel*, 9Marks (Wheaton, IL: Crossway, 2018), 75.

[43] Cf. Dale Ralph Davis, *1 Samuel: Looking on the Heart*, Focus on the Bible (Ross-Shire, UK: Christian Focus, 2000), 189.

5. Conclusion

To sum up, the pastor as biblical theologian is a godly man called by the church whose ministry is marked by careful, Christ-centered exposition of the whole Bible to edify the people of God. The pastor as biblical theologian shares the *presuppositions* of the apostles, cultivates personal and corporate *practices* for whole Bible intake, and embraces the glorious *purpose* of magnifying Christ in all areas of life. Such a pastor may or may not hold advanced degrees and write books. He may or may not have a public platform to speak presciently into the pressing and perplexing cultural issues of the day. But he is saturated in the Scriptures and able to teach the saints how to read their Bibles in a way that exalts Jesus. He offers needed encouragement and wisdom so that God's people can remain firm and established, not wavering from the hope of the gospel.

STRANGE TIMES

Dr Strange in the Multiperspectival Paradox

— Daniel Strange —

Daniel Strange is director of Crosslands Forum, a centre for cultural engagement and missional innovation, and contributing editor of Themelios.

Let's play a game of 'Guess Who?' Now that we're out and about again, it's been my privilege in the last few months to find myself in the company of two statesmen of the conservative evangelical theological world who have made a formative impression in my thinking over the years, but whom previously I had never met in person. These senior scholars were educated at both Harvard and Cambridge (where they overlapped) before long teaching stints in seminaries and schools. Both have been prolific in their written output, outputs which have included forays into other theological disciplines (including New Testament, Hermeneutics, and Systematic Theology), and what would be thought of as 'non-theological' subjects. Both have espoused and modelled, to my mind at least, what could be called the highest view of a 'high view' of biblical authority and *sola Scriptura*. Both have been much lauded and both have faced much criticism. Although both have 'campaigned' on (at least) one issue together, interestingly it is precisely what I have taken as *contrasting* features of their contributions that form an interestingly complex but ultimately complementarity juxtaposition when it comes to our theology, theological posture, and theological education. Any ideas to whom I am referring?

Vern Poythress's method of *Symphonic Theology* (and with John Frame also known as 'multiperspectivalism') has always given me a gut feeling of 'rightness' about it, and one that I have been brushed by.[1] I say 'brushed' because I know I haven't been as rigorous or methodological as I might have been in deploying it consciously (of which more anon). Although it is an entire theological 'method' with a very large edifice made up of theological, philosophical, and linguistic theory lying under its surface, the tip of the multiperspectival iceberg is pretty easy to see. Moreover, one does not have to be Reformed (let alone a devotee of apologist Cornelius Van Til, linguist Kenneth Pike, or even novelist Dorothy L. Sayers!),[2] to sympathize broadly with its thrust and posture. Multiperspectivalism is an application of the confessional cornerstone of a Christian worldview—the Creator-creature distinction.

---

[1] See Vern S. Poythress, *Symphonic Theology: The Validity of Multiple Perspectives in Theology* (Phillipsburg, NJ: P&R Publishing, 1987); Vern S. Poythress, 'Multiperspectivalism and the Reformed Faith', in *Speaking the Truth in Love: The Theology of John M. Frame*, ed. John J. Hughes (Phillipsburg, NJ: P&R Publishing, 2009), 173–200; John Frame, 'A Primer on Perspectivalism', *Frame-Poythress*, 6 June 2012, https://frame-poythress.org/a-primer-on-perspectivalism-revised-2008/. For a critique of multiperspectivalism as a method see Mark W. Karlberg, 'On the Theological Correlations of Divine and Human Language: A Review Article', *JETS* 32 (1989): 99–105.

[2] See Poythress, 'Multiperspectivalism and the Reformed Faith', 184.

Human beings are not the sovereign personal absolute Creator God but are limited, finite, and sinful creatures. God's knowledge is archetypal, our knowledge is always ectypal. Therefore, *and always under the authority of Scripture*, which itself evidences multiperspectival diversity in its unity,[3] the more perspectives we take time to understand and appreciate, the richer our understanding of the truth will be and the less prone we will be to misunderstanding and error. Limited creatures with limited perspective need more perspectives in order to better live and serve in a world created by the omniperspectival God. Multiperspectivalism recognises my limitations not as an inherent evil or problem, but as a God-given feature of my identity, but a feature that can and does sinfully strives for domination and mastery through reduction: by either making all perspectives subservient to my own, or reducing the complexity of the world to my small window on it.

As Don Carson writes, and referencing *Symphonic Theology* explicitly, 'not all of God's truth is vouchsafed to one particular interpretive community—and the result will be that we will be eager to learn from one another, to correct and to be corrected by one another, provided only that there is a principled submission to God's gracious self-disclosure in Christ and in the Scriptures. The truth may be one, but it sounds less like a single wavering note than like a symphony.'[4]

The implications for the symphonic theological method can be outlined for different disciplines including biblical studies, biblical theology, and systematics, together with my own 'areas' of interest, culture, religion, missiology, and apologetics. At its best a multiperspectival approach fosters faithful contextualisation and indigeneity, and a posture of patience and charity in listening to those who are different from us. It takes seriously the richness of language and our tendency to overstate and/or oversimplify. Multiperspectivalism can stimulate a curiosity as we learn from one another, and a desire for evangelical collaboration recognising its necessity in dealing with cultural complexity. Apologetically, multiperspectivalism gives us a point of contact and pre-emptive attack with unbelief and idolatrous ideological perspectives in recognising that error is always parasitic on the truth. Ironically, I would contend that it is precisely multiperspectivalism cut loose and untethered from biblical authority, and

---

[3] For example, in the sixteenth century, Martin Chemnitz speaks of the gospels displaying 'a very concordant dissonance'. Cited in Timothy Ward (who himself speaks of canonically limited polyphony), 'The Diversity and Sufficiency of Scripture', in *The Trustworthiness of God: Perspectives on the Nature of Scripture*, ed. Paul Helm and Carl R. Trueman (Grand Rapids: Eerdmans, 2002), 192.

[4] D. A. Carson, *The Gagging of God: Christianity Confronts Pluralism* (Leicester: Apollos, 1996), 552. It might be helpful to list Poythress's twelve maxims of *Symphonic Theology*, 69–92:

1. Language is not transparent to the world.
2. No term in the Bible is equal to a technical term of systematic theology.
3. Technical terms in systematic theology can almost always be defined in more than one way. Every technical term is selective in the features it includes.
4. Boundaries are fuzzy.
5. No category or system of categories gives us ultimate reality.
6. Different human writers of the Bible bring differing perspectives to bear on a given doctrine or event.
7. The differences between biblical writings by different human authors are also divine differences.
8. Any motif of the Bible can be used as the single organizing motif.
9. We use different motifs not to relativize truth but to gain truth.
10. We see what our tools enable us to see.
11. Error is parasitic on the truth.
12. In theological debates, we should pre-empt the other person's strong points.

as a result 'gone to seed' which describes the epistemological foundations, or better non-foundations of Charybdis-like cultural movements and cultural moments with which we are all trying to understand and engage with at the moment, be it various forms of 'critical theory' and 'intersectionality'. There is both opportunity as well as challenge here for biblical multiperspectivalism to both subvert and fulfil its counterfeits.

The problem—or perhaps more accurately the 'paradox'—that I have found in wanting to adopt more consciously a multiperspectival approach is that whenever I've come to the cake, I've become paralysed, knife frustratingly hovering and unable to make that first cut. If, biblically, theologically, epistemologically, one perspective always can be expanded to include another, and another, and so one, then where does one start? Indeed where does one stop? How does one teach and say something when theoretically starting from this one thing you could say everything? I'm sure this theological equivalent of the golfing 'yips' is a matter of temperament, and if I'm being honest, a matter of intellect. There is no doubt Poythress is a genius and polymath who has the mental and emotional capacity to discern, hold together, and teach multiperspectivally (and to teach multiperspectivally about multiperspectivalism!). I'm not ashamed to say that my own capacities are less.[5] That said, I do think in more haphazard and subliminal fashion I have been influenced for the good by symphonic theology. Moreover, maybe I need not beat myself up too much here. I hope he doesn't mind me sharing this anecdote, but the highlight of my time with Poythress was the little exchange when I asked a rather inane question concerning how he thought multiperspectivalism had been received over the years. Without missing a beat and with a little glint in the eye his response was something like, 'well of course, I wouldn't want everyone to embrace it would I?' As I said, genius.

Like it or not, there has always been a directness and perspicuity to Wayne Grudem's writing that I have always admired and found refreshing from what can be abstruse and even 'emperor has no clothes' pretentious pretentions of contemporary 'fashionable' theological discussion. Was it only me who chuckled when they saw that Grudem's contribution to John Frame's own *festschrift* was a chapter outlining why Frame was *wrong* in his ethical position that it is sometimes legitimate to lie?[6] I love this! Joking aside, for a young evangelical theology student in a very liberal department in the early 1990s Grudem's contribution to *Scripture and Truth* on the self-attestation of Scripture was a lifeline for many of me and I know many others in similar situations.[7] Hearing Grudem interviewed at a conference

---

[5] In personal correspondence Poythress has noted how he would respond to my paralysis alongside a general encouragement that one just needs to take the plunge and not worry. He does recognise the need pedagogically for a single main perspective and overarching theme such as the 'kingdom of God' in the Gospels, or 'union with Christ' in Pauline letters, but then also the development of multiple perspectives within that theme so there is richness of resources to draw on. As to where one stops, 'the obvious response is, one does not. Or (a second perspective, more situational) one stops when one runs out of time. If we understand that each of us is contributing to a much larger building of the church in Christian mission, then one just does one's bit, confident that God will fit it in (Eph 2:20–22; 1 Pet 2:4–6; 1 Cor 3:10–15): Wise words that we so need to hear and apply to our hearts and scholarly pretentions.

[6] See Wayne Grudem, 'Why It Is Never Right to Lie: An Example of John Frame's Influence on My Approach to Ethics', in *Speaking the Truth in Love: The Theology of John Frame*, ed. John J. Hughes (Phillipsburg, NJ: P&R Publishing, 2009), 778–801. Interestingly Poythress wrote a subsequent article siding with Grudem on the matter. See Vern S. Poythress, 'Why Lying Is Always Wrong: The Uniqueness of Verbal Deceit', *WTJ* 75 (2013): 83–95.

[7] See Wayne Grudem, 'Scripture's Self-Attestation and the Problem of Formulating a Doctrine of Scripture', in *Scripture and Truth*, ed. D. A. Carson and John D. Woodbridge (Grand Rapids: Baker Books, 1992), 19–59.

last month about his life and career was a genuinely moving experience for all those present.[8] For me it was a rare instance where I would use the word 'piety' in a positive rather than pejorative sense. At that same conference I attended, Grudem presented a seminar version of an essay he had published some years ago: 'When, Why, and for What Should We Draw New Boundaries?'[9] Listening to Grudem was a welcome reminder—and I will argue a *complement* to Poythress's multiperspectivalism—that as Christians we need to 'draw lines when drawing lines is rude'.[10]

Once again, the capacity and necessity to create boundaries is an application of the confessional cornerstone of a Christian worldview—the Creator-creature *distinction*. We image a Creator God who creates, separates, and distinguishes by ourselves placing boundaries, making distinctions and separations, and distinguishing truth from error. In terms of theological anthropology, the doctrine of the 'antithesis' is the divinely revealed distinction and ultimately eternal separation of humanity into two *and only two* groups: the seed of the serpent and seed of the women, those in Adam and those in Christ, those who are blind, those who can see, those who are dead and those who are alive, goats and sheep, the city of man and city of God.

At its best, discrimination and boundary setting are not inherently confining or destructive, but when applied according to the divine order (that is, according to a biblically defined structure and interpretation of reality), ensure beautiful, God-exalting, clarifying, and life-giving peace. Conversely it is the blurring or erasing of God-given boundaries that generate sub- and non-Christian worldviews, which evidence and perpetuate rebellion, confusion, and futility. The blurring and erasing of the Creator-creature distinction is the definition of idolatry.[11]

The New Testament writers repeatedly make distinctions and create boundaries for the building up and protection of Christ's church. It is in a pastoral rather than pedantic spirit that Paul exhorts Titus to hold firmly to the trustworthy message as it has been taught, to encourage others by sound doctrine, *and* to refute those who oppose it (Titus 1:9). The healthiness of orthodoxy is to be contrasted with gangrenous false teaching. To exhort, encourage, and refute, one needs not only an affirmation of what the trustworthy message is, but also a corollary denial of what it is not, or by implication, what it cannot be.

In the mirror image to what said of multiperspectivalism, it is distinction making and boundary setting cut loose and untethered from biblical authority which describes a Scylla-like modernistic Enlightenment positivism and what Chris Watkin calls modern western cultures damaging and violent 'congenital predisposition to think in dualisms'.[12] In a sense you call this an idolatrous mono-perspectivalism. Apologetically and as stated above, there is both opportunity as well as challenge here for biblical distinction and our distinction making to both subvert and fulfil its idolatrous counterfeits.

---

[8] It was also illuminating to hear Grudem explain the purpose and intended audience of his *Systematic Theology* which to my mind answers the guild's (unfair) criticisms of this publishing phenomenon.

[9] Wayne Grudem, 'When, Why, and for What Should We Draw New Boundaries?', in *Beyond the Bounds: Open Theism and the Undermining of Biblical Christianity*, ed. John Piper, Justin Taylor, and Paul Kjoss Helseth (Wheaton, IL: Crossway, 2003), 339–70.

[10] To quote of one of Carson's chapter titles in *Gagging of God*, 347.

[11] See Peter Jones, *One or Two: Seeing a World of Difference: Romans 1 for the Twenty-First Century* (Escondido, CA: Main Entry Editions, 2010).

[12] Christopher Watkin, 'The Third Way is Dead. Long Live the Third Way!', *The Gospel Coalition Australia*, 10 May 2022, https://au.thegospelcoalition.org/article/the-third-way-is-dead-long-live-the-third-way/.

So, we have Poythress and Grudem and my personal associations with them in terms of multiperspectivalism and boundary setting respectively.[13] I am not seeking to pit one against the other (notice I have not regarded Grudem or 'boundary setting' as a 'mono-perspectivalism') but rather *under the authority of Scripture* I see both as coming to the aid of the other as we seek to safely and biblically navigate between Charybdis and Scylla both in position and posture. A perspectival *paralysis* or 'death of a thousand qualifications' can be helped by seeing a need for *process* in coming to making decisions and judgements on boundary setting. To adapt the famous Chesterton quip, the object of expanding perspectives, as of opening the mouth, is to shut it again on something solid. Conversely, a boundary and distinction setting which might be *precipitous* might be helped by the posture of multiperspectival *patience.* As both 'drives' are held together and encounter the other, a humility might overcome a hubris, and a confidence might overcome a timidity. In this sense I am arguing that there are biblical and sub-biblical ways to be *both* a dove and a hawk.

Furthermore, and particularly relevant to a *Themelios* audience, I think the two 'drives' which I see in a Grudem and a Poythress and which I've been commending as complementary have implications for theological education particularly in a seminary setting. Let give some pointers which might act as discussion starters.

First, in our seminaries and schools we are not to be ashamed or embarrassed of having confessional boundaries which should be carefully drawn and enforced, with care and with prudence, but enforced nonetheless. As Grudem expounds in his essay, we do this because false teaching harms the church; if false teaching is not stopped, it spreads and does more damage; if false teaching is not stopped, we will waste time and energy in endless controversies rather than doing valuable kingdom work; and Jesus and the NT authors hold church leaders responsible for silencing false teaching within the church.[14] Ironically, the more boundaries are agreed and are understood, the more time and freedom there might be to explore within those boundaries rather than the need to constantly patrol them.

Second, in *Symphonic Theology*, Poythress talks of the value of expanding perspectives and stretching operations, 'fields of study and areas of life that are frequently compartmentalized in people's minds actually belong together…, '[15] and 'the boundaries that we have set up between our compartments are in some cases arbitrary and artificial.'[16] He writes:

> We can still make rough distinctions for the sake of convenience between specialists in ethics and specialists in systematic theology. If we are not alert however, the terms can all to easily mislead us into thinking that we are dealing with rigidly distinct departments…. Bible students who are inclined to compartmentalize should stretch their terms. They should use them as perspectives to cover the whole of the Bible. Then afterward they should go back to the earlier compartments and ask whether old boundaries are the only ones that are possible. They can retain old boundaries if they

---

[13] I am not claiming that Grudem is 'against' multiperspectivalism or that Poythress is 'against' boundary setting and distinction making.

[14] See Grudem, 'When, Why, and for What Should We Draw New Boundaries?', 341–48.

[15] Poythress, *Symphonic Theology*, 27.

[16] Poythress, *Symphonic Theology*, 27.

wish but should recognize that boundaries are often drawn arbitrarily at one point on a continuum.[17]

While I'm not denying that in theological education interdisciplinarity is more common now than it was, what would a more intentionally applied multiperspectivalism do to our theological curricula and to our theological faculties that might be enriching? The compartmentalisation of departments and of teaching staff within those departments still seems to persist in many of our institutions. Note, I'm not arguing for a chaotic mash and mush of disciplines but maybe a more modest proposal: a recognition within and between theological (and yes, 'non-theological disciplines') disciplines of the others existence and perspective as we come to all sit under the normative authority of God's Word. Given the principle of boundary expansion, let's have the freedom to experiment and be creative as we design our seminary curricula.[18]

Third, in terms of the students we are looking to produce in our seminaries and schools, a multiperspectival approach will have the perspectives of character formation, skills and knowledge as implied by the other and enriched by the other. Such profiles, if following biblical criteria, will include the need to learn (in terms of character, skills, and knowledge) biblical boundary setting as sound doctrine is encouraged and error is refuted.

Fourth, for all those in seminary education, and especially for those at post-graduate level who should have achieved a level of spiritual and academic maturity, there is a need for such students to be exposed to other perspectives—biblical, sub-biblical, and non-biblical. We need to do this for a number of reasons in our pedagogy, discipleship, ethics, apologetics, and mission. In terms of Poythress's symphonic maxims, we will learn here that 'error is parasitic on the truth', and that in theological debates, 'we should pre-empt the other person's strong points'. There will always be something to learn from other perspectives even if that learning, to use an Os Guinness saying, is that 'contrast is the mother of clarity'.[19] However such 'exposure' in the classroom should be conducted on certain foundations, within certain boundaries, and with a confessional 'safety net'. I bring some bitter experience to this point having studied theology and religious studies as a young evangelical in a department where there were no foundations, boundaries, or safety nets. For me, the attendant issue was not so much my faith being challenged, or the danger of it being deconstructed or destroyed, although no doubt this will a danger for some. As an aside here, in any theological education, it's one thing to worry about wrapping believers up in 'cotton-wool' or even 'hot-housing' them in echo chambers, it's another thing to be pastorally sensitive as to what we expose the spiritually young, weak, and immature to. Playing it 'safe' in theological education can be both a mark of folly, and a mark of wisdom.

Returning to my own experience, the issue was not of danger, it was that with no foundation or boundaries, positive theological formulation and construction was virtually impossible. After a while, tracing discussions back to first principles and sources of authority in *every single* lecture quickly becomes frustrating and quite tedious. You can't build on air. Moreover, in studying other sub-biblical perspectives from within confessional boundaries we will be prompted not simply to describe different

---

[17] Poythress, *Symphonic Theology*, 27–28.

[18] For example, in my previous seminary we built and taught a multi-disciplinary year-long 'mega-module' on the book of Isaiah which consisted of faculty from different departments coming to bring their disciplinary perspectives to Isaiah. Some aspects of the module worked, some aspects were a glorious failure, but over a few years we did refine the module with, in my opinion, a certain degree of success.

[19] Os Guinness, 'Relevance or the Gospel', *Church Leaders*, 13 September 2010, https://tinyurl.com/2p89ev78.

perspective after perspective, but to offer prescriptions and make decisions that we can apply to our lives and our ministries.

Finally, the trajectory of multi-perspectivalism within clear confessional boundaries must push us out of simply discussing *theological* education to consider education more broadly. I think here particularly our need for a Christ-centred, liberal arts education with the *telos,* to quote Milton, that 'the end of learning is to repair the ruins of our first parents by regaining to know God aright, and out of that knowledge to love him, to imitate him, to be like him.'[20] Goals such as 'formation', 'encyclopaedia', 'integration', and 'vocation' can be built upon and safeguarded by multiple perspectives as we fulfil our call to have dominion, exploring God's world *but through the light of God's Word.* I say this as something of a *cri de coeur* given the absence of any such institution in the UK. Craig Bartholomew has recognised this gap in a recent paper.[21] His narration of what he calls 'the unknown idea of Christian Higher Education'[22] makes for painful reading as he describes the non-neutral antichristian ideology in the UK university sector that often masquerades as 'neutrality', with all the contradiction, compartmentalization, and noetic disintegration, the results of which sound like a cacophony, not a symphony. Both Grudem and Poythress have seen the need, and been brave enough to write in different areas applying Christ's lordship to different *perspectives* of human learning with the corollary *antithetical* boundary that 'You shall have no other gods before me.' Indeed Poythress seems on his own steadily to be building an entire liberal arts curriculum, writing about 'a God-centered approach' to subjects including science, language, mathematics, logic, sociology, chance, the sovereignty of God, and history, to name just seven![23] Let's follow the example of these senior scholars and brothers in Christ as we seek to join them in building an ever richer symphonic sound that will glorify God, calling the nations to come under the authority of the Lord Jesus Christ.

P.S. Yes, I felt compelled to attempt some kind of Marvel title here—if not now, then when? And no, at the time of writing, I've not yet seen the latest Doctor Strange film.

---

[20] John Milton, 'Of Education', in *Complete Poems and Major Prose,* ed. Merritt Y. Hughes (Indianapolis: Hackett, 2003), 631. Cited in Jeffrey C. Davis and Philip G. Ryken, ed., *Liberal Arts for the Christian Life* (Wheaton, IL: Crossway, 2012), 16.

[21] Craig G. Bartholomew, 'A Jewel in the Crown of North America: Christian Higher Education', *Ethics in Conversation* 23.3 (2019).

[22] To parody, of course, George Marsden's seminal work, *The Outrageous Idea of Christian Scholarship* (New York: Oxford University Press, 1997).

[23] For example, Vern S. Poythress, *Redeeming our Thinking About History: A God-Centered Approach* (Wheaton, IL: Crossway, 2022).

Mark as the Backstory to the Gospel: Mark 1:1 as a Key to Mark's Gospel

— Peter C. Orr —

Peter Orr is lecturer in New Testament at Moore Theological College in Newtown, Australia.

****

Abstract: This article argues that the first 3 words of the Gospel of Mark: ἀρχὴ τοῦ εὐαγγελίου ["the beginning of the Gospel"] are best understood as the title of the book. Mark identifies his work as a description of the origin or backstory of the preached gospel that his readers were familiar with. The article examines what this implies for the relationship of Mark to Peter and Paul. It then explores the implications of this understanding for reading Mark.

****

New Testament writers sometimes tell us why they have written. Luke composed "an orderly account" for Theophilus so that he might "have certainty concerning the things [he had] been taught" (Luke 1:3–4).[1] Peter pens his first letter "exhorting and declaring that this is the true grace of God" and calling his readers to "stand firm in it" (1 Pet 5:12). These purpose statements help us read in line with the author's intention. When they are absent (e.g., Paul's letter to the Romans), it is more challenging to correctly orientate ourselves to the letter and not skew its purpose by pursuing our own agenda (e.g., reading Romans as if it something akin to a systematic theology rather than a letter to a church with multiple purposes).[2]

In this article I argue that Mark 1:1, while not a purpose statement for the book, is a title and similarly helps us to correctly orientate ourselves to the Gospel. There is a growing consensus in commentaries on Mark for this reading, and I will show why there are good reasons for adopting it. I also want to explore some of the implications of understanding 1:1 this way.

Many have observed that Mark 1:1 "plays an important role and acts as a key-verse—not only for chapter 1, but for the whole gospel."[3] However, scholars debate its precise function. The confusion is compounded by some of the complexities in the immediate context of the beginning of Mark. In

---

[1] All Scripture quotations follow the ESV unless otherwise indicated.

[2] See Will Timmins, "Why Paul Wrote Romans: Putting the Pieces Together," *Themelios* 43 (2018): 387–404.

[3] Eve-Marie Becker, *Der früheste Evangelist: Studien zum Markusevangelium*, WUNT 380 (Tübingen: Mohr Siebeck, 2017), 298.

fact, writing in 1942, Wikgen could speak of the "oblivion that has been visited upon [readers] by the Commentaries" in their discussion of the opening section of Mark.[4]

There are textual questions: were υἱοῦ θεοῦ at the end of verse 1 and ὁ and καί in verse 4 original? There are lexical questions: what do ἀρχή (beginning? norm? foundation?) and εὐαγγέλιον (the written Gospel of Mark? the preached gospel?) refer to? There are grammatical questions: Is Ἰησοῦ Χριστου an objective genitive ("the gospel *about* Jesus Christ") or a subjective genitive ("the gospel [*preached by*] Jesus Christ")?[5] There are structural questions: How should we break up the first section, and how far does it extend (to verse 8? verse 13? verse 15). There are genre questions: How should we identify the first section? Is it a prologue, a preface, an overture, or an introduction?[6]

These questions are worth considering but they too often remain on the pages of commentaries and monographs as they seem too obscure or intractable to help readers and teachers of Mark. In this article, I want to focus on one issue about which we can be confident, and which significantly impacts our reading of the Gospel.

My thesis is that if we understand 1:1 as the title for the book, then we can read the work as the origin or backstory of the gospel as it was being preached when Mark was writing. A first century Christian who read Mark would have understood the "gospel" as a message to be heard, not as a book to be read. Mark uses εὐαγγέλιον this way throughout his book (1:14, 15; 8:35; 10:29; 13:10; 14:9)—that is, always as a message that is preached and heard. Only after Mark wrote and his book became known as a "Gospel" were there two related but distinct understandings of the word "gospel" (i.e., a written book about Jesus's life or a preached message about him). However, as Mark writes, the "gospel" was only known as a preached message. If Mark titles his book "the beginning of the gospel," he provides his readers with a detailed backstory to the gospel they had heard preached.

Thinking about Mark as the "backstory" to the gospel invites us to relate it to the two, for want of a better word, "leading" apostles in the New Testament: Peter and Paul. Having first defended this reading of 1:1, we will consider his relationship with these two apostles before in our final section considering the difference this makes to reading the Gospel.

1. The Beginning of the Gospel (Ἀρχὴ τοῦ εὐαγγελίου)

The relationship of ἀρχὴ τοῦ εὐαγγελίου to its context has been considered by Cranfield, who lists ten options,[7] and Boring, who considers twelve.[8] The main question is whether 1:1 functions as a title

---

[4] Allen P. Wikgren, "ΑΡΧΗ ΤΟΥ ΕΥΑΓΓΕΛΙΟΥ," *JBL* 61 (1942): 20.

[5] By far the dominant view in the commentaries is that it is an objective genitive though some like France suggest Mark could intend both; see R. T. France, *The Gospel of Mark: A Commentary on the Greek Text*, NIGTC (Grand Rapids: Eerdmans, 2002), 53.

[6] See the discussion in Francesco Filannino, *The Theological Programme of Mark*, WUNT 2.551 (Tübingen: Mohr Siebeck, 2021), 30–35

[7] C. E. B. Cranfield, *The Gospel According to St. Mark*, Cambridge Greek Testament Commentary (Cambridge: Cambridge University Press, 1959), 34.

[8] M. Eugene Boring, "Mark 1:1–15 and the Beginning of the Gospel," *Semeia* 22 (1991): 48–50. Boring does not enumerate them all. He also does not only consider the relationship of 1:1 to the context but how the other verses relate.

(or an *incipit*[9]) for the entire work or whether it *introduces* the book either on its own or part of a larger section (e.g., 1:1–8; 1:1–11; 1:1–13; 1:1–15). Below we examine some of the more common suggestions of how to understand 1:1 in its context.

1.1. The Beginning of the Book

If the phrase introduces the book, Mark could be doing something similar to the LXX of Hosea 1:2: "This is the beginning of the word of the Lord to Hosea" (ἀρχὴ λόγου κυρίου πρὸς Ωσηε).[10] Mark would thus offer a "somewhat abrupt introduction" to what he has written.[11] Read this way, the phrase means something like, "Here begins the gospel." Mark would thus be identifying his book as a "gospel"—that is, the phrase "the beginning of the gospel" would mean "the beginning of this book."[12] Most, however, recognize that this *literary* use of the word εὐαγγέλιον did not arise until the middle of the second century.[13] Further, as we have noted, every other use εὐαγγέλιον in Mark refers to the preached message.

1.2. The Beginning of the Gospel Was Prophesied in the Scriptures

This reading connects the first two verses together: "The beginning of the gospel of Jesus Christ, the Son of God was just as it is written in Isaiah the prophet...."[14] There is a strong grammatical argument for this reading, namely that 1:2 begins with a subordinating conjunction (καθώς) which introduces the quotation from Isaiah (and Mal 3:1 and Exod 23:20).[15] This conjunction typically subordinates the following clause to a previous verbal clause. Further, every other example in the NT and LXX of the particular phrase "as it is written" (καθώς γέγραπται) functions to connect what has just been said to the Scripture reference that follows.[16] This is certainly the way that it is used in Mark 9:13 ("Elijah has come, and they did to him whatever they pleased, *as it is written* of him") and 14:21 ("the Son of Man goes *as it is written* of him").

However, there are problems with taking 1:2 as subordinate to 1:1.[17] First of all, 1:1 is not a clause and so a verb needs to be supplied—usually ἦν (or ἐστιν). It is certainly possible that Mark understood

---

[9] Dennis E. Smith, "Narrative Beginnings in Ancient Literature and Theory," *Semeia* 22 (1991): 4: "a brief phrase" used "to introduce a document or selection from a document."

[10] My own translation.

[11] Morna D. Hooker, *The Gospel according to Saint Mark*, BNTC (London: Continuum, 1991), 33.

[12] Francis J. Moloney, *The Gospel of Mark: A Commentary* (Grand Rapids: Baker Academic, 2002), 31.

[13] Filannino, *Theological Programme of Mark*, 51 n. 43.

[14] Filannino (*Theological Programme of Mark*, 15 n. 7) gives an extensive list of those who take this position inducing Robert A. Guelich, *Mark 1–8:26*, WBC 34A (Dallas: Word, 1989), 10; Robert Gundry, *Mark: A Commentary on His Apology for the Cross* (Grand Rapids: Eerdmans, 1993), 30–31; Mary Ann Tolbert, *Sowing the Gospel: Mark's World in Literary-Historical Perspective* (Minneapolis: Fortress, 1989), 239–48.

[15] See Christian Rose, *Theologie als Erzählung im Markusevangelium: Eine narratologisch-rezeptionsästhetische Studie zu Mk 1,1–15*, WUNT 2.236 (Tübingen: Mohr Siebeck, 2007), 88, and Tolbert, Sowing the Gospel, 243.

[16] 2 Kings 14:6; 23:21; 2 Chron 23:18; 25:4; Matt 26:24; Mark 9:13; 14:21; Luke 2:23; Acts 7:42; 15:15; Rom 1:17; 2:24; 3:4, 10; 4:17; 8:36; 9:13, 33; 10:15; 11:8, 26; 15:3, 9, 21; 1 Cor 1:31; 2:9; 2 Cor 8:15; 9:9. See also, 1 Esdras. 3:9; Tobit 1:6; Daniel (Theodotion) 9:13. This list was generated by Bible Works and matches that of Filannino, *Theological Programme*, 15 n. 8.

[17] Clayton Croy ("Where the Gospel Text Begins: A Non-Theological Interpretation of Mark 1:1," *NovT* 68 [2001]: 126) ends up suggesting that 1:1 is actually a "second century redactional gloss."

ἦν in the first verse, nevertheless context is usually required to determine an ellipsis and the first verse of Mark's Gospel does not provide that context. Further, as Croy notes, it is hard to see verse 1 as the fulfillment of Isaiah's prophecy since Mark 1:1 "does not predicate, let alone narrate, anything."[18] In what sense is verse 1 the fulfillment of verses 2–3?

We will return to the syntactical function of καθώς below. At this point we can observe that Matthew (3:3–4) and Luke (3:4–6) both insert material about John the Baptist *before* repeating the quotation of Mark 1:2–3. That is, they move their equivalent of Mark 1:4–8 to before their equivalent of Mark 1:2–3. While this is "a strong indication that Mark, as it stands, violated the expected order of 'fulfillment— then prophecy,'"[19] it is also a strong indication that Matthew, Luke, and John (who puts the quotation on the lips of John the Baptist himself in 1:23) understand the quotation to refer to the ministry of John the Baptist.[20] The Isaiah quotation certainly lends itself to be read with the John the Baptist material.

This reading creates an abrupt syntactical transition to 1:4 with no conjunction introducing the description of John the Baptist. Where Matthew, Luke and John all understand the Isaiah quotation of 1:2–3 to refer to the ministry of John the Baptist, this reading connects the quotation to 1:1, and John the Baptist is given no introduction.

1.3. The Beginning of the Gospel Was the Ministry of John the Baptist

On this reading the Scripture quotation of 1:2–3 is a parenthesis, and the first four verses should be understood: "the beginning of the Gospel of Jesus Christ Son of God (as it is written in Isaiah …) was John baptizing in the desert."[21] Lane, for example, suggests that the "primary reference in Ch. 1:1 is to the ministry of John and the fulfillment of the hope in Israel."[22]

This reading (as did the previous one) connects καθώς γέγραπται to 1:1 but also connects it to the ministry of John. There is no need for a conjunction at the beginning of verse 4 since ἀρχή is the subject of ἐγένετο and Ἰωάννης is the predicate nominative. This is not impossible; however, one would expect the subject to be marked with an article when the predicate is a proper noun.[23] Further, as Filaninno observes, "in other cases where Mark interrupts a sentence to insert a parenthesis or a brief, explanatory, digression he always employs a textual element to recall the sentence interrupted."[24] It also renders

---

[18] Croy, "Where the Gospel Text Begins," 113.

[19] Croy, "Where the Gospel Text Begins," 112.

[20] This partially answers Tolbert (*Sowing the Gospel*, 243), who suggests that it is much simpler "to recognize that Jesus Christ, Son of God (1:1), is the messenger sent by God to show the way we are to follow (1:2) and that the beginning of this good news is found in the prophecy of Isaiah, for God in Isaiah's time foretold the sending of this special emissary into the world."

[21] This is an adaptation of the translation provided by Filannino, *Theological Programme*, 17. His footnote 13 lists commentators who take this reading including William L. Lane, *The Gospel According to Mark: The English Text with Introduction, Exposition, and Notes*, NICNT (Grand Rapids: Eerdmans, 1974), 42. See also Ezra Palmer Gould, *A Critical and Exegetical Commentary on the Gospel according to St. Mark*, ICC (New York: C. Scribner's Sons, 1896), 2–3

[22] Lane, *The Gospel According to Mark*, 45.

[23] Daniel B. Wallace, *Greek Grammar Beyond the Basics: An Exegetical Syntax of the New Testament* (Grand Rapids: Zondervan, 1996), 43–44.

[24] See Filannino, *Theological Programme*, 18, and the examples he considers from Mark 3:16; 5:6; and 7:1–5.

the Scripture citation as somewhat parenthetical when by all accounts it is fundamental for Mark's Christology and soteriology.[25]

Guelich rejects this reading on the grounds of content, noting that both "the quotation and the Baptist materials stress John's role as the *precursor* of the promised, coming one."[26] It would seem "out of character" for Mark to not include as part of the "beginning" the one "who actually preached this gospel in 1:14–15."[27] As Filaninno notes, if taken "to the letter" this reading would imply that the beginning of the gospel of Jesus Christ coincide "with the coming of John the Baptist and his preaching and baptism."[28] Particularly since ἀρχή can mean "foundation," this reading seems to attribute an importance to John that exceeds his place in the rest of the narrative.

1.4. The Beginning of the Gospel of Jesus Christ the Son of God

The final reading to consider is that the phrase with which Mark starts his book which has no verb and no predicate most naturally functions as a title to the book as a whole.[29] Mark titles his book "The Beginning of the Gospel about Jesus Christ, the Son of God."[30] There are several biblical precedents for using a phrase to serve as the title of a book, such as Proverbs 1:1 (παροιμίαι Σαλωμῶντος υἱοῦ Δαυιδ, "The proverbs of Solomon, son of David") and Isaiah 1:1 (ὅρασις ἣν εἶδεν Ησαιας, "The vision which Isaiah saw").[31]

However, we have already considered that elsewhere καθώς *usually* and καθώς γέγραπται *always* point backward, suggesting that verse 1 is syntactically connected to verse 2. On the former, it is rare but not unheard of for καθώς on its own to point forward (e.g., John 15:9; Acts 7:17; Gal 3:6; Phil 1:7).[32] 1 Timothy 1:3 serves as a helpful parallel. The first two verses of the letter are Paul's introduction of himself and Timothy. The καθώς that begins verse 3 is used in a syntactically unusual way. Not only does it point forward, but it also seems to have no corresponding apodosis.[33]

Even if none of these examples of καθώς behaves in precisely the same way as the one found in Mark 1:2, they show that the conjunction can be employed in syntactically unusual or incomplete situations. If we take καθώς as pointing forward in 1:2, the correspondence for the quotation is found in John

---

[25] On its importance, see Rikk E. Watts, "Mark," in *Commentary on the New Testament Use of the Old Testament*, ed. G. K. Beale and D. A. Carson (Grand Rapids: Baker Academic, 2007), 113–20.

[26] Robert A. Guelich, "'The Beginning of the Gospel': Mark 1:1–15," *BR* 27 (1982): 7.

[27] Guelich, "The Beginning of the Gospel," 7.

[28] Filannino, *Theological Programme*, 18.

[29] As the first phrase in the book it thus differs from Hosea 1:2.

[30] There is some doubt concerning whether "son of God" in 1:1 is original since it is missing in some very significant early manuscripts. For succinct arguments for its originality, see Guelich, *Mark 1–8:26*, 6; Mark L. Strauss, *Mark*, ZECNT (Grand Rapids: Zondervan, 2014), 61.

[31] Filannino (*Theological Programme*, 20 n .17) lists the following additional examples: Eccl 1:1; Song 1:1; Jer 1:1; Hos 1:1; Joel 1:1; Amos 1:1; Obad 1:1; Mic 1:1; Nah 1:1; Hab 1:1; Zeph 1:1; Mal 1:1.

[32] Strauss (*Mark*, 62 n. 17) is incorrect when (following Guelich, *Mark 1:1–8:26*, 7) he states, "καθώς never begins a sentence in Mark or elsewhere in the NT (except in the unrelated καθώς/οὕτως combination)." He is correct, however, that in a formula with γέγραπται it elsewhere always refers to what precedes rather than to what follows.

[33] See the discussion in I. Howard Marshall, *A Critical and Exegetical Commentary on the Pastoral Epistles*, ICC (London: T&T Clark, 2004), 362.

the Baptist's ministry in 1:4–8: "Just as it is written in Isaiah … John appeared, baptizing…." This is an unusual but not impossible way for Mark to start his book.[34]

While it is true that καθὼς γέγραπται elsewhere always points back, it is also true that *each* reading of 1:1–2 creates syntactical problems. Further, it may be that employing this phrase in an unusual way allows Mark to highlight the function of the following quotation. That is, by placing this phrase in the syntactically unusual position, Mark indicates that all the subsequent narrative corresponds at some level to the scriptural citation.[35] As we noted, this quotation is fundamental for what Mark wants to say about Jesus and this unusual construction and its placement at the beginning of the book proper cohere with that.

Reading 1:1 as a title and so understanding the καθὼς of 1:2 to point forward does create awkward syntax, but it seems that the "extraordinary function of the unit has interfered with normal syntax."[36] In fact, as we have seen, each of the options we have considered create syntactical problems.[37]

The meaning of ἀρχή ranges from "beginning" (BDAG definition 1) to "first cause" (BDAG definition 2) to "authority" (BDAG definition 6). Boring, in addition, suggests "foundation" or "norm." The position of the word at the *start* of the book and its use elsewhere in Mark (10:6, "the beginning of creation"; 13:8, "the beginning of the birth pains"; 13:19, "from the beginning of the creation that God created until now") suggest that a temporal meaning is best understood here. Mark is narrating how the preached gospel began. He is giving its origin story.

How does this internal title *The Beginning of the Gospel of Jesus Christ, the Son of God* relate to the traditional title of the book *The Gospel According to Mark*? The consensus is that although the traditional title of Mark was attributed to it early, it is not original since it presupposes other Gospels—that is, you only need to identify it as "according to Mark" when other "gospels" are circulating.[38] The later title implies the existence of other Gospels and relates Mark to them but does not perform the same function as 1:1.

Thinking about this book as the "backstory" to the gospel invites us to think about Mark in relationship to the two, for want of a better word, "leading" apostles in the New Testament: Peter and Paul. Put simply, Peter is the historical source of Mark's writing while Paul is his theological conversation partner.

2. Peter: Mark's Historical Source

Traditionally Mark has been associated with the apostle Peter, while Luke has been associated with Paul.[39] In Eusebius's *Ecclesiastical History* (3:39) he discusses "the extant five books of Papias" (a 2nd

---

[34] Further, as Boring, "Mark 1:1–15 and the Beginning of the Gospel," 50, points out, "a document that ends with γάρ ("for") can well begin with καθὼς. Just as Mark brings his narrative to an end in mid-sentence, so that the reader must write the conclusion in her or his own life (see below), so Mark begins *in media res*, with the action of God long since underway and in fact coming to its fulfillment (1:14!)."

[35] M. Eugene Boring, *Mark: A Commentary*, NTL (Louisville: Westminster John Knox, 2006), 34.

[36] Boring, *Mark*, 34.

[37] Boring, *Mark*, 35.

[38] See Strauss, *Mark*, 28.

[39] The material from this point on is largely adapted from my book *Mark: The Beginning of the Gospel* (Wheaton, IL: Crossway, forthcoming), used by permission of Crossway.

century bishop of Hierapolis). At one point he quotes what Papias says about Mark: "Mark, having become the interpreter of Peter, wrote down accurately, though not in order, whatsoever he remembered of the things said or done by Christ" (3:39:15).[40] This quote is subject to considerable debate, but we need simply note the clear, early association made between Mark and Peter. A little later, Irenaeus, bishop of Lyons, also wrote about how the Gospels came to be written: "Mark, the disciple and interpreter of Peter, did also hand down to us in writing what had been preached by Peter. Luke also, the companion of Paul, recorded in a book the Gospel preached by him" (*Against Heresies* 3.1.1). Here again, we have Mark described as the "interpreter of Peter," while Luke is associated with Paul.

There are also indications in Mark's Gospel itself that point to Peter's influence. There is an inclusio in the narrative that has Peter as the first (1:16) and last (16:7) named disciple.[41] Richard Bauckham suggests that this may be an ancient literary device to indicate Peter as the eyewitness on whose testimony the narrative depends.[42] There are other details that highlight Peter, such as the double reference to Simon Peter in 1:16 (Jesus saw "*Simon* and Andrew the brother of *Simon*") and the highlighting of Peter in 16:7 ("go, tell his disciples *and Peter*").[43]

Peter is certainly the most prominent disciple in the Gospel, mentioned by Mark more frequently (proportionally) than by Matthew or Luke. At points in the narrative Peter is the disciple who is the focus, perhaps most notably in his dialogue with Jesus in Mark 8:31–38 (cf. 9:5; 10:28; 11:21; 14:29, 37, 54–72).[44] Further, while Mark frequently "narrates what different characters see and hear," "the act of remembering is only attributed to Peter."[45] In 11:21 Peter remembers the fig tree Jesus cursed, and in 14:72 he remembers Jesus's prediction of his denial. These and other features that highlight Peter's perspective suggest that Mark is writing his Gospel primarily through the lens and perspective of Peter.[46]

One potential objection to this view is the fact that Mark often portrays Peter in a negative light. However, it is more accurate to say that the portrayal of Peter is complex and certainly not wholly negative. In any case, the first readers of Mark would know that Peter ultimately underwent a transformation, and the Gospel itself indicates that this would happen (e.g., 16:7).

None of these features provides incontrovertible proof of Petrine influence on Mark's Gospel, but together with the testimony of Papias and Irenaeus they point to a likely link between Peter and Mark's Gospel. Mark, it seems, has penned his Gospel from Peter's perspective.

---

[40] Eusebius, *Ecclesiastical History, Books 1–5*, trans. Kirsopp Lake, LCL 153 (Cambridge, MA: Harvard University Press, 1926), 297.

[41] Richard Bauckham, *Jesus and the Eyewitnesses: The Gospels as Eyewitness Testimony*, 2nd ed. (Grand Rapids: Eerdmans, 2017), 124–25.

[42] Bauckham, *Jesus and the Eyewitnesses*, 132–45.

[43] Michael Bird, "Mark: Interpreter of Peter and Disciple of Paul," in *Paul and the Gospels: Christologies, Conflicts and Convergences*, ed. Michael F. Bird and Joel Willits, LNTS 411 (London: T&T Clark, 2011), 35.

[44] Bauckham, *Jesus and the Eyewitnesses*, 126.

[45] Finn Damgaard, "Persecution and Denial—Paradigmatic Apostolic Portrayals in Paul and Mark," in *Mark and Paul: Comparative Essays, Part II: For and against Pauline Influence on Mark*, ed. Eve-Marie Becker, Troels Engberg-Pedersen, and Mogens Müller, BZNW 199 (Berlin: de Gruyter, 2014), 297.

[46] Bauckham, Jesus and the Eyewitnesses, 155–82.

3. Paul: Mark's Theological Partner

This close connection between Mark and Peter meant that any possible relationship between Mark and Paul was left largely unexplored until the 19th century with the publication of two monographs by the German scholar Gustav Volkmar.[47] Volkmar argued that Mark's Gospel was essentially an allegorical defense of Paul. He suggested that Jesus in Mark represents Paul; Jesus's family stands for the Jerusalem church led by James; and the Pharisees correspond to Paul's opponents.

Volkmar's argument was largely refuted by Martin Werner in a 1923 monograph.[48] As such, although the relationship between Paul and Mark was periodically touched on in scholarship, it was not until the publication of an article by Joel Marcus in 2000 that scholarly focus turned to the question.[49] Marcus's article has sparked a mini-revival in the study of Mark's dependence on Paul, and if we can speak of a scholarly consensus, it seems that it is now held that Mark wrote under the theological influence of Paul.

One of the clearest connections between Paul and Mark is their use of the word "gospel" (εὐαγγέλιον). The word "gospel" occurs four times in Matthew (4:23, 9:35, 24:14, 26:13), twice in Acts (15:7, 20:14) and not at all in Luke or John.[50] Its appearance 8 times in Mark makes it the NT book with the most occurrences outside of Paul (the only two other occurrences are in 1 Pet 4:17 and Rev 14:6). In the New Testament, this is a particularly Pauline and Markan word. Even the phrase with which Mark starts his work, "the beginning of the gospel," is found in Paul's writings when he reminds the Philippian church of their partnership with him "in the beginning of the gospel" (ἐν ἀρχῇ τοῦ εὐαγγελίου; Phil 4:15).[51]

As well as frequency of usage, the ways in which Mark and Paul employ the word "gospel" also have strong parallels. Paul tends to refer to "the gospel" without modifiers (e.g., Rom 1:16; 10:16; 1 Cor 4:15 etc.).[52] Apart from 1:1 and 1:14 Mark writes the word without any modifiers, in contrast with Matthew who tends to use modifiers (e.g., "the gospel of the kingdom," 4:23; 9:35; 24:14).

For Paul, the gospel can be an "episodic narrative"[53] as seen most famously in 1 Corinthians 15:3–8: "[1] Christ died … [2] was buried … [3] was raised … [4] appeared," but also more succinctly in 1 Thessalonians 4:14: "we believe that [1] Jesus died and [2] rose again." It seems that part of Mark's reason for writing is to "render the Pauline oral gospel episodic narrative for the first time into a written long-form episodic narrative."[54]

---

[47] Gustav Volkmar, *Die Religion Jesu* (Leipzig: Brockhaus, 1857); and *Die Evangelien oder Marcus und die Synopsis der kanonischen und ausserkanonischen Evangelien nach dem ältesten Text mit historisch-exegetischem Commentar* (Leipzig: Fuess, 1870).

[48] Martin Werner, *Der Einfluss paulinischer Theologie im Markusevangelium: eine Studie zur neutestamentlichen Theologie*, BZNW 1 (Giessen: Töpelmann, 1923).

[49] Joel Marcus, "Mark–Interpreter of Paul," *NTS* 46 (2000): 472–87.

[50] Although Luke frequently uses the verb εὐαγγελίζω.

[51] Paul here is referring to the beginning of the Philippians' association with the gospel. So, G. Walter Hansen, *The Letter to the Philippians*, PNTC (Grand Rapids: Eerdmans, 2009), 318.

[52] Willi Marxsen, *Mark the Evangelist: Studies on the Redaction History of the Gospel*, trans. James Boyce et al. (New York: Abingdon, 1969), 127.

[53] Margaret Mitchell, "Mark, the Long-Form Pauline εὐαγγέλιον," in *Modern and Ancient Literary Criticism of the Gospels: Continuing the Debate on Gospel Genre(s)*, ed. R. M. Calhoun, D. P. Moessner, and T. Nicklas, WUNT 451 (Tübingen: Mohr Siebeck, 2020), 211.

[54] Mitchell, "Mark, the Long-Form Pauline εὐαγγέλιον," 211.

Paul and Mark share a number of additional theological convictions. These include the inability for people to "naturally" understand the cross (cf. Mark 8:32; 1 Cor 1:18); the continuity and discontinuity of the law in the Christian life, as illustrated by the fact that they both expressly teach that the food laws do not remain in force (cf. Mark 7:19; Rom 14:20); the temporal priority of mission to Israel and then to the world (cf. Mark 7:27; Rom 1:16); and the relationship between the Christian and the state (cf. Mark 12:17 and Rom 13:1).[55]

For Joel Marcus, however, their shared understanding of the cross is their clearest point of similarity. For both Mark and Paul, the death of Jesus as well as bringing salvation, is an "apocalyptic event," which reveals what could not otherwise be known.[56] Paul speaks of the cross in apocalyptic terms in 1 Corinthians 1–2 (e.g., the cross is the "secret and hidden wisdom of God," 2:7). As Mark narrates the crucifixion, he highlights the apocalyptic phenomena that occurred around Jesus's death (particularly the darkness of 15:33 and the torn curtain of 15:38). His narrative climaxes with a moment of "apocalyptic revelation" when the centurion grasps his identity as the son of God—precisely at the moment of his death (15:39).[57]

These parallels between Mark and Paul are significant. As Marcus puts it, "The other Gospels do not concentrate on the cross as single-mindedly as Mark does. Nor do they share to the same extent the Markan emphasis that this apocalyptic demonstration of divine power took place in an arena of stark human weakness."[58] He notes that Mark is the only Gospel that narrates the first confession of Jesus's sonship as occurring at the cross.[59]

There may be a particular connection between Mark's Gospel and Paul's letter to the Romans. There is (inevitably!) debate about the location from which Mark wrote his Gospel, but a good case can be made that he wrote from Rome.[60] For example, it has been noted that ten of the eighteen "Latinisms" in the NT (Greek transliterations of Latin loan-words, such as δηνάριον [Mark 6:37; 12:15; 14:5]; and πραιτώριον [15:16]) are found in Mark's Gospel. This is "a frequency which is higher than any other Greek literary text of the period."[61] The "most likely place for Latinisms to predominate is in the city of Rome, where the Latin and Greek languages were closely intermingled as nowhere else at the time."[62]

If Mark did write from Rome (and we are only raising it as a possibility), it is interesting to note that the two descriptions of the "gospel" at the beginning of Romans ("the gospel of his Son" [1:9] and "the gospel of God" [1:1]) correspond to those at the beginning of Mark "the gospel of Jesus Christ, the son of God" [1:1] and "the gospel of God" [1:14]).

---

[55] For more see Mar Pérez I Díaz, *Mark, A Pauline Theologian*, WUNT 2.521 (Tübingen: Mohr Siebeck, 2020), 45–190.

[56] Marcus, "Mark–Interpreter of Paul," 479.

[57] Marcus, "Mark–Interpreter of Paul," 480.

[58] Marcus, "Mark–Interpreter of Paul," 482.

[59] Marcus, "Mark–Interpreter of Paul," 483. Cf. Matt 16:16; Luke 1:32, 34; John 1:49.

[60] For a more comprehensive defense of this position see Brian J. Incigneri, *The Gospel to the Romans: The Setting and Rhetoric of Mark's Gospel*, BibInt 65 (Leiden: Brill, 2003).

[61] Michael P. Theophilus, "The Roman Connection: Paul and Mark," in *Paul and Mark: Comparative Essays, Part I: Two Authors at the Beginnings of Christianity*, ed. Oda Wischmeyer, David C. Sim, and Ian J. Elmer, BZNW 198 (Berlin: de Gruyter, 2014), 50.

[62] Incigneri, *The Gospel to the Romans*, 102.

There are strong parallels in theological emphases between Mark and Paul, particularly his letter to the Romans.[63] That is not to say that there aren't parallels with other New Testament writers. However, the shared theological emphases between Mark and Paul suggest a closer affinity between the two writers. It is worth noting, for example, that Mark and Romans also both draw heavily on the book of Isaiah to explain Jesus's person and work.[64]

4. Reading Mark with Peter and Paul: Mark as Backstory

Michael Bird has very helpfully shown that it is reductionistic to line Mark's Gospel up with either Peter *or* Paul. In fact, the New Testament associates Mark with both Paul (e.g., Acts 12:25; Col 4:10; 2 Tim 4:11; Philem 1:24) *and* Peter (1 Pet 5:13). He suggests that the Gospel of Mark reflects the influence of both and is best thought of as "Petrine testimony shaped into an evangelical narrative conducive to Pauline proclamation."[65]

How does this help us read Mark's Gospel? In the first place it reminds us that Mark is writing both history *and* theology. He is writing a historical account of what Jesus said and did. Though not an eyewitness himself,[66] Mark writes his account in conversation with one of the main eyewitnesses who was with Jesus for almost the entire duration of the events that are described. At the same time, Mark is not simply writing "pure history," if such a thing even exists. Comparing Mark to the other Gospels shows that he has made choices concerning the order of his narrative and what he includes and omits. These choices are made for theological reasons. When, for example, we read of people's repeated inability to grasp the truth about Jesus, Mark is showing us the theological point that without Jesus opening a person's eyes (as he does so dramatically in 8:22–26), they cannot grasp the truth of who he is.

It is particularly the connection with Paul which will help us as we read the Gospel of Mark. It is important to remember that although the Gospels come first in our New Testament (because they describe the earliest events in the period), it is Paul's letters (with 1 Thessalonians probably the first one written) that were the first widely circulated Christian writings.[67] And so, while Mark and Paul both write about the gospel, they do so from different perspectives and employing different genres. Paul unfolds the significance of the gospel for the churches that he writes to, while Mark gives the beginning, the backstory of the gospel as it is found in the life and teaching of Jesus.

Mark is writing in the context of an already known, understood gospel, particularly in the form in which it was preached by Paul. And so, as much as we can and should read Mark on his own terms, by titling his work as "the beginning of the gospel," he is deliberately inviting his work to be read in conversation with the already known and preached gospel. This is not an argument that Mark necessarily writes with a copy of Paul's letter to the Romans in front of him (although this is not impossible),

---

[63] Albert C. Outler "The Gospel According to St. Mark," *Perkins School of Theology Journal* 33–34 (1980): 7 (cited in Theophilus, "The Roman Connection," 45) went as far as to describe Romans as Mark's 'Q.'"

[64] For Mark see Rikk E. Watts, *Isaiah's New Exodus in Mark* (Grand Rapids: Baker Academic, 2000); for Romans see J. Ross Wagner, *Heralds of the Good News: Isaiah and Paul "In Concert" in the Letter to the Romans*, NovTSup 101 (Leiden: Brill, 2002).

[65] Bird, "Mark," 32.

[66] The suggestion that the young man in 14:51 who flees naked is a reference to Mark is intriguing but unlikely.

[67] It may be that the Gospel writings themselves draw on early written sources, but these do not seem to have been widely circulated (such that they only survive in the form in which they are found in the Gospels).

but that he is writing in conversation with (particularly) the form of Pauline Christianity that we see expressed in Paul's letters.

There are a number of implications that flow from this relationship between Mark and Paul. First, we should not expect that every concept that Mark introduces will receive the fullest explanation. We see this even with his reference to the "gospel." As I noted, εὐαγγέλιον is introduced in the very first verse and is referenced six other times in the book (1:14, 15; 8:35; 10:29; 13:10; 14:9), but it is nowhere defined. Mark assumes that his readers will have a basic understanding of the content of the gospel—the preached message about Jesus—and he offers a basic commentary on that gospel message. Twice Mark refers to the widespread proclamation of the gospel (13:10, "all nations"; 14:9, "the whole world"). Mark writes into a context where this has already begun to happen.

Second, Mark's Gospel was written for Christians. This does not mean that a non-Christian could not read it and come to understand the gospel—not at all. There is obviously enough in Mark's Gospel to bring a non-believer to faith (as no doubt has happened throughout history). However, this does not negate the fact that Mark wrote for Christians with an awareness of the basic gospel message. There is a parallel with Luke's Gospel, which Luke tells us is written to give a Christian (whether Theophilus is a real or stylized person) "certainty concerning the things" that he had been taught (Luke 1:4).

Third, understanding Mark to be writing in self-conscious conversation with Paul will help us at different points of interpretation. One of the challenges in reading the narrative sections of the Bible is that sometimes it can be hard to know why a writer has included a particular account. What theological point are they making? Reading Mark in conversation with Paul (in particular) gives us a control, in that often the theological point being made will have a parallel in Paul.

Fourth, this reading of Mark helps us in the other direction as we read Paul's letters. We can see the theological points that Paul makes grounded and narrated in the life of Jesus. This does not simply establish their truthfulness (showing that Paul is faithfully discharging his role as an apostle of Christ) but it also allows us to see them demonstrated and lived out. For instance, in 1 Corinthians 2:14 Paul writes that the "natural person does not accept the things of the Spirit of God, for they are folly to him, and he is not able to understand them because they are spiritually discerned." We see this reality played out across the narrative of Mark's Gospel as people consistently fail to grasp the truth about Jesus.

Thinking of Mark as the "backstory" to the gospel finds a partial parallel in the writings of C. S. Lewis. I say "partial" because analogies like this can easily take on a life of their own! However, it may help to think of the relationship between Mark and Romans (say) as *somewhat* similar to the relationship between *The Magician's Nephew* and the more famous *The Lion, the Witch and the Wardrobe*, which was written first in 1950. *The Magician's Nephew* was written five years later (with three books in between) but narrates events that occurred before the story contained in *The Lion, the Witch and the Wardrobe*. The books each stand alone as wonderful works of fiction, but readers who have read both have a richer, fuller and more complete understanding of the overall story arc.[68]

Mark writes to narrate "the beginning of the Gospel." He writes to give the backstory to the proclamation of the message about Jesus. The title also anticipates the end of the book. Famously, the book finishes with the women fleeing from the empty tomb in amazement and not saying anything to anyone "for they were afraid" (16:8).[69] There is no appearance of the risen Christ, and it seems as if

---

[68] I refuse to enter into the highly charged debate about the "proper" reading order of the Narnia series!

[69] The Greek is even more abrupt with the last word being the word "for" (γάρ). Because of this abruptness, a number of longer endings can be found in some manuscripts, but it seems unlikely that any of these are original.

the Gospel ends in an anticlimactic way. However, the identity of this volume as "the beginning of the Gospel" fits with the abruptness of the ending. Mark writes in a context where the Gospel is known and where people *have* communicated the gospel, unlike the women who fled because of fear. He also writes with an implied encouragement that his readers will continue to be involved in the proclamation of the gospel. The abrupt ending reflects the fact that "Mark's Gospel is just the *beginning* of the good news, because Jesus's story has become ours, and we take it up where Mark leaves off."[70]

It is right to approach Mark's Gospel as a coherent and stand-alone account of Jesus's life. It can be read wholly and meaningfully on its own terms. However, Mark's Gospel, as the first Gospel to be written, invites us to read it in conversation with the rest of the NT (and, indeed, the OT), as it narrates for us the *"beginning* of the gospel."

---

[70] Joel Marcus, *Mark 8–16: A New Translation with Introduction and Commentary*, AB 27A (New Haven: Yale University Press, 2009), 1096, emphasis original.

Revisiting "the Time of Abiathar the High Priest": Interpretation, Methodology and Ways Forward for Understanding Mark 2:26

— *William B. Bowes* —

William B. Bowes is a PhD candidate in New Testament and Christian Origins at the University of Edinburgh.

****

Abstract: Mark 2:26 has presented itself as a difficult textual and historical problem for interpreters. Mark narrates Jesus describing an action of David which is said to happen during the priesthood of Abiathar, but in the Old Testament source this detail appears inaccurate and is absent from the Matthean and Lukan versions. This article will first examine three types of problems that arise in interpreting this text and will then evaluate two types of solutions that have been proposed. The aim of this article is to highlight the limitations of previous approaches and to argue for a third type of solution as best option for understanding the text, which is based in a narrative reading of Mark's Christology.

****

In the introductory section of his 2005 bestselling book, *Misquoting Jesus*,[1] Bart Ehrman pointed to one verse in the Gospel of Mark as being the reason for him renouncing his belief in the divine inspiration of Scripture and eventually leading to his abandonment of Christianity entirely. The verse was Mark 2:26, a saying of Jesus narrated by the evangelist in the context of one of several episodes of conflict with the religious authorities. In this case, the broader pericope (2:23–28) concerns a dispute over the actions of Jesus's disciples in picking grain on the Sabbath, which appeared to the Pharisaical interlocutors to be in violation of the Torah. In response, Jesus appeals to the actions of David in 1 Samuel 21:1–9 as both a precedent and justification, concluding with pronouncements on the purpose of the Sabbath and about his own Christological identity and authority. In his reference to David taking the priest's showbread during his flight from Saul, Mark has Jesus saying that David's actions took place ἐπὶ Ἀβιαθὰρ ἀρχιερέως, or, as is commonly rendered, "in the time of Abiathar the High Priest." Ehrman noted in this verse what many before him have observed, namely that in the text of 1 Samuel 21, the

---

[1] Bart Ehrman, *Misquoting Jesus: The Story Behind Who Changed the Bible and Why* (New York: HarperCollins, 2005).

priest interacting with David was Ahimelech, the father of Abiathar, and not Abiathar himself, who would only later become High Priest. After attempting to develop a solution to this problem, Ehrman came to believe that Mark was in error, and, in his words, "the floodgates opened."[2] Ehrman concluded that the text of the New Testament as a whole was untrustworthy, and has since continued to propagate that message.

While Ehrman's response to this problem is more extreme than that of the typical interpreter, it is true that the temporal phrase in 2:26 has stymied readers for centuries and continues to be an exegetical incubus for commentators. For example, Darrell Bock is representative of many scholars when, referencing the problem in a recent commentary, he concludes: "no clear resolution exists."[3] Some commentators, while they may acknowledge the problem, do not attempt to explain it.[4] For others, the discussion of the issue occupies no more than a sentence,[5] or may be relegated to only a short footnote.[6] Still others avoid the discussion entirely by not even mentioning the problem and focusing on other aspects of the passage.[7] Regardless of the length or detail of the respective analysis, what most interpreters seem to share in common is a lack of confidence in the sufficiency of the answers that have been proposed.

Given the many difficulties that this passage has presented for understanding the relationship between Jesus's words and Mark's words, and more broadly of Scripture and historical accuracy, a thorough examination of the problem and its possible solution(s) is warranted. The questions raised by this passage and the interpretive methods used to develop plausible explanations are relevant for any reader of Mark's Gospel, but they are especially relevant to those reading from a place of conviction regarding the supernatural inspiration of the text. However, in this analysis my goal is not to argue deductively from such a position as an *a priori* assumption, but rather to present and evaluate the litany of explanations that have been proposed, and then to propose what I see as the best explanation for interpreting the specific phrase ἐπὶ Ἀβιαθὰρ ἀρχιερέως and the best explanation for its place in the whole of Mark's Gospel. In so doing, I intend to advocate for a high view of the text and its author as an *a posteriori* induction.

This examination will not endeavor to prove that Mark's Gospel as a whole is without any error, but rather it will advocate for reading Mark 2:26 (and 2:23–28) from a narrative perspective in light of Mark's broader literary and Christological aims.[8] That is, I contend that Mark as a narrator deserves far

---

[2] Ehrman, *Misquoting Jesus*, 9.

[3] Darrell L. Bock, *Mark*, NCBC (Cambridge: Cambridge University Press, 2015), 155. cf. James A. Brooks, *Mark: An Exegetical and Theological Exposition of Holy Scripture*, NAC 23 (Nashville: Broadman & Holman, 1991), 66: "no explanation is completely satisfactory"; Robert Stein, *Mark*, BECNT (Grand Rapids: Baker Academic, 2008), 146: "no satisfactory solution has come forward"; Kim Huat Tan, *Mark*, NCCS (Eugene, OR: Cascade, 2015), 42: "the jury is still out on this question."

[4] As in Mary Ann Beavis, *Mark*, Paideia (Grand Rapids: Baker Academic, 2011), 63.

[5] As in Lamar Williamson, *Mark*, Interpretation (Louisville: Westminster John Knox, 2009), 73.

[6] As in Warren Carter, *Mark*, Wisdom Commentary 42 (Collegeville, MN: Liturgical Press, 2019), 59 n. 35.

[7] As in Charles Bobertz, *The Gospel of Mark: A Liturgical Reading* (Grand Rapids: Baker Academic, 2016), 30–31; Larry Hurtado, *Mark*, Understanding the Bible (Grand Rapids: Baker Books, 1989), 48–49.

[8] I will elaborate on what a narrative approach entails below. It is distinct from a form-critical approach which examines pericopae in order to identify subdivisions and units, analyzing their compilation from oral sources, or a redaction-critical approach, which focuses on the ways in which the text's author edited the source materials.

more credit for his selection and ordering or material than he has been given, and that the solution to this issue does not ultimately lie in a more flexible or general understanding of Mark's Greek (though that may help), but in understanding Mark's inclusion of this phrase as intentional.[9] That is, I suggest seeing it not as a mistake or later gloss but as a quintessentially Markan highlight not reproduced in the Matthean and Lukan versions, where the same narrative unfolds differently, with different emphases and ends in mind for each author. Prior to proposing my preferred explanation, however, I will begin with an overview of the various ways that interpreters have addressed the problem. Afterward, I will elaborate on the nuances of narrative-critical methodology before suggesting what I see as the best way forward for interpreting the passage.

1. An Evaluation of Various Aspects of the Problem

Despite the fact that "there are almost as many opinions about this story as there are exegetes,"[10] a review of the literature reveals that interpreters tend to group the problems associated with this passage into three categories, as outlined below. First, we will examine the possibility that the problem occurred in the transmission of the content of the saying, evaluating evidence and arguments for this position. Second, we will turn to the possibility that the issue is related to how the phrase should be translated from the original language, noting various perspectives on how this could have happened. Third, we will consider the idea that there is a problem in the source text being referenced by Mark, and how this could have influenced the narration of the episode.

1.1. A Problem of Transmission

Conceptualizing the issue as a problem of textual transmission is the most common position among modern interpreters.[11] That is, while some express it in stronger language than others, the contention is

---

[9] When I say that Mark intentionally included the phrase, I do not mean that Mark invented the phrase or the dialogue. Rather, I do believe that Mark preserves and relays what Jesus actually said in an historical encounter. I assert as much because of the obviously Semitic nature of the pericope (which are not likely to fit later contexts), its unusual features (such as the fact that the dialogue has no connection with Jesus's miracles and the controversy is not related to what Jesus himself does, but only his disciples), and the offense that would have been created by various aspects of the text (such as Jesus's series of controversial statements in vv. 27–28, or the fact that he does not appear to adhere to an acceptable form of Rabbinic debate in vv. 25–26), all of which are unlikely to have been invented later. This is in contrast with E. P. Sanders, *Jewish Law from Jesus to the Mishnah: Five Studies* (London: SCM, 1990), 20–21; Arland Hultgren, "The Formation of the Sabbath Pericope in Mark 2:23–28," *JBL* 91 (1972): 43; or Lewis Hay, "The Son of Man in Mark 2:10 and 2:28," *JBL* 89 (1970): 72, who represent the view that this is an ahistorical exchange invented by the early church to justify their departure from Jewish Sabbath practice.

[10] John Meier, "The Historical Jesus and the Plucking of the Grain on the Sabbath," *CBQ* 66 (2004): 563.

[11] Cf. Francis Maloney, *The Gospel of Mark: A Commentary* (Grand Rapids: Baker Academic, 2012), 69; Morna Hooker, *The Gospel According to Saint Mark*, BNTC (Peabody, MA: Hendrickson, 1993), 103; C. E. B. Cranfield, *The Gospel According to St. Mark: An Introduction and Commentary*, CGTC (Cambridge: Cambridge University Press, 1959), 116; Carter, *Mark*, 59 n. 35; C. Clifton Black, *Mark*, ANTC (Nashville: Abingdon, 2011), 97; Donald English, *The Message of Mark: The Mystery of Faith*, Bible Speaks Today (Downers Grove, IL: InterVarsity Press, 1992), 74; Hugh Anderson, *The Gospel of Mark*, NCBC (Grand Rapids: Eerdmans, 1981), 110.

that this is an error on the part of Mark,[12] on the part of Mark's source,[13] on the part of a scribe who copied the text,[14] or on the part of the Jesus himself.[15] Most frequently, this is explained as a memory lapse by Mark, who simply inherited an oral tradition that he inaccurately reproduced.[16] Indeed, if one evaluates each of these possibilities individually, the idea that Mark's source would have erred in communicating an inaccuracy is unlikely, given the fact that such accounts of Jesus's words and actions were circulated orally and repeated for decades before Mark's writing,[17] and if a mistake or error was made, it would not have persisted as long.[18]

That an early copyist corrupted the text is not impossible, but the manuscript evidence is inconclusive on this point.[19] It is more commonly argued that since both Matthew and Luke almost certainly used Mark as a source and do not have ἐπὶ Ἀβιαθὰρ ἀρχιερέως in their accounts, it is plausible that they were aware that this phrase was original and decided to omit it, rather than that they knew an early copy of Mark that did not have this phrase (thus meaning that a scribe would have added it after the late first century).[20] Recently, Haelewyck has mounted perhaps the most detailed argument for the idea that the phrase was unoriginal, and represents scribal corruption.[21] While it has been shown that early church fathers like John Chrysostom and Jerome were aware of the problem in their early copies of Mark's

---

[12] This is the view, as discussed above, of Ehrman (*Misquoting Jesus*, 9); recently reasserted by Matthew Thiessen, *Jesus and the Forces of Death* (Grand Rapids: Baker Academic, 2020), 157.

[13] For a recent discussion on Peter as a source for Mark, see Richard Bauckham, *Jesus and the Eyewitnesses: The Gospels as Eyewitness Testimony*, 2nd ed. (Grand Rapids: Eerdmans, 2017), 129–50.

[14] This is suggested by Sherman Johnson, *A Commentary on the Gospel According to St. Mark* (London: A&C Black, 1960), 68; Brooks, *Mark*, 66.

[15] This is suggested by Meier, "The Historical Jesus and the Plucking of the Grain on the Sabbath," 573–79.

[16] In the words of Lamar Williamson, *Mark*, 73: "a lapse of memory or slip of the tongue"; Also Eduard Schweitzer, *The Good News According to Mark*, trans. Donald H. Madvig (Louisville: Westminster John Knox, 1970), 72; D. E. Nineham, *The Gospel of St. Mark*, PNTC (London: Penguin Books, 1964), 107; Elizabeth Struthers Malbon, *Mark's Jesus: Characterization as Narrative Christology* (Waco, TX: Baylor University Press, 2009), 166; Joel Marcus, *Mark 1–8: A New Translation with Introduction and Commentary*, AYB 27 (New Haven, Yale University Press, 2002), 241.

[17] I concur with the majority of commentators who place the date of composition sometime in the range of AD 60–75. Even if one places Mark's writing at AD 60, this exchange would have been repeatedly circulated orally for nearly three decades.

[18] The conundrum then becomes, in the words of John Wenham, "Mark 2:26," *JTS* 1 (1950): 156: "how to account for the retention of the phrase for so long in the oral tradition when the error was so readily recognized."

[19] The phrase is attested most strongly in Western manuscripts of Mark's Gospel. Other manuscript traditions appear to omit the phrase (D W it syˢ). Still others (A C Q 1 F) introduce τοῦ before ἐπὶ Ἀβιαθὰρ ἀρχιερέως, which achieves a more general temporal meaning.

[20] As argued by Shannon Morgan, "When Abiathar was High Priest (Mark 2:26)," *JBL* 98 (1979): 410; and Robert Guelich, *Mark 1–8:26*, WBC 34A (Nashville: Thomas Nelson, 1989), 122. Why Matthew and Luke omitted the phrase cannot be known with certainty. Scholars who insist that they intentionally did so, in the words of R. T. France, *The Gospel of Mark*, NIGTC (Grand Rapids: Eerdmans, 2002), 142: "to remove the embarrassment of a historical error," are begging the question. Matthew and Luke had different narrative intentions in what they included and highlighted, and in various places they both and add on to Mark's accounts for their own reasons.

[21] Jean-Claude Haelewyck, "Réflexion sur la Méthode en Critique Textuelle à Partir de L'épisode des Épis Arrachés en Mc 2,23–28," *RB* 126 (2019): 401–14.

Gospel,[22] Haelewyck points out that others such as Ambrosiaster and Augustine appear to have not known it.[23] He adds as well that when manuscripts or translations do appear without the phrase, even though they are fewer, they are still historically early and geographically widespread, which leads him to conclude that the phrase was a misguided gloss.[24]

That Jesus was in error in his citation of Scripture has been rather difficult for most interpreters to accept, given that even highly skeptical scholars would grant that we can know with a good degree of historical certainty that Jesus was a knowledgeable teacher well-versed in the Hebrew Scriptures.[25] In every other place in the four Gospels where Jesus cites Scripture, he does so with a command of the text that would indicate an intimate knowledge not only of the entire Old Testament narrative but of the details of numerous individual pericopes, which he would have not only been able to read but also recite from memory.[26] One of the few scholars to attempt to make the case that Jesus himself erred is Meier, who contends that Jesus embarrasses himself in this exchange, proceeding "in the presence of these scriptural experts to mangle and distort the test of the story."[27] More specifically, Meier suggests that any honest and rigorous historian is required to come to the conclusion that "the historical Jesus was a Scriptural ignoramus," and "not only an ignoramus but a completely inept debater who foolishly challenges Scripture experts to a public contest," only to disqualify himself by botching the reference.[28]

1.2. A Problem of Translation

Also frequent in the discussions of this issue is the suggestion that ἐπὶ Ἀβιαθὰρ ἀρχιερέως is an example of a phrase that either has been poorly translated into English (which may not be able to express the varieties of temporal nuance possible when ἐπί is combined with a genitive),[29] or has been poorly translated from an original Aramaic form into Greek.[30] In Mark 2:26, it is clear that ἐπί has a temporal nuance, and in most cases can this temporal nuance can simply be expressed with the word "when," indicating that something took place in a very specific period associated with the surrounding words (as it is in Acts 11:28). However, this is certainly not always the case, since in other cases it can be a broad temporal marker, carrying a more general connotation (as it is in Mark 12:26). The ambiguity that can result from using ἐπί temporally is clear from the many ways that Mark 2:26 tends to be rendered in

---

[22] Craig Evans, "Patristic Interpretation of Mark 2:26," *VigChr* 40 (1986): 184–85.

[23] Haelewyck, "Reflexion," 404.

[24] Haelewyck, "Reflexion," 414. "Early" refers to before the fifth century.

[25] For example, this is conceded as the consensus even by Meier ("The Historical Jesus and the Plucking of Grain on the Sabbath," 579).

[26] Luke 4:17 indicates that Jesus could read. In the Gospels, he directly quotes from or extensively alludes to the entire Pentateuch, Hosea, Isaiah, the Psalms, Malachi, Jonah, 1–2 Samuel, 1–2 Kings, 1–2 Chronicles, and Daniel.

[27] Meier, "The Historical Jesus and the Plucking of Grain on the Sabbath," 574.

[28] Meier, "The Historical Jesus and the Plucking of Grain on the Sabbath," 579.

[29] ἐπί is a flexible term with a wide semantic range. BDAG 363–67 lists eighteen uses and meanings of it.

[30] It is almost certain that in the historical dialogue, Jesus would have spoken Aramaic with the religious leaders. We can probably conclude that Mark is translating in his reproduction of the episode. For more on Jesus's use of Aramaic, see P. M. Casey, "In Which Language Did Jesus Teach?" *ExpTim* 108 (1997): 326–28.

English translations.[31] Other temporal uses of ἐπί in the New Testament which are specifically employed for eponymous dating (as in Luke 3:2) have often been noted as comparisons and even contributors to the problem, since there appears to be less ambiguity surrounding how those passages should be translated.

One of the more creative versions of this idea involves issues that could have arisen in the translation of an original Aramaic form of the saying. This view was first raised by Maurice Casey, who argues that since the original historical dialogue would have been in Aramaic, the original Aramaic form of Mark 2:23–28 would have been somewhat different, and thus 2:26 was obtusely (or perhaps wrongly) rendered when it came into Greek and was copied.[32] Casey renders ἐπὶ Ἀβιαθὰρ ἀρχιερέως as: ביומי אביתר כהן רב, a retroversion which, in Casey's view, carries in itself both a problem and the solution to that problem, since כהן רב ("great/high priest") is "an accurate description of what Abiathar was famous as, and does not necessarily carry the implication, clear in Mark's Greek, that he was כהן רב at the time of the incident."[33] Casey notes as well that the combination of ἐπί with a genitive is a sound translation of the Semitic idea of being "with someone" at the specific time, since LXX Job 38:12 translates מימיך ("since your days") as ἐπὶ σοῦ ("in your time").[34] Thus, he can argue that the passage (and all of Mark 2:23–28) "is intelligible only if we make assumptions which would have been normal in (Mark's) environment," knowing that the evangelist was a first century Jew familiar with Jerusalem.[35]

A further elaboration on this basic premise has been proposed by Brooks, who contends that the original Aramaic may have had not only "Abiathar" but "the father of Abiathar" or "ab(ba)-Abiathar," which could possibly have been omitted by a copyist since the first two Aramaic letters would have been the same as the first two letters of Abiathar's name, as shown here with the hypothetical word in red:[36] ביומי אבאביתר כהן רב. Despite the fact that Brooks calls this "perhaps the best explanation,"[37] the problem with both his idea and Casey's, of course, is that there remains no extant copy of an Aramaic written form of Mark's Gospel, or even any Aramaic source materials. Beyond this, we possess no strong evidence that a written Aramaic Gospel or early Aramaic form of a sayings-source even existed, making this theory largely conjectural.

1.3. A Problem of Textual Referent

A study of the Hebrew manuscripts where either Abiathar or Ahimelech is mentioned shows that there is confusion even in Mark's sources as to the identity of both men, with variant readings in different books. For example, the Masoretic Text of 2 Samuel 8:17, 1 Chronicles 18:16, and 1 Chronicles 24:6 have name lists which describe Ahimelech as the *son* of Abiathar, and not the *father* of Abiathar as he is called

---

[31] A comparison of five English translations captures how elliptic ἐπί can be: "In the days of Abiathar the high priest" (NIV); "when Abiathar was high priest" (RSV); "in the time of Abiathar the high priest" (NASB); "during the days when Abiathar was high priest" (NLT); "under Abiathar the high priest" (Douay-Rheims).

[32] See Casey, "Culture and Historicity," 1–23.

[33] Casey, "Culture and Historicity," 8.

[34] Casey, "Culture and Historicity," 8.

[35] Casey, "Culture and Historicity," 8.

[36] Brooks, *Mark*, 66.

[37] Brooks, *Mark*, 66.

in 1 Samuel 22:20; 23:6; and 30:7.[38] The Qumran version of 1 Samuel 21 (4QSam[b], frags. 6–7 and 14–19) is also different than the Masoretic Text, and actually makes the name of the priest less prominent.[39] Moreover, the Septuagint tends to align more closely to 4QSam[b] than to our Masoretic Text, and the Targums depart from all of these.[40] Thus, in Botner's words, "the textual history of 1 Sam 21:1–10 could be a contributing factor to the presence of the curious phrase ἐπὶ Ἀβιαθὰρ ἀρχιερέως in Mark 2:26."[41]

In addition to these difficulties in the source texts, in the Markan dialogue Jesus also appears to "Midrashize" the passage in terms of his inclusion or inference of details that are not explicit (but may be implicit) in the source text itself, such as the fact that David "entered" the sanctuary at Nob, that he gave some of the bread to "those with him," or that the episode with David is assumed by Jesus to have taken place on the Sabbath. It must be granted that none of these details clearly contradicts what is written in 1 Samuel 21:1–9, but none of them would be clear from what is in the text itself. In the first case, for David to have "entered the house of God" would not have been unusual, but almost seems to be a superfluous detail in Jesus's retelling and requires using one's imagination in order to elaborate on the little detail that the source text provides. In the second case, some commentators have made much of Jesus's detail about the men "with" David, presuming that since 1 Samuel 21:1 seems to overemphasize that David was alone with the priest, that this detail constitutes another inaccuracy.[42] The point in Mark 2:26 is clearly that David gave the bread to these men later, and not that they came into the sanctuary with him. Since David is asked about the ritual purity of his men relative to the bread in 1 Samuel 21:4 and mentions that they were to meet him in 1 Samuel 21:2, it follows that they were not far from the scene.[43] In the third case, that this instance took place on the Sabbath appears to have been a common view in later Rabbinic texts,[44] and given the presence of the showbread in the first place, that it was Sabbath can be assumed since the priests made and consumed the showbread on the Sabbath.[45]

---

[38] Some have suggested that Abiathar, the son of Ahimelech, may have in turn named his own son Ahimelech after the name of his father. For more on this possibility, which was not uncommon in antiquity, see James Edwards, *The Gospel According to Mark*, PNTC (Grand Rapids: Eerdmans, 2001), 95. Others even suggest that the text may be confused on the precise identity of Ahimelech. For example, David Tsumura, *The First Book of Samuel*, NICOT (Grand Rapids: Eerdmans, 2007), 529: "(Ahimelech) could be the same person as Ahijah, the son of Ahitub (1 Sam 14:3) since *melech* may be a divine element like *yah*."

[39] Max Botner, "Has Jesus Read What David Did? Probing Problems in Mark 2:25–26," *JTS* 69.2 (2018): 14.

[40] Meier, "The Historical Jesus and the Plucking of Grain on the Sabbath," 571. See also David Firth, *1 and 2 Samuel*, AOTC (Downers Grove, IL: InterVarsity Press, 2020), 213–14.

[41] Botner, "Has Jesus Read What David Did?," 14–15.

[42] Cf. France, *Mark*, 146; John Donahue and Daniel Harrington, *The Gospel of Mark*, SP 2 (Collegeville, MN: Liturgical Press, 2002), 111 n. 25.

[43] Botner notes that that the Qumran text 11QT[a] ("Statutes of the King") describes how a group of men typically would travel with Israel's king at all times, and even in special instances like 1 Samuel 21:1, these men would have been close by and immediately rejoined David after a brief separation ("Has Jesus Read What David Did?," 10). Ahimelech's fear in 1 Samuel 21:1 shows that the absence of the men would have been considered highly unusual.

[44] For texts that infer the showbread episode to be on the Sabbath, see b. Menahot 95b; Yalqut Shim'oni 2.130.

[45] See Leviticus 24:5–9.

2. An Evaluation of Various Possible Solutions to the Problem

Given this examination of the various categories of problems that interpreters note in analyzing this passage, we now turn to two categories of solutions that have been proposed. This will be followed by a third category, representing my articulation of what I see as the most promising view. The first considers linguistic approaches that allow for a more flexible reading, noting the broadness of the terminology. The second examines historical and cultural aspects that inform the context of the passage and may shed light on the ways in which early audiences may have understood it. Finally, the third considers Mark's narrative intent and Christological emphases as a way of understanding what he wrote and how he framed it.

2.1. The Lexical-Linguistic Solution

Generally speaking, for those who do not assume that the phrase is an error or a gloss, the most frequently cited solution is an emphasis on the flexibility of ἐπί, presuming it to allow for wide range of time that extends beyond the episode narrated in 1 Samuel 21:1–9.[46] This is presented in three forms, the first being that ἐπί can mean more than "when" (thus being a very specific timeframe) but "in the lifetime of" or "during the time of" (being a more general period).[47] 1 Maccabees 13:42 is an example of a similar reference, where an entire calendar year is marked by the high priesthood of Simon Maccabeus. For those who adopt this position, the primary reason why Jesus would mark this time period by the lifetime of Abiathar is because Abiathar was simply the more prominent and memorable high priest, and thus Jesus was calling to mind the general period and not the exact episode.[48] As Tan puts it, this could be comparable to the modern equivalent of someone making the statement, "the queen was born this year," even though the queen was not given this title at her birth.[49]

The second form of this solution sees this use of ἐπί as corresponding to the usage in Mark 12:26, where ἐπί marks not a time period but a passage of Scripture.[50] In this case, it is proposed that Jesus is locating the showbread episode in 1 Samuel by referring to it, so to speak, as "the section of Scripture related to Abiathar the high priest."[51] The third form of this solution understands ἐπί here as being possibly rendered "in the presence of," which is a locative rather than a temporal sense, assuming that

---

[46] This solution seems to be preferred by more conservative commentators. Those preferring this option include Eckhard Schnabel, *Mark: An Introduction and Commentary*, TNTC 2 (Downers Grove, IL: InterVarsity Press, 2017), 77; Mark Strauss, *Mark*, ZECNT (Grand Rapids: Zondervan, 2014), 145–46; Brooks, *Mark*, 66; Tan, *Mark*, 41–42; Heikki Sariola, *Markus und das Gesetz: Eine Redaktionskritische Untersuchung* (Helsinki: Suomalainen Tiedeakatemia, 1990), 100.

[47] Argued by Strauss, *Mark*, 146.

[48] Articulated by William Lane, *The Gospel According to Mark*, NICNT (Grand Rapids: Eerdmans, 1974), 115.

[49] Tan, *Mark*, 42. See also John Wenham, *Christ and the Bible*, 3rd ed. (Eugene, OR: Wipf & Stock, 2009), 83. This suggestion has its detractors, with examples being Ezra Gould, *St. Mark*, ICC (Edinburgh: T&T Clark, 2000), 49; France, *Mark*, 146 n. 52.

[50] The part in question reads: ἐν τῇ βίβλῳ Μωυσέως ἐπὶ τοῦ βάτου, translated, "in the Book of Moses, in the passage about the bush."

[51] For scholars who consider this a viable solution, cf. Bock, *Mark*, 155; Stein, *Mark*, 146; Brooks, *Mark*, 66. This explanation has provoked criticism from scholars such as Evans, "Patristic Interpretation of Mark 2:26," 183; Eugene Boring, *Mark: A Commentary*, NTL (Louisville: Westminster John Knox Press, 2006): 88; France, *Mark*, 146 n. 52. The problem with this assertion is that when a section of Scripture is designated by a person (or term), it

Abiathar was present with Ahimelech.[52] This locative sense is possible if one assumes that the point of Jesus's reference is not at all about the time period or the precise passage itself, but only about the unlawful or transgressive action of David in taking the showbread in the presence of the priest(s), and, indirectly, the unlawful or transgressive action of the priest(s) in providing David and his men with the bread.[53]

2.2. The Historical-Cultural Solution

There are two variations of this solution, which I have called "historical-cultural" because it involves neither a mistranslation of the text nor a misunderstanding of the intention of the words, but rather assumes that there is another, overlooked historical or cultural reason that allows for a correspondence between Jesus's saying and the precise details of the account in 1 Samuel 21. The first variation, dating back even to Chrysostom, explains that Mark's text is accurate because Abiathar actually had two names.[54] That is, there is an exact historical correspondence between Ahimelech and Abiathar in 1 Samuel 21 because Abiathar was also called Ahimelech. This would also be a creative way to explain the textual issues that arise in 2 Samuel and 1 Chronicles as noted above regarding the problematic references to both men, and would not be entirely unnatural in a culture where generations of men often adopted family names.[55]

The second variation assumes that it would have been acceptable at the time to refer to both Ahimelech and Abiathar as "high priest" because they either could have served in a co-regency or would have taken the title simply as part of being part the same priestly family.[56] As the narrative ensues and Saul puts Ahimelech to death, the text (specifically 1 Sam 22:11) does indicate that not only Ahimelech but his "whole family" were priests at Nob, certainly making it likely that Abiathar was present with his father when David took the showbread.[57] Those adopting this view are quick to point out that in other places throughout the Gospels, the evangelists frequently refer to the plural "chief priests" to designate eminent men of that order (as in Matt 2:4; 26:3; 27:62; Mark 14:10, 43; John 11:47), even though in Jesus's time, Caiaphas would have been the one formally holding that specific title.[58] Luke 3:1–2 is an oft-

---

is typically when that person or term occurs earlier in the section referenced, not later as with Abiathar (as noted in Lane, *Mark*, 116 n. 86).

[52] Articulated clearly by Sariota, "Markus und das Gesetz," 100. cf. Casey, who says that "(Abiathar's) presence may reasonably be deduced from the narrative in 1 Samuel" ("Culture and Historicity," 8).

[53] Sariota, "Markus und das Gesetz," 100. For another defense of this view, see J. D. M. Derrett, "Judaica in St. Mark," *Journal of the Royal Asiatic Society of Great Britain and Ireland* 1 (1975): 92.

[54] Craig Evans, "Patristic Interpretation of Mark 2:26," 184. This view is argued by J. C. Ryle, *Mark*, Crossway Classic Commentaries (Wheaton, IL: Crossway, 1993), 27.

[55] For a brief treatment of this practice, see Zvonko Rode, "The Origin of Jewish Family Names," *Names* 24.3 (1976): 165–79.

[56] Also presented as a possible solution by Ryle, *Mark*, 27; and most recently by Nicholas Perrin, "The Temple, A Davidic Messiah, and a Case of Mistaken Priestly Identity (Mark 2:26)," in *From Creation to New Creation: Biblical Theology and Exegesis*, ed. Daniel Gurtner and Benjamin Gladd (Peabody, MA: Hendrickson, 2013), 166.

[57] This solution is proposed by Marie-Joseph Lagrange, *Evangile Selon Saint Marc* (Paris: Librairie Lecoffre, 1929), 53.

[58] Noted clearly by Ryle, *Mark*, 28.

cited example of how loose such priestly references can be, since Luke mentions the high priesthood of "Annas and Caiaphas" when Annas had been removed from his priestly position fourteen years prior.[59]

3. A Third Solution Based on a Narrative Lens for Markan Christology

While these approaches have their strengths, I do not see them as providing a full scope for how to read this text in light of how Mark's unique Christological portrayal. I propose that to avoid misreading Mark's text it is necessary to recognize Mark as the author behind his text, and to view him not as a robotic compiler of tradition but as a brilliant narrator and theologian who intentionally organized his material, adapting it based on the way he intended for it to be read and the picture of Jesus that he intended to portray. I see a narrative approach as key not only to hearing Mark's voice in his Gospel but Jesus's voice through Mark's narration, as Mark shapes his work to communicate a particular perspective. In this light we can view the omissions of the phrase from Matthew's and Luke's accounts less as a reaction to a discrepancy and more as a way to eliminate confusion and intentionally highlight the aspects of the pericope that they intended to highlight, which, in both cases, may be the more significant Christological identity claim at the end of the dialogue, rather than the point that Jesus was making in the dialogue itself. Before we examine how Markan Christology plays a key role in understanding our passage, first it will be necessary to describe what a narrative approach entails.

3.1. A Narrative Lens as a Methodological Approach

A narrative approach seeks to analyze the narrative form and function of a text, with the narrative "taken to be a self-referential world with its own structures, patterns signals, codes and values," all of which create meaning and lead to a coherent overall message.[60] For Mark, what matters is how he engages in particular strategies of characterization when it comes to Jesus, or the contributing factors of his narrative itself to his Christological portrait. Reading Mark's account of Jesus with this lens helps us to situate Jesus's interactions with others in their broader context, and not simply to treat them as isolated episodes. If we see the narrative itself as having a unique capacity to communicate Christological ideas, the narrator's literary characterization (as well as the sequence) are essential to how the audience is supposed to understand Jesus as a character and ascertain the right meaning of the whole story.[61] Considering authorial characterization in an approach to Mark's Christology is to see Mark as emphasizing Jesus's assumption of certain roles in relation to other people as important for

---

[59] Noted by Perrin, "The Temple, A Davidic Messiah, and a Case of Mistaken Priestly Identity," 168.

[60] Edwin Broadhead, "Christology as Polemic and Apologetic: The Priestly Portrait of Jesus in the Gospel of Mark," *JSNT* 15 (1992): 22 n. 4. Another way of saying this is that the *what* of a narrative (the content) and the *how* of the narrative (the rhetoric and structure) are analyzed as a complete whole. For more, see James Resseguie, "A Glossary of New Testament Narrative Criticism with Illustrations," *Religions* 10.3 (2019): 1. The focus is on the text itself, attending to its constitutive features in a way intentionally distinct from traditional historical-critical methods.

[61] Michal Dinkler, "A New Formalist Approach to Narrative Christology: Returning to the Structure of the Synoptic Gospels," *HTS* 73 (2017): 2. By "sequence," I mean that the narrative develops meaningfully, and that order is key to interpretation of the whole. For more on the complexity with which Mark does this, see Richard Hays, *Reading Backwards: Figural Christology and the Fourfold Gospel Witness* (Waco, TX: Baylor University Press (2016), 17.

the communication of an essential theological message.[62] Because of the artistry that is assumed in this approach, this requires that we view Mark far more highly as an author, not considering him simply as a receiver and compiler.[63] A simple example of his artistry is found in the clear structural divisions within the storyline, and the various intercalations that Mark uses.[64]

It must be asserted, however, that a focus on the features of Mark's story and his authorial techniques does not treat "texts as mere stories rather than as records of significant moments in history."[65] For us to say that Mark has written a highly structured text and narrated the various elements so as to produce a particular portrait of Jesus need not mean that he is not communicating accurate information about what Jesus said and did historically. We can still say that Jesus intentionally mentioned Abiathar and meant for his disciples and Pharisaical hearers to understand the Christological implications of his claim, while also saying that Mark intentionally placed this episode at its precise location in his narrative and intended to connect it with sayings and events which unfold later.

Because the characters within Mark exist within the narrative text, "what we know about them is controlled both as to the extent of the information and the manner of its presentation ... they play particular roles within the overall sequence of events, while they themselves are also influenced and shaped by those events."[66] Therefore, we can say that what Mark highlights about Jesus's identity is part of the storyline itself. Mark's portrayal of Jesus is built around particular themes and character development which unfold through the narrative to reach a climax, bringing both internal characters and external audience to a decision regarding the identity of Jesus and their response. With this explanation in mind, I propose that the most significant Christological emphases that Mark attempts to highlight in 2:23–28 are Jesus as "son of David" and Jesus as priest.

3.2. Specific Markan Christological Emphases as a Hermeneutical Key

Mark's characterization of Jesus unfolds throughout the narrative as a "communicative design," in that Mark is careful to situate the revelation of certain aspects of Jesus's identity at significant plot points.[67] In the context of Mark 2:26, we can see two Christological emphases at play which develop

---

[62] This assumes that Mark's Christology is advanced by considering the relationships between Jesus and others. Jesus's identity is understood by the reader when the reader can comprehend the relationships between different characters, and how those characters respond to Jesus.

[63] As Michal Dinkler (*Literary Theory and the New Testament* [New Haven: Yale University Press, 2020]: 19) puts it, narrative critical approaches are often adopted as a rejection of "the endless stream of seemingly unanswerable questions posited by historical criticism, or the lack of regard for the text in its final form except as it points to its earlier stages of production."

[64] An example is the bracketing of the Jairus narrative with the healing of the hemorrhaging woman, which increases the pace and suspense of the text and the meaning of what follows. As observed by Ciliers Breytenbach, *The Gospel of Mark as Episodic Narrative* (Leiden: Brill, 2020), 16: "there can hardly be any doubt that the Gospel of Mark is a carefully structured text." This contrasts with form critics and even with the second century commentator Papias, who is famously quoted as saying that Mark just recorded what he remembered, and his work had no order (per Eusebius, *Hist. Eccl.* 3.39.15).

[65] Mark Alan Powell, "Narrative Criticism," in *Hearing the New Testament: Strategies for Interpretation*, ed. Joel Green (Grand Rapids: Eerdmans, 1995), 253.

[66] Joel Williams, "The Characterization of Jesus as Lord in Mark's Gospel," in *Character Studies and the Gospel of Mark*, ed. Christopher Skinner and Matthew Hauge, LNTS 483 (Edinburgh: T&T Clark, 2014), 116–17.

[67] Williams, "The Characterization of Jesus as Lord in Mark's Gospel," 118.

sequentially and contribute to the Markan Christological portrait: Jesus as the messianic "son of David" and Jesus as a priest. In understanding the importance of these narrative characterizations and in observing how they unfold, we will be able to understand why Mark intentionally highlights Jesus's reference to Abiathar.

3.2.1. Jesus the "Son of David"

The title/figure of the "son of David" as applied to Jesus is present in Mark, but its appearances are enigmatic. It seems important for Mark to show Jesus playing a Davidic role, but in the passages where the title or idea appears, it is met either with reticence, the need for qualification, or little comment at all. Even though passages like Mark 12:35–37 suggest a reservation in how the title is used given popular ideas about a Davidic deliverer-king, the words or idea of the "son of David" still appear without qualification either from Jesus or the evangelist in Mark 10:48 and 11:9–10.[68] The difficulty of interpreting what are often seen as veiled or vague references has led some to deny the importance of the idea, exemplified in Boring's assertion that "Mark's Christology has no Davidic typology and is extremely cautious about interpreting Jesus in Davidic terms."[69] I see this as incorrect, and suggest rather that understanding Mark's Davidic emphases is essential for rightly interpreting the Abiathar reference, which is the first explicit mention of David in the narrative and the first comparison between David and Jesus.[70]

If one examines the occurrences of Davidic language associated with Jesus, Smith is right to say that "it would appear that Mark in no way denies the Davidic messiahship of Jesus," even when "he is more reticent about its nature."[71] We can see from the appellation given by Bartimaeus, to the symbolic nature of the colt Jesus rides on, and on to the acclamation of the crowd receiving him in Jerusalem that while the evangelist avoids depicting Jesus as a nationalist-political messiah, there is nonetheless a clear message that Jesus is David's heir (even if in a primarily spiritual sense).[72] Beyond these overt references, most scholars accept that there is an allusion to Psalm 2:7 at Jesus's baptism, which would have had messianic connotations at Mark's time, as it did in some Jewish pseudepigraphal texts.[73] The Davidic idea in Psalm 2:7, which Mark highlights in the very beginning, is that the anointed king of the Psalm would be a future son of David.

---

[68] For more on the paradoxical reticence we find in some of these references and how this relates to Mark 2:23–28, see Marcus, *Mark 1–8*, 245.

[69] Boring, *Mark*, 91. For a discussion of developments in the rejection of Davidic elements in Mark's Christology, see Botner, *Jesus Christ as the Son of David in the Gospel of Mark*, 1–38 (especially pp. 15 and 19). Other scholars do not even mention the idea of the "son of David" in their treatments of Markan Christology at all. For example, it is not mentioned by Sigurd Grindheim, *Christology in the Synoptic Gospels: God or God's Servant* (Edinburgh: T&T Clark, 2012), 35–80.

[70] Interestingly, most scholars who assume that Mark intended Davidic typology in his Christological paradigm do not mention Mark 2:23–28 in their discussion of passages relevant to the "son of David" idea (for example, it is absent in Stephen Smith, "The Function of the Son of David Tradition in Mark's Gospel," *NTS* 42 [1996]: 523–39).

[71] Smith, "The Function of the Son of David Tradition in Mark's Gospel," 532.

[72] Smith, "The Function of the Son of David Tradition in Mark's Gospel," 532.

[73] Botner, *Jesus Christ as the Son of David in the Gospel of Mark*, 52; cf. Psalms of Solomon 17 or 1 Enoch 37–41.

As Botner observes, Mark had a "penchant for drawing on royal psalms at pivotal junctures in the narrative," interspersed throughout the narrative with enough regularity to make the emphasis obvious.[74] In the aforementioned royal procession of Jesus to Jerusalem, the crowds cite Psalm 118 without objection from Jesus or qualification by Mark, which, in combination with the reference to Zechariah 9:9, anticipates an anointed Davidic son.[75] Not only that, but we see the allusion to Psalm 2:7 appear once more at Jesus's transfiguration (Mark 9:7), and again in the context of Jesus's trial in the question from Caiaphas (Mark 14:61), bookending the narrative. Finally, the idea that Jesus claimed to be a Davidic ruler is affirmed in his crucifixion, per the *titulus crucis*, which hails Jesus as "the king of the Jews," in the spirit and form of David. As Perrin puts it, "Jesus enters Jerusalem as the true son of David, teaches as the true son of David, and dies as the true son of David."[76]

The most enigmatic "son of David" reference is surely Mark 12:35–37, which has been used to suggest that Jesus intended to distance himself from the title.[77] However, I contend that it is better to understand this instance as Jesus pointing out how the religious leaders of his time failed to understand what it meant for him to be a Davidic messiah.[78] Part of the problem that Jesus was addressing was an idea of the messiah that was too small. In his question to the crowd, he critiques how a messianic "son of David" could come from David in only a physical sense if in Psalm 110, if David calls this messianic figure "Lord." Rather than Jesus refuting this messianic association, it seems more like that he is suggesting that the religious leaders are wrong to associate their understanding of this title with the messiah, because the messiah is not merely David's son, but he is David's Lord who establishes a kingdom far beyond that of David.[79] Given that the narrative position of this question to the crowd is after Jesus's royal procession into the city, it is likely that the crowd would have understood him to be referring to himself. Additionally, the sequentially previous parable of the vineyard tenants can illuminate the ways in which Jesus considers the religious leaders to be misunderstanding his sonship, as the heir destined for death.

Now that we have established the importance of the "son of David" idea to Mark's narrative, how does it relate to the grain-picking episode of 2:23–28? Of the few explicit mentions of David in Mark's Gospel, this passage is the first, and as the first, I contend that paves the way for the other references to David that follow in the narrative sequence. It is hardly questionable that in the dialogue with the Pharisees, Jesus is making a comparison between David and himself, but the real question regards the nature of this comparison. At one level, it is David's authority to override a cultic and legal barrier which Jesus uses as the basis for his approval of "the 'unorthodox' actions of his disciples."[80] But from a narrative perspective, the mention of David is not simply a blithe reference as a way to establish a precedent for violating Torah, but is intentionally mentioned in order to establish a connection between the person of David, his authority, and his context in 1 Samuel 21, and the person of Jesus, his authority, and his

---

[74] Botner, *Jesus Christ as the Son of David in the Gospel of Mark*, 60.

[75] For a fuller discussion, see Botner, *Jesus Christ as the Son of David in the Gospel of Mark*, 146–53. For Mark's audience, Jesus's entry would have drawn to mind 1 Kings 1:38 and Solomon's route to his coronation.

[76] Perrin, "The Temple, A Davidic Messiah, and a Case of Mistaken Priestly Identity," 171.

[77] As suggested by Boring, *Mark*, 348.

[78] Noted by Perrin, "The Temple, A Davidic Messiah, and a Case of Mistaken Priestly Identity," 171.

[79] See the discussion in France, *Mark*, 483–85.

[80] France, *Mark*, 144.

context at that point in Mark's narrative.[81] To see this in clearer relief, we need to recall the broader narrative details of both Jesus's early ministry and David's early ascendancy.

In both the cases of David in 1 Samuel 21 and Jesus in Mark 2, we have a ruler and his band of men who represent a new, unrecognized kingdom, with this ruler and his followers wandering through the countryside, currently embroiled in conflict with the regnant religious and political authorities, and in both cases the leadership is considered illegitimate and unfavored by God.[82] In David's case, as the true anointed king he comes to the priest at Nob and violates otherwise sacral prohibitions, but the narrative in 1 Samuel indicates that "the divine appointment of David justified his action," leading Jesus's interlocutors (and Mark's audience) to the question what identity Jesus has that could justify his similar actions.[83] Jesus's specific choice of wording in Mark 2:26 is also important, as he adds the (seemingly unnecessary) detail that David gave the showbread to those who were "with him," and later in Mark 3:14, the narrator adds that Jesus gave authority to the Twelve, that they might be "with him." While on the surface this seems innocuous, it is possible that Mark intended this connection to be clear to his readers in order to establish yet another comparison between David and his men and Jesus and his disciples.[84] As Perrin puts it, Mark thus "prepares us to surmise that Jesus's gathering of the Twelve is modeled on David's gathering of his movement."[85]

If indeed Mark's phraseology was so careful and his narrative connections so intentional regarding these Davidic connections, I suggest that his inclusion of Jesus's mention of Abiathar over Ahimelech was also careful and intentional. In David's context, Ahimelech would be killed by King Saul's order shortly after the episode at Nob, and Abiathar would serve in a more significant capacity as priest under David's kingship. However, Abiathar is not only mentioned because he is more memorable,[86] but rather because of what he represents. In David's context, Abiathar started well, and served for a long period, but ended badly due to his participation in the revolt of Adonijah against Solomon, David's anointed son. As a result of his participation in and association with the plot against the son of David, Abiathar was the only high priest to ever be deposed in the Old Testament.[87] In Mark's context, Jesus is highlighting Abiathar to insinuate that the Pharisees represent Abiathar, who was present during David's taking of the showbread and participated in his transgression, and would eventually be shown to be illegitimate, because of the Pharisees' participation in rebelling against Jesus as the true "son of David," who is far

---

[81] As Guelich says, the point of the passage is not even about providing "an OT precedent for the disciples' conduct," but rather is about "typology between David and Jesus" (*Mark*, 123).

[82] For more on these connections, see Hurtado, *Mark*, 48. Joel Marcus also notes that Mark "accentuates Jesus's kingly role…by the way in which he describes the disciples' plucking of grain, since it creates the impression that a path is being cleared…as would be done in preparation for a royal visit" (*Mark 1–8*, 245).

[83] Hurtado, *Mark*, 49.

[84] As noted by Botner, "Has Jesus Read What David Did?," 495.

[85] Perrin, "The Temple, A Davidic Messiah, and a Case of Mistaken Priestly Identity," 174.

[86] This is often a reason given by commentators to explain his appearance in Mark 2:26, but for no reason other than he was more prominent than Abiathar. For an example, see Adela Yarbro Collins, *Mark: A Commentary*, Hermeneia (Minneapolis: Fortress, 2007), 203 n. 130.

[87] Nicholas Perrin, *Jesus the Priest* (Grand Rapids: Baker Academic, 2019), 198. Abiathar's deposition would also fulfill the Old Testament word regarding his ancestor Eli, who had his descendants cursed in 1 Kings 2:26–27.

greater than David and is establishing a greater kingdom. Additionally, just as Abiathar was deposed for his participation in the rebellion, Caiaphas would later be deposed as high priest.[88]

As Perrin puts it, Jesus intends to communicate what Mark expands, namely that Abiathar is "an emblem of a rebellious and therefore failed priesthood," which explains Jesus's present scenario and anticipates his own enthronement as the greater "son of David."[89] From this, we can infer that Jesus is associating the resistance of the Pharisees to his ascendancy in light of Abiathar's failed rebellion and resistance to Solomon, thereby declaring them to be illegitimate. This all takes places in the context of the early parts of Jesus's ministry, where Mark highlights his annunciation and establishment of God's Kingdom, and his ushering in of a new age where he is the messianic "son of David."[90] This reading shows that the passage is just as polemical as it is Christological, in that it seeks not only to associate Jesus with David, but the religious leaders with Abiathar. Therefore, as Botner concludes, the wording encourages Mark's audience "to engage the events of 1 Sam 21:2–10 within their wider narrative framework, and thus to grapple with the impending conflict between claims to authority by those who are currently in power, and by a new figure claiming to be God's messiah."[91]

3.2.2. Jesus the Priest

While the idea of Jesus as a priest, and as one establishing a new priesthood, is often overlooked in treatments of Mark's Gospel, I argue that it is essential to Mark's larger narrative and especially to understanding the significance of Jesus's statements in Mark 2:26. As Broadhead observes, "the priestly image, though briefly developed, has been woven into the larger tapestry of the Gospel of Mark and contributes to its wider Christological portrait. More importantly, the image of Jesus as priest probably plays a decisive role in the ongoing life of the church which lives by this gospel."[92] There are five passages where this Christological emphasis is most clearly developed: Mark 1:21–45; 2:1–12; 2:23–28; 3:13–17; and 7:14–23.[93] The first of these passages establishes Jesus's priestly exorcistic authority in his domination of the spiritual realm, and in his didactic authority, as one teaching differently than the current authorities. The second establishes his remissive authority in priestly fashion as one who is able to forgive the sins of the paralytic. This is then followed by our passage, which precedes Jesus giving of his own spiritual and didactic authority as priest to his disciples in 3:13–17. Lastly, in 7:14–23, Jesus acts as priest in displaying a ritual or cultic authority to make pronouncements over what is clean and unclean. From a narrative perspective, the proximity and sequence of these stories is important for interpreting their development, a development which involves establishing Jesus as a priest who is increasingly opposed by the regnant priestly authorities.

Regarding Jesus as a priest in 2:23–28, in placing himself within the role of the one justifying or allowing his disciples to pick the grain, Jesus "allows his followers to do on the Sabbath what was by

---

[88] As reported by Josephus, *Jewish Antiquities* 18.95–97.

[89] Perrin, "The Temple, A Davidic Messiah, and a Case of Mistaken Priestly Identity," 175.

[90] As noted by Strauss, *Mark*, 145.

[91] Botner, "Has Jesus Read What David Did?," 496.

[92] Broadhead, *Christology as Polemic and Apologetic*, 22.

[93] Articulated first by Broadhead, *Christology as Polemic and Apologetic*, 23.

law reserved for the priest of Israel," since in David's context, only the priests could eat the showbread.[94] To be high priest in Jesus's first century context meant to be "Yahweh's duly appointed, duly installed divine representative to Israel—and by extension to the world."[95] Jesus's actions in this priestly capacity, especially as related to his message of the inauguration of a new kingdom, a new order, and a new era of history, meant that he intended to change the entire ritual-cultic economy, and to establish a new priesthood from his own followers.[96] These followers, as those endowed with priestly rights by association with Jesus, can be justified in picking the grain on the Sabbath because they are part of this new order with its new king and partake in its privileges.

This establishment of a new order obviously meant resistance from the regnant system and, in turn, Jesus's denunciation or rejection of that system, exemplified in his association of the religious leaders with Abiathar. Of course, this also involved Jesus's indictment and judgment of the Temple, with which the priesthood of Jesus's time had long been associated.[97] While only in nascent form here, we see this become fully developed in the dramatic events around the Temple grounds in Mark 11–13, culminating in Jesus's judgment of the Temple and his prediction of its destruction. When understood in light of Mark's broader narrative goals, the mention of "Abiathar the high priest" can be understood as integral to his message, a message that sees the followers of Jesus and not the first century priestly order as the true future temple and priestly order.[98]

3.3. A Narrative-Christological Solution to Mark 2:26 as an Incorporative, Holistic Paradigm

Given all the strands that come together if we consider Mark 2:26 in light of narrative Christology, we are provided with a solution that allows for us to consider Mark's inclusion of the saying as intentional, and indeed as key to understanding his portrait of Jesus and the disciples. That is, considering the narrative threads that come together in Mark's understanding of Jesus as priest and "son of David," we can understand how Mark 2:23–28 represents not only a series of significant Christological points, but also the beginning of Jesus's polemic against the religious leaders, who, as the narrative unfolds, increasingly oppose him and his disciples. This paradigm allows for us to view Mark highly as a narrator, and can help us begin to understand why Matthew and Luke, with their distinct narrative aims, omitted the saying. This narrative framework can be considered incorporative and holistic in that it can both supplement and inform the strengths of other proposed solutions. For example, while I do not find the lexical-linguistic solution ultimately necessary, I do find aspects of the historical-cultural solution helpful. Specifically, if we can understand Abiathar to have been present with Ahimelech when David arrived at Nob, and if we can understand the flexibility with which many first century Jews used the title of high priest, then we can understand both how Jesus's mention of "Abiathar the high priest" is both a historically accurate claim for him to make and a useful detail for Mark to highlight in his own narrative development.

---

[94] Broadhead, *Christology as Polemic and Apologetic*, 28–29. Broadhead helpfully notes that the same thing happens in 7:14–23, where Jesus applies the standard of clean and unclean for his followers as only a priest would.

[95] Perrin, *Jesus the Priest*, 143.

[96] Perrin, *Jesus the Priest*, 54.

[97] Nicholas Perrin describes this at length in *Jesus the Temple* (Grand Rapids: Baker Academic, 2010).

[98] Perrin, "The Temple, a Davidic Messiah, and a Case of Mistaken Priestly Identity," 166.

4. Conclusion

Rather than the typical assertion (formulated in Ehrman's *Misquoting Jesus*) that Mark's mention of ἐπὶ Ἀβιαθὰρ ἀρχιερέως was an error, I have argued in this article that Mark (and Jesus before him) intentionally included it. There is no ambiguous language to blame, but rather, through the utilization of a narrative approach, I have shown that Mark purposefully highlighted these words and placed this pericope at its place in his narrative sequence in order to make a point about the relationship between the person and message of Jesus and that of the religious authorities. Both Jesus and Mark understood that David met Ahimelech, but they understood that the presence of Abiathar with Ahimelech could be easily inferred, and that as the more significant high priest associated with David who was eventually proved illegitimate by his actions toward David's son, Abiathar was uniquely representative of the priestly authorities standing in opposition to Jesus, the true "son of David," and greater high priest.

Presuming that Mark highlighted this episode as part of his unfolding narrative Christological portrait allows us to leave behind the idea of a Markan "slip" and to view the text more highly, given Mark's complex and detailed structuring of his Gospel. Viewing Mark 2:26 through a narrative lens helps us to understand it as part of a deftly crafted, coherent, and connected storyline with a clear purpose, arranged by a narrator who intended for certain ideas, words and events to be presented as they are, and who carefully developed those over the course of his work. This approach and the conclusions that can be rendered from it are important for the establishment of the integrity of the text and its correspondence to historical events, and serves to defend, in *a posteriori* fashion, the strength of what we have in the text, reminding us not to forget the author who stands behind the text. This level of insight would be impossible had Mark simply wrote that David went to the sanctuary at Nob "in the time of Ahimelech the high priest."

Rejecting Syncretism:
Paul and the Python

— Scott D. MacDonald —

*Formerly a missionary instructor with the Baptist Theological Seminary of
Zambia, Scott D. MacDonald serves as associate professor of theology with the
Canadian Baptist Theological Seminary and College in Cochrane, Alberta.*

****

Abstract: Syncretism—the blending of two or more religious paradigms—threatens
Christian witness around the world. And the church in Africa continues to struggle
with the popularity of local religious practices. In many locales, the *ng'anga* (an African
religious diviner) prominently features in the lives of many church-going people. In
response, Paul's mission to Philippi, recounted in Acts 16:16–18, provides needed clarity
concerning Christianity's relationship to other religious powers and to syncretism.
This article outlines the religious backdrop of Philippi, Paul's missionary method in
the Greek religious context, and the consequences that arise from Paul's exorcism of
the πύθων. In sum, Paul's reaction to the divining spirit of Philippi leaves no room for
syncretistic behavior among Christians today. Accommodation and any reliance upon
other religious powers compromises the quality of the gospel and the reputation of the
savior.

****

As servants of Christ deliver the good news of Jesus's life, death, and resurrection both near and
far, ancient spiritual actors and religious competitors abound. In sub-Saharan Africa, every
other urban street corner bears a sign promoting the abilities of some traditional power man
from a rural or distant location, a place with charms difficult to undo by an average local witchdoctor.[1]
Even in supposedly secular cities in other parts of the world, vestiges of ancient paganism remain as as-
trologers and diviners offer their services in the public sphere without shame. Spiritual power is seemingly never beyond a human's reach.

Depending on our cultural upbringing, such spiritual resources are our first or last resource in a
time of need—an accepted and trusted form of support or a desperation-induced "last ditch" option.
Occult practitioners claim to provide the knowledge we need, repair the relationships we crave, hinder
the people we hate, and empower the economic endeavors on which we rely. They are the so-called
"way-makers" and "problem-solvers" of the spiritually attuned.

---

[1] One common statement in Zambia is "I will go to Kaputa," and it is used as a threat. Because Kaputa lies at
the furthest reaches of Zambian territory, many people consider the village's charms effective.

How should the Christian relate to the *ng'anga* (i.e., the *sangoma*, the witchdoctor)?[2] Sadly, the testimony from too many Christians in many places is mixed. In a moment of need, one might recite the Bemba proverb "*Ukwimba kati kusansha na Lesa*," meaning "Charms are mixed with God for them to work."[3] Believers may easily justify a quick visit to the witchdoctor or use charms if they believe that God works in and through them!

Martin Mwamba, a pastor and talk show host with Faith Radio in Kitwe, Zambia, recounts an experience:

> One day a woman texted me during the program. She said she had been working, and after retiring she had gotten her pension money, and now when going back home she was robbed. She continued, "I will take off my church uniform as a Christian and go *kuli shi in'anga* ('to the witchdoctor') and bewitch them." Then her question was, "Is it right for a Christian to visit the witchdoctor?" The phone response from other listeners was interesting and shocking. Some suggested that she should go because God takes too much time to respond, and others said it was fine because witchdoctors give fast solutions, adding that they (witchdoctors) are also used by the same God.[4]

Hearing this kind of urgency-based decision making, Mwamba's assertion is reasonable: "Even people in churches today in Africa would prefer to consult diviners and witchdoctors … to receive a quick solution to their daily problems."[5] After all, no one wants to wait for God![6]

Occultists easily capture Christian customers. Surprisingly enough, many "witchdoctor shrines" are veritable havens of Christian objects like Bibles and practices like singing praise songs.[7] And witchdoctors readily play along with the cultural idea that God empowers their work, offering to pray to God for effectiveness with charms and reciting a Scripture verse or two.[8] Confusion abounds, and Christians readily step into the confusion by seeking their desired results despite the syncretism.

Syncretism is the "blending of one idea, practice, or attitude with another. Traditionally among Christians it has been used of the replacement or dilution of the essential truths of the gospel through

---

[2] Some people may balk at the use of the term "witchdoctor," preferring to opt for a less pejorative phrase "African religious practitioner" or "traditional healer." However, this article largely retains the use of the English "witchdoctor" to reflect the overwhelming norm of English-speaking Zambian Christians. *Ng'anga* is the ChiChewa word for witchdoctor (a language indigenous to Zambia and Malawi), and *sangoma* is the Zulu term for diviners in South Africa.

[3] Martin Mwamba, "'God Empowers African Charms' (Ukwimba Kati Kusansha na Lesa): A Biblical Response to an African Proverb," *Kērussōmen* 2.2 (2016): 39.

[4] Mwamba, "God Empowers African Charms," 41. The caller uses the Bemba term *in'anga*. Mwamba helpfully provides the translation.

[5] Mwamba, "God Empowers African Charms," 41.

[6] Speaking of animistic humanity's relationship to divination, Steyne argues, "Man believes that if he can enter the world of mystery, he may be able to change circumstances…. God's providence is not sufficient for life. Man must determine his own destiny." Philip M. Steyne, *Gods of Power: A Study of the Beliefs and Practices of Animists* (Houston: Touch Publications, 1989), 220–21.

[7] Mwamba, "God Empowers African Charms," 42.

[8] "It is not surprising that when these witchdoctors lose their market, they may even start to masquerade as 'prophets' and 'apostles'" adds Mwamba, "God Empowers African Charms," 42.

the incorporation of non-Christian elements."[9] The *ng'anga* has played a central role in the African's religious life throughout Africans' collective memories. Despite Christianity's inroads throughout Africa over the past century, the role and importance of the *ng'anga* has not evaporated. Many Christians sadly still find a need for them, and witchdoctors adjust and modify their practices to suit the Christian environment. Syncretism, the blending of African and Christian religious concepts, persists.

The irony is that many pulpits resound with sermons against syncretism. Preachers unflinchingly expound Jesus's statement from John 14:6: "I am the way, and the truth, and the life. No one comes to the Father except through me." "Jesus alone" is declared, yet the cultural norm remains firm: witchdoctors have a place in the life of Christians.

Many an African Christian still feels the draw of the *ng'anga*. The appeal of animism is not unique to Africa. While the African Christian visits the *ng'anga*, a European Christian convert dabbles in astrology, and an American teenager consults a Ouija board. The pull of spiritual knowledge and power is strong in Africa, but do not think that the rest of the world is immune! Thus, syncretism arises in every culture where Christianity enters, and "church history is filled with the struggle against syncretism from political, social, religious, and economic sources."[10] And the best response to our syncretistic attachments is a fidelity to Scripture, which both rebukes and affirms aspects of our church traditions and cultural norms.

One underutilized text in countering syncretism is Acts 16:16–18. Luke records the following account from the second missionary journey:

> As we were going to the place of prayer, we were met by a slave girl who had a spirit of divination and brought her owners much gain by fortune-telling. She followed Paul and us, crying out, "These men are servants of the Most High God, who proclaim to you the way of salvation." And this she kept doing for many days. Paul, having become greatly annoyed, turned and said to the spirit, "I command you in the name of Jesus Christ to come out of her." And it came out that very hour.[11]

While we could look to other missional encounters with spiritual power persons throughout Acts (e.g., Simon the Sorcerer, Elymus, the Sons of Sceva), the Philippian confrontation serves as an example to Christians throughout the world today. We must reject all forms of syncretism. Our missional testimony to non-Christians only heightens this necessity.

1. The Background of Acts 16:16–18

As we consider Acts 16:16–18, let us first locate where this episode occurs in Paul's missional endeavors. Between leaving Antioch in Acts 15:36 and returning in 18:22, Paul's work broke considerable

---

[9] A. Scott Moreau, "Syncretism" in *Evangelical Dictionary of World Missions*, ed. A. Scott Moreau (Grand Rapids: Baker Books, 2000): 924. Imbach defines syncretism as "the process by which elements of one religion are assimilated into another religion resulting in a change in the fundamental tenets or nature of those religions…. Syncretism of the Christian gospel occurs when critical or basic elements of the gospel are replaced by religious elements from the host culture." S. R. Imbach, "Syncretism" in *Evangelical Dictionary of Theology*, ed. Walter A. Elwell (Grand Rapids: Baker Books, 1984): 1062.

[10] Imbach, "Syncretism," 1063.

[11] Biblical citations come from the ESV, unless otherwise noted.

new ground as the Lord turned the missionary team toward Greece.[12] "Following his vision at Troas (Acts 16:8–10), the apostle Paul started the first church in ancient Greece at Philippi (c. AD 49–50, Acts 16:11–40)."[13] Like Paul's earlier ministry, which led to a confrontation with the sorcerer Elymus on the island of Cyprus (Acts 13:6–12), this journey involves another spiritual challenge in the city of Philippi.

Lest we mistakenly brand Paul as a troublemaker, Paul's missionary method does not call for the immediate confrontation of any religious figures in a particular region. On Cyprus, Barnabas and Paul are not looking for Elymus. Instead, they proclaim the word of God to those who wish to hear it, such as Sergius Paulus (Acts 13:7). In Philippi, again, Paul's priority is preaching, even after his initial meeting with the slave girl (Acts 16:16–18)! Creating religious conflict (which would ultimately result in his imprisonment) and exorcising a πύθων are not Paul's primary objectives. Only when the situation proves intolerable, hindering his proclamation ministry in a new mission field, does Paul confront the slave girl and the spirit within her.

The Greek religious context is evident upon Paul and Silas's entry into Philippi. As the slave girl attaches herself to their ministry, it is as if the current religious powers greet Paul at the gate and refuse to let go. While a casual reader of an English translation (e.g., "a spirit of divination" in the ESV, "a spirit by which she predicted the future" in the CSB) might mentally divorce this spirit-inhabited girl from the broader religious climate, the Greek text πνεῦμα πύθωνα at least indirectly ties the girl and her owners to the Greek oracular system.[14] Keener explains that this spirit is "the same sort of spirit that stood behind the most famous of all Greek oracles, the Delphic oracle of Apollo whose priestess was called a pythoness."[15] And Herodotus confirms that oracles, inspired by a πύθων, were not limited to Delphi.[16] Paul is pestered by what was considered a valued part of ancient society, an oracle treasured for guidance and insight. Leaders even consulted them before battle, for "Greeks and Romans put great

---

[12] P. Trebilco, "Itineraries, Travel Plans, Journeys, Apostolic Parousia," *DPL* 450.

[13] L. M. McDonald, "Philippi," *DNTB* 788.

[14] A few English translations (e.g., YLT, LSV, BSB) employ the rendering "a spirit of Python" to clarify the connection. Unger also states that the girl's "power of prognostication" as a πύθων links her to "the same evil supernaturalism that inspired the famous heathen oracles at ancient Delphi." Merrill F. Unger, *Biblical Demonology: A Study of the Spiritual Forces Behind the Present World Unrest* (Wheaton, IL: Scripture Press, 1952): 80. Michael S. Heiser affirms this link in *Demons: What the Bible Really Says about the Powers of Darkness* (Bellingham, WA: Lexham Press, 2020): 199. Keener says, "Although a 'python' itself would normally be a negative image, Greeks viewed it positively in any context related to prophecy. 'Spirit of a pythoness' would entail a spirit like the one that possessed the Pythia, Apollo's oracular priestess, with what was considered highly reliable prophetic information." Craig S. Keener, *Acts: An Exegetical Commentary* (Grand Rapids: Baker Academic, 2012–2015): 3:2422.

[15] Craig S. Keener, *The IVP Bible Background Commentary: New Testament*, 2nd ed. (Downers Grove, IL: InterVarsity Press, 2014): 370–71.

[16] Herodotus states, "The Satrae, as far as we know, have never yet been subject to any man; they alone of the Thracians have continued living in freedom to this day; they dwell on high mountains covered with forests of all kinds and snow, and they are excellent warriors. It is they who possess the place of divination sacred to Dionysus. This place is in their highest mountains; the Bessi, a clan of the Satrae, are the prophets of the shrine; there is a priestess who utters the oracle, as at Delphi; it is no more complicated here than there." Herodotus, *The Histories*, trans. A. D. Godley (Cambridge, MA: Harvard University Press, 1920), 7.111.

stock on augury and divination."[17] The consequences Paul receives for exorcising the spirit are therefore understandable and somewhat predictable in the Greco-Roman religious context.

The word πύθων merits closer reflection, as "there appears a semantic development from the specific Delphic dragon to an oracular spirit in general."[18] While πύθων evokes the Greek religious background, the term is historically fluid in meaning, referring to the Dragon, divining spirits, and even to ventriloquists.[19] In reality, this slave girl in Philippi is a "very pale reflection" of the oracle of Delphi.[20] But this observation in no way means that a spirit is uninvolved, as if the girl is somehow a mere trained ventriloquist; the text explicitly identifies a spirit in the girl. Foerster asserts, "Acts 16:16 tells us that the girl was a soothsayer-ventriloquist and that she thus stood in relation to the demonic."[21] And Conzelmann points to the exorcism, diminishing the possibility of mere ventriloquism.[22] Casting out the spirit reminds us of the ministry of Christ in the Synoptics. Ventriloquism is unlikely, as "Luke is trying to make it clear that a soothsaying demon is speaking from within the slave girl."[23] While having the ability to divine, this girl amounts to something like a poor copy, a "knockoff" of the more established Greek oracles.[24] Paul is not in Delphi, but he encounters a local, less impressive expression of the oracular system, an accepted (or tolerated) aspect of Greek polytheism.

---

[17] John B. Polhill, *Acts*, NAC 26 (Nashville: Broadman & Holman, 1992): 351. He continues, "No commander would set out on a major military campaign nor would an emperor make an important decree without first consulting an oracle to see how things might turn out. A slave girl with a clairvoyant gift was thus a veritable gold mine for her owners."

[18] J. W. van Henten, "Python," *DDD*, 670. The article later clarifies: "Acts 16:16 refers to a slave-girl who was possessed by an oracular spirit. *Pythōn* occurs as apposition to *pneuma*. The passage can be interpreted against the background of the semantic development of *Pythōn*.... Acts 16:16 should not be necessarily understood as a reference to a female ventriloquist. The passage may refer in a more general sense to a predicting demon."

[19] The πύθων is "the serpent or dragon that guarded the Delphic oracle; it lived at the foot of Mt. Parnassus, and was slain by Apollo. Later the word came to designate a spirit of divination, then also of ventriloquists, who were believed to have such a spirit dwelling in their belly" (BDAG 896).

[20] "[The slave girl] is described by Luke as 'having a pythonic spirit' or being a 'pythoness' that is, a person inspired by Apollo, the Greek deity specially associated with the giving of oracles, who was worshiped as the "Pythian" god at the oracular shrine of Delphi in central Greece. His priestess there was the Pythian prophet par excellence; the girl of whom Luke speaks was a very pale reflection of her." F. F. Bruce, *The Book of the Acts*, NICNT (Grand Rapids: Eerdmans, 1988): 312.

[21] Werner Foerster, "πύθων," *TDNT* 6:920. The early church understood the gods and the divining spirits to be demons. Asserting that the pagan gods are not actually gods, *The Clementine Homilies* state that their claim to divine the future "does not prove them to be gods; for it does not follow, if anything prophesies, that it is a god. For pythons prophesy, yet they are cast out by us as demons, and put to flight." *The Clementine Homilies* 9.16.3 (*ANF*, 8:278).

[22] Hans Conzelmann, *Acts of the Apostles*, trans. James Limburg, Hermeneia (Minneapolis: Fortress, 1987): 131. He says, "Luke transfers the label from the ventriloquist to a spirit which speaks through the ventriloquist (in fact, Luke is probably not thinking of ventriloquism at all; the use of the verb κράζω, "to cry out," in vs 17 is appropriate for spirit possession). In this way the account is more closely patterned after the Synoptic exorcisms."

[23] *EDNT* 196.

[24] Pervo further denigrates the standing of the oracular slave girl. "The woman's advertising might seem like a good thing, but Paul had absolutely no use for this kind of vulgar religion, which resembled the superstitions hawked in public squares by unscrupulous quacks." Richard I. Pervo, *Acts: A Commentary*, Hermeneia (Minneapolis: Fortress, 2009): 404.

2. The Divining Spirit's Deception

With Philippi lacking a synagogue, Paul enjoys fruitful outreach at the riverside prayer location (Acts 16:13–14), yet Luke quickly introduces the thorn in their side: "a slave girl who had a spirit of divination" (παιδίσκην τινὰ ἔχουσαν πνεῦμα πύθωνα). As he continues his ministry, Paul is ultimately annoyed. The reason for his frustration and the subsequent exorcism seemingly clash with message she repeated: "These men are servants of the Most High God, who proclaim to you the way of salvation" (Acts 16:17). But Paul's reaction indicates that this message is not as helpful as it sounds.

The πύθων is not interested in merely being a repetitive pest.[25] A more sinister deception lies behind its words.[26] "It is more likely … that she is not taunting but relativizing their message to make it acceptable in a polytheistic framework."[27] Christianity is entering the Gentile world, but its doctrine is inflexible. The spirit slyly contorts how the Philippians would perceive the missionaries and their message. Consider the phrase "of the Most High God" (τοῦ θεοῦ τοῦ ὑψίστου).

> "Most High God" is ambiguous, a common designation for God in Jewish texts but also occurs in pagan sources for Zeus or for the Jewish God with whom pagans sometimes identified Zeus. Magical texts show that pagans respected this supreme God, often identified with the Jewish God, as the most powerful. The spirit ambiguously reduces the missionaries' deity to a chief role in polytheism.[28]

Furthermore, "the way of salvation" (ὁδὸν σωτηρίας) obscures the message. Some commentators endorse the translation "a way" (as seen in the NASB), not "the way."[29] Polhill explains, "None of this would have been very clear to Gentiles…. The Greco-Roman world was full of 'saviors.' Savior/deliverer, salvation/deliverance were favorite terms. The emperor dubbed himself 'savior' of the people."[30] This spirit is not confirming Jesus's assertion of being "the way" (ἡ ὁδός)! Instead, it foists Jesus into polytheistic context, where pagans could receive him on their terms. The message of the Christ is syncretized, adjusted by the spirit to suit the religious atmosphere.

---

[25] While not intended as a direct response to Parsons, the argument of this article does oppose his claim that the spirit performed a somewhat "positive" role, as such "external validation was necessary" for the entrance of Christianity into that region. Mikeal C. Parsons, *Acts*, Paideia (Grand Rapids: Baker Academic, 2008), 231.

[26] For more on the demonic activity of deception, see Scott D. MacDonald, *Demonology for the Global Church: A Biblical Approach in a Multicultural Age* (Carlisle, Cumbria: Langham Global Library, 2021), 43–46.

[27] Keener, *Acts*, 3:2457.

[28] Keener, *The IVP Bible Background Commentary*, 371. Beyond the numerous historical and archeological references to Zeus being the "Most High" recorded by Paul Trebilco in his article "Paul and Silas—'Servants of the Most High God' (Acts 16.16–18)," *JSNT* 36 (1989): 51–52, an overt example is seen in the title and content of *Homeric Hymn* 23: "To the Son of Chronos, Most High."

[29] Newman and Nida prefer "the way" by appealing to the author Luke. "Luke certainly intends for his readers to understand that there is but one way of salvation; and for this reason 'way of salvation' must be understood in the sense that Luke himself would have taken it, 'the way of salvation.'" Barclay M. Newman and Eugene A. Nida, *A Translator's Handbook on the Acts of the Apostles*, UBS Translator's Handbooks (New York: United Bible Societies, 1972), 318. However, what if Luke's intention is to reflect the syncretistic deception of the spirit and the necessity of the exorcism? The argument from Luke's intention is not as strong as it appears.

[30] Polhill, *Acts*, 351. He continues, "These acclamations may have been true enough, but they were open to too much misunderstanding for pagan hearers. The truth could not be so easily condensed for those from a polytheistic background. Jesus might be seen as just another savior in the bulging pantheon of Greek gods."

3. *Paul's Delay*

The divining spirit persists, refusing to abandon Paul's company for "many days" (πολλὰς ἡμέρας). When Paul met Elymus, the confrontation with a "son of the devil" is brief, resulting in the blinding of the religious opposition (Acts 13:11). In Ephesus, cloth that touched Paul is expelling demons, with the sons of Sceva attempting to replicate his powerful works (19:12–16). As an apostle of Christ, Paul seemingly lacks nothing for the ministry of exorcism, yet he delays for many days with this divine spirit, waiting until he is annoyed.

A couple of ideas deserve suggestion. First and least likely, Paul fails to recognize that a spirit is involved, and when he realizes the presence of the spirit, he exorcises it. Luke's telling of the narrative points us away from this proposal. There is no moment of realization, only a girl with a divining spirit and a progressively annoyed Paul. Second and more plausibly, Paul knows what she is, but he treats her like a sideshow, unworthy of attention. Only when she persists, Paul's ire leads to action. Third and most likely, Paul knows what she is, but he prioritizes preaching, supposing that any early confrontation with her will likely lead to great conflict and hinder his ability to preach. So, Paul delays as long as possible, but not so long as to leave the issue of syncretism unaddressed.

Paul ensures the healthy entry of the gospel into Philippi. Yet, Paul could not let the spirit continue. Consider Chrysostom's evaluation:

> Why did the demon utter these words, and why did Paul forbid him? The one acted maliciously, the other wisely. For [Paul] did not want to make him believable. If Paul had admitted his testimony, the demon would have deceived many of the believers, since he was accepted by Paul.... The demon uses agreement for the purpose of destruction.[31]

If Paul said nothing, letting the spirit continue to speak and endlessly associate with him in Philippi, the damage to the fledgling Christian community could be incalculable. These new believers could simultaneously accept Paul and the spirit's testimony as authorized witnesses! Thus, according to his missional priorities, Paul delays, but he does not endlessly ignore and compromise the content of his mission.

4. *The Exorcism and Its Consequences*

The matter can wait no longer. Paul is "greatly annoyed" because the attachment and testimony of the slave girl threatens his witness in Philippi. Yet a public confrontation with a πύθων would surely elicit some consequences. The child is owned. Greek paganism saturates the city. As foreigners, causing any sort of disturbance is dangerous enough! But for the sake of the gospel, an exorcism is necessary.

The entire exorcism is less than a verse, only amounting to the last two sentences of verse 18: "Paul, having become greatly annoyed, turned and said to the spirit, 'I command you in the name of Jesus Christ to come out of her.' And it came out that very hour." Luke's framing of this exorcism portrays the apostle as a picture of his master. Jesus, like Paul, silenced and cast out demons with but a few words (e.g., Luke 4:35).

---

[31] Francis Martin, ed., *Acts*, ACCSNT 5 (Downers Grove, IL: IVP Academic, 2006), 203. The quote is originally from Chrysostom's *Homilies on the Acts of the Apostles* 35.

The consequences of this exorcism of the slave girl are swift. First, the πύθων releases its grip on the girl. New Testament exorcisms normally involve compassion upon the inhabited. For instance, Matthew records that Jesus exorcised a demon from a mute man (Matt 9:32–34), and this little narrative lies between the cries for mercy from two blind men (9:27) and Jesus's compassion upon the crowds (9:36). In other words, an exorcism demonstrates God's compassion on the oppressed. But Acts 16:16–18 does not describe mercy upon the oppressed as a motivation behind the exorcism. Instead, Paul acts out of hostility toward the spirit and its strategic actions to undermine his ministry. Yes, the girl is free from the spirit, yet she is still enslaved to her owners and the text emphasizes the spirit's exit—"it came out that very hour" (ἐξῆλθεν αὐτῇ τῇ ὥρᾳ).

Second, the exorcism exalts Christ. Paul's exorcism command clearly proclaims the superior power—"the name of Jesus Christ." The conflict with the πύθων shakes accepted religious powers and practices, while simultaneously presenting Jesus as the Savior from such entanglements. Keener says,

> A pagan hearer of Luke's narrative, for whom python spirits were positive or, at worst, neutral, would find baffling the exorcism recounted here in Acts.... But the exorcism made perfect sense on monotheistic Jewish and Christian presuppositions. It is not surprising that John Chrysostom read the narrative as a confrontation with Apollo, here recognized as a demon (*Hom. Acts* 35).[32]

Paul and his mission team are preaching in the lands associated with the Greek gods, and this exorcism demonstrates that Christ has entered not a colleague, but as a rival who would expose the gods as "no gods" (Gal 4:8). The power of the Christ routs the πύθων, and it is not long before Gentiles flock to his salvation banner (Acts 16:29–34).

Third, local outcry arises. In some respects, the reaction of the community is overblown thanks to the spurious and ethnically-based adjurations of the slave girls' owners (16:20–21). In Greek circles, "The exploitation of such diviners for commercial gain regularly drew criticism."[33] Pervo adds, "To put such individuals out of business will be a community service."[34] Yet money matters, and so the owners drag Paul and Silas to court and press the issue through the magistrates, while a mob joins in the attack.

Fourth, the Philippians physically persecute Paul and Silas. The meeting with the magistrates is a complete sham, aiming to appease public consensus rather than pursuing the cause of justice.

> In practically less time than it takes to tell, [the owners of the slave girl] arraigned the missionaries on their foul charges, supported by the testimony of the urban mob. The panicked magistrates caved in to this threat and, without inquiry or examination, had

---

[32] Keener, *Acts*, 3:2429. Keener also notes that Bede "favored the Apollo connection" in his comments on Acts 16:16.

[33] Conzelmann, *Acts of the Apostles*, 131. Conzelmann specifically points to Lucian of Samasota for this argument.

[34] Pervo, *Acts*, 405. Pervo argues that putting the slave girl out of business would be a "public service" because, "in this instance, the majestic god Apollo is represented by a street person of the lowest status, whose advertisement is far from Apollonian and whose career collapses at a single pronouncement by Paul. Her fate resembles that of the alleged sons of a high priest of the God of Israel in 19:13–17." However, this argument understands the exorcism as the exposing of the slave girl's weakness, when it would be better to predominantly see the exorcism as a reflection of Christ's power. The simplicity of the exorcism is remarkable in comparison to the elaborate systems and tools which were common then and now.

the alleged perpetrators viciously whipped and slapped into firm custody. Those who
had loosened the bonds of a demon found themselves in shackles.[35]

Dragged through the streets, beaten with rods, locked and immobilized in a Philippian prison, the persecution is harsh. But Paul and Silas have planted the gospel in the city. A demonized girl is free. And Christ is distinct from the polytheistic system of the day.

5. Acts' Rebuke of Syncretism Today

Imagine the state of the Philippian church had Paul declined to exorcize the πύθων. A lack of persecution would have ensured the free movement of the missionaries. The church might have grown rapidly, with many people who subscribe to the diviner's "ministry" accepting this "Christ." The number of "converts" would swell, yet in times of need or desperation, these so-called "Christians" might see no issue with consulting the local diviners. They might say, "God uses the πύθων too, since one introduced this Jesus to us when Paul arrived." This syncretized state of the Philippian church is exactly what Paul intended to avoid. Instead, Paul's courage leads to a partner church, confident in the gospel (Phil 1:5).

How then shall we respond to the present syncretism of our time, captivating hearts and corrupting Christian communities? First, in the words of Byang Kato, let us remember, "non-Christian religions prove man has a concept of God, but they also show man's rebellion against God (Rom. 1:18–23)."[36] When Christian missionaries enter a new place or people (like Paul and Silas in Philippi), the existing non-Christian religion needs far more than accommodation and adjustment. Rather, the entrance of the Lord of Lords necessitates a spiritual conflict with human and demonic rebels.

Second, let us prepare to suffer for a gospel that refuses the notion that other gods and religious systems are equals with Jesus Christ. In many places of Africa and the West, the zeitgeist calls for equality, peaceful dialogue, and mutual affirmation.[37] Conventional wisdom discourages or even derides evangelism, much less exorcism. Direct conflict with other religious powers is often verboten. But when the gospel is in peril as it was in Philippi, we need "Polycarps, Athanasiuses, and Martin Luthers, ready to contend for the faith at any cost."[38] Imitating the early missionaries singing in a Philippian prison (Acts 16:25), may Paul's joy in suffering for Christ be our own.

Third, let us expose the frailty of these powers. As Psalm 89:6 asks, "For who in the skies can be compared to the LORD? Who among the heavenly beings is like the LORD?" The divining spirit in Philippi is pathetically weak compared to Christ. Yes, it holds sway for a moment, but the spirit did not foresee or prevent its own defeat![39] People look to the *ng'anga*, but their demonic "solutions" are so temporary and insignificant compared to work of Jesus Christ on our behalf.

---

[35] Pervo, *Acts*, 406.

[36] Byang H. Kato, *Theological Pitfalls in Africa* (Kisumu: Evangel, 1975), 181.

[37] I vividly remember an oral examination with my missiology professor at Stellenbosch University (South Africa). He posed a scenario in which I was a pastor in a town where there was also an imam. He asked if I would proselytize the imam. When I responded that I would, he coldly responded, "I would disagree with you on that."

[38] Kato, *Theological Pitfalls*, 184.

[39] Lenski observes, "The spirit in this girl accomplished no more by means of his divining than our fortune-tellers do today. Why, this spirit could not and did not know what was awaiting him, namely that in a few days he would be driven out of the girl by the power of Jesus!" R. C. H. Lenski, *The Interpretation of the Acts of the Apostles* (Minneapolis: Augsburg, 1961), 663.

People in the church who dabble with witchdoctors and occultism are ultimately deceived; they find no true, lasting solution. "To believe '*Ukwimba kati kusansha na Lesa*' is to believe a lie. We must choose to trust and wait on God in every circumstance, and His Word must be our final authority as we encounter conflict with our African traditional proverbs and beliefs."[40] Jesus alone is our savior, and as Paul demonstrates in Philippi, the Christ did not come to work with the *ng'anga*. He came to set us free.

---

[40] Mwamba, "God Empowers African Charms," 44.

Themelios 47.2 (2022): 288–302

The Fantasy of the Frantic Apostle:
Paul and the Parousia

— Allan Chapple —

Allan Chapple is honorary research fellow at Trinity Theological College in Perth, Western Australia.

******

Abstract: There is a widespread belief that Paul understood his Gentile mission as the brief final chapter of salvation-history, preceding—or even triggering—the imminent return of Jesus. The first half of this essay discusses four major problems that make this view implausible: Paul's understanding of the extent of the world, of God's saving purpose, and of his specific task, and what his plans and activities reveal. The second half provides an alternative account of what the evidence discloses about the connections between Paul's missionary convictions and activities and his beliefs about the end. The conclusion indicates where this discussion takes us.

******

Paul believed that God had called him to preach the gospel to the Gentiles in order to bring about the end-time conversion of the nations … [and] that his service from Jerusalem to Illyricum put him well on the road to converting the nations and thus hastening the parousia.[1]

The faster Paul reached the "ends of the earth," bringing with him the "full number of Gentiles" (Rom 11:25), the sooner Jesus would return.[2]

I t is not uncommon to meet such statements in studies of Paul, claiming that he was engaged in a campaign to evangelize the world before its imminent end.[3] Had this been the case, everything about him would have had a frantic air—but this essay aims to demonstrate that that Paul is almost certainly a fantasy, a figment of the imagination. There are just too many contradictions with the data of his letters and the book of Acts for this view of Paul to be credible. A thorough demonstration would

---

[1] C. Marvin Pate, *Romans*, Teach the Text Commentary (Grand Rapids: Baker Books, 2013), 287–88.

[2] David B. Capes, Rodney Reeves, and E. Randolph Richards, *Rediscovering Paul: An Introduction to His World, Letters, and Theology* (Downers Grove, IL: IVP Academic, 2007), 104.

[3] Another recent study exemplifying many of the problems discussed in this essay is Seyoon Kim, "Paul as an Eschatological Herald," in *Paul as Missionary: Identity, Activity, Theology, and Practice*, ed. Trevor J. Burke and Brian S. Rosner, LNTS 420 (London: T&T Clark, 2011), 9–24.

obviously require a book rather than a brief study like this, which only outlines the case against the "frantic apostle."[4] What makes this worth doing is the way this imaginary Paul keeps turning up in all sorts of places. The case against him is presented here in two sections: the first summarizes how this view of Paul misrepresents him, and the second sketches what I think is the right alternative. A third section then gives a brief answer to the necessary question, why does this matter?

1. The Case against the "Frantic Apostle"

A convenient way of presenting this case is to concentrate on *four* key ideas that are embedded in the view of Paul represented in the two quotations above.

1.1. This Paul Was Ignorant of the Size of the World

Another proponent of this view describes Romans 15:19 as "an enormous exaggeration when measured by geographical reality"[5]—a polite way of saying that Paul was simply mistaken. He could only have believed that his activities from Jerusalem to Illyricum meant that he was "well on the road to converting the nations" if his world was merely Roman and Mediterranean. But there are good reasons for confidence that he was much better informed about the world than that.

One is his reference to Scythians (Col 3:11), who came from modern day Crimea and Ukraine. Another is the high probability that a well-instructed, well-connected Jew like Paul (Acts 22:3–5; Gal 1:14) would have known of the Jewish communities in Parthia, Media, and Mesopotamia (Acts 2:9). Thirdly, the fact is that Paul and his contemporaries were rather well informed about numerous regions between the borders of the Roman Empire and the "ends of the earth."[6]

More than three centuries earlier Alexander and his army had fought their way to India, and the legacy of his exploits was one of the foundations on which the Romans developed extensive trade networks with the east coast of Africa, the Arabian Peninsula, the Indian subcontinent, parts of southeast Asia, and China.[7] They also looked westward, for Julius Caesar's campaigns in Gaul and Britain meant that both were on the Roman map, along with what they called "Germania." Although we can't know how much Paul knew about such places, we can be confident that his commission to take the gospel to "all the nations" (lit.: Rom 1:5; 16:25–26; 2 Tim 4:17) gave him a *motive* to find out as much as possible about what this would involve, and that he also had the *means* for doing so.[8] There is no reason

---

[4] Because this is only an introductory survey, I refer to scholarly literature only where access to such information is likely to be helpful to readers who might not be aware of it. Bible quotations are taken from the NIV2011, except where I give a more literal translation ("lit.")

[5] Ernst Käsemann, *Commentary on Romans*, trans. Geoffrey W. Bromiley (Grand Rapids: Eerdmans, 1980), 395.

[6] Eckhard J. Schnabel, *Early Christian Mission* (Downers Grove, IL: InterVarsity Press, 2004), 1:445. The evidence for this statement is in pages 445–99.

[7] See Matthew Adam Cobb, *Rome and the Indian Ocean Trade from Augustus to the Early Third Century CE*, Mnemosyne Supplements 418 (Leiden: Brill, 2018); Berit Hildebrandt with Carole Gillis, eds., *Silk: Trade and Exchange Along the Silk Roads Between Rome and China in Antiquity*, Ancient Textiles Series 29 (Oxford: Oxbow, 2017); Raoul McLaughlin, *The Roman Empire and the Indian Ocean: The Ancient World Economy and the Kingdoms of Africa, Arabia and India* (Barnsley, UK: Pen & Sword, 2014).

[8] See the evidence presented in Schnabel, *Early Christian Mission*, 1:470–71.

to think he was less well-informed than Thomas, for example, who apparently knew enough to plan on, and succeed in, taking the gospel to India.[9]

Therefore: What Paul is likely to have known about the size of the world makes it very unlikely that he ever expected the evangelization of the nations, and thus the return of the Lord, within his own lifetime.

1.2. This Paul Had Astonishingly Small Expectations about God's Saving Work

This too is embedded in the claim that he was "well on the road to converting the nations" and takes two different forms: one focuses on what Paul was actually aiming to do and the other on what he would achieve.

What was Paul aiming to do? One commentary on Romans 15:19 gives this answer:

> [When] Paul says that in this region he has completed the Gospel of Christ, he does not mean that he (or anyone else) has preached the Gospel to every person in it, but that it has been covered in a representative way. The Gospel has been heard; more could not be expected before the *parousia.*[10]

This understands Paul as a herald, the chief means in that world of broadcasting important information. Having made his announcement (κήρυγμα) in a public setting, the herald (κῆρυξ) would move on and announce it (κηρύσσειν) in a new location. What the hearers made of the announcement was not his concern; he was responsible only to make it known. But this wasn't Paul's outlook—not because he wasn't a herald, but because he wasn't just a herald.[11] That is why he expected a great deal more before the parousia than simply getting the gospel heard.

He makes this clear in Romans, for example, long before we come to 15:19. He did not proclaim the gospel with a take-it-or-leave-it attitude: he wanted hearing to result in believing, and thus in calling on the Lord, because he wanted his hearers to be saved (Rom 10:8–17). This is all there at the beginning of the letter: he aimed at securing "the obedience of faith" (lit.) among the Gentiles by bringing them the gospel, the means by which God saves all who believe (Rom 1:1, 5, 9, 16). But we do not even have to read Romans to realize that this Paul-as-herald view is mistaken, for it is contradicted by the existence of the letter. How could he justify deviating from his commission as a herald to compose long and complex letters to people who had already heard and embraced what he announced?

What would Paul's ministry achieve? Here we return to the initial quotation of C. Marvin Pate. Let's suppose, first, that "well on the road" means that this work was about one-third complete, and secondly, that all of Paul's churches between Jerusalem and Illyricum—in Syria and Cilicia, Galatia and

---

[9] On the likelihood of Thomas's mission to India, see Robert Eric Frykenberg, *Christianity in India: From Beginnings to the Present,* Oxford History of the Christian Church (Oxford: Oxford University Press, 2008), 91–115; Samuel Hugh Moffett, *A History of Christianity in Asia, Volume I: Beginnings to 1500,* 2nd ed. (Maryknoll, NY: Orbis, 1998), 25–36; Schnabel, *Early Christian Mission,* 1:880–95; W. Brian Shelton, *Quest for the Historical Apostles: Tracing their Lives and Legacies* (Grand Rapids: Baker Academic, 2018), 178–84.

[10] C. K. Barrett, *The Epistle to the Romans,* 2nd ed., BNTC (London: Black, 1991), 253.

[11] For Paul as κῆρυξ: 1 Tim 2:7; 2 Tim 1:11; his κήρυγμα: Rom 16:25; 1 Cor 1:21; 2:4; 15:14; 2 Tim 4:17; Titus 1:3; and his κηρύσσειν: Rom 10:8; 1 Cor 1:23; 9:27; 15:11–12; 2 Cor 1:19; 4:5; 11:4; Gal 2:2; 5:11; 1 Thess 2:9; plus that of others: Rom 10:14–15; Phil 1:15; Col 1:23; 1 Tim 3:16; 2 Tim 4:2.

Asia, Macedonia and Achaia, and wherever else—had a total of some ten thousand members.[12] This means that when he had completed the "conversion of the nations," the entire company of those waiting to greet the returning Lord would fit into the amphitheater of a typical Roman city. Quite frankly, that looks much more like an embarrassing piece of tokenism than a great and universal salvation. But it is obvious that Paul did not expect God to save only a tiny portion of the world's population.

This is demonstrated, first, by three features of his exposition in Romans 11 of God's saving work. First, he is expecting a future that he describes as "riches" (11:12), a metaphor that obviously indicates great abundance. Secondly, he is also very confident that the present "remnant" of Israel (11:5) will become a "fullness" (πλήρωμα, 11:12 [lit.]), to match that of all the Gentiles who will be saved (πλήρωμα, 11:25). Whatever size a πλήρωμα might be, it is at the opposite end of the spectrum from a crowd of spectators in one amphitheater. And thirdly, whatever Paul means precisely by "all" (πᾶς, 11:26) and "everyone" (πάντες, 11:32), such expectations are obviously huge and expansive.

The second counter to this view is the fact that Paul attached great importance to God's covenant promises to Abraham, as his expositions in Romans 4 and Galatians 3 demonstrate. And since Abraham's end-time family was to be both *universal* in scope ("all peoples on earth": Gen 12:3) and *immense* in size ("as numerous as the stars in the sky and as the sand on the seashore": Gen 22:17), how could Paul possibly regard the results of his own ministry as the complete fulfilment of those promises? When measured against what God has promised, even tens of thousands of converts could only be the first fruits at best, and a *very* long way from the complete harvest.

Therefore: Paul's convictions about the greatness of God's saving purpose and power make it most unlikely that he ever expected the full and final salvation of Jews and Gentiles, and thus the return of the Lord, within his own lifetime.

1.3. This Paul Believed That He Must "Convert the Nations"

In order to keep the discussion within reasonable bounds, we will concentrate on *four* key problems with this claim.

First, it gives Paul's work a completeness and finality he doesn't claim. The stark contrast between the fruit of Paul's labors and God's promises to Abraham is obviously important here. Such a contrast is also evident in Paul's own words: in comparison with his expectations of a vast and comprehensive outcome to God's saving work, his hopes and goals for his own work are very modest.

Although he is confident of the future salvation of "all Israel" (Rom 11:26), he still longs and prays for the Israelites' salvation (Rom 10:1) and works to that end—but his sights are not set any higher than saving "some of them" (Rom 11:14). The obvious contrast between "some" and "all" effectively rules out the frequent claim that Paul expected his own missionary labors to win "the full number of the Gentiles"—and thus indirectly to trigger Israel's final salvation (Rom 11:11–14, 25–26).[13] In God's great mercy, all of this will happen (Rom 11:30–32)—but obviously not just through Paul's ministry. This limitation is true of his work as a whole, as we learn from two descriptions in 1 Corinthians of his

---

[12] The limitations of our knowledge make this figure no more than a generous guess.

[13] These claims reflect a common problem in the studies we are critiquing: the tendency to assume connections where none are stated. Because Paul mentions in the same chapter both his own ministry to Jews and Gentiles and also the salvation of the full complement of both of them (their πλήρωμα: 11:12, 25), many studies claim that he expects his ministry to bring about this comprehensive salvation (11:13–14, 25–26). However, he does not say so, there or anywhere else—and what he does say about his ministry in that chapter contradicts such a view.

general approach. He makes himself "all things to all people" (1 Cor 9:22b) and aims to "please everyone in every way" (1 Cor 10:33)—but this is not an unprincipled pursuit of human approval.[14] Because his goal is the salvation of as many people as possible (1 Cor 9:19; 10:33), he does all that he can to remove any barriers (1 Cor 9:20–22) and to avoid giving any offence (1 Cor 10:32–33) that might prevent the gospel being heard. Yet here too the harvest he anticipates is not "all" or even "most," but only "some" (1 Cor 9:22b).

Second, this view wrongly depicts Paul as a "lone ranger." He is represented as viewing the conversion of the nations is *his* responsibility, with the timing of the Lord's return dependent on how quickly he gets this done. But Paul does not speak of himself in these ways—and what he does say about his mission reveals a markedly different view.

His policy of not "building on someone else's foundation" reveals his awareness that he was not the only one engaged in foundation-laying evangelism and church-planting (Rom 15:20; cf. 2 Cor 10:15–16). While some of his associates did such work, as Epaphras did in Colossae (Col 1:3–8), in this passage he is more likely to be thinking of the work of other apostles and church leaders.[15] His own work was by no means a solitary affair, for his letters refer to a great many people who were involved with him at different times and in different ways.[16] Although some worked under his direction over several years, it is very striking that he doesn't regard them as subordinates who assisted him in *his* work but as his partners in "the work of the Lord." A clear example is his telling the church in Philippi that he often thanks God for their "partnership in the gospel" (Phil 1:3–5). A different kind of leader would probably have referred to this as "helping me in my work," for (as this letter reveals) it was by no means an equal partnership.

Third, there are real problems with describing Paul's task as "converting the nations." These problems are of different kinds, but their combined effect makes this description unhelpful at best.

Paul doesn't use such terminology in describing his commission, and it is difficult to make it fit with what he does say. A "conversion" normally refers to the point at which someone accepts the gospel, "calling on the name of the Lord" for the first time.[17] But Paul is not focused on this starting-point ("being converted") but on the final outcome ("being saved")[18]—which is why he prays and works for perseverance and progress, for growth and depth, in his churches.[19] This is also why he wrote to his churches: his letters are not the work of an itinerant evangelist but of a faithful pastor, whose goal is not

---

[14] Paul is insistent that he does not—and must not—seek such approval: 1 Cor 4:3–5; 2 Cor 5:9–14; 10:16–18; 12:19; Gal 1:10; 1 Thess 2:3–6.

[15] Examples are found in 1 Cor 3:5–6; 9:5–6; 15:11; 16:12; Titus 3:13.

[16] On the important subject of Paul and his large network of co-workers, begin with Paul W. Barnett, *Paul and His Friends in Leadership: How they Changed the World* (Abingdon, UK: The Bible Reading Fellowship, 2017); see also Schnabel, *Early Christian Mission*, 2:1425–45.

[17] Rom 10:9–13; 1 Cor 1:2; 12:3; Col 2:6. There are many other ways in which Paul refers to this first "turning": e.g., Rom 5:17; 6:17; 1 Thess 1:9–10; 2:13; 2 Thess 1:8; 2:11.

[18] Rom 10:1; 11:14; 1 Cor 1:21; 5:5; 9:22; 10:33; 15:1–2; 2 Cor 5:20–6:2; 1 Thess 2:16; 1 Tim 2:3–7; 4:16; 2 Tim 2:10.

[19] e.g., 1 Cor 11:2; 15:1–2, 58; 16:13; 2 Cor 10:15; Phil 1:9–11, 25–27; 2:16; 4:1; Col 1:9–11, 23; 2:6–7, 19; 4:12; 1 Thess 3:8, 12; 4:1, 10; 2 Thess 1:3–4; 2:15.

winning converts but establishing churches that last.[20] If Paul had been sent to convert the nations, how would he know when his task was done? What would count as a nation's "conversion"? And what would signal that the nations as a whole had been converted? It is difficult to find any indications in his letters as to how Paul would answer these questions.

Fourth, the way Paul describes and conducts his mission doesn't fit such a goal. There are several key features of Paul's descriptions of his task and of the way he goes about it that are at odds with the idea of "converting the nations."

He depicts himself as an initiator rather than a finisher, with an obvious example being his statement that he has "fully proclaimed the gospel of Christ" (Rom 15:19). He is not claiming to be "well on the road to converting the nations," as Pate believes. He means that he has completed his assignment in the regions between Jerusalem and Illyricum—and verse 20 makes it clear what that assignment is.[21] He has a *pioneering* task, making the gospel known where it has not yet been heard. By doing so he initiates a process that he himself does not complete: his work is essential and foundational, but it is not everything that must be done.

Sometimes he makes this explicit: he tells the Corinthians, for example, that he planted the seed in God's farmland, but others water it (1 Cor 3:6–9); he laid the foundation for God's edifice, but others build on it (1 Cor 3:9–15); he fathered their church by means of the gospel, while others ("guardians") have a role in their upbringing (1 Cor 4:15). He also expresses this idea indirectly, such as designating certain people as the "first fruits" (ἀπαρχή) of a particular city or region (Rom 16:5; 1 Cor 16:15; 2 Thess 2:13). This OT metaphor depicts a location's first converts as a sign that the "harvest" there has only just begun.[22] Paul's labors have begun the process—but there is still much more to be done.

It is because he understands himself as a gospel pioneer that he takes it for granted that many others will continue what he begins—an expectation that emerges in several ways in his letters. One of these is especially noteworthy because he makes nothing of it: he addresses 1 Corinthians to "the church of God in Corinth" (1 Cor 1:2), but the major letter he sends a year or two later is addressed to that church "together with all his holy people throughout Achaia" (2 Cor 1:1). Through the work of unnamed others, the gospel has spread out from Corinth and taken root in other centers, with Cenchreae being the only one we know about (Rom 16:1). This expectation underlies his references to the gospel as active and powerful: it "comes" (Col 1:6; 1 Thess 1:5), it "bears fruit and grows" (Col 1:6), it "rings out" (1 Thess 1:8), it "works" (1 Thess 2:13), and it "runs" (2 Thess 3:1 [lit.]). Such language is clearly meant to instill confidence in the gospel as God's powerful means of effecting his saving purpose—but it is also an implicit acknowledgement of the work of those through whom all this happens. His intention to travel from Rome to Spain (Rom 15:23–24, 28–29) means choosing to bypass completely the important province of Narbonensis. The most likely explanation for this surprising omission is Paul's confidence that the gospel will be taken there in a "pincer movement" by workers heading west from the churches in Rome and east from churches he expects to establish in Spain.[23] This raises the much-debated subject of whether Paul expected his churches to engage in evangelism and church-planting activities after

---

[20] See the essays in Brian S. Rosner, Andrew S. Malone, and Trevor J. Burke, eds., *Paul as Pastor* (London: Bloomsbury T&T Clark, 2018).

[21] I have discussed some aspects of this in "Paul and Illyricum," *RTR* 72.1 (2013): 20–35.

[22] See Exod 23:16, 19; 34:22, 26; Lev 2:11–14; 23:9–14, 17, 20; Num 18:12–13; 28:26; Deut 18:4–5; 26:1–11.

[23] I have discussed these and related matters in "Why Spain? Paul and His Mission-Plans," *JSPL* 1 (2011): 193–212.

he had moved on.[24] The fact that his letters are largely silent on this matter has been taken as evidence that he had no such expectations—but it is more likely to reflect his knowledge that they did do so, in response to what they had learned from both his teaching and his example. That is surely one of the key reasons he regards his task as complete in all the regions from Jerusalem to Illyricum (Rom 15:19, 23): he has established churches in enough centers to ensure that the gospel will keep spreading through the areas between and beyond them.

This is the background which provides the best explanation for the fact that Paul increasingly spent time looking after his churches—time that was therefore not devoted to evangelism and church-planting in new locations. He did this because he could not expect the gospel to spread widely from his churches unless it was also penetrating deeply within them. The ongoing outward progress of the gospel would not happen unless his churches remained stable and faithful, holding fast to the gospel and not corrupting it; living worthily of the gospel and not bringing it into disrepute; and standing firm in the face of persecution. That is why we have his letters, which arise out of the necessary pastoring role that complements his pioneering role, the *intensive* church-building aspect of his mission that goes with its *extensive* church-planting aspect.

This continuing involvement with his churches was quite time-consuming. Composing his letters and arranging for their distribution required a good deal of time and effort.[25] The letters themselves reveal that he spent time each day praying for his churches.[26] He also had to put time into supervising the team of trusted associates he sent to particular churches when needs and problems arose.[27] And when he could, he spent more time with those churches himself.[28] These commitments are hard to reconcile with the "frantic apostle" of the initial quotations.

Therefore: The way Paul envisaged the gospel taking root and spreading throughout the world makes it most unlikely that he expected that the evangelization of the nations, and thus the return of the Lord, would occur within his own lifetime.

1.4. This Paul Believed That His Work Was the Key to the Return of Jesus.

This is a Paul whose mission-statement could be summarized as "the faster I get it done, the sooner he will come!" Yet the evidence we have just considered undermines this view: if the task of converting the nations wasn't his alone, then his work was not *the* key to the coming of the end. Even more damaging is the fact that Paul nowhere suggests that his work was "hastening the parousia." In fact, he never draws

---

[24] See, for example, I. Howard Marshall, "Who Were the Evangelists?," in *The Mission of the Early Church to Jews and Gentiles*, ed. Jostein Ådna and Hans Kvalbein, WUNT 127 (Tübingen: Mohr Siebeck, 2000), 251–63; Christoph W. Stenschke, "Paul's Mission as the Mission of the Church," in *Paul's Missionary Methods in His Time and Ours*, ed. Robert L. Plummer and John Mark Terry (Nottingham: Inter-Varsity Press, 2012), 74–94; James P. Ware, *Paul and the Mission of the Church: Philippians in Ancient Jewish Context* (Grand Rapids: Baker Academic, 2011).

[25] See E. Randolph Richards, *Paul and First-Century Letter Writing: Secretaries, Composition and Collection* (Downers Grove, IL: InterVarsity Press, 2004).

[26] Rom 1:8–10; 1 Cor 1:4; 2 Cor 11:28; Eph 1:15–23; 3:14–21; Phil 1:3–11; Col 1:3–12; 1 Thess 1:2–3; 2:13; 3:10–13; 2 Thess 1:3–4, 11–12; 2:13, 16–17; Phlm 4–6.

[27] e.g., 1 Cor 4:17; 2 Cor 8:17–18; Eph 6:21–22; Phil 2:19–23; Col 4:7–8; 2 Tim 4:11–12; Titus 1:5; 3:12.

[28] e.g., 1 Cor 4:18–21; 2 Cor 12:20–13:3; Phil 1:22–26; 2:24; 1 Tim 3:14–15.

any link of this kind between his apostolic mission and the end.[29] This silence is especially striking in *three* areas in particular.

First, although he refers in various ways to the ethnic breadth and geographical scope of his apostolic task, he never speaks of any temporal limit—except that of his own death (2 Tim 4:6–8). And this is often viewed as a change of mind on Paul's part:

> The younger Paul seems confident he will be alive until the parousia, but … in his last days Paul realizes that his churches will go on without him…. While we can only speculate regarding the causes, we may question whether Paul's imprisonments, advanced age and/or near-death experiences may have persuaded him that he would not always be around for his churches.[30]

This is simply not the case. He did not move from the former expectation in his earlier letters to its opposite sometime later. What we do find in Paul is this: he sometimes expresses both perspectives in the same letter;[31] he tells his churches to be prepared for either possibility (Rom 14:7–9; 2 Cor 5:6–10; Phil 1:20–24; 1 Thess 5:10); and his canonical letters belong only to the second half of his apostolic career—and because he had often come close to death in the first half (2 Cor 11:23–27, 32–33), "the younger Paul" had been confronted with the possibility of an early death well before the earliest of his letters. As a result, any unrealistic expectations about how long he would live had been dealt with already.

Second, his many references to his travels, those in the past or those he is planning, give no indication that his decisions about them have been influenced—let alone controlled—by expectations about an imminent end.[32] Yet if his work was indeed the key to Jesus's return, this would have been the decisive factor in all of his plans and travels, and therefore a frequent element in what he says about them. For some, there is an obvious rejoinder: why would Paul need to make this explicit, when he and his readers were convinced that the Lord would return very soon indeed? Why bother to say what could be taken for granted? This defense only compounds the problem, however. When such an idea is not stated, its absence could be a sign that everybody believed it—or evidence that nobody did! It is not enough to assert the first of these; it must be demonstrated. So if Paul never links his travels with any sense of a rapidly approaching end, what does he say about them? In this regard, the Paul we meet in his letters and in Acts is comparatively unhurried. He spent long periods in cities like Syrian Antioch, Corinth, and Ephesus.[33] Brief stays elsewhere were generally not planned but forced upon him.[34] Yet if Paul had understood himself as ushering in the parousia, he would surely have regarded his enforced departure from Thessalonica, for example, as a providential sign that he should move on because his work there was done. Instead, he longed and prayed to return so that he could continue the work he

---

[29] See especially Rom 1:5; 15:15–20; 1 Cor 1:17; 9:1–2; 15:8–10; 2 Cor 10:8; 13:10; Gal 1:1, 11–16; 2:7–9; Eph 3:7–11; 1 Tim 1:12–16; 2:5–7; Titus 1:1–3.

[30] Capes, Reeves, and Richards, *Rediscovering Paul*, 255, 266.

[31] Rom 13:11–12 *and* 8:11, 23; 1 Cor 1:8; 15:51–52 *and* 6:14; 7:39; 15:29–32; Phil 1:6, 10; 3:20–21 *and* 1:20–21; 1 Thess 3:13; 4:15–17; 5:23 *and* 4:13–14, 16; 5:10.

[32] Rom 15:20–29; 1 Cor 4:18–21; 11:34; 16:5–9; 2 Cor 1:15–17, 23; 2:12–13; Gal 1:17–22; 4:13–14; Phil 1:25–27; 2:23–24; 1 Thess 2:1–2; 3:10–11; Titus 3:12; Phlm 22.

[33] Acts 11:26; 14:26–28; 15:30–35; 18:11, 22–23; 19:8–10; 20:31.

[34] Acts 13:50–51; 14:19–20; 17:1–8, 13–14; Phil 1:27–30; 1 Thess 2:2, 17–18.

believed he had only begun (1 Thess 2:17–18; 3:10–11). He also stayed in various centers and travelled through various regions more than once—and there were other occasions when he wanted to do so but was prevented by factors outside his control.[35] Moreover, he was quite prepared to change his plans in response to changing circumstances, even when this meant delaying the start of new work (e.g., Rom 1:11–13; 15:20–22; 2 Cor 1:23–2:1; 2:12–13); and he was realistic about the limitations imposed by such factors as his own physical and emotional condition and the seasonal weather (1 Cor 16:6; 2 Cor 2:12–13; Gal 4:13–14; Titus 3:12). This general picture of an unhurried Paul is reinforced by the great deal of time and effort he devoted to collecting a monetary gift from his churches for the church in Jerusalem (Rom 15:25–27; 1 Cor 16:1–4; 2 Cor 8:1–9:15)—which meant delaying the expansion of his work into new regions. He tells the believers in Rome that he intends to go from Corinth to Jerusalem, then from Jerusalem to Rome, and then from Rome to Spain (Rom 15:23–28)—a series of journeys that would take a great many months, even if the travel conditions were favorable and if nothing in either Jerusalem or Rome hindered him (Rom 15:31–32). It is very difficult to reconcile this Paul with the Paul who must work with great urgency because of the fast-approaching end. Or is it? It is often said that this time-consuming project was in fact a product of his convictions about the end:

> It must have been … designed to foster unity between the Jewish and Gentile wings of
> the Church; but it was far more than this, for, as the context shows, it was intended to
> play a vital part among the events of the last days.[36]

The obvious problem here is that the context (15:14–33) gives not the slightest hint of such an outlook. In fact, it points in quite a different direction: what Paul expects to happen once he has "completed this task" (15:28) is not that the Lord will return but that he will finally achieve his long-held ambition of going to Rome—and he will then go on to Spain. His other discussions of this important project also lack any indication that it plays a role in the coming of the end (1 Cor 16:1–4; 2 Cor 8–9; and possibly Gal 2:9–10).

Third, this view of Paul is very difficult to reconcile with the way he responds to being a prisoner. If he was intent upon completing his evangelistic task as quickly as possible, so that the Lord would return, any confinement would have been a hugely frustrating setback. Yet despite having to spend years in custody, Paul gives no hint of seeing this as a calamity that prevented him from completing his work. In fact, he never refers to this situation in negative terms; instead, he often speaks of himself as the Lord's prisoner and welcomes the opportunities this gives him to make the gospel known to those around him.[37]

Therefore: The idea that Paul connected the Lord's return to the completion of his own mission sees that link where Paul does not make it and also overlooks important evidence that he never made such a connection.

We have considered four areas in which the idea of Paul as the "frantic apostle" is at odds with the evidence of his letters and the book of Acts. This leads to the obvious conclusion that this concept of

---

[35] Acts 14:21–23; 15:23, 41 [cf. Gal 1:21]; 16:6, 9–12; 18:23; 19:21; 20:1–3; 1 Cor 4:18–19; 11:34; 16:5–7; 2 Cor 13:1–2; Phil 1:25–27; 2:24; 1 Thess 2:17–18; 3:10–11; 1 Tim 1:3; 3:14–15.

[36] Barrett, *Romans*, 255.

[37] Rom 16:7; 2 Cor 11:23; Eph 3:1; 4:1; 6:19–20; Phil 1:7, 12–18; Col 4:3–4; 2 Tim 2:8–10; 4:16–17; Phlm 1, 10–12, 23.

Paul should be abandoned. And this leads to the obvious question: what should we put in its place? What is the right way of interpreting Paul and his mission?

2. Paul and the End

If Paul was not the "frantic apostle," how did he understand his commission and go about fulfilling it? What impact did his beliefs about the end have on the conduct of his ministry? The key elements of his view can be summed up in the following *five* points.[38]

First, in line with Jesus's own teaching (e.g., Mark 13:32–33; Luke 12:40; 21:34–36), Paul believed that nobody knows when the end will come (e.g., 1 Thess 5:1–3; 2 Thess 2:1–2, 5–6). The fundamental reason for this is that it is God's prerogative to appoint the time (1 Tim 6:13–15; cf. Mark 13:32; Acts 1:6–7; 17:31).

Second, since the end could arrive at *any* moment, it is necessary to be ready for it at *every* moment (1 Thess 5:1–8). But being ready for what *could* happen now is very different from being certain that it *would* happen now—and there is no evidence that Paul ever confused the two.

Third, although he speaks of himself and his readers as waiting for the Lord's coming—and thus as living with a very important "until"[39]—he never indicates how long he thinks this waiting will last.[40] But he does describe it as patient as well as eager and hopeful (Rom 8:23–25), saying that they are waiting "with perseverance" (δι' ὑπομονῆς, 8:25).

Fourth, everything that Paul says about the end arises out of his convictions about Easter: he understands the coming triumph of the end as the necessary climax and crowning of the decisive events of Christ's death and resurrection.

Because Jesus's final coming and what God did through him at Easter are the twin poles of one great reality, there is an immensely powerful bond between them. If we think of the Easter events as a powerful magnet pulling the end closer, describing the end as "near" or "soon" is best seen as an implicit recognition of how great that magnetic force is. In other words, the nearness of the end is not a conclusion reached by looking forward to make a chronological calculation, but by looking backward to make a theological evaluation: it results from a right understanding of the epochal significance of Jesus's death and resurrection.

A good example is when Paul tells the Corinthians that "the time is short" and that "the world in its present form is passing away" (1 Cor 7:29, 31). They then discover the basis for this view in Paul's statement that "the culmination of the ages has come" (1 Cor 10:11): that is, in the decisive events of Easter, the end has arrived early, before the end. Paul is convinced that *the* critical moment is not ahead of us but already behind us: Jesus's resurrection has begun his reign, and it also guarantees his final triumph in the overthrow of death and his people's resurrection to eternal life in God's kingdom (1 Cor 15:20–26, 42–57). So what is true of this world is also true of this life: "its present form is passing away."

This also explains why Paul says believers are "eager" for the end to come (Rom 8:23; 1 Cor 1:7; Gal 5:5; Phil 3:20). This is not a sign of expecting it very soon; it is the result of what has happened already,

---

[38] Because what follows is little more than an outline sketch, it leaves many passages in Paul and many scholarly issues untouched.

[39] 1 Cor 1:8 [lit.]; 4:5; 11:26; 15:25; Eph 1:14; Phil 1:6; 1 Thess 4:15; 1 Tim 6:14; 2 Tim 1:12.

[40] Note Rom 8:23, 25; 1 Cor 1:7; Eph 1:14; 4:30; Phil 3:20; 1 Thess 1:10; 4:15; 2 Tim 1:12; Titus 2:13.

both to them and to the Lord. The Spirit generates this eagerness, because his presence within them is both the guarantee (ἀρραβών) and the foretaste (ἀπαρχή) of the resurrection-life they will enter when the Lord comes (Rom 8:11, 23; 2 Cor 1:22; 5:5; Eph 1:14). That is also when his heavenly glory—to which he was exalted by resurrection[41]—will be revealed.[42] And believers "love" this coming (2 Tim 4:8 [lit.]), not only because of what they will receive then but also—and most of all—because of what *he* will receive: the universal acclamation he should have as Lord of all (Phil 2:10–11). Against this background, when "short" is applied to time, it is more qualitative than quantitative: because the end has already begun, its glorious climax cannot *not* happen—and it presses in to crown that decisive beginning. How long the period between Easter and that great Day lasts depends on whether the pressure pulling them together is the most powerful force at work between them—but is it?

Fifth, Paul believes that there is another powerful force affecting the timing of the end—but this one has the opposite impact, keeping the end at a distance rather than bringing it nearer. This powerful reality is the kindness and patience of God.

Human sin makes the "day of God's wrath" inevitable—but "the riches of his kindness, forbearance and patience" keep holding that Day back, to give time for repentance (Rom 2:4–6). And when it comes to delaying the exercise of his wrath, God's patience is very great (Rom 9:22), a most amazing "forbearance" (ἀνοχή). In Romans, Paul refers to two eras marked by this divine forbearance. The first ended with the death of Jesus, in which human sin finally received the rightful judgment God had been holding back from the very beginning (3:25–26). The second will end on the last Day, when God will no longer restrain his wrath to give opportunity for repentance (Rom 2:4–5). This raises an obvious question: why would Paul expect God's exercise of forbearance in the present to be any less enduring than it was in the past? Why would it continue this time only for a few decades and not for millennia? If the interval between Easter and the end is a measure of God's kindness and patience, how could it be anything but very lengthy indeed?

But what about Paul's statement that "the Lord is near" (Phil 4:5)? Doesn't this show that he was expecting the parousia very soon? This assumes that he is using "near" in a temporal sense—but it is much more likely that he is using it spatially, referring not to the Lord's parousia but to his presence. Because they are so often seen as a reference to the parousia, these words can serve as a test case of how strong this interpretation is.[43] I have four reasons for rejecting it.

First, every other NT use of "near" in a temporal sense refers not to the Lord but to an important event, sometimes specified as the coming of the kingdom or of the Lord, and sometimes referred to only as the "time," the "hour," the "day," or the "end."[44] As a result, if Paul had been referring to the nearness of the parousia, he is much more likely to have used the same wording as James: "the Lord's coming is near" (Jas 5:8).

Additionally, the primary indicator of what Paul means by this statement is, as always, the context (Phil 4:4–9), which involves several important connections. The first links the Lord's nearness with

---

[41] Rom 6:4; 8:11, 17; 1 Cor 15:23–26, 42–44, 47–49; 2 Cor 4:14, 17; Eph 1:20–22; 2:6; Phil 2:8–11; 3:20–21; Col 3:1–4; 1 Thess 1:10; 4:14, 16; 2 Tim 2:8–12a; 4:1, 8, 18.

[42] The parousia will be his "revelation" (ἀποκάλυψις: 1 Cor 1:7; 2 Thess 1:7) and his "appearance" (ἐπιφάνεια: 2 Thess 2:8; 1 Tim 6:14; 2 Tim 4:1, 8; Titus 2:13).

[43] Two other passages are often used as evidence that Paul believed the parousia was imminent: 1 Cor 7:29–31 and 1 Thess 4:15–17, both of which are discussed earlier in this article.

[44] e.g., Matt 4:17; 10:7; 26:18, 45; Luke 21:8, 31; Rom 13:12; Heb 10:25; Jas 5:8; 1 Peter 4:7; Rev 1:3; 22:10.

coming to him in prayer, and thus replacing anxiety with petition and thanksgiving (v. 6). The second links this statement (v. 5b) and Paul's exhortation (v. 6) with God's gift of "peace" (v. 7)—not "peace with God" through Christ's reconciling work (e.g., Rom 5:1; Eph 2:14–17; 6:15; Col 1:20), but the Spirit-given peace in the believer's life (e.g., Rom 8:6; 14:17; 15:13; Gal 5:22; 2 Thess 3:16), especially the sense of assurance that goes with being grasped, graced, and guarded by the Lord (Phil 1:29; 3:12; 4:7). Third, Paul closes this set of exhortations with the affirmation that God, the giver of peace, "will be with us" (4:9): that is, what is true now—he is present ("near")—will always be true ("with us").

Further, Philippians who knew the Scriptures well would recognize this pattern of connections without difficulty.[45] That is because—as the clear thematic parallels demonstrate—Paul is alluding to what the Psalms say about God's nearness. There, each of the affirmations that he is "near" (Pss 34:18; 119:151; 145:18) expresses a sense of security, being linked with assurances that he hears his people's prayers, and that he can be trusted to rescue and protect them (Pss 34:15–22; 119:145–156; 145:13–20).

Fourth, while these Psalms provide the closest parallels to what Paul says, the connection between his people's prayers and God's nearness to hear and to rescue is found elsewhere in the OT (note especially Deut 4:7; Ps 69:16–18; Isa 55:6; Lam 3:55–58). The clearest statement of the strength of this connection is in Proverbs 15:29, where the expected contrast with God being "far" from the wicked is that he is "near" to the righteous. What we have instead—the assurance that he "hears the prayer" of the righteous—shows us what it means to say that he is "near."

For these four reasons, it seems clear that Paul intends "the Lord is near" (Phil 4:5) to be understood spatially rather than temporally: as the Scriptures often testify, the Lord's real and constant presence with us is an encouragement to pray and a source of peace.

If Paul was not the "frantic apostle," driven by the certainty of an imminent end, did he take the opposite view, believing that the Lord's return was in the far distant future? The short answer is that we do not and cannot know, because although he said various things about the "what" and the "why" of the parousia, he never made predictions about the "when."[46] Yet there are some possible indicators as to which he thought was more likely.

We have seen that he is unlikely to have formed clear views about how far away the parousia was, chiefly because it was impossible to predict when the gospel would have taken root in all the nations— yet he almost certainly knew enough about the world to realize that this goal would not be reached quickly. What he believed about the magnitude of God's grace pointed in the same direction.[47] In his patience and forbearance God gives sinners time for repentance (Rom 2:4)—and great patience will give plenty of time! And God's grace promises and effects a great salvation involving all the peoples of the world—and the reaping of that great harvest had hardly begun.

An obvious place to look for his views about the timing of the end is the only one of his letters which reveals that he expects to die soon (2 Tim 4:6–8). This letter is often read as though all that Paul had worked so hard to achieve, and even Paul himself, was coming unstuck and in danger of complete

---

[45] For what follows, see my essay, "'The Lord Is Near' (Philippians 4:5b)," in *In the Fullness of Time: Biblical Studies in Honour of Archbishop Donald Robinson*, ed. David Peterson and John W. Pryor (Homebush West, NSW: Lancer, 1992), 149–65.

[46] See Rom 11:25–27; 1 Cor 4:5; 15:23–28; Phil 3:20–21; Col 3:1–4; 1 Thess 1:9–10; 3:13; 4:14–17; 2 Thess 1:6–10; 2:8; 2 Tim 4:1, 8; Titus 2:11–14.

[47] Note how often he uses the language of abundance or wealth in connection with God's grace: Rom 5:15–21; 1 Cor 1:4–7; 2 Cor 4:15; 8:1–9; 9:8–15; Eph 1:6–7; 2:6–7; 1 Tim 1:14; Titus 2:11; 3:4–7.

collapse.[48] Many have betrayed him; his churches are being devastated by false teaching; Timothy shows signs of being too timid for the challenges of leadership in such tough times; and Paul is desperately lonely—so that, despite the serious problems that he would be leaving behind, Timothy must drop everything and come to comfort Paul in his final days.[49] While not completely false, this approach misses the heart of what Paul is saying and doing in this letter. Yes, things are very tough—but so is Paul. He is no stranger to hardships of many kinds (2 Tim 1:12; 2:3, 10; 3:10–11), and now that his part in the work is over (4:6–7), he is not throwing in the towel. Timothy is to come as soon as he can (4:9, 21a) so that Paul can entrust him with the leadership of the mission—for which the letter is preparing Timothy and all who are with him (4:22b).[50] That is why it says so much about the relationship between them, in marked contrast to the more "down to business" approach of his letter to Titus and the previous letter to Timothy. The opening reference to Timothy's tears (1:4), although often taken to imply that he needs to toughen up, is indicating that Paul's affection for Timothy ("I long to see you") is fully reciprocated. This and other such reminders of the length and depth of their relationship make it clear why Paul regards Timothy as the right person to take on such a great responsibility. This is also why the letter refers to twenty-three named individuals and seven different groups of people.[51] One of Timothy's major tasks as leader will be supervising a large network of co-workers of different kinds in many locations.

And it also explains why the letter gives so much attention to the fundamentals of Christian ministry: it is not because Timothy doesn't know them, but because he must never let go of them—as could happen all too easily when he is under great pressure on all fronts. And because the letter reminds those around Timothy of those fundamentals, they will be able to encourage him to maintain the right focus and priorities in his new role—and also to do the same in their own ministries.[52] The letter reveals a Paul committed to the progress of this essential work: far from being demoralized and worn out, as many claim, he is still doing as much as his confinement allows. He wants Mark there to assist him in his ministry (4:11b), not to be his valet in his final days. He is still supervising the work, keeping in touch with the activities of his associates and the situation of his churches (1:15, 2:17–18; 3:6–9; 4:10, 12, 19, 21). He does not refer to his suffering for the gospel as a thing of the past but as an ongoing reality (1:8; 2:3, 9): it is bound to continue because he intends to use every opportunity to make the gospel known (1:11–12; 4:17–18). The strongest indication of Paul's intention is his emphasis on succession, on stability and continuity in the work of the gospel. Again, this is flagged in the opening paragraph: as the family histories of Paul and Timothy demonstrate (1:3–4; cf. 3:14–15), imparting the truth to the

---

[48] At the popular level, a good example is Handley C. G. Moule, *The Second Epistle to Timothy* (London: The Religious Tract Society, 1905), *passim*; for scholarly examples see Luke Timothy Johnson, *The First and Second Letters to Timothy*, AB 35A (New York: Doubleday, 2001), 319–20; Thomas D. Lea and Hayne P. Griffin Jr., *1, 2 Timothy, Titus*, NAC 34 (Nashville: Broadman, 1992), 44–45; Ben Witherington III, *Letters and Homilies for Hellenized Christians, Volume 1: A Socio-Rhetorical Commentary on Titus, 1–2 Timothy and 1–3 John* (Downers Grove, IL: IVP Academic, 2006), 302, 307.

[49] 2 Tim 1:7–8, 15; 2:16–18; 3:6–9; 4:3–4, 9–10, 16, 21.

[50] There have been many suggestions about what the scrolls and parchments were (2 Tim 4:13), and why Paul wanted them. I think the most likely is that they were—or included—his copies of the letters to his churches (Richards, *Letter Writing*, 214–23). Entrusting them to Timothy would be a fitting symbol of handing over the leadership to him.

[51] The only letter of Paul to name more individuals is Romans.

[52] The letters to Timothy and Titus were most likely preserved because they give a clear overview of fundamental aspects of Christian leadership, applicable far beyond the situations for which they were written.

next generation is a vital means by which God advances his saving work. So what is true of Timothy's faith must also be true of his ministry: he must hand on to the next generation of leaders what Paul has entrusted to him (1:13–14; 2:2, 8–9; 3:10, 14)—so that they in turn will hand it on to others (2:2, 14, 23–25). This also explains why it is so important for Paul to have Timothy with him (4:9, 21a), despite the major problems he would leave behind (1:15; 2:14–18, 23–26; 3:1–9). Handing over responsibility for the mission will involve telling him more than he could say in a letter. However, if he is unable to get to Rome before Paul is condemned and executed, the letter will serve as a helpful guide to the essentials—not only for Timothy, but also for the whole network of gospel workers he will now lead.

It is clear, therefore, that the Paul of 2 Timothy expects *his* end quite soon (4:6–8)—but he does not assume that this will mean *the* end, for he is arranging for his mission to continue without him.

Therefore: although we can never be certain, there are good reasons for thinking that Paul is unlikely to have expected the end to come very soon. We must not push this too far, however. Paul might well have thought that "some way off" is more likely than "very soon"—but that would not mean that the last Day no longer had a significant place in his convictions and conduct, for it is just as prominent in 2 Timothy as it was in his earliest letters.[53] Paul makes it clear that their responsive love for their loving Lord should mean that faithful believers do not love this world but love his appearing (4:8, 10), and that what matters to them is his approval (2:15) and his reward (4:8). There is therefore no reason to see the last Day as less important for Paul in his last days than it used to be earlier in his ministry. Nor is there any reason to expect such a change, because Paul's convictions about the end meant that believers should live each day ready for the Lord to come—and equally ready to keep working if he doesn't (e.g., 1 Cor 15:22–23, 58; 1 Thess 3:10–13; 2 Tim 4:1–2, 5; Titus 2:11–14).

3. Why Does This Matter?

We must ask this question because our exegetical labors should never be an end in themselves, as though all that matters is being right: "God, I thank you that I am not like other exegetes." What's at stake here is *semper reformanda*: that is, God's word in the power of God's Spirit continuing to change our lives and ministries and churches, as greater understanding of God's word brings us to love him more deeply and serve him more faithfully.

So, what makes this discussion worth having? While this is not the only answer, it is always essential that God's people give careful attention to the issue at the heart of this discussion. That is because the question of how Paul's beliefs about the parousia shaped his approach in taking the gospel to the nations has a direct bearing on what should be a major concern for all of us: that is, what can we learn from him about this great task?[54] The answer is largely dependent on the level of continuity and discontinuity between his mission and ours—and that in turn depends on how much influence his expectations about the parousia had on his missionary convictions and conduct.

If our Paul is the "frantic apostle" of Part 1, there is a major qualitative distinction between his situation and ours. If Paul had believed that his mission to the Gentiles could and should be completed before the imminent parousia, this would have had a major impact on every aspect of his work—in

---

[53] 2 Tim 1:12, 18; 2:10–13, 18; 4:1–2, 6–8, 14, 18. This compares favorably with its place in his first letters: Galatians (5:5, 21; 6:8) and 1 Thessalonians (1:10; 2:12, 19; 3:13; 4:6, 13–17; 5:1–10, 23).

[54] A helpful starting-point is Eckhard J. Schnabel, "The Task of Missionary Work in the Twenty-First Century" in his *Paul the Missionary: Realities, Strategies and Methods* (Downers Grove, IL: IVP Academic, 2008), 374–458.

much the same way that war necessitates severe restrictions that do not apply in peacetime. Both the scope and manner of his activities would have been affected: it is not just that he would have to do everything with great speed; there would also be a severe limit on how much he could do. And because his goals and methods would have been developed in what was seen as an emergency situation, major changes would be needed before we could apply them in our quite different setting.

Working out what these changes should be will obviously require a good deal of careful work—but the changes would not be limited just to missionary goals and methods. As the previous sections of the essay have demonstrated, it is not possible to quarantine the expectation of an imminent end from what Paul believed about other matters. This makes it necessary to ask how far the theological impact of this expectation would go. What other consequences would there be, in addition to those we have noted? And are these only peripheral—or do they go to the heart of Paul's theological convictions? If being mistaken about the parousia involved being wrong elsewhere, our longstanding convictions about the status and function of Paul's letters would need to be reconsidered. It would be foolish to jump to conclusions too quickly here—but equally, it would be short-sighted not to ask these questions.

On the other hand, what if Paul allowed for the possibility that the parousia might not occur in the immediate future? This makes the difference between his situation and ours primarily quantitative, with the future stretching much further than he is likely to have envisaged. Crucially, this means that there is no principial reason why his approach to world mission would not suit our setting. It will obviously require a lot of careful and collaborative work to identify how much of it we can appropriate and to establish how to implement his principles and paradigms in contexts very different from his. There is a good example of what such work looks like in the missiological writings of Roland Allen and in contemporary evaluations of his ideas.[55]

Like every generation of Christians before us, we must continue the vital work of making the gospel known throughout the world. The Paul who pioneered this mission to the nations will obviously offer a great deal more of the missiological input we need than a Paul who believed that this mission would end with him.

An essential last word: It is all too easy to over-correct in response to a perceived imbalance—so I realize this is what I might have done in this essay. That is why the respectful interaction of critique and response is such a necessary part of our life together as God's people. Without it, we will not see God's truth as clearly as we should, or hold it as firmly as we should, or obey it as fully as we should, or pass it on as faithfully as we should. It is important, therefore, that this essay is not the last word on this important subject.[56]

---

[55] See especially Roland Allen, *Missionary Methods: St Paul's or Ours? A Study of the Church in the Four Provinces* (London: Robert Scott, 1912); Allen, *The Spontaneous Expansion of the Church and the Causes which Hinder It* (London: World Dominion Press, 1927). The work edited by Plummer and Terry (*Paul's Missionary Methods in His Time and Ours*) was published to mark the centenary of Allen's *Missionary Methods*, his best-known work, with chapters 8–14 devoted to an analysis of his ideas and their impact. See also the recent contribution by Elliot Clark, *Mission Affirmed: Recovering the Missionary Motivation of Paul* (Wheaton, IL Crossway, 2022).

[56] I'm grateful to Dr Brian Tabb and an anonymous reviewer for helpful input which made this essay better than it would have been.

Love, Hope, Faith: Christopher Nolan and the Apostle Paul in Dialogue

— EJ Davila —

EJ Davila is the youth pastor at Eastwood Baptist Church in Gatesville, Texas, and is a copyeditor at Wipf and Stock Publishing.

****

Abstract: This article examines Christopher Nolan's three most recent films, *Interstellar* (2014), *Dunkirk* (2017), and *Tenet* (2020), through the lens of Christianity's preeminent theological virtues: love, hope, and faith, respectively. In dialogue with the apostle Paul, I argue that Nolan takes Paul's cruciform theology of virtue (consisting of vertical and horizontal relationships) and intentionally flattens it to the purely horizontal, resulting in a presentation of these virtues that, while emotive, ultimately strips them of their significance.

****

Few filmmakers have reached the commercial, critical, and cultish fame of Christopher Nolan. As of August 2021, Nolan's twelve directorial films have grossed nearly $5 billion at the box office,[1] two of his films (*Memento* and *The Dark Knight*) are preserved in the United States' National Film Registry[2] (for films deemed "culturally, historically or aesthetically significant")[3] and six of his films (*Memento, Batman Begins, The Prestige, The Dark Knight, Inception, The Dark Knight Rises*, and *Interstellar*) are listed on IMDB's user-voted top-250 films of all time.[4] Without a doubt, then, Nolan is one of the most important and innovative filmmakers of the last two decades; so much so that in an age of reboots and sequels, Nolan's original works continue to garner positive reviews, draw audiences to the theater, and incite philosophical conversations on the nature of time.

Indeed, if we asked someone to summarize Nolan's filmography with a single word, they would probably answer *time*. Time, after all, features in several of Nolan's biggest films. *Memento*'s nonlinear

---

[1] "Christopher Nolan," *The Numbers*, accessed August 10, 2021, https://www.the-numbers.com/person/106410401-Christopher-Nolan#tab=technical.

[2] "Complete National Film Registry Listing," *Library of Congress*, accessed August 10, 2021, https://www.loc.gov/programs/national-film-preservation-board/film-registry/complete-national-film-registry-listing/.

[3] "About this Collection," *Library of Congress*, accessed August 10, 2021, https://www.loc.gov/collections/selections-from-the-national-film-registry/about-this-collection/.

[4] "Top Rated Movies," *IMDB*, accessed August 10, 2021, https://www.imdb.com/chart/top/?ref_=nv_mv_250.

narrative oscillates between future and past before arriving at the middle of the story. *Inception* takes us into a dream within a dream within a dream, with each level of the dream operating at a different pace. *Interstellar* features the relativity of time and the transcendent nature of love (and gravity). *Dunkirk* intertwines three distinctive timelines. *Tenet* introduces inverted entropy, enabling characters to interact with one another as they move backwards and forwards through time.

While time may be the most apparent theme that ties Nolan's films together, his most recent three films, *Interstellar* (2014), *Dunkirk* (2017), and *Tenet* (2020), share another focus, namely, a thematic examination of three Christian virtues: love, hope, and faith, respectively. In this informal trilogy, Nolan, who was raised Catholic, presents a secular analogue to these Christian virtues, reshaping them for a culture that is becoming increasingly less Christian and less theistic. The result is three narratives in which God is displaced by humanity, which serves as both giver and recipient of the examined virtues. Nolan's reconfiguration makes his films more palatable for wider audiences, but it also threatens to undercut Nolan's very presentation of virtue and humanity. In what follows, then, I examine each film in dialogue with the apostle Paul, noting how Nolan's anthropological vision of love, hope, and faith lacks a coherent theological foundation and thereby fails to offer a compelling exposition of these preeminent virtues.

1. Interstellar: Love That Transcends Time and Space

In 1 Corinthians 13, Paul extols the virtue of love: "love is patient, love is kind, … love never fails…. And now these three things remain: faith, hope, love. But the greatest of these is love" (vv. 4, 8, 13).[5] Christopher Nolan would likely agree. Of the three films I examine, it is the first, *Interstellar*, that most clearly evinces a thematic virtue, namely, the transcendent power of love.

Set in the near future, *Interstellar* presents an increasingly inhospitable Earth, ravaged by generations of neglect and exploitation. In an attempt to find a new home, a remnant of NASA scientists launch the aptly named Lazarus missions, sending a group of scientists through a wormhole with the task of evaluating twelve distant planets on their viability for human life. When three of these planets are deemed potentially hospitable, Cooper (Matthew McConaughey)—a former NASA engineer—and a crew of NASA scientists embark on an interstellar journey to confirm the viability of these planets and to thereby ensure humanity's post-Earth survival.

The cosmic scope of *Interstellar* weaves together themes of mystery and exploration, allowing Nolan to imbue the film with a palpable supernatural aura evocative of the Christian tradition.[6] Akin to the Holy Spirit, for instance, a "ghost" directs Cooper to NASA's secret base by communicating to him via gravity in the bedroom of his daughter, Murph (Mackenzie Foy). Moreover, as NASA acknowledges, the wormhole which enables their intergalactic travel is not a naturally occurring phenomenon; "they"— unidentifiable but seemingly benevolent beings—placed it there, inviting the audience to ponder the existence of a compassionate "other" who intervenes on humanity's behalf.

At its core, however, *Interstellar* is not so much about space exploration or even human survival; it is about love, exemplified primarily in the relationship between Cooper and his daughter, Murph.

---

[5] All translations, unless otherwise noted, are my own.

[6] Unlike *Dunkirk* and *Tenet*, *Interstellar* was co-written by Christopher Nolan's brother, Jonathan Nolan. Since Christopher Nolan wrote the final draft and is the director of the project, all references to "Nolan" refer to him.

Indeed, Cooper's main impetus for participating in the perilous, intergalactic trek is not his concern for the human race but his love for his children and his desire to secure a world in which he can grow old with them. Cooper articulates this in his farewell to his daughter: "I love you, Murph. Forever. And I'm coming back."[7]

But Cooper's promise proves difficult to keep. After a mishap on Miller's planet—a water planet whose approximation to a supermassive black hole slows the passage of time—twenty-plus years pass on Earth in what feels like a few hours to Cooper; thus, when Cooper reviews two decades of video communication from Earth, he discovers that his children are now as old as he is and that they no longer believe he will return home.

Having created a void—temporal, spatial, and relational—between Cooper and Murph, Nolan presents the film's grand exposition of love: with limited fuel, the crew must choose which of the two remaining planets they will visit. Dr. Brand (Anne Hathaway) petitions for Edmunds's planet, but Cooper, wary of her judgement, questions her subjectivity. In response, Dr. Brand confesses her love for Edmunds and cautions against dogmatic scientism: "maybe we've spent too long trying to figure all this with theory." Cooper attempts to re-ground the discussion in reason: "You're a scientist, Brand." But Dr. Brand is insistent:

> I am. So listen to me when I tell you that love isn't something we invented—it's observable, powerful. Why shouldn't it mean something? … Maybe it means more—something we can't understand, yet. Maybe it's some evidence, some artifact of higher dimensions that we can't perceive…. Love is the one thing we're capable of perceiving that transcends dimensions of time and space. Maybe we should trust that, even if we can't yet understand it.

Here, Dr. Brand sounds much like the apostle Paul. Love, she says, transcends time and space and binds us together inexplicable ways. Moreover, love is not merely a human construct. It "isn't something we invented." Rather, love breaks in from the outside, and is, perhaps, "some artifact of high dimensions" calling out from the great beyond.

Dr. Brand's exposition of love hints towards the film's climax and thematic resolution. Following a bout with the antagonistic Dr. Mann (a not-so-subtle character name), Cooper and Dr. Brand manage to retake control of their damaged spacecraft, the Endurance, but now they are being drawn into the gravitational pull of Gargantua, a supermassive black hole. Critically low on fuel, Cooper uses Gargantua's gravitational pull to slingshot the Endurance toward the last viable planet, Edmunds's planet, while Cooper detaches himself to ensure that Dr. Brand can escape Gargantua's pull and complete the mission. Cooper's sacrifice is not in vain. Gargantua swallows him up, but the black hole does not macerate him upon entry; rather, "they" intervene once again and save Cooper by constructing a tesseract—an infinite, five-dimensional tunnel that allows Cooper to communicate with his daughter via her bedroom bookshelf at any point in time. Once Cooper realizes that he is the "ghost" of Murph's childhood, he relays her the necessary quantum data to ensure humanity's survival beyond the deterioration of Earth. In doing so, Nolan's primary theme crescendos with a father's love transcending time and space to save his daughter and, by extension, all humanity. For Cooper, then, Dr. Brand was not simply pontificating when she professed, "Love is the one thing we're capable of perceiving that transcends dimensions of

---

[7] This is the first articulation of "love" in the film.

time and space." Rather, she was prophesying what was to come, for in the end, love indeed triumphs, proving Paul's succinct phrase true: "Love never fails."

At this point, Nolan and Paul seem to be humming the same tune on the transcendent power of love, but when we listen closely, we hear the dissonance. To begin, Paul envisions love first and foremost as a divine activity. That is not to say that love is always one directional (i.e., God to human or vice versa), but that the love people share with one another is always predicated upon God's love for humanity.[8] Paul may not articulate this theology of love as concisely as 1 John 4:10: "This is love. Not that we loved God, but rather that God loved us and gave his son as an atoning sacrifice for our sins." Nevertheless, Paul reaches the same conclusion. In his letter to the Romans, for instance, Paul declares the priority of God's love as manifested in the redemptive death of the Messiah: "God demonstrated *his love for us*, for while we were still sinners, Christ died for us" (Rom 5:8). Within the wider context of Romans—and indeed the wider context of Paul's epistolary corpus—Paul conceptualizes humanity as enslaved to the powers of Sin and Death, incapable of effecting its own liberation.[9] And yet at the moment when all hope was lost and humanity was "dead in transgressions and sins" (Eph 2:1), God intervened "because of the *great love with which he loved us*" (Eph 2:4).

For Paul, then, love necessarily begins with the vertical: love descends from heaven in the act of a Father sending his Son to effect salvation and reconciliation. But love is not merely a vertical act. There is a horizontal element as well when love multiplies through the Son—the true image of God and man (Rom 5:12–21; Col 1:15–20)—and into the community, the people of God, enabling them to be a people of charity and compassion. For Paul, this horizontal outpouring of love is inextricable from the fundamental identity of the church; for as recipients of God's transformative love, the church must manifest this same sacrificial love in its daily, communal activity lest love be reduced to an intangible idea divorced from God's redemptive purpose. It is for this reason that Paul frequently exhorts the church to be characterized by love: to "do everything in love" (1 Cor 16:14), "to owe no one anything, except love to another" (Rom 13:8; cf. Gal 5:12–13), and to "clothe yourselves with love" (Col 3:14).[10]

Paul, then, conceptualizes love as a cruciform image of vertical (God and human) and horizontal (human and human) relationships.[11] Nolan appears to follow suit, imbuing *Interstellar* with images that

---

[8] Commenting on the 1 Corinthians 13 exposition of love, Dunn notes, "It is hard to doubt that Paul in thus describing love had in mind the love of God in Christ." James D. G. Dunn, *The Theology of Paul the Apostle* (Grand Rapids: Eerdmans, 1998), 596.

[9] On the personification of Sin and Death, see Beverly Roberts Gaventa, "The Cosmic Power of Sin in Paul's Letter to the Romans: Toward a Widescreen Edition," *Int* 58 (2004): 229–40. On p. 231, Gaventa notes, "In Romans in particular, sin is Sin—not a lower-case transgression ... but an upper-case Power that enslaves humankind."

[10] As these three citations indicate, love for Paul is not merely a quality or an emotion; it is an activity. Similarly, when Paul writes the famous passage "Love is patient, love is kind; it is not jealous ..." (1 Cor 13:4), he uses verbs, not adjectives, to describe the movement of love. On this point, Garland writes: "Love is dynamic and active, not something static. [Paul] is not talking about some inner feeling or emotion. Love is not conveyed by words; it has to be shown. It can be defined only by what it does and does not do." David E. Garland, *1 Corinthians*, BECNT (Grand Rapids: Baker Academic, 2003), 616.

[11] By "cruciform" I mean "in the form of the cross." In what follows, I frequently refer to the intersection of the vertical and horizontal planes of love, hope, and faith as resembling that of the cross, where these virtues find their fullest expression and telos. The vertical plane designates the relationship between God and humanity; the horizontal is that between human and human. I often refer to God's activity through Jesus as "vertical," but in doing so I do not intend to screen out the horizontal nature of Jesus's life, death, and resurrection, for as the God-

evoke the Christian tradition: Earth's reversion to dust, the "ghost," the benevolent "they," Dr. Brand's exposition of love, the booming church organ in Hans Zimmer's score,[12] Cooper's sacrifice. But at the climax of the story, Nolan dismantles the vertical love from the outside and reveals that, in the end, it was humanity all along. Cooper articulates this revelation in the tesseract: "We brought ourselves here." "We're the bridge." "Don't you get it yet, Tars? 'They' aren't '*beings*' … they're *us* … trying to help … just like I tried to help Murph." Thus, the "ghost" which conjures images of the Holy Spirit is actually Cooper. The enigmatic "they" so evocative of the inbreaking love of God is actually a future incarnation of humanity. And both Dr. Brand's exposition of love, which echoes Paul's similar exaltation, and Cooper's sacrifice, which is so redolent of Jesus' self-giving, are both diluted from emblematic manifestations of divine love to dignified images of human effort.

By moving in this direction, Nolan has ensnared himself. He wants to preserve love as the consummate virtue (as in the Christian tradition; cf. 1 Cor 13:13; Gal 5:22–23), but he has not provided a theological justification for doing so. That is, if love simply *is*—a purely anthropological, horizontal phenomenon—what appeal can be made for its preeminence? Perhaps Nolan anticipates this challenge and responds via Dr. Brand's petition, "Why shouldn't it mean something?" But Dr. Brand's appeal is hardly persuasive. Indeed, by begging the question, Nolan shows that his conception of love, as anthropological as it is, demands a leap of faith.[13]

> Love is the one thing we're capable of perceiving that transcends dimensions of time and space. Maybe we should trust that, even if we can't yet understand it. (Dr. Brand, in *Interstellar*)

> I pray that you may have the power to comprehend, with all the saints … to know the love of Christ which *transcends* knowledge. (Eph 3:18–19)

2. Dunkirk: Hope for Deliverance

Nolan's first historical drama, *Dunkirk* recounts the week leading up to the Dunkirk evacuation—sometimes called the "Miracle of Dunkirk"—climaxing with the civilian-helmed rescue of British soldiers from the eponymous French coastal town. Although the film is constrained by the historicity of the Dunkirk evacuation, Nolan still imbues the story with his characteristic emphasis on *time*, presenting *Dunkirk* as an interweaving of three distinctive timelines: (1) "The Mole" timeline tracks Tommy (Fionn Whitehead), a young, taciturn British soldier who attempts to escape Dunkirk the week leading up to the evacuation. (2) "The Sea" timeline follows Mr. Dawson (Mark Rylance) and the crew of his yacht,

---

man, Jesus is at the very center of the cruciform intersection and thus perfects both the vertical and horizontal. Still, I refer to this activity primarily as "vertical" because it is an act of divine intervention that cannot be effected by humanity alone.

[12] The church organ featured in Zimmer's Oscar-nominated original score was Zimmer's first choice: the "1926 four-manual Harrison & Harrison organ in London's 12th-century Temple Church." Jon Burlingame, "Hans Zimmer's *Interstellar* Adventure: Composer Unveils Secrets of Organ, Choir, Orchestra in Nolan Film," *Film Music Society*, 6 November 2014, http://www.filmmusicsociety.org/news_events/features/2014/110614.html.

[13] As the juxtaposed quotes below testify, it is this leap of faith that, despite their irreconcilable differences, gives Nolan and the apostle Paul a common ground on which to stand, namely, the transcendent and ineffable nature of love.

Moonstone, as they travel to Dunkirk on the day of the evacuation. (3) "The Air" timeline focuses on Farrier (Tom Hardy), a Spitfire pilot whose aerial deftness proves salvific in the final hour before the evacuation commences.

If *Interstellar* unambiguously explores the virtue of love, *Dunkirk* similarly examines the virtue of hope. This emphasis is made explicit in the opening title cards:

> The enemy have driven the British and French armies to the sea.
>
> Trapped at Dunkirk, they await their fate.
>
> Hoping for deliverance.
>
> For a miracle.[14]

Hope is necessarily experienced in the absence of and the anticipation for some greater fulfillment: food for the hungry, direction for the lost, or, as in *Dunkirk*, home for the forsaken. Naturally, then, *Dunkirk* approaches hope from the negative, inviting the audience to experience and meditate on the depravity of war and its accompanying hopelessness.

We encounter this hopelessness at the inception of the film: As the aforementioned title cards exposit the perilous situation, pamphlets which read "WE SURROUND YOU" fall from the sky like parodic pieces of manna. Here, Hans Zimmer's score introduces the ticking of a clock—a sound which permeates the score—signaling that time is a scarce resource. Moreover, death is so common that Tommy is unfazed by the sight of Gibson (Aneurin Bernard) burying a soldier; in fact, Tommy helps Gibson with the hasty interment and quickly enlists his new acquaintance in his deception to sneak aboard a departing ship.

Comparable to his approach in *Interstellar*, Nolan imbues *Dunkirk* with what could be considered biblical imagery, much of which compounds the mounting hopelessness. The opening title cards refer to the German forces as "the enemy," stripping them of their historical identity and clothing them as a cosmic adversary. The enemy repeatedly descends from the sky like demonic persecutors, dive-bombing the stationary soldiers. Dunkirk, the land upon which the enemy encroaches, is a mass of rising smoke, appearing like hell on earth, or perhaps more accurately, a purgatorial limbo. And the waters of Dunkirk—like the indomitable sea which threatens to dismember the boats of Jonah (Jonah 1:4–16) and the disciples (Mark 4:35–41)—swallow up every vessel that endeavors to escape, coercing Tommy and his compatriots back the beach.

The Dunkirk coast is so demoralizing, so hopeless, that one soldier drowns himself to exit the interminable torment. Similarly, when the Shivering Soldier (Cillian Murphy), the first soldier to board Mr. Dawson's yacht, discovers that they are traveling to Dunkirk, he shouts at Mr. Dawson, "I'm not going back!" and in his panic, deals a fatal blow to George (Barry Keoghan), a seventeen-year-old boy. When we meet the same Shivering Soldier at an earlier point in "The Mole" timeline, he is composed and decisive as he exhorts Tommy and Alex (Harry Styles), "You have to stay calm.... Don't panic.... We're heading back to the beach." The horrors at Dunkirk, however, have degraded his resolve in only a few days.

---

[14] Similarly, the *Dunkirk* trailer features the following title card: "Hope is a weapon." Warner Bros. Pictures, "Dunkirk—Trailer 1," YouTube video, 14 December 2016, https://www.youtube.com/watch?v=F-eMt3SrfFU.

As the title cards indicate, then, the apparent futility of escape beckons for a miracle of deliverance. Just such a miracle occurs at the climax of the film, for just when all hope seems lost, an armada of civilian-helmed boats capable of navigating the shallow beachfront arrives to transport forsaken soldiers back home. Their triumphant arrival is threatened when a Stuka dive-bomber begins its descent, but a fuel-less Farrier glides in with angelic grace, guns down the Stuka, and ensures the evacuation's success.

With Tommy and Alex safely arriving in England, the Dunkirk evacuation is a success, and Nolan's vision of hope is realized. Before expositing Nolan's views, however, it may be more advantageous to note Paul's theology of hope so as to show how the two approaches differ.

For Paul, hope, as with love, is predominantly a vertical relationship. That is, humanity's hope is rightly oriented and rooted in God's salvific activity, hence Paul's salutation: "Paul, an apostle of Christ Jesus according to the command of God our savior and Christ Jesus our hope" (1 Tim 1:1). Accordingly, to be estranged from God is to be hopeless: "You were at that time without Christ, excluded from citizenship of Israel, strangers of the covenants of promise, having no hope, and without God in the world" (Eph 2:12).

Such hope is not abstract or self-indulgent; rather, Paul's hope stands in the Jewish tradition that looks forward with fervent expectation to a time of redemption, resurrection, and restoration.[15] For Paul and the early church, the life, death, and resurrection of Jesus modify these expectations while preserving the essential hope: an age will come when God will deliver his people from all forms of suffering, raise his people to new life, and restore creation to its perfected state. Again, this hope is not a form of abstract escapism to the "spiritual," it is confident anticipation that God has not forsaken his covenantal promises. Accordingly, Paul can endure—and encourage his churches to endure—all manners of suffering because he trusts that God's salvific work, though inaugurated in the present, will be fully realized at some indeterminate point of the future, in a manner that is both continuous and discontinuous with the present experience.

We see this hope expressed, once again, in Paul's letter to the Romans:

> Not only that, but we also boast in our sufferings, knowing that the suffering produces endurance, and endurance produces character, and character produces hope, and *hope does not disappoint*, because the *love* of God has been poured into our hearts through the Holy Spirit which has been given to us. (Rom 5:3–5)

This passage immediately precedes the previously quoted text, "God demonstrated his love for us, for while we were still sinners, Christ died for us" (Rom 5:8), and reveals how, for Paul, love produces much more than theological musings. Love, rather, produces an orientation of endurance and expectation that radically transforms the believing community to persevere in its worship and ministry despite various toils and snares. Such perseverance is possible precisely because it does not depend on the fallibility of humans but on the union of Christ and the church and on the God who raises the dead. That is, if the church is the body of Christ, as Paul frequently affirms (Rom 12:4–5; 1 Cor 10:17; 12:27; Eph 4:15–16; Col 1:24), it will suffer as Christ's body suffered and will also be restored as Christ body was restored. Thus, while suffering may be inevitable, so is restoration, in this age or the next. Paul articulates this point in 2 Corinthians, a letter that lays bare Paul's frequent sufferings and shortcomings:

---

[15] On the hope of Israel, see N. T. Wright, *The New Testament and the People of God*, Christian Origins and the Question of God 1 (Minneapolis: Fortress, 1994), 280–338.

> But we felt that we had received the sentence of death so that we would not rely on ourselves, but rather upon the God who raises the dead, who delivered us from such a deadly peril and will continue to deliver us. *On him we have set our hope*, and he will continue to deliver us. (2 Cor 1:9–10; cf. 1 Thess 4:13–14)

Here and elsewhere in the letter Paul makes it clear that he perseveres not of his own power, but of his belief in the "God who raises the dead." In doing so, Paul invites the Corinthians to see his sufferings not as a weakness, but as a mark of his fidelity and hope through which Christ's power is on full display.[16]

As with love, then, Paul predicates hope on the God who works through Jesus Christ, enabling Paul to look horizontally (his ministry to others) because he is simultaneously looking vertically (evoking again a cruciform image). In *Dunkirk*, however, Nolan follows the same pattern as *Interstellar* by flattening the vertical aspect in favor of a purely horizontal manifestation of hope, showing that salvation does not come from above, but rather when we look to one another or even in ourselves.[17]

Nolan confirmed this interpretation in an interview with *Time*:

> We live in an era where the virtue of individuality is very much overstated. The idea of communal responsibility and communal heroism and what can be achieved through community is unfashionable. *Dunkirk* is a very emotional story for me because it represents what's being lost.[18]

And Mr. Dawson articulates the same point in response to the Shivering Soldier's demand to forego the trip to Dunkirk: "We have a job to do."[19]

At its core, then, *Dunkirk* is story of human triumph. Yes, "the enemy" is human too, but by excising their identity from the narrative, Nolan is able to accentuate the perseverance of the central characters against a nameless, faceless, and quasi-mythological adversary. Accordingly, *Dunkirk* shows that hopelessness may be evoked by the "other," but hope should be directed toward one another.

All of this is not to say that *Dunkirk* is superficial. The film's emotional force lies in the fact that it is a true, historical event, and a recent one at that. Accordingly, *Dunkirk* invites us to remember our past and thus inspires us to be better by risking our own lives in service of others, a point with which Paul

---

[16] On this point, Timothy B. Savage concludes: "The Apostle guides us to the paradoxical … conclusion that it is only in cruciform sufferings like his that the Lord can perform his powerful work, introducing glory into an age of darkness, salvation into a world of despair, a new age within the old and life and power to more and more people" (*Power through Weakness: Paul's Understanding of the Christian Ministry in 2 Corinthians*, SNTSMS 86 [Cambridge: Cambridge University Press, 1996], 189). For more on Paul's views of suffering, see Savage, *Power through Weakness*, esp. 164–86; Dunn, *The Theology of Paul the Apostle*, 482–87; Scott J. Hafemann, "Suffering," *DPL* 919–21; and Brian J. Tabb, "Paul and Seneca on Suffering," in *Paul and Seneca in Dialogue*, ed. David E. Briones and Joseph Dodson, Ancient Philosophical Commentary on the Pauline Writings (Leiden: Brill, 2017), 88–108.

[17] The visual rejoinder to this point is that Farrier's timely intervention occurs "from above," but this does not upend the claim that Farrier is one aspect of the planned Dunkirk evacuation. Still, it is notable that Farrier's descent from the sky and capture by "the enemy" evokes the scriptural narrative of Jesus' incarnation and death, though certainly colored by the film's anthropological lens.

[18] Eliza Berman, "Christopher Nolan: *Dunkirk* Is My Most Experimental Film since *Memento*," *Time*, 19 July 2017, https://time.com/4864049/dunkirk-christopher-nolan-interview/.

[19] Mr. Dawson embodies the selfless, communal responsibility Nolan wants to inspire. This explains why Nolan has the character depart without the Navy, despite being requisitioned. Mr. Dawson's heroism is more apparent without the Navy aboard directing the mission.

would no doubt agree. But as with *Interstellar*, by the time the story ends, we must ask "Why?" Why trust one's neighbor when it is one's neighbor who incited the war to begin with? Why put one's hope in something as mercurial as the human race? And for what exactly are we hoping? Peace? Love? Life? By screening out the vertical, Nolan has left us stranded, staring at the horizon, unsure of what is to come.

> Until, in God's good time … The New World, with all its power and might steps forth to the rescue and the liberation of the old. (Tommy, reading Winston Churchill's speech in *Dunkirk*)[20]

> For I consider the sufferings of the present age not worthy to be compared to the coming glory which is to be revealed to us. For the creation waits with eager longing for the revelation of the children of God. For the creation was subjected to futility, not of its own will, but by the will of the one who subjected it, *in hope*, because this same creation will be set free from its slavery to decay for the freedom of the glory of the children of God. For we know that the whole creation has been groaning and laboring together until now. Not only that, but we ourselves who have the firstfruits of the Spirit, are groaning inwardly as we await adoption, the redemption of our bodies. *For in hope we were saved*. (Rom 8:18–24)

3. Tenet: Faith and Fatalism

The relationship between *Tenet* and the final theological virtue, faith, is more opaque than the relationship between *Interstellar* and love or *Dunkirk* and hope, but a gentle inquiry reveals it nonetheless. Indeed, this relationship is perceptible, though subtle, before the film even begins as the title of the film, *Tenet*—a word which denotes a principle or belief, particularly a religious one—prompts the audience to ponder the role of faith within the forthcoming narrative.[21]

Matters get more complicated, however, when we delve into *Tenet*'s labyrinthine plot. The film follows the charismatic Protagonist (John David Washington), a CIA operative, involved in a covert organization, Tenet, whose mission is to prevent "World War Three." A relatively straightforward idea, Nolan complicates matters by suffusing the narrative with his characteristic manipulation of time: Tenet possesses objects with "inverted entropy," a property which causes the objects to move backwards in time. Andrei Sator (Kenneth Branagh), a Russian oligarch, controls several "turnstiles," machines capable of inverting those who pass through, enabling them to move backwards in time in order to share future information and to "intervene" with the past. Armed with turnstiles and communication from the future, Sator intends to collect the nine pieces of the inversion algorithm in order to effectively end the world by completely reversing time at the behest of future generations for whom Earth has become inhospitable. Accordingly, the Protagonist must navigate the world of elite arms-dealers and master the

---

[20] Churchill's personal religious beliefs aside, it is interesting that Nolan chooses to end the film with a quote so evocative of Christian eschatology. It is unlikely that Paul would dissent with anything in this brief quote, although, as the subsequent quote from Romans shows, he would have much to add.

[21] The other significance of the *Tenet* title is the central location of "TENET" in the Sator Square, a five-word Latin palindrome that consists of the words SATOR, ROTAS, OPERA, AREPO, and TENET, all of which appear in the film. Moreover, the Sator Square is reflected in *Tenet*'s palindromic plot structure.

complexities of overlapping timelines en route to saving humanity from complete annihilation via time reversal.

As with the previously examined films, *Tenet* contains what could be interpreted as biblical imagery: Following the title card, *Tenet*, the Protagonist is "born again" when he awakes from a medically induced coma, brought on by what he thought was a suicide pill, with the following greeting, "Welcome to the afterlife," signaling the radical new world he enters in partnership with Tenet. Throughout the film, the Protagonist evinces a willingness to sacrifice himself for others: after securing the target, he risks his life to save the civilians in the opera house; on several occasions he antagonizes the formidable Sator in order to protect Sator's wife, Kat (Elizabeth Debicki), despite their tenuous relationship. Nolan himself commented on this aspect of the Protagonist character, noting that he and Washington were "looking for an aspect of selflessness to the character," for "some degree of spirituality" or "a generosity of spirit."[22] Similarly, Neil (Robert Pattinson) displays the same selflessness when, at the film's denouement, he reenters the hypocenter, knowing that it leads to his death and the Protagonist's survival. So, while subtler than *Interstellar* or *Dunkirk*, *Tenet* seems to consciously evince the Christian tradition.

More perceptible perhaps is the film's discussion of free will, a controversial theological topic among differing Christian traditions which, to simplify the matter greatly, centers on the relationship between the concept of God's omniscience and humanity's culpability in accepting or rejecting God's means of atonement. Generally speaking, the Calvinist tradition has emphasized a version of predestination in which God's sovereignly elects individuals irrespective of their volition to accept God's grace, whereas the Arminian tradition has argued that God's election is predicated upon God's foreknowledge of which individuals, if given the opportunity, would accept God's grace. Both sides agree that God foreordains the elect and directs history in accordance with God's will, but the latter tradition accommodates the ostensible phenomenon of free will into the equation; after all, free will, as a lived experience, seems to be an inextricable aspect of the human identity which forces us to question to what extent we are actors compelled to play our parts as written and to what extent we are improvising our roles.[23]

Tenet wrestles with these same questions. Once the Protagonist is tutored on the nature of inversion, he asks "What about free will?" The scientist, Barbara (Clémence Poésy), responds, "Don't try to understand it. Feel it." Despite Barbara's petition, the film continues to exposit the nature of inversion and its relationship with free will. Later, the Protagonist asks Neil what would happen to Kat in the present if Sator killed her in the past. Neil responds that it's impossible to know, to which the Protagonist asks an unscientific question: "What do you believe?" Neil's answer, "What's happened's happened," becomes the fatalistic mantra of the film, an appeal to the immutable nature of the past, present, and the future.

Like many theologians, however, Nolan recognizes that dispensing of free will may devolve into the remittance of personal accountability, and so he nuances the free will discussion at the film's conclusion. As Neil is preparing to reenter the hypocenter, the Protagonist asks him, "But can we change things? If we do it differently?" Neil responds, "What's happened's happened. Which is an expression of faith in

---

[22] Writers Bloc Presents, "Writers Bloc Presents: Christopher Nolan, Tom Shone and Kenneth Branagh," You-Tube video, 2 December 2020, https://www.youtube.com/watch?v=PqGrR2Upz0M/.

[23] No doubt this simplification will draw the ire of some theologians, but for the purpose of this paper, this brief outline is all that can be offered. For a survey of views on elections, see Chad Owen Brand, ed., *Perspectives on Election* (Nashville: B&H Academic, 2006).

the mechanics of the world, not an excuse to do nothing." The Protagonist asks if this is "fate," to which Neil answers, "Reality."

Here Nolan is attempting to solve the dilemma on the basis of faith, but Nolan's definition of faith is quite different from that of the apostle Paul and thus complicates his solution. In a move that should seem familiar by now, Nolan collapses the vertical aspect of Paul's theology of faith into the horizontal, creating an anthropological imitation of Paul's worldview.

As with love and hope, faith for Paul is a cruciform virtue for which the vertical necessarily precedes and intersects with the horizontal. We see this in Paul's exposition of justification—God's designation of righteousness.[24] In his letter to the Romans, Paul writes:

> The righteousness of God is through the *faithfulness of Jesus Christ* for all who believe. There is no distinction, for all have sinned and fall short of the glory of God; they are now justified freely by his grace through the redemption which is in Christ Jesus, whom God presented as a sacrifice of atonement by his blood, *received by faith*. (Rom 3:22–25; cf. Gal 2:15–16)[25]

Here Paul plainly states that sinfulness is a universal condition ("all have sinned") for which humanity has no remedy. That is, humanity is wholly unrighteous and is thus incapable of self-designating righteousness. If humanity is to be liberated from the powers of Sin and Death, it needs God—through the Messiah—to intervene and set things right. Justification, then, cannot be achieved with human effort; it is granted solely through the church's faith—its recognition and reception—of divine activity, a point Paul similarly articulates in his letter to the Ephesians: "For it is by grace you have been saved, *through faith*. And this is not of your own doing. It is God's gift—not by works, so that no one can boast" (Eph 2:8–9; cf. 1 Cor 2:4–5). For Paul, then, redemptive faith cannot be directed horizontally; it must be oriented vertically toward the intercession of God through the life, death, and resurrection of the Messiah. That said, Paul's conception of faith is no mere intellectual exercise. As with love and hope, the vertical necessarily pours into the horizontal as faith manifests in the church's faithfulness to God *and*

---

[24] That God initiates and sustains the relationship between God and humanity is paramount to Paul's theology of faith. On this point, Dunn notes, "This, then, is what Paul meant by justification by faith, by faith alone. It was a profound conception of the relation between God and humankind—a relation of utter dependence, of unconditional trust. Human dependence on divine grace had to be unqualified or else it was not Abraham's faith, the faith through which God could work his own work." Dunn, *The Theology of Paul the Apostle*, 379. Though he disagrees with Dunn's understanding of "justification" in Paul, Moo likewise emphasizes God's initiation of the divine-human relationship: "Justification by faith is the anthropological reflex of Paul's basic conviction that what God has done in Christ for sinful human beings is entirely a matter of grace." Douglas J. Moo, *Romans*, 2nd ed., NICNT (Grand Rapids: Eerdmans, 2018), 100. For a historic overview on the oft-contentious doctrine of "justification," see Alister E. McGrath, *Iustitia Dei: A History of the Christian Doctrine of Justification*, 4th ed. (New York: Cambridge University Press, 2020).

[25] On the translation "faithfulness of Jesus Christ," I follow N. T. Wright, *Paul and the Faithfulness of God*, Christian Origins and the Question of God 4 (Minneapolis: Fortress, 2013), 529: "'The faithfulness of Jesus the Messiah' is, in the person of this one representative figure, 'the faithfulness' that God required from Israel if the promise was to be valid for the whole world, as always promised. This 'faithfulness', it turns out, is a synecdochic reference to Jesus' death, *seen as* 'the faithfulness of Israel to God's saving plan' on the one hand and also as 'the faithfulness of Israel's God to his covenant promise and purpose' on the other." This translation in no way rejects the role of faith as personal belief, as made clear in verse 25 ("received by faith").

neighbor, transforming and enabling the believing community to bear the fruit of love, joy, peace, etc. (Gal 5:22–23).

For Paul, then, the church must believe in something or someone outside of itself. Humanity is too depraved to act as its own savior and must be rescued by the inbreaking love of the God via the God-man Jesus. To do the unimaginable and substitute faith in God for faith in humanity—those who have sinned and fallen short of God's glory (Rom 3:23)—is to eliminate faith altogether and to recapitulate the idolatry which has beleaguered humanity from time immemorial. And yet this is exactly what Nolan does in *Tenet*.

Throughout *Tenet*, the Protagonist is kept in the dark concerning the inner machinations of Tenet. Everyone around him, Neil, Priya (Dimple Kapadia), Ives (Aaron Taylor-Johnson), and Sator, are more informed about the nature of Tenet, inversion, and the looming threat surrounding the algorithm. Sator mocks the Protagonist's ignorance at the film's climax, "You fight for a cause you barely understand.... Your faith is blind. You're a fanatic." He then posits his own apotheotic role as humanity's savior by claiming he is creating a new world and is perhaps "a god of sorts." The Protagonist retorts that Sator does not believe in God or "anything outside your own experience," adding that without belief "you're not human. You're a madman."

This climactic dialogue exposits Nolan's views on faith. On the one hand, he censures Sator's self-deification as untenable and inhuman. Faith in something grander, he argues, is an essential aspect of the human identity. On the other hand, however, undercuts his first point by failing to provide a substantial entity in which one should believe. In fact, it seems as if Nolan contradicts himself here, for whereas he vilifies Sator's ambition, it is the Protagonist himself who becomes the object of faith when Neil reveals that the Protagonist is the mastermind behind Tenet and has thus been orchestrating the events of the film. The Protagonist explicates this point in the film's final scene: "I realized I wasn't working for you. We've both been working for me. I'm the protagonist." With this epiphany, the Protagonist asserts himself as mastermind of the operation and demonstrates that his participation in Tenet is no longer "blind faith," it is a recognition of his own centrality.

To be sure, Nolan retains an aspect of verticality in Neil's exhortation that "reality" is "an expression of faith in the mechanics of the world," but this appeal to the deterministic laws of physics is vacuous in that these laws bend to the algorithm formulated by the anonymous, future scientist, and it is the Protagonist's manipulation of inversion via the Tenet operation that effects humanity's salvation. Nolan thus wants to dehumanize Sator's lack of belief outside of himself ("The rest is belief, and I don't have it") while also asserting that humanity acts as its own deliverance. Accordingly, like the palindromic structure of *Tenet*'s plot, Nolan's conception of faith folds in on itself.

> What's happened's happened. Which is an expression of faith in the mechanics of the world, not an excuse to do nothing. (Neil, in *Tenet*)

> The life I now live in the flesh, I live by faith in the Son of God who loved me and gave himself for me. (Gal 2:20)[26]

---

[26] The disparity between Nolan and Paul is perhaps most apparent in these final juxtaposed quotes. Unlike *Interstellar* and *Dunkirk* where the orientation of love and hope are delegated to the narrative, *Tenet* includes an explicit recipient of one's faith, namely, "the mechanics of the world." For Paul, as Galatians unambiguously affirms, God alone is a worthy recipient of faith.

4. Conclusion

In this article, I have examined Christopher Nolan's three most recent films, *Interstellar*, *Dunkirk*, and *Tenet*, through the lens of the preeminent theological virtues of love, hope, and faith, respectively. In each case, I have demonstrated that Nolan takes Paul's cruciform (vertical and horizontal) theology of virtue and flattens it to the purely horizontal; thus, whereas Paul understands love as the sacrificial descent of the Son, hope as anticipation of God's restoration of all creation, and faith as the transformative reception of God's grace, Nolan makes humanity the giver and recipient of these virtues, so that in each film humanity effects its own salvation.

At this point, it is necessary to ask whether this argument is unfair or not. After all, film as a medium is about visual storytelling, and one could hardly expect every film that touches on love, hope, and faith to somehow exhibit the cruciform theology of virtue that we see in Paul. For this reason, what I have attempted to show is not that Nolan's films simply have an impoverished view of virtue, but that Nolan has intentionally coopted the imagery and language of Christian virtue and reshaped it in order to elicit a particular response from his audience. Lest a reader think I am too critical here, Nolan confirmed as much when questioned on the role of Christianity in his films:

> I think the influence of Christianity in my films in mostly cultural in terms of my upbringing. You know I was raised Catholic…. I would say that Christianity is just a cultural influence as it is for so many people growing up in the Western culture.[27]

Nolan, then, is not endeavoring to create "Christian" films, but neither is he willing to surrender the preeminent virtues. Nolan understands their evocative power, and so he incorporates them via secularization, crafting exceptional films that provoke us to love, inspire us to hope, and encourage us to believe. But by screening God out of the picture, the theological elements of the films, while emotive, are exposed as a veneer, a white-washed tomb that upon inspection, promises more than it delivers.

For something more substantial, the church must return again and again to the words of the apostle Paul, who reorients us back to God and calls us to become a cruciform people of love, hope, and faith.

---

[27] Writers Bloc Presents, "Writers Bloc Presents: Christopher Nolan, Tom Shone and Kenneth Branagh," You-Tube video, 2 December 2020, https://www.youtube.com/watch?v=PqGrR2Upz0M/.

Give Honor and Vote?
A Reflection on the Christian's Voting Conscience and Romans 13:1–7

— Robert D. Golding —

Robert Golding is the lead pastor of First Christian Reformed Church of Artesia, California.

****

Abstract: Paul's instruction in Romans 13:1–7 can be applied to Christian voting behavior in the West. Since Paul tells the Romans to honor debauched pagans, Christians can vote for similarly debauched political candidates with clear consciences. There are clear distinctions between Paul's teaching and the Western political context. However, the underlying continuities are clear and they are based in God's sovereignty, not political structure. Furthermore, the ancient Roman practice of giving honor to rulers only regarded the office, not the office holder's morality.

****

The majority of scholars agree (though there is a significant number of detractors) with the traditional interpretation that Paul's interlude in Romans 13:1–7 on civil obedience is instruction to Christians to properly behave as subjects to unchristian Roman authority.[1] Douglas Moo rightly

---

[1] The Empire in Paul school sees Romans 13:1–7 as spiritual subversion to the emperor cult. They see Paul denigrating civil authorities in this passage (and others) because those authorities increasingly saw themselves as divine. However, this school still seems to understand Paul to be instructing civil obedience. Though Paul is denigrating their status as divine, he is recognizing their natural status as harbingers of order on a natural level. *In the latter way,* they should be submitted to. N. T. Wright gave an address in which he said, "Reminding the emperor's subjects that the emperor is responsible to the true God is a diminution of, not a subjection to, imperial arrogance. *But if this is so, then the Christian owes to the emperor, not indeed the worship Caesar claimed, but appropriate civil obedience. The subversive gospel is not designed to produce civil anarchy*" ("Paul's Gospel and Caesar's Empire," *Reflections* 2 [1998]: https://ntwrightpage.com/1998/01/01/pauls-gospel-and-caesars-empire/, italics mine). In the revised version of this address, Wright reproduces the first sentence above verbatim but omits the italicized portion ("Paul's Gospel and Caesar's Empire," in *Paul and Politics: Ekklesia, Israel, Imperium, Interpretation: Essays in Honor of Krister Stendahl*, ed. Richard A. Horsley [Harrisburg, PA: Trinity Press International, 2000], 172). If this omission indicates a change of mind, Wright would probably not agree with my thesis. If he still believes what is written in italics, it seems he would. This paper is about exegeting Paul, not Wright (both are difficult tasks). At any rate, some schools would disagree and some would agree. Cf. N. T. Wright, *Paul and the Faithfulness of God*, Christian Origins and the Question of God 4 (Minneapolis: Fortress, 2013), 2:1302–4. T. L. Carter argues similarly that Paul is using irony to denigrate Roman authorities in "The Irony of Romans 13," *NovT* 46 (2004): 209–28. Contra Wright's view see, Dorothea H. Bertschmann, *Bowing before Christ—Nodding to the*

said, "It is only a slight exaggeration to say that the history of the interpretation of Rom. 13:1–7 is the history of attempts to avoid what seems to be its plain meaning."[2] While I acknowledge a plethora of vying interpretations of this passage (see footnote 1), I make my exegetical arguments without stopping along the way to respond to the other available interpretations (aside from those that are pressing) to avoid turning a modest article into a book.

In the majority interpretation, Paul is laying out the way in which Christians should live before their pagan rulers. This instruction is not limited to the Christians in Rome because Paul goes out of his way to make his command universal in scope: "'every soul' is to submit; there is 'no authority' except by appointment of God."[3] Paul knows that the vast majority of governing authorities are not Christ–followers (this will be explained below), and this is therefore the impetus for his remarks. Since the rulers are not part of God's family, what should the dynamic be between God's children and the children of Adam? In this article, in which I assume the aforementioned interpretation and context, I argue that Paul's teaching in Romans 13:1–7 frees the conscience of Christians to vote for political candidates that display radically unchristian behavior. This is because Paul is taking for granted that the rulers in Rome are depraved pagans yet he instructs the Roman church to engage in a symbiotic relationship with them. Since Paul tells the Romans to give honor to depraved pagans, Christians today can vote for similarly depraved pagans with clear consciences.

1. Context

Romans, Paul's most theologically rich (extant) epistle, was likely written from Corinth around AD 57 (though some scholars place it as early as 47, none typically attribute it any later than 57) during the reign of emperor Nero (AD 54–68) but before his infamous persecution of Christians began.[4] Though it is debated whether the Jews in Rome actually left following the diaspora mandate of emperor Claudius (Acts 18:2)[5] most scholars agree that Paul is writing to a predominantly Gentile church with Jews included as a minority.[6] Our passage occurs as an integral unit (rather than, as some say, an insertion

---

State? Reading Paul Politically with Oliver O'Donovan and John Howard Yoder, LNTS 502 (London: Bloomsbury T&T Clark, 2014); Seyoon Kim, *Christ and Caesar: The Gospel and the Roman Empire in the Writings of Paul and Luke* (Grand Rapids: Eerdmans, 2008). Others say that Paul is only referring to Christian Roman authorities (like those mentioned in chapter 16). Against this view see, Paul David Feinberg, "The Christian and Civil Authorities," *Master's Seminary Journal* 10.1 (1999): 90–92. Though there are other interpretations that do not cohere with my thesis, I have tried to note the significant ones and references to viable rebuttals. I cannot discuss all competing views due to length restrictions.

[2] Douglas J. Moo, *The Epistle to the Romans*, 2nd ed., NICNT (Grand Rapids: Eerdmans, 2018), 823. For a helpful review of various recent readings that also notes the influence of the Cold War on the Empire school see, Bernard C. Lategan, "Romans 13:1–7: A Review of Post-1989 Readings," *Scriptura* 110 (2012): 259–72. Cf. Jan Botha, *Subject to Whose Authority? Multiple Readings of Romans 13*, Emory Studies in Early Christianity 4 (Atlanta: Scholars Press, 1994).

[3] Moo, *The Epistle to the Romans*, 824.

[4] D. A. Carson and Douglas J. Moo, *An Introduction to the New Testament*, 2nd ed. (Grand Rapids: Zondervan, 2005), 394.

[5] Cf. Suetonius, *Divus Claudius* 25.4.

[6] For a summary of various contextual theories see Craig Keener, *Romans*, New Covenant Commentary (Eugene, OR: Cascade, 2009), 11–16.

made by Paul or someone else)[7] in Paul's gospel presentation with two apocalyptic "wings" on either side of it, both of which urge Christians to be set apart from the world in their union with Christ.[8] The contextual question then, is how this passage operates within a section that is calling for separation when 13:1–7 seems to be extolling the exact opposite. That is, why does Paul tell the Romans not only that they must be in subjection (ὑποτασσέσθω, 13:1; διὸ ἀνάγκη ὑποτάσσεσθαι, 13:5) but that they must give respect (φόβον) and honor (τιμήν, 13:7) to the governing authorities (ἐξουσίαις ὑπερεχούσαις, 13:1) after he tells them in the left "wing" to not be conformed to the world (μὴ συσχηματίζεσθε τῷ αἰῶνι τούτῳ, 12:2) and to overcome evil with good (ἀλλὰ νίκα ἐν τῷ ἀγαθῷ τὸ κακόν, 12:21)? The right "wing" (the material after our passage) is, in part, an unpacking of these separation imperatives in which Paul shows the Romans how they should cast off the works of darkness (ἀποβαλώμεθα οὖν τὰ ἔργα τοῦ σκότους, 13:12). How then does submission fit within this context?

2. Distinctions with Overlap

Dorothy Bertschmann provides a more focused version of the traditional interpretation of Romans 13:1–7 in seeing this passage as indicating an overlap between the reign of Christ and the reign of man. Paul, for Bertschmann, is first and foremost compelling the Roman Christians to live under the absolutely sovereign reign of Christ, and he is showing how the will of Christ aligns some aspects of secular rule with his own reign. Christ's rule mandates that Christians love their neighbors (Matt 19:19; Mark 12:31), pay their taxes (Matt 22:21; Mark 12:17), and seek to live peaceably (Matt 26:52). This kingly reign—though subverted by unregenerate man in some, if not most, respects—is not wholly resisted by secular authorities. In the words of Robert Stein, "Governments, even oppressive governments, by their very nature seek to prevent the evils of indiscriminate murder, riot, thievery, as well as general instability and chaos, and good acts do at times meet with its approval and praise."[9] Bertschmann provides a helpful Venn diagram in which the reign of man and Christ are represented by two distinct circles with isolated emphases, but they also have a section that overlaps where love of neighbor, "doing nothing bad," and "no terror to good work" are seen within both of the respective circles.[10] In this way, Paul's command to be separate from the world yet submissive to authorities can be seen to be complementary. There are areas of divergence (e.g., Christians should not be haughty like many secular rulers, 12:16) but also convergence (e.g., Christians should seek domestic peace as the secular rulers do, 12:18).[11] In a word, some things the secular rulers want are the same things Christ the King wants. This is the interpretation I will operate from moving forward.

---

[7] James D. G. Dunn, *Romans 9–16*, WBC 38B (Dallas: Word, 1988), 758.

[8] Bertschmann, *Bowing before Christ—Nodding to the State?*, 132–33.

[9] Robert H. Stein, "The Argument of Romans 13:1–7," *NovT* 31 (1989): 334.

[10] Dorothea H Bertschmann, "The Good, the Bad and the State: Rom 13.1–7 and the Dynamics of Love," *NTS* 60 (2014): 245.

[11] Another helpful distinction is seen in that "Taxes were used to finance roads and run the government but also to support Roman armies and temples devoted to the worship of the emperor." Craig S. Keener, *The IVP Bible Background Commentary: New Testament*, 2nd ed. (Downers Grove, IL: InterVarsity Press, 2014), 450.

3. *"Governing Authorities"*

Josephus uses the term "governing authorities" (ἐξουσίαις ὑπερεχούσαις) like Paul, to refer to those who ruled in the name of Rome over the Jews in Palestine.[12] As mentioned above, Nero would be the emperor when Paul was writing. Despite the later persecution of Christians, Paul wrote at a time "when there was considerable confidence abroad that his [i.e., Nero's] administration would be just and humane."[13] The "authorities, officials, [or] government"[14] to which Paul was referring were ultimately under Nero and the plural seems to indicate that Paul was primarily referring to the former, though all three were probably in view.[15] So, Paul is referring here to rulers under Nero who were not (yet) persecuting the church. This will be important to keep in mind as we move forward.

3.1. Servants and Ministers of God

Paul twice refers to the authorities as servants or deacons (διάκονός, 13:4) and once as ministers (λειτουργοί, 13:6). The amicable relationship that Paul and the Roman Christians were enjoying with their secular overlords by no means indicated that all was well in the world. The rulers were by and large pagan, and they were prone to all the sins that Paul lambasts in his epistle (cf. Rom 1:18–31). The terms that Paul uses to refer to them, therefore, were not spiritual in a narrow sense. That is, Paul was not referring to Nero, for example, as a deacon of Christ. The term διάκονος can be applied to Nero or his subordinates as well as the apostles (2 Cor 6:4) with wildly different locution.

Nero, at best, was neutral to the gospel at this point. This is where Bertschmann's Venn diagram helps us. Nero was opposed to the gospel where his circle, if you will, does not overlap with Christ's. But, on the other hand, Nero was a servant of God (θεοῦ διάκονός) when his policies (or those of his subordinates) *had the effect* of supporting the gospel indirectly (this is explicitly the case in our passage when the rulers carry "out God's wrath on the wrongdoer," 13:4). To be sure, Paul is not saying that the Roman authorities are sitting behind their legislative desks pondering how they might further the agenda of God. They serve many gods (θεοὶ πολλοί), "yet for us there is one God" (1 Cor 8:6a). But, the one God is capable of instituting secular authorities—who seek to serve other gods—who nevertheless serve his purposes. In this way, Paul is simply reiterating a common biblical theme: all human rulers are put in place by God, and they ultimately serve his purposes (Isa 45:1; Jer 25:9; 27:6, 43:10; Dan 2:21, 4:17; 5:18–21, 26; John 19:11; 1 Pet 2:13–14).

---

[12] Josephus, *Jewish War* 2.350. One competing view not mentioned in note 1 is traced back to Oscar Cullman which states that Paul is referring here to spiritual powers (like demons). Oscar Cullmann, *Christ and Time: The Primitive Christian Conception of Time and History* (London: SCM, 1951), 191–210. For an interpretation against Cullman's view see Bertschmann, *Bowing before Christ—Nodding to the State?*, 133–35. According to Käsemann, most exegetes have rejected this view. Ernst Käsemann, *Commentary on Romans*, trans. Geoffrey Bromiley (Grand Rapids: Eerdmans, 1994), 353. It should be mentioned here, in passing, that Paul would also have in his mind people like Erastus who was both the city treasurer and an upstanding member of the church (Rom 16:23; 2 Tim 4:20; Cf. Phil 4:22) but it would be outlandish to assume that Paul has *only* people like him in mind when he makes these sweeping statements.

[13] Victor Paul Furnish, *The Moral Teaching of Paul: Selected Issues* (Nashville: Abingdon, 2009), 122.

[14] BDAG 353.

[15] Joseph A. Fitzmyer, *Romans: A New Translation with Introduction and Commentary*, AB 33 (New York: Doubleday, 1993), 666.

It has been regularly observed that Paul is not condoning or prohibiting the *character* of the rulers he is referring to in this passage. Tertullian, Origen, and Chrysostom all understood this passage to be mandating honor for the *authority* of secular rulers.[16] Beverly Gaventa has shown that Paul's reference to Pharaoh in Romans 9:17 "treats Pharaoh as an agent of God for the good … Paul pays no attention whatever to Pharaoh's own inclinations, or to his actions. They are not important … asserting the role of the authorities 'for the good' need not mean either that they themselves will the good or that they will do the good."[17] Therefore, in chapter 13, "these designations [διακονία, λειτουργός] indicate not character but relationship."[18] Paul is saying that the Romans should submit to the authorities by virtue of their relationship to them, not because of their intrinsic worth or morality. This is why we need to keep the rest of Romans in mind when reading 13:1–7; Paul knows that unbelievers are prone to hellish sin (cf. 1:18–31)! Paul never entertains a middle ground between the sheep and the goats. It should be obvious, then, that Paul's command to submit is on the basis of the divinely ordained *office*. Everyone knows the Roman authorities are not exemplars of moral virtue (more on this below) but they must be submitted to because—despite their immorality—they function as God's harbingers of peace.

3.2. Worthless Fellows

Was it common knowledge in Paul's context that the Roman authorities were often dodgy people? Perhaps Paul and the Romans naively thought that they were generally upstanding and exemplary. Nero is commonly thought of as one of the most debauched Roman emperors. As was mentioned above, his true evil was not fully unveiled until later in life when his voracious persecution of the church began. However, scholars have shown that his debauchery was evident from an early age: "The young Nero developed sexual characteristics so numerous and so conflicting that it is astonishing to find them all in one and the same person.… Nero was a good husband, who nevertheless had strongly homosexual tendencies; in addition, he had many extra-marital relations with women; his character also contained sadistic elements."[19] In his biography of Nero, Tacitus recounts Nero's entrance into Rome from Campania in AD 59 (two years after most scholars think Paul wrote Romans) as follows: "exulting over his people's slavery, he proceeded to the Capitol, performed the thanksgiving, and then plunged into all the excesses, which, though ill-restrained, some sort of respect for his mother had for a while delayed."[20]

---

[16] Moo wrongly claims (without providing a reference) that Tertullian and Origen saw this passage as indicating respect and honor only to God. Moo, *The Epistle to the Romans*, 822 n. 346. Though Origen does say "we ought to refer 'fear and honor' *more* to him [God]" (which does not exclude fearing and honoring man to a lesser degree) he also indicates—in line with Jewett's findings below—that Christians *should* honor rulers so that they will not be oppressed. Origen, *Commentary on the Epistle to the Romans. Books 6–10*, trans. Thomas P. Scheck, FC 104 (Washington, DC: Catholic University of America Press, 2002), 228 (9.30). See also Tertullian, *On Idolatry* 15; John Chrysostom, *Homilies on Romans* 23.

[17] Beverly Roberts Gaventa, "Reading Romans 13 with Simone Weil: Toward a More Generous Hermeneutic," *JBL* 136 (2017): 16.

[18] Gaventa, "Reading Romans 13 with Simone Weil," 17.

[19] Otto Kiefer, *Sexual Life in Ancient Rome* (New York: Barnes & Noble, 2003), 509. The appellation "good husband" affixed here to man who "had many extra-marital relations" is indicative of the fact that even modern secular scholars who do not share a Christian sex ethic are able to see Nero's depravity.

[20] Tacitus, *Annals*, in *Complete Works of Tacitus*, ed. Moses Hadas, trans. Alfred John Church and William Jackson Brodribb, reprint ed. (New York: Modern Library, 2008), 14.13.

In order to bolster his image, Nero "actually invited all the people of Rome"[21] to the amphitheater for some "juvenile sports" which, according to Tacitus led to "a rank growth of abominations and of all infamy. Never did a more filthy rabble add a worse licentiousness to our long corrupted morals."[22]

Tacitus is not the only ancient historian to note Nero's licentious morality. Rebecca Langlands aptly summarizes Suetonius's biography of Nero: "On this firm foundation [i.e., young men and married women] Nero will build his edifice of depravity, going on to desecrate a religious figure and throw the very institution of marriage into confusion with the behaviour that Suetonius goes on to describe: forcing a Vestal Virgin to have sex, trying to marry a freedwoman through deception, marrying then a castrated boy as his wife, and provoking rumours that he lusted after his own mother and even consummated this lust."[23] Nero was a notorious and incestuous homosexual, pedophile, adulterer, and murderer. Of course, Nero's depravity is nothing new. But, it is instructive to note that it was, in all likelihood, conspicuously apparent in the historical context of Paul's words to the Romans in the first seven verses of chapter 13 as Nero's debauchery did not spring into existence after the letter to the Romans was sent.

Though it is difficult to say with absolute certainty that Paul knew about Nero's debauchery, it was infamous nonetheless and it would be almost inconceivable to deny that at least a portion of his Roman audience were aware, especially due to their geographical proximity to his various escapades (they and he were principally in Rome). It is hard to imagine Paul and the Romans not thinking of Nero when he wrote, "Therefore God gave them up in the lusts of their hearts to impurity, to the dishonoring of their bodies among themselves" (Rom 1:24). Indeed, the litany of sins that Paul catalogues which begins after his description of "men committing shameless acts with men" (1:27) could easily fit within one of the ancient biographies of Nero if one simply switched the nominative plural to the singular: "[He is] filled with all manner of unrighteousness, evil, covetousness, malice. [He is] full of envy, murder, strife, deceit, maliciousness. [He is like the] gossips, slanderers, haters of God, insolent, haughty, boastful, inventors of evil, disobedient to parents, foolish, faithless, heartless, ruthless. Though [he] know[s] God's righteous decree that those who practice such things deserve to die, [he] not only do[es] them but give[s] approval to those who practice them" (Rom 1:29–32). Arguably not a single description in these verses would not apply to Nero. Some claim that Paul is here and in other places adopting "sexual virtue and vice as his anti-imperial code language,"[24] which was a common technique in ancient political confrontation.[25] This would have Nero and his ilk squarely in mind as Paul wrote.

As was mentioned above, Nero was not the only person potentially in mind when Paul referred to the authorities. It would be hard to imagine Nero becoming who he was if the society in which he was brought up was not similarly debauched. This is precisely what we find. In her book *The Politics of Immorality in Ancient Rome*, Catharine Edwards shows that the "commonplace" theme of lust and licentiousness that so many scholars have noted as a "frequent occurrence" is "a preoccupation of countless Roman texts which we must surely see as reflecting the anxieties of those who wrote them."[26]

---

[21] Tacitus, *Annals* 14.14.

[22] Tacitus, *Annals* 14.15.

[23] Rebecca Langlands, *Sexual Morality in Ancient Rome* (Cambridge: Cambridge University Press, 2006), 365.

[24] Richard A. Horsley, ed., *Paul and the Roman Imperial Order* (Harrisburg, PA: Trinity Press International, 2004), 157.

[25] Langlands, *Sexual Morality in Ancient Rome*, 1–36.

[26] Catharine Edwards, *Politics of Immorality in Ancient Rome* (Cambridge: Cambridge University Press, 2009), 176.

Of course, this is the famous apologetic of 5th century Augustine who, appealing to the likes of Cicero, attributed the downfall of Rome to its vices.[27] Ubiquitous sin was not only indicative of Nero. One could attempt to make the argument that the subordinate civil leaders were not given to serious sin like those inveighed by the "countless Roman texts," but this would require evidence (of which I have seen none, other than the aforementioned lower level civil leaders who were upstanding members in the Roman church).[28] That is to say, all signs indicate that this Nero-like licentiousness was indicative of many, if not most, Roman authorities. One is hard pressed to find non-Christian exemplars of virtue during this period. Ernst Käsemann insists that "the apostle is in fact writing under a dictatorship with largely corrupt and capricious representatives, not to speak of the petty despotism of departments and officials."[29]

3.3. Honor to the Honorable

What about Paul's qualifier "to those who are owed" (τὰς ὀφειλάς, 13:7)? It is reasonable to conclude that the instruction to render both honor and respect are negated, in the case of Nero or Nero-like subordinates, due to their dishonorable and shameful conduct. Paul does not say, "give honor and respect to all authorities." Rather, he says, in effect, "give honor and respect to all authorities to whom you owe honor and respect." The question, then, is this: How does Paul determine whether a secular authority deserves respect?[30]

Robert Jewett cites multiple examples of both primary and secondary sources which show that honor (τιμή) was due to both the emperor and his subordinates in ancient Rome on the basis of the service they provided. Personal character and morality was not part of the equation. Honor was bestowed in a pragmatic sense—the emperor was due honor on the basis of his work for the people, and the people gave honor as a means of getting from the emperor what they wanted. Therefore, "Paul was willing to accept the system that demanded honor for the emperor and his officials whether they deserved it or not."[31] Käsemann recognizes that not only were the authorities to whom Paul was referring not limited to the emperor (as mentioned above) but that assessments of their relative goodness were purely political and not moral:

> The phrase ἐξουσίαι τεταγμέναι ["appointed rulers," citing a variant reading] describes prominent Roman officials [not just Nero].... Correlative to the power of the sword, which at least in part was transferred to Caesar's deputies is the practice of commending and honoring worthy citizens and communities in official correspondence. In this connection καλός ["beautiful, good"] and ἀγαθός ["good"] are not moral qualities but characterize political good conduct.[32]

---

[27] Augustine, *The City of God* 2.21.

[28] See the last sentence in note 12 above.

[29] Käsemann, *Commentary on Romans*, 356.

[30] Cranfield argued that the authorities in view here were not physical. This interpretation does not have much support today. See C. E. B. Cranfield, *A Critical and Exegetical Commentary on the Epistle to the Romans*, ICC (Edinburgh: T&T Clark, 1975), 1:267–72.

[31] Robert Jewett, *Romans: A Commentary*, Hermeneia (Minneapolis: Fortress, 2007), 803.

[32] Käsemann, *Commentary on Romans*, 353.

Therefore, honor is to be seen as something that is due to those political officials who operate as they should in terms of providing order and peace. If a debauched sinner creates an orderly and peaceful society, in Paul's mind, he should be honored.[33]

In fact, we see Paul employ this logic in Acts 22:30–23:5. When the high priest orders Paul to be struck, he responds with, "God is going to strike you, you whitewashed wall! Are you sitting to judge me according to the law, and yet contrary to the law you order me to be struck?" (23:3). However, once Paul realizes that the high priest—who had been instituted by God—made the order, he responds, "I did not know, brothers, that he was the high priest, for it is written, 'You shall not speak evil of a ruler of your people'" (23:5). Paul is here exemplifying the teaching of Romans 13:1–7 only a short time after he wrote it. Though the office-holder's actions were sinful in Paul's estimation, the office deserved to be honored nonetheless. What is more, the ruler to whom Paul is rendering honor (by not speaking evil of him) is actually abusing his office. Paul renders appropriate honor regardless.[34] Of course, the high priest is a religious ruler, and Romans 13:1–7 is referring to secular authorities, but the underlying logic is the same—submit to those who are above you because God put them there.

Paul is not saying the Romans should ignore the sin of their rulers, whitewash it, or see their "honorable" service as atoning for their sins. The overlap of the reign of Christ and that of man is not complete. There are large swaths of human leadership that need to be brought under the Christian ethic, as mentioned above. N. T. Wright aptly summarizes this tension:

> Paul was always ready to honor the office even while criticizing the present holder.... Being able to say "the existing powers are ordained by God" while living under a system that, as he makes clear elsewhere, was bristling with potential or actual blasphemy and injustice, is part of Christian maturity—a part he urges his Roman readers to make their own.[35]

The next section examines how we might do just that.

4. Application: Clear Conscience Christians

Lest we contextualize Paul and the Romans to the point of relegating all application to history, we do well to remember that, although Romans 13:1–7 has a clear historical, literary, and theological setting that prohibits using it as a tool for foisting various political agendas, "Paul's discussion of the relation of Christians to civil authorities, nevertheless, remains on the level of general principles."[36] These general principles can be used to help guide political interaction today. The findings of this study do not indicate that Christians should wholly endorse whatever secular government they find themselves under. Paul and the apostles clearly instruct and enact opposition to bad leadership (cf. Acts 5:29). However, the insights above do indicate that Paul had a category for honoring leaders that did not include morality within its consideration. Paul and the Romans were capable of giving honor to debauched sinners because they were providing a good service, they were enacting (in that limited sense) the will of God,

---

[33] Fitzmyer takes this further by saying that rank, not performance, demands respect (*Romans*, 670).

[34] Thanks to Guy Waters for providing this entire insight to me. He does not necessarily endorse my position.

[35] N. T. Wright, "Romans," in *Acts–First Corinthians*, ed. Leander E. Keck, NIB 10 (Nashville: Abingdon, 2002), 721–22.

[36] Fitzmyer, *Romans*, 664.

and they were instituted by God. Therefore, Christians today should simultaneously rebuke the sins of their political leaders, while rendering them due honor for the God-ordained services they provide.

Christians in modern America seem to move in the opposite direction. It is common to hear Christians say that they are refraining from voting for a political candidate because both candidates are morally reprehensible. In America, voting for a person is seen as not only as an endorsement of political services (i.e., what the candidate seeks to do for society politically) but also as an endorsement of the candidate's character. To be sure, voting and democracy would be completely foreign concepts to Paul and the church in Rome. However, their capacity to give honor while simultaneously rejecting sin (or, *a fortiori*, character flaws) should free the American Christian's conscience to vote for a political candidate that displays non-Christian actions, even sinful ones. There is nothing inherently contradictory with desiring a certain political candidate to take office, even though his scruples are far from exemplary. Surely, Paul, the Romans, and every Christian alive during the egregious later reign of Nero were all pining for the days of Claudius who brought relative peace to the land, despite his being a sinful pagan. This biblical category (as mentioned above, it is not limited to Rom 13:1–7) of honoring those who are sinful unbinds the conscience of those Christians who seek to vote for various political candidates in order to promote social order and gospel proclamation by means of religious liberty.[37]

Of course, one could argue that voting for a candidate in a democratic system is *de facto* an endorsement of the individual's behavior. The purpose of this paper is to show that such an argument— from a biblical perspective—is, at best, an uphill battle. Paul clearly operated from a paradigm that had categories for honoring those who were morally debauched. This paradigm is analogous to the system of democratic voting. For Paul, one is able to acknowledge political good in a spiritually depraved individual. For a citizen of a democracy, one is (or, at least, should be) capable of acknowledging potential political value while simultaneously rejecting spiritual and moral sinfulness. To a lesser extent, this is apparent in all sectors of theology. Theologians regularly acknowledge and reject moral failures of their forbearers who they nevertheless appropriate at a theological level. One thinks of Barthians rejecting

---

[37] A careful caveat must be put in place here. Integral to Paul's argument in Romans 13:1–7 is 12:1–2. The honor that the Romans were to give to their pagan rulers was to be conditioned by a mind (and life) transformed by Christ. Paul put it this way: "Do not be conformed to this world, but be transformed by the renewal of your mind, that by testing you may discern what is the will of God, what is good and acceptable and perfect" (12:2). Paul is regularly hesitant, if not unwilling, to instruct his hearers with the law. Key to his understanding of the reign of Christ was the nullification of any notion of works-righteousness. It is by the law of Christ that Christians operate (1 Cor 9:21; Gal 6:2). Therefore, Paul rarely draws a line in the sand in determining what his hearers should and should not do in regards to actions that fall outside the clear ordinance of Scripture. For example, he does not tell Christians to eat or not eat meat sacrificed to idols (1 Cor 8). Rather, he tells the Corinthians, "But take care [βλέπετε] that this right of yours does not somehow [πώς] become a stumbling block to the weak" (1 Cor 8:9). Literally he tells them to "watch out" (βλέπετε). The indefinite word "somehow" (πώς) indicates that the Corinthians are to exercise judgment. They are to pay attention, pray, and think in order to determine if something they are doing (e.g., eating meat) might be detrimental to another believer's faith. Paul does not give them the answer; they must determine what the "somehow" might be. The Christian is free in cases where his or her conscience is not bound by the Scriptures to exercise prayerful wisdom. Therefore, this paper does not give Christians the "liberty" to mandate various voting procedures, whatever they may be. The Christian is free to vote, but he is not constrained. He should pay attention, think, pray, and seek to determine how he might best fulfill the law of Christ. It might be by voting for an upstanding candidate, a debauched one, or not voting at all. One thing Christians must not do is legalistically proscribe or prescribe specific political actions that are not *expressly* condemned or commanded in Scripture. Voting for morally dubious candidates is, as we have seen, not only *not* expressly condemned, it is biblically warranted.

Barth's adultery, or Edwardsians rejecting Edwards's slaveholding. Indeed, embracing anything anyone does as a Christian requires some level of moral rejection since "No one is good except God alone" (Mark 10:18 // Luke 18:19). Therefore, it seems clear that desiring a certain person to obtain a certain political office should not require the wholesale endorsement of the individual (recall the concept of Bertschmann's Venn diagram). To be sure, wholesale endorsement seems to be the case in American politics. This indicates political idolatry, not biblical pagan-Christian relations. The Bible offers a better, more nuanced, way. We should honor the good things bad politicians do. Obtuse, black-and-white thinking is not Pauline, reformed, or Christian. As reformed thinkers in whatever sphere, we *must* distinguish.[38] This is not a difficult or new concept. Indeed, it dates back at least as far as the 1st century when Paul wrote Romans.

---

[38] I allude here to Turretin, who beautifully demonstrates a frequent propensity to distinguish between wholesale endorsement or rejection of various theological ideas, all the while maintaining impeccable orthodoxy. For example, Turretin engages the age-old question of whether "the will of God is the primary rule of justice." In other words, is right and wrong based on God's freewill or his intrinsic being (this is akin to the Euthyphro dilemma)? Rather than simply choosing one option or the other, Turretin distinguishes between the two by saying, "the will [of God] … is the first rule of justice extrinsically and in reference to us, but not intrinsically and in reference to God." Turretin says right and wrong is based on God's will for us humans when it comes to things like OT ceremonies (these were commanded by God as per his good pleasure, but he could have been pleased to command something else or nothing instead). On the other hand, right and wrong is not based on his will when it comes to something like loving God, which is necessarily right due to God's intrinsic goodness. This demonstrates, in my opinion, a high-water mark in Christian thinking, to which we would do well to return. Francis Turretin, *Institutes of Elenctic Theology*, ed. James T. Dennison, trans. George Giger (Philippsburg, NJ: P&R Publishing, 1997), 232–34.

The Standard-Bearer: Pastoral Suffering in the Theology of John Calvin

— Leland Brown —

Leland Brown is a pastor at East Cooper Baptist Church in Mount Pleasant, South Carolina, and a PhD student at the Southern Baptist Theological Seminary.

****

Abstract: This article examines John Calvin's theology of pastoral suffering, an overlooked but relevant aspect of his theology for pastors struggling with the trials and difficulties of ministry. Calvin pictured the pastor as the chief agent of edification for God's people, and therefore, the primary target for the assaults of Satan. Pastors will therefore suffer in the ways that all believers suffer but also suffer peculiarly as pastors–especially from opposition in their churches, criticism, slander, and possibly martyrdom. Calvin encouraged pastors to prepare themselves for sufferings, to set their eyes on Christ, and to patiently and gently deal with those causing their sufferings.

****

While many pastors might turn to John Calvin for faithful exposition and solid reformed theology, he may be the last resource they consider when the elders are about to vote for their termination or when the all-caps email comes hours after Sunday's sermon. Even to Calvin's theological friends and fans, he is often merely a great theologian–most of us do not see him as a resource for the struggles and sufferings of ministry. My purpose in this article is to offer Calvin as a profound resource to those suffering both the mundane and more intense trials of pastoral ministry.

Recent scholarship has retrieved Calvin as a more beleaguered and suffering pastor than the typical portrayals of him as the victorious reformer of Geneva. Elsie McKee has attempted to "reintroduce" pastor John Calvin as "a religious exile whose wife and infant child die prematurely, while he himself suffered increasingly ill health, in a lifelong ministry to other religious refugees, the resident alien-pastor to a people of a beleaguered city-state, precariously situated between large, hungry neighbors."[1] McKee argues that even the most unsympathetic reading of the biographical details of Calvin's life demonstrates that he was far from a privileged religious dictator and much more than a systematizing theologian who believed in double-predestination and participated in Michael Servetus' trial. When we consider that Calvin's ministry was opposed for most of his time in Geneva and that he was not

---

[1] Elsie McKee, "(Re)Introducing Pastor John Calvin," *Journal of Presbyterian History* 87.2 (2009): 53.

even made a citizen of Geneva until five years before his death, we see that in addition to being a great theologian, Calvin was an opposed pastor who suffered much at the hands of his own people and spent the lion's share of his ministry *not* getting his way.

With that in mind, it should be no surprise that Calvin wrote a great deal about the peculiar sufferings that attend pastoral ministry. For Calvin, the pastor was edifier-in-chief—the key agent in God's work of building up the church. But as edifier-in-chief, the pastor was also sufferer-in-chief because he bore the brunt of Satan's opposition to the church's spiritual well-being. What follows is Calvin's general sketch of the pastor, with a focus on edification as the essential pastoral task. Coupled with this picture is Calvin's articulation of pastoral ministry as spiritual warfare against Satan, who assaults ministers above and beyond the way he attacks all believers. Finally, I will show the peculiar sufferings Calvin said pastors would bear—opposition from their own people, slander and its resulting public disgrace, and potentially even martyrdom—and the counsel he gave pastors on how to bear these things well. We will see Calvin as a profound resource both for the work of modern pastoral ministry and for various trials that attend ministry.

1. Calvin's Picture of the Pastor

Calvin described the pastor as the most important officer of the church, a gifted and called man whose Word-centered ministry built up the church. For Calvin, the pastorate was essential for the spiritual health of the church and focused on what he called edification—the spiritual growth and well-being of God's people.

1.1. Pastors Are Gifted and Called to Edify

With Ephesians 4:1–16 as his key text, Calvin placed the office of pastor within an order of offices with which God gifts the church for its spiritual maturity and growth. There were four post-apostolic offices according to Calvin: doctor, elder, deacon, and pastor.[2] Doctors were the teachers of the church who taught the Scriptures and trained other ministers to do so. Elders oversaw the moral and spiritual discipline of the congregation, while deacons cared for the poor. Pastors were charged with preaching the gospel, administering the sacraments, and overseeing the spiritual care of a particular congregation.[3] These four offices formed the "quadriform ministry, providing a symphony for unity of the church."[4] Important for understanding his view of pastoral suffering is how Calvin focused on the gifts given to pastors for the church's health. Though the other offices were important, it was the pastor who chiefly pursued and (under God's blessing) produced the edification of the church.[5] Calvin did not ignore the role and gifts of other believers, but he emphasized above all else that it was pastors who built up the church.[6]

---

[2] John Calvin, *Institutes of the Christian Religion*, ed. John T. McNeil, trans. Ford Lewis Battles, Library of Christian Classics (Philadelphia: Westminster John Knox, 1960), 4.3.5.

[3] William Reid, "John Calvin, Pastoral Theologian," *RTR* 41.3 (1982): 68.

[4] Reid, "John Calvin, Pastoral Theologian," 66.

[5] John Calvin, *The Epistle of Paul to the Ephesians*, trans. William Pringle, reprint ed., Calvin's Commentaries 21 (Grand Rapids: Baker Books, 1979), 281 (Eph 4:12).

[6] Calvin, *The Epistle of Paul to the Ephesians*, 281 (Eph 4:12).

Calvin emphasized that it was God himself who ordained and empowered pastors to build up the church. Commenting on 1 Corinthians 3:1, Calvin said, "'What else,' says he, 'are all ministers appointed for, but to bring you to faith through means of their preaching?'"[7] Ministers are sovereignly appointed by God for the faith of God's people. For Calvin, faith was at the center of Christian experience.[8] This faith came by hearing the gospel preached, and since pastors were those chiefly charged with preaching, they were God's gift to the church—their preaching was the primary means of the church's good.[9] Calvin found this choice of God to use humans in his work to be an occasion for joy and wonder, writing, "Here we have an admirable commendation of the ministry—that while God could accomplish the work entirely himself, he calls us, puny mortals, to be as it were his coadjutors, and makes use of us as instruments."[10] The primary wonder was that God would stoop so low as to use men as his means for building the church. Another wonder from this truth that God works through the preaching and labor of pastors was that he is glorified regardless of the results of a pastor's preaching. God is honored and pleased by faithful pastoral ministry whether he chooses to save individuals through it or not.[11]

Calvin regularly articulated the weight of the pastoral calling and argued that men who would take on such a weighty office must be called by God and have this call demonstrated through outward evidence of giftedness for the work. Calvin understood there to be two callings on a pastor's life: the internal calling and the external calling. In the internal call, a man was conscious before God that he was called by him to preach the gospel; the distinctive feature of the internal call was that it was not and could not be tested by the church.[12] On the other hand, the external call could and must be tested by the church in four categories: the giftedness of the candidate, the possession of sound doctrine, a holy life, and necessary ministry skills.[13] This conception of the external call demonstrates that Calvin thought it necessary for prospective pastors to be shown able to edify the church in order to be called to edify the church. Regarding ordination, Calvin said, "We must always take care that [prospective pastors] are not unfit for or unequal to the burden imposed upon them; in other words, that they are provided with the means which will be necessary to fulfill their office."[14] The burden of a pastor is to edify God's church; therefore, prospective pastors must demonstrate the skills necessary for this work before taking it up.

1.2. Edification as Pastoral Motivation

Pastors must not only be skilled to edify the church; they must also be motivated solely by this goal. Pastoral motivation was a consistent theme in Calvin's comments on pastoral ministry; the number of passages in which he speaks of it is remarkable.[15] A particularly revealing example is Calvin's

---

[7] John Calvin, *The Epistles of Paul the Apostle to the Corinthians*, trans. William Pringle, reprint ed., Calvin's Commentaries 20 (Grand Rapids: Baker Books, 1979), 125 (1 Cor 3:5).

[8] Shawn D. Wright, "John Calvin as Pastor," *SBJT* 13.4 (2009): 8.

[9] Reid, "John Calvin, Pastoral Theologian," 67.

[10] Calvin, *The Epistles of Paul the Apostle to the Corinthians*, 131 (1 Cor 3:9).

[11] Calvin, *The Epistles of Paul the Apostle to the Corinthians*, 160 (2 Cor 2:15).

[12] Craig Tucker, "Calvin and the Call to Ministry," *RTR* 76.2 (2017): 106.

[13] Tucker, "Calvin and the Call to Ministry," 107.

[14] Calvin, *Institutes* 4.3.12.

[15] For a sample of passages that speak of pastoral motivation in these terms, see Calvin's Commentaries on John 20:15–20; Acts 20; 1 Cor 3:8–9; 2 Cor 5:13; 12:14–16; 1 Thess 2; 3:8.

commentary on 1 Corinthians 4:2, which according to Calvin mitigated against any ministers who "have any other object in view than the glory of Christ and the edification of the church."[16] True ministers exclusively desire "from the heart" to serve Christ and advance the kingdom. Otherwise, they are what Augustine called "hirelings," those teachers that serve a middle place between true shepherds and wicked false teachers.[17] Edification to the glory of God is a pastor's role in the church; it must also be his sole motivation.

1.3. Pastors Edify through Preaching

Pastors edify their people through faithful and wise preaching. For Calvin, "The basic and fundamental character of the pastoral ministry is the proclamation of the gospel, both publicly and privately. In so doing the pastor is exercising the cure of souls."[18] The public preaching of a pastor ought to be faithful to the whole counsel of God, understandable to hearers, and directed at application—in other words, his preaching must be suited for edification. Calvin emphasized wisdom in directing one's preaching to the most important and useful doctrines, encouraging pastors to focus their preaching on the doctrines and truths that are "chiefly necessary" for their people's benefit and to "dwell" on these doctrines regularly.[19] The manner, content, and frequency of preaching must be aimed at the spiritual benefit of the hearers. Calvin had harsh words for those that would bring irrelevant speculations into the pulpit: "God does not wish to indulge our curiosity, but to instruct us in a useful manner. Away with all speculations, therefore, which produce no edifications!"[20] (Today we might hear Calvin say, "Away with your 7-minute sermon illustrations that produce no edifications!") A pastor must discipline and focus his preaching for the spiritual maturity of his people.

A pastor preaches both publicly and privately. Calvin admonished pastors to not merely engage in edifying public preaching but to also imitate the apostolic model of going "house to house" (Acts 20:20), giving private instruction and admonition to his people.[21] Calvin remarked that

> Christ hath not appointed pastors upon this condition, that they may only teach the Church in general in the open pulpit; but that they may take charge of every particular sheep, that they may bring back to the sheepfold those which wander and go astray, that they may strengthen those which are discouraged and weak, that they may cure the sick.... Wherefore the negligence of those men is inexcusable, who, having made one sermon, as if they had done their task, live all the rest of their time idly.[22]

According to Calvin, Scripture's use of the terms "shepherd" and "overseer" for pastors implied the personal and personalized care for individual people in the congregation. He also reasoned that pastors

---

[16] Calvin, *The Epistles of Paul the Apostle to the Corinthians*, 151 (1 Cor 4:2).

[17] Calvin, *The Epistles of Paul the Apostle to the Corinthians*, 151 (1 Cor 4:2).

[18] Reid, "John Calvin, Pastoral Theologian," 68.

[19] John Calvin, *Commentaries on the Epistles to Timothy, Titus, and Philemon*, trans. William Pringle, reprint ed., Calvin's Commentaries 21 (Grand Rapids: Baker Books, 1979), 133 (1 Tim 4:11).

[20] John Calvin, *Commentaries on the Epistles to Timothy, Titus, and Philemon*, 221 (2 Tim 2:14).

[21] Reid, "John Calvin, Pastoral Theologian," 68.

[22] Calvin, *Commentary upon the Acts of the Apostles*, Vol. 2, trans. William Pringle, reprint ed., Calvin's Commentaries 18 (Grand Rapids: Baker Books, 1979), 244 (Acts 20:20).

must admonish and instruct privately because "common doctrine" can "wax cold."[23] This expression means that doctrine preached to all can easily be misunderstood or left unapplied in hearers' hearts. Therefore, pastors must bring personal admonition and application of the gospel suited to the condition of the individuals he ministers to: the various wandering, discouraged, or sick sheep. As we will see, this call to admonish and instruct people individually is one of the reasons pastors suffer.

1.4. Implications

In a day where pastors are often loaded with administrative tasks and expected to be vision casters/organizational leaders/relational gurus/pundits on every cultural issue, Calvin's focus on the one main thing ministry is about is a refreshing and much-needed reminder. Pastors are gifted and called by God for *one thing*: the spiritual maturity of God's people through the public and private teaching and preaching of the gospel. When pastors give themselves to this one thing, they have the awe-inspiring honor of participating in God's work and being the instruments of God's sovereign and efficacious grace. If ministers are to be effective, they must arrange their days, examine their hearts, and give themselves most to this central task God has entrusted to them, whatever the costs may be. As will be shown, Calvin argued the costs would be high.

2. Pastoral Ministry as Spiritual Warfare

In C. S. Lewis's *The Magician's Nephew*, Aslan describes a good king at war as the one who is the "first in the charge and the last in the retreat."[24] For Calvin, Christians were constantly at war with the spiritual forces of darkness, and pastors were to be the first in the charge and last in the retreat: as the edifiers-in-chief, they were therefore the sufferers-in-chief. Two primary images relate Calvin's picture of spiritual warfare in the ministry: first, that of pastors being "armed" by Christ in their gifts for their office; second, pastors are "standard-bearers" in the army of God—those who lead God's people and therefore suffer the fiercest assaults of the devil.

2.1. Pastoral Gifting as "Arming"

Calvin portrayed the gifting of pastors for ministry as their arming for battle. Calvin reasoned that a pastor's giftedness and sound doctrine must be tested before he is ordained because "those whom the Lord has destined for such high office, he first supplies with the arms required to fulfill it, that they may not come empty-handed and unprepared."[25] A pastor's spiritual gifts are weapons in his hands; his preparation for ministry is preparation for war. Therefore, no candidate should be ordained for ministry unless he already has these weapons available. After describing pastoral gifting as arming, Calvin noted that this was the pattern of the Lord Himself, who, "when about to send his apostles, provided them with the arms and instruments which were indispensably requisite."[26] Three of the passages that Calvin

---

[23] Calvin, *Commentary upon the Acts of the Apostles*, Vol. 2, 244 (Acts 20:20).

[24] C. S. Lewis, *The Magician's Nephew*, reprint ed. (New York: HarperCollins: 2001), 83.

[25] Calvin, *Institutes* 4.4.11.

[26] Calvin, *Institutes* 4.4.11.

cited in support of this statement refer to the gifts of speech given by the Spirit.[27] In other words, when pastors exercise their gifts and preach the gospel to edify the church, they engage in acts of war and must be armed by the Spirit to do so. Moreover, these armaments are "indispensably requisite" for anyone who would engage in pastoral ministry.

2.2. Pastors as "Standard-Bearers"

Pastors must be armed because they contend with Satan himself, who rages against the advance of the gospel. Calvin's commentary on 2 Corinthians 10:3–4 brings together the themes of edification, ministry as warfare, and pastoral suffering together, showing why pastors necessarily suffer in their work. Calvin's comments on the phrase "the weapons of our warfare" are worth quoting at length:

> In comparing the ministry of the gospel to a warfare, he uses a most apt similitude. The life of a Christian, it is true, is a perpetual warfare, for whoever gives himself to the service of God will have no truce from Satan at any time, but will be harassed with incessant disquietude. It becomes, however, ministers of the word and pastors to be standard-bearers, going before the others; and, certainly, there are none that Satan harasses more, that are more severely assaulted, or that sustain more numerous or more dreadful onsets ... For we must take this into account, that the gospel is like a fire, by which the fury of Satan is en-kindled. Hence it cannot but be that he will arm himself for a contest, whenever he sees that it is advanced.[28]

Calvin described the ministry of the gospel as warfare; war is an "apt similitude" for ministry. At the end of the passage, he reasoned why gospel ministry is warfare: the gospel is a fire that "en-kindles" (that is, sets on fire) the fury of Satan. Calvin wrote often of Satan's work against individual Christians, but here he specifically articulated Satan's fury against the general advance of the gospel through its faithful ministers.[29] The edifying ministry of the gospel, at the heart of pastoral calling, *infuriates* Satan, who "arms himself for a contest" whenever he sees the work of the gospel advanced— that is, whenever he sees a faithful pastor exercising his office.

So, although all Christians will suffer the onslaughts of Satan, ministers are special targets of his assaults because they are the "standard-bearers" of the church. In medieval and premodern warfare, standard-bearers were the soldiers who carried the distinctive flag of a military unit and led the unit to battle. Evidently, Calvin understood the standard-bearer as both the leader of the unit and the best target for an enemy's attacks. He was especially exposed to the enemy's sight because he carried the unit's standard. Additionally, capturing an enemy's standard was one of the best ways to demoralize and dishonor an opposing force, making the standard-bearer a particularly good target for attack.[30] Using this image, Calvin designated pastors as the distinctive leaders who bear the gospel as the banner of the church and advance the cause of the gospel by their faithful ministry to the church. This weighty

---

[27] The three passages are Luke 21:15; 24:49; and Acts 1:8. It appears that the other passages Calvin cites here (Mark 6:15 and 1 Tim 5:22) are supporting the requirement of sound doctrine for ministry and not being hasty in ordaining men for ministry.

[28] Calvin, *Commentaries on the Epistle of Paul the Apostle to the Corinthians*, 321–22 (2 Cor 2:13).

[29] See Adrian Hallett, "The Theology of John Calvin. Part Three: the Christian's Conflict with the Devil," *Churchman* 105.4 (1991): 10, for the ways in which Calvin speaks of the devil's assaults on Christians in general.

[30] Jim Bradberry, *The Routledge Companion to Medieval Warfare* (London: Routledge, 2004), 288–89.

privilege makes pastors the most frequent targets for Satan's assaults, because he knows that the best way to disrupt and dishonor the church is to destroy its leaders.

2.3. Clarifications

I will make two clarifications before moving on to Calvin's picture of a pastor's peculiar sufferings. First, though Calvin pictured pastors as incessantly at war, he did not picture them as at war against *their people or any other people* and did not advocate for the kind of domineering leadership that is today often associated with warfare images of ministry and the Christian life. With podcasts like "The Rise and Fall of Mars Hill" and various leadership scandals gripping the evangelical world, it is important to emphasize that when Calvin speaks of war he means war against the devil in the bold and gracious proclamation of the Gospel to all and the tender care and admonishment of God's people.[31] Pastors do not wage war against people; they wage war against the spiritual forces that harm and trap people. Second, Calvin's warfare imagery is balanced by both his counsel to pastors and his personal pastoral care. Calvin encouraged pastors to be patient and tender with their people, especially when their people opposed and slandered them. He specifically cautioned pastors to subject themselves to the judgement of the church when they were in conflict, to use moderation in their reproofs so as not to wound the minds of their people, and never give even the appearance of delight over their critics if they prevailed in church conflicts.[32] Calvin's own pastoral care, demonstrated especially in his letters, also shows remarkable sensitivity and patient care even in the instances when he admonished those to whom he wrote.[33]

3. How Pastors Will Suffer

3.1. Peculiar Pastoral Sufferings

Pastors will not only suffer chiefly in the life of the church, they will also suffer peculiarly. In Calvin's picture of the Christian life, all believers would suffer a variety of temptations and trials from Satan, ranging from health afflictions and physical enemies to a wide variety of spiritual temptations.[34] He also argued that Satan was under God's government and that God used the afflictions of Satan for the "exercise" of the saints, for their growth and spiritual maturity.[35] Calvin's general counsel to sufferers was to submissively entrust themselves to God's providential care and to content themselves with God's promises in their sufferings.[36] Pastors would bear these various trials but also face peculiar pastoral suffering: opposition from their own people, slander, public disgrace and martyrdom. Pastors are to

---

[31] "The Rise and Fall of Mars Hill" is a podcast that details various leadership abuses in the ministry of Mark Driscoll.

[32] Calvin, *Commentary on the Epistle of Paul the Apostle to the Corinthians*, 152–53, 168 (1 Cor 4:2; 4:14).

[33] For Calvin's pastoral care in his letters, see Raymond Potgieter, "Discerning Calvin's Pastoral Care from His Letters," *In die Skriflig/In Luce Verbi* 48.1 (2014), https://indieskriflig.org.za/index.php/skriflig/article/view/1830/2872.

[34] Hallett, "The Theology of John Calvin," 16. See also Calvin's commentary on John 9:3, which Hallett cites.

[35] Hallett, "The Theology of John Calvin," 9–10.

[36] Nicholas Wolterstorff, "If God Is Good and Sovereign, Why Lament?," *CTJ* 36 (2001): 48–49.

deal with these sufferings by exercising courage and fixing their eyes on the Lord.[37] Calvin derived each of these particular pastoral sufferings from his exegesis of biblical texts and, in some cases, his own ministry experience.

3.2. General Opposition

Because of the work of Satan, faithful pastors will experience opposition from people within their own congregations. Calvin's experiences of opposition in Geneva come out in his commentary on 1 Timothy 6:4, where he goes beyond Paul's admonition to "keep the commandment unstained" to describe why this command is so hard to fulfill. Besides all the external sufferings pastors face, such as the prospect of martyrdom, slander and other vexations, "How many things there are within that are far worse! Ambitious men openly attack us … impudent men insult us, hypocrites rage against us, those who are wise after the flesh do us harm, and we are harassed in many different ways on every side."[38] The worst aspect of pastoral suffering in Calvin's thought—worse than death in this passage—was the opposition of ungodly men from within a pastor's own congregation. Opposition from the ambitious, impudent, and hypocritical within the church are the "far worse" sufferings of ministry.

3.3. Slander and Criticism

This opposition often manifested itself in slander, criticism, and their resulting public disgrace, which Calvin conceived of as a tactic of Satan to draw away the hearts of people from faithful gospel ministers.[39] Calvin explained that Paul's command in 1 Timothy 5:9 to verify charges brought against an elder by witnesses was necessary because of the universal reality that "none are more liable to slanders and calumnies than godly teachers."[40] Ministers may stagger and blunder under the weight of their office, and the ungodly will gladly rise to censure them for those legitimate, though small, faults. But even if pastors "perform their duty correctly, so as not to commit any error whatever, they never escape a thousand censures."[41] While Calvin's words here may sound cynical, they appear to explain, in part, his own historical legacy (many Christians only know his name with "–ism" at the end) and the unceasing barrage of criticism that modern pastors have faced in the last two years over decidedly secondary and tertiary issues.

Calvin explicitly connected the pastoral duty of personal admonishment to these verbal attacks against him. A pastor who is opposed to the sins of his people and who speaks plainly to them about their sins will have many enemies, who presumably speak against him in repayment for his admonitions because they resist what God requires of them through the words of their pastor.[42] (Again, this comment of Calvin's is balanced by his example of tender admonishment.) This slander against the pastor's person

---

[37] Reid, "John Calvin, Pastoral Theologian," 67. Courage is a regular theme in scholarly writings about Calvin's conception of the pastor. However, in this literature, the courage required of pastors is not explicitly connected to the kinds of sufferings pastors would experience.

[38] John Calvin, *Commentaries on the Epistles to Timothy, Titus, and Philemon*, 166 (1 Tim 6:14).

[39] Calvin, *Commentaries on the Epistles to Timothy, Titus, and Philemon*, 140 (1 Tim 5:9).

[40] Calvin, *Commentaries on the Epistles to Timothy, Titus, and Philemon*, 140 (1 Tim 5:9).

[41] Calvin, *Commentaries on the Epistles to Timothy, Titus, and Philemon*, 140 (1 Tim 5:9).

[42] Calvin, *Commentaries on the Epistles to Timothy, Titus, and Philemon*, 140 (1 Tim 5:9). Calvin specifically says, "we need not wonder, therefore, if they whose duty it is to reprove the faults of all, to oppose the wicked desires of all, and to restrain by their severity every person whom they see going astray, have many enemies"

results in public disgrace. Calvin keenly felt the difficulty of public disgrace in his own ministry and wrote, "This is no slight test for subjecting a man to trial, for to a man of a noble spirit nothing is more unpleasant, than to incur disgrace."[43] Calvin went on in this passage to say that the disgrace that comes from verbal attacks is a test from the Lord to see if a minister's heart is wholly set on pleasing God.

3.4. Martyrdom

Though any believer may suffer martyrdom, ministers especially must prepare themselves for it. Calvin took Jesus' prediction of Peter's death in John 20:18 as indicative of what some pastors would suffer and what all must be ready for: "as Satan continually makes new and various attacks, all who undertake the office of feeding must be prepared for death … the doctrine of which he was a minister must be at length ratified by his own blood."[44] As in previous passages, Satan initiates the attacks that particularly fall upon those who undertake the "office of feeding," that is, the pastorate. In the same way in which ministers should expect slander and opposition, they should actively prepare themselves for death. Additionally, the idea in this passage that a pastor's death for his ministry ratifies his doctrine furthers the picture of Calvin's understanding of suffering as an essential feature of pastoral ministry. The faithful death of a pastor validates the fact he actually believed the doctrine he preached and truly was a servant of the Lord; it was the final test and best indicator of a minister's faithfulness.

4. How Pastors Should Handle Suffering

Calvin did not only warn pastors that they would suffer, he also counseled them in how to prepare for and handle suffering in ministry. Interestingly, this counsel was distinctive from the counsel he gave believers for handling the normal trials of the Christian life.

4.1. Courage and Preparation

While Calvin counseled suffering believers to entrust themselves submissively to God's providence when suffering, he admonished pastors to proactively prepare themselves to suffer and consider whether they had the courage and bravery necessary to fulfill their office.[45] Calvin gave "unwavering firmness of courage" to hold to one's doctrine unto death as a prerequisite for elders.[46] The previously quoted passage from Calvin's commentary on 2 Corinthians 10:3–4 also averred that a pastor must be "furnished with courage and bravery for contending; for he is not exercised otherwise than in fighting."[47] Since unceasing spiritual battle is the reality of ministry, all who would be pastors "should carefully consider with themselves, whether or not they were able to bear so heavy a burden."[48] Because ministry

---

[43] Calvin, *Commentary on the Epistle of Paul the Apostle to the Corinthians*, 252 (2 Cor 6:8).

[44] Calvin, *Commentary upon the Gospel according to John, Vol. 2*, ed. Henry Beveridge, trans. Christopher Fetherstone, reprint ed., Calvin's Commentaries 19 (Grand Rapids: Baker Books, 1979), 292.

[45] For Calvin's general encouragement for believers suffering, see Wolterstorff, "If God Is Good and Sovereign, Why Lament?," 48–49.

[46] Calvin, *Commentaries on the Epistles to Timothy, Titus, and Philemon*, 295 (Titus 1:9).

[47] Calvin, *Commentary on the Epistle of Paul the Apostle to the Corinthians*, 321 (2 Cor 10:3–4).

[48] Calvin, *Commentaries on the Epistles to Timothy, Titus, and Philemon*, 73–74 (1 Tim 3:1). Calvin's preoccupation with the difficulty and suffering of ministry is especially prevalent in this passage, because he was commenting on 1 Tim 3:1, which speaks of the excellence and nobility of the pastoral office. Calvin was so concerned

will always be filled with difficulties and sufferings, the frank assessment of one's ability to bear those difficulties is an essential part of examining one's call to ministry.

4.2. Setting the Heart on Christ

Considering the sufferings attendant to faithful ministry, pastors must set their hearts and minds wholly on Christ's future return and present love. In his commentary on 1 Peter 5:4, Calvin listed the wide variety of discouragements and difficulties of ministry, many of which have been outlined thus far, and said, "Lest, then, the faithful servant of Christ should be broken down, there is for him one and only one remedy—to turn his eyes to the coming of Christ."[49] The return of Christ will bring the pastor his great reward and now motivates his faithful labors in the midst of many difficulties. Though he said setting one's eyes on the return of Christ was the "one and only remedy," Calvin also encouraged pastors to set their eyes on the love of Christ. In his commentary on John 20, after demonstrating that no pastor can serve faithfully if he only looks to the approval of men, Calvin asserted that "no man, therefore, will steadily persevere in the discharge of this office, unless the love of Christ shall reign in his heart, in such a manner that, forgetful of himself and devoting himself entirely to Christ, he overcomes every obstacle."[50] Pastors who look to the love of Christ will be enabled to forget their comforts and reputations and be able to persevere in a work which so often costs them those comforts and reputations.

5. Conclusion

In summary, Calvin's thought consistently connects the central work of pastoral ministry with the experience of pastoral suffering. As edifier-in-chief, a pastor is sufferer-in-chief, the first in the charge and the last in the retreat. Ministers are attacked by the forces of darkness more than other believers because the good of the church through a pastor's faithful ministry most infuriates the devil. Far from expecting the podcast, book deal, and universal admiration of his people, Calvin would tell pastors today to expect opposition, slander, public disgrace, vexations on every side, and perhaps death. He would also remind ministers that one willing to bear these things humbly will share particularly in his Lord's ministry and reward, who suffered for a rebellious people and was glorified because of his suffering (Phil 2:8–11). In conclusion, I will suggest an evaluation of Calvin's teaching on pastoral suffering and commend two ways in which Calvin can be a helpful resource to all pastors and especially those presently suffering.

How should we evaluate Calvin's teaching on the prevalence and nature of pastoral suffering? At a first glance, it appears that his experience of opposition in Geneva colors some of his reading of biblical texts about pastoral ministry. There seems to be an overemphasis on suffering and a few instances of outright reading pastoral suffering into biblical texts in a few passages in Calvin's commentaries.[51]

---

with articulating the difficulty of ministry he assumed Paul was alluding to a Greek proverb that connected the excellence of a task to its difficulty. Normally a careful Bible expositor, this appears to be an instance where Calvin was reading the difficulty of ministry into a text where it is not explicit, revealing how central suffering was to his picture of pastoral ministry.

[49] Calvin, *Commentaries on the Catholic Epistles*, trans. John Owen, reprint ed., Calvin's Commentaries 22 (Grand Rapids: Baker Books, 1979), 146.

[50] Calvin, *Commentary upon the Gospel according to John, Vol. 2*, 288 (John 20:15).

[51] See footnote 48 for my comments about Calvin's interpretation of 1 Tim 3:1.

However, the general thrust of Calvin's teaching on pastoral suffering actually reveals a close reading of Scripture; Calvin evidently allowed the Scriptures to shape his understanding of ministry in profound ways. For example, the Pastoral Epistles devote substantial space to instructing pastors about how to deal with opposition, rebellious congregations, or slanderous false teachers. Second Timothy is taken almost entirely up with these issues, and the following passages all have them at the forefront: 1 Timothy 4:1–4, 5:17–24; 6:3–10; Titus 1:10–16; 3:9–10. Aside from those passages, one could argue that the entirety of 1 and 2 Corinthians is an extended saga of a pastor patiently admonishing the rebellious flock he loves and dealing with the slanderous false teachers who oppose his authority. All this being said, the Scriptures seem to attest to Calvin's view of both profound and peculiar pastoral suffering, specifically that dealing with opposition and verbal attacks are central trials that are part of any pastor's job description.[52]

That is the first way Calvin can be a resource for struggling pastors: he encourages them to see suffering as an *essential* feature of pastoral ministry. If suffering comes with the vocation, pastors can prepare for and have theological categories for difficult seasons and people in ministry. Put another way, Calvin's theology of ministry will help pastors be less shocked when they receive a biting piece of criticism, experience a family or health crisis, or discover that a powerful elder is after their job. If ministers will follow Calvin in seeing these sorts of things as a part of the pastoral job description (and also as under God's sovereign goodness, working for their good and storing up for them their reward), they will bear them better. If present statistics on pastoral longevity and mental health are any indication, pastors need Calvin's help and counsel. Calvin also gives pastors a category for how the seemingly minor relational sufferings of ministry can wreck them emotionally. In a century full of horrors like the plague and the stake, Calvin said that opposition from one's own church was the *worst* way a pastor could suffer. That is a striking assertion in its historical context and, though you may not agree with Calvin wholeheartedly, it probably means that if Calvin heard you were up all night languishing over the words of that angry email you received from a church member, he would suspend judgement, offer you sympathy, and encourage you to re-fix your eyes on your Lord.

That brings us to the second way Calvin is a resource to struggling ministers: he offers them a path forward, not out of their sufferings, but through them with patience. Present evangelical leadership culture tends to assume that unpopular and opposed leaders are either doing something wrong or need to go look for a better position; Calvin assumes they are doing something right and that they need to stay. He is that rare voice that commends patiently staying the faithful, difficult and unpopular course in ministry. Additionally, Calvin commends a much-needed balance between personal tenderness and convictional courage in the way pastors remain faithful. If heeded, Calvin's admonition to exercise courage but to also be tender with and willing to suffer for one's people would cure a thousand ministry leadership ills. With the present challenges and looming future evangelical leaders face, Calvin's balanced counsel to courageously and tenderly stay the suffering course could not come at a better time.

The irony could hardly be greater: the theologian most frequently caricatured as a cold, ivory-tower systematizer may be the beleaguered and discouraged pastor's best dead friend and counselor. Allow Calvin to be more than a great theological resource for you: let him be the sympathetic help and guide when you are seeking to be faithful but are pressed and vexed on every side.

---

[52] For readers interested in studying more of what Calvin had to say about ministerial trials and sufferings (there is much more than the space of this article allows), Calvin's commentaries on the Pastoral Epistles and 1 and 2 Corinthians are the best places to start.

Hell for a Single Sin:
A Response to Robert Golding's Asymptotic Theory of Those in Hell

— Paul Dirks —

Paul Dirks is Lead Pastor of New West Community Church near Vancouver, British Columbia, and the author of Is There Anything Good About Hell? *(Decretum, 2021).*

****

Abstract: This article is a response to Robert Golding's recent essay, "Making Sense of Hell," in which he contends for the logic of eternal punishment on the basis of a progressive and asymptotic conception of sin and sinners in hell. I will argue that this innovation is unnecessary and that both the Scriptures and the "infinite-obligation" proof by Anselm of Canterbury demonstrate that hell is just and necessary for even a single sin.

****

It was refreshing to read Robert Golding's recent article in *Themelios* on eternal punishment.[1] In a sea of compromise around this topic, his commitment to the doctrine of hell is commendable, and he has surely accomplished his goal of strengthening the resolve of pastors to preach on eternal damnation. In particular, his explanation of sin as privation leading to the loss of the goodness or the full humanness of the reprobate in hell is crucial to answering one of the greatest objections to the biblical doctrine of eternal punishment—that the torment of those we love will mar our everlasting felicity. As Golding points out, what we love in unbelievers now is of God and will no longer be expressed in the lake of fire.[2] The saints will not pine eternally over the loss of their loved ones but will look in horror upon what they have become, and have chosen to be, without God.

In spite of the article's many strengths, this response offers a friendly critique to one of its central aspects—the asymptotic nature of sin and sinners in hell.[3] Using Jonathan Edward's views on the eternal and progressive increase of the saints towards God in heaven, Golding argues for a correlative move away from God—a never-ending increase of sinfulness of the reprobate in hell. Moreover, the

---

[1] Robert Golding, "Making Sense of Hell," *Themelios* 46 (2021): 145–62.

[2] Golding, "Making Sense of Hell," 154–55.

[3] "An asymptotic curve is one that continually approaches a straight line without touching at any point, which is employed to describe our ascent into greater and greater communion with the infinite God in Christ." Golding, "Making Sense of Hell," 146 n. 7.

article posits that this eternal regression from God explains the merit of eternal punishment, answering possible objections regarding divine justice towards sins that are finite in duration and/or proportion.

I will respond to this theory in two ways. Firstly, it will be demonstrated that the final judgment is presented in Scripture as a monumental interposition in the lives of the wicked. I will make use of the views of Henri Blocher to argue that this fact undermines Golding's construal of a continual, progressive, or asymptotic state of sinning by the reprobate and I will suggest a synthesis of Blocher's and Golding's thoughts on sin in hell. Secondly, it will be shown that Golding's theory is unnecessary to defend the eternal punishment of the wicked, and that the logic of both Scripture and reason demand eternal retribution in hell as punishment for even a single sin. Three scriptural passages will be briefly considered in addition to Anselm's proof in *Cur Deus Homo*. In conclusion, it will be argued that this more traditional "hell for a single sin" view not only magnifies the grievousness and debt of sin, it also more greatly magnifies the work and atonement of our Lord Jesus.

1. The Interposition of the Judgment

Golding's article relies strongly upon an asymptotic theory of human relations to God.[4] The terminology taken from mathematics, "asymptotic" is aptly descriptive of Jonathan Edward's view of the saints' infinite progress in likeness to God in heaven, without ever arriving at being God or possessing the fullness of his characteristics.[5] The author draws from Edwards to posit a parallel movement of the reprobate in hell: "I present the hell as a place of infinite duration for people who are progressively moving further and further from their true existence as subsistence in God, which can be viewed as asymptotic in the same way that the saints progressively move closer and closer to God in eternal communion with him in heaven."[6]

Golding matches this eternal regression with the privation theory of sin—that sin is inherently a lack of the goodness of God. Although he admits that the reprobate retain the goodness of being, the total depravity of the wicked on this side of hell becomes utter depravity in the eternal fire, as God's common grace is removed.[7] Referencing Calvin, he states,

> the goodness we perceive in other people is nothing other than subsistence in God that should lead us to him. I argue that those subsistences are all but removed from the damned and therefore the glorified saints have no reason to look to the damned with affection, for their felicity is completely to be found in goodness, which is completely in God. The damned are vessels made for dishonorable use (Rom 9:21). Before judgement, they were worthy of affection because they were potentially redeemable and they

---

[4] "Just as a person cannot go infinitely backwards or forwards because each step would be a step to nowhere since at the end of the journey infinity would stand far away, it seems logical to say that we can never reach the climax of a move away from or towards God's infinite perfection." Golding, "Making Sense of Hell," 147.

[5] Jonathan Edwards, "Heaven Is a World of Love," in *Ethical Writings*, ed. Paul Ramsey and John E. Smith, The Works of Jonathan Edwards 8 (New Haven: Yale University Press, 1989), 366–96.

[6] Golding, "Making Sense of Hell," 146.

[7] Golding, "Making Sense of Hell," 152–53.

> contained some of God's goodness. After judgement, they are no longer redeemable,
> and any goodness they once contained will then be gone.[8]

I agree with the author on this point and the apologetic it presents against those who deny the eternal torment of the wicked. What is unclear, however, is why this removal of God's goodness supports an infinite process or progression.[9] The Scriptures are silent about such a process and instead place its emphasis upon one momentous and singular event at the climax of human history—the final judgment.

The final judgment is presented in the New Testament as a drastic and decisive event which ends this current age. Although eternity streams out from it evermore, it bears the hallmarks of both *telos* and *terminus* as each person receives the fruit of the deeds of their lives. In this ultimate judgment there are elements of reversal (Luke 16:25) and revelation (1 Cor 4:5), but more particularly for our purposes, review. Our Lord Jesus states in Matthew 16:27, "For the Son of Man is going to come with his angels in the glory of his Father, and then he will repay each person according to what he has done." The recompense on the day of judgment is specifically said to be for things which have *already* taken place. The apostle Paul adds in 2 Corinthians 5:10 that man's due is received for things done "in the body, whether good or evil," clarifying that this time of probation is linked to the duration of our flesh prior to the resurrection. As Tertullian argues, it is this life currently lived in the body which is the basis of judgment after the resurrection.

> Now, since the entire man consists of the union of the two natures, he must therefore
> appear in both, as it is right that he should be judged in his entirety; nor, of course, did
> he pass through life except in his entire state. As therefore he lived, so also must he be
> judged, because he has to be judged concerning the way in which he lived. For life is the
> cause of judgment, and it must undergo investigation in as many natures as it possessed
> when it discharged its vital functions.[10]

The scriptural emphasis upon a future judgment for this life suggests that the continual state of sin and sinning in the wicked prior to the judgment will not continue uninterrupted throughout eternity. Furthermore, the scriptural teaching on final judgment undermines the need for a progressively sinful state to establish the justice of eternal damnation. When Christ, then, states in Revelation 22:11, "Let the evildoer still do evil, and the filthy still be filthy, and the righteous still do right, and the holy still be holy," we ought to interpret this as signifying a progressive state up until the judgment, but not continuing in precisely the same way afterwards. For the Lord goes on to urge, "Behold, I am coming soon, bringing my recompense with me, to repay each one for what he has done," (Rev 22:12) punctuating the interposition of the final judgment in the progressive states of both the righteous and the wicked as the past is brought up before the Judge who not only was, but is, and is to come (Rev 1:8).

A second theme intersecting with the interposition of the judgment is God's current patience not only with sinners but also with sin. God is currently restraining his wrath against sinners due to his willingness that none perish but that all would come to repentance (2 Pet 3:9). At the judgment, however, God's patience will be at an end, and the sword long looming over the wicked will finally descend in distributive justice. As already noted, this decisive act is marked by a discontinuity between the current

---

[8] Golding, "Making Sense of Hell," 155.

[9] Golding equivocates on whether this loss of goodness occurs immediately after the judgment or eventually, presumably in his asymptotic process. Golding, "Making Sense of Hell," 152.

[10] Tertullian, *On the Resurrection of the Flesh* 14 (*ANF* 3:555).

age and what is to come eternally for the unrepentant sinner. Just as Asaph found illumination in the temple after lamenting the seeming blessedness of the unrighteous (Ps 73:17), so too as the entire world becomes God's temple, will the saints find that the probing clarity of the Lamb-Sun will bring to light the condemnation of the wicked (Rev 21:22–27).

But what of the final judgment's effect upon sin itself? Henri Blocher explores this question in his essay "Everlasting Punishment and the Problem of Evil."[11] He asks, "Would it be normal for God to allow for sin to go on for ever since he allows it now? That logic appears to bypass entirely the Biblical theme of divine *patience*. Is not the point that God tolerates at present what he will *no longer* when his patience comes to an end?"[12] He later states, "What is amazing, in Biblical vision, what is abnormal, incredible, is not that God should suppress sin–rather, that he should not do so immediately! How can it be that the Lord, in whom all men live, and move, and have their being, of whom and unto whom are all things, *endures*, for so long *vessels of wrath*?"[13]

Blocher's exclamation concerning the current presence of evils ought to cause sober reflection on the implications of a continual, progressive, and eternal increase of sin in hell. What will it look like for the reprobate in hell to "continue to egregiously sin against God and his children in increasingly evil ways"?[14] Are we to conceive of hell as a sordid cesspool of the most vile and heinous sins imaginable? Golding suggests that we should, but the language he uses is considerably lighter than the language the Scriptures use even of current sin.[15] Are we to take the debauched and depraved actions of Canaan, Sodom, and Tyre and amplify them hundredfold in order to begin to describe what we will find in the pit of Gehenna? The horrors of this world are often too much for the human heart—consider the trauma of soldiers who have witnessed violent atrocities on the battlefield or those who review abhorrent video content to catch child pornographers. For all the objections a person may have to the eternal punishment of the wicked, most men would recoil in *greater* horror at the infinite increase in the magnitude and number of such sins. If it is therefore the desire to logically justify the eternal torment of the wicked which underpins Golding's theory, whatever the concerns may be with the traditional doctrine of hell, they are not ameliorated by appealing to an eternal increase in sin.[16]

In his essay, Blocher also raises the fact of Christ's return as a triumph over sin and sinners.[17] In the letter to Colossians, the apostle Paul states that "all things" will be reconciled to Christ by the blood of his cross, procuring a "peace" (Col 1:20). Philippians 2:8–11 likewise states, "that at the name of Jesus every knee should bow, in heaven and on earth and under the earth, and every tongue confess that Jesus Christ is Lord, to the glory of God the Father." Both the righteous and the wicked will confess Christ as Lord, bow before Him in submission, and glorify God. It is worth noting that these actions are nothing less than what *defines* salvation this side of the judgment. When sinners confess Christ, bow the knee to

---

[11] Henri Blocher, "Everlasting Punishment and the Problem of Evil," in *Universalism and the Doctrine of Hell*, ed. Nigel Cameron (Carlisle: Paternoster, 1992), 283–312.

[12] Blocher, "Everlasting Punishment and the Problem of Evil," 299.

[13] Blocher, "Everlasting Punishment and the Problem of Evil," 305 (italics original).

[14] Golding, "Making Sense of Hell," 156.

[15] Golding, "Making Sense of Hell," 156.

[16] This argument could conceivably be turned into Golding's favor—surely a good God would be just to punish those contributing to such a pit of filth and degradation? My point is that it raises concerns equally as problematic—why would a good God allow infinitely increasing murder, rape, and violence?

[17] Blocher, "Everlasting Punishment and the Problem of Evil," 303.

Christ, and glorify God through Him prior to the judgment they are saved. However, when the wicked confess, bow, and glorify God through Christ at the judgment they are not saved—they are delivered up to the eternal prison for punishment. Once more we are faced with a significant discontinuity between this life and the next.

Knitting these threads together, Blocher concludes that the reprobate in hell will no longer sin at all.[18] This claim however, evinces a misunderstanding of sin and pushes the biblical data too far. As Golding argues, sin is fundamentally privation. The privation theory of sin, first suggested by Origen[19] and later developed by Athanasius and Augustine,[20] was an intrinsic part of the early church's answer to the problem of evil. God is entirely good and creates only what is good, and so any evil is not a creation of God but a lack of that original goodness. In *Against the Heathens*, Athanasius argues,

> Now certain of the Greeks, having erred from the right way, and not having known Christ, have ascribed to evil a substantive and independent existence. In this they make a double mistake: either in denying the Creator to be maker of all things, if evil had an independent subsistence and being of its own; or again, if they mean that He is maker of all things, they will of necessity admit Him to be maker of evil also. For evil, according to them, is included among existing things.[21]

Bavinck agrees, clarifying the positive act of sin, "Neither, for that matter, is sin a substance, but consists in lawlessness (ἀνομια); it is an actualized privation."[22] Blocher's statement that there will be no sin in hell seems to therefore fundamentally argue for the goodness of those in hell. There is no neutral relation to the Lord; "Whoever is not with me is against me" (Matt 12:30). Even if hell will not be full of murder or mayhem, will Judas love Christ or Esau trust God's promises in its fiery pit? It would be an impossibility due to their hardened character (Heb 12:17).

In spite of the error in Blocher's final conclusion, his views help elucidate the arresting nature of the judgment. It would be incongruous that after a momentous interposition in the sinning of the wicked they should afterwards start up again and continue in an unabated increase eternally, leaving the judgment as a mere momentary footnote in redemptive history. I propose therefore a synthesis of Blocher's view that there is no sin in hell and Golding's view of ever-increasing and maximal sin in hell. Given the nature of sin as privation, there *will* be a continuation of sin in hell after the judgment, but not an eternal increase. More speculatively, it seems likely to me that the sins of the reprobate in hell will be directed against God alone, their evil effects towards the rest of the universe muted in their private

---

[18] Blocher, "Everlasting Punishment and the Problem of Evil," 307.

[19] "The apostle indeed appears to use the expression 'those things that are not' not for things that exist nowhere but for things that are wicked, considering 'those things that are not' to be things that are bad. For he says, 'God called those things that are not as those that are.' ... 'Not being' and 'nothing' are synonyms, and for this reason those 'who are not' are 'nothing,' and all evil is 'nothing,' since it too is 'not being.' And evil, which is called 'nothing,' has been made without the Word, not being included in 'all things.'" Cited from Joel C. Elowsky, ed., *John 1–10*, ACCSNT 4A (Downers Grove, IL: InterVarsity Press, 2006), 22.

[20] "Sin, indeed, was not made by Him; and it is plain that sin is nothing, and men become nothing when they sin." Augustine, *Tractates on John* 1.13 (*NPNF*[2] 7:13)

[21] Athanasius, *Against the Heathen* 6.1 (*NPNF*[2] 4:6)

[22] Herman Bavinck, *Reformed Dogmatics*, ed. John Bolt, trans. John Vriend (Grand Rapids: Baker Academic, 2008), 4:92.

prisons, as God laughs and holds the wicked in derision in their vain blasphemies and hatred towards Him (Ps 2:4).

2. The Measure of a Single Sin

Not only is the eternal increase of sin in hell inconsistent with the biblical emphasis upon the final judgment, but it is also unnecessary as a logical ground for eternal punishment, which the Scriptures represent as the due requital for even a single sin. Golding employs his asymptotic theory apologetically to answer the concern that "since humans only transgress in limited ways on earth, it seems warranted to claim that they should only sustain limited punishment in hell."[23] Although he notes that there may be truth to the traditional response that sin is a crime "against an unlimited Person and thus deserves unlimited retribution," Golding suggests that the abstract quality of this argument has little intuitive force.[24] His asymptotic theory steps into this void. The claim is that the eternally increasing nature of the reprobate's sin in hell provides this force. The presentation of the "poor Old Buddhist grandmother" is therefore a straw-man caricature, for every reprobate will progress to the villainy and malevolence of a Hitler or Manson.[25]

As already acknowledged, all of God's common-grace goodness will be removed from those cast into hell resulting in a being no longer pitiable or worthy of the love of the saints. Nevertheless, contrary to Golding, a progressive state of sin is not necessary to demonstrate the justice of eternal punishment. We will consider a trio of scriptural passages which suggest this fact, and then examine Anselm's proof in *Cur Deus Homo* which provides a ratcheting and accurate measurement of the penalty of a single sin due to our infinite obligation to God. Rightly understood, these provide a rational, if not intuitive, argument for the traditional doctrine of hell.[26]

2.1. A Single Piece of Fruit

The account of the fall in Genesis 3 argues strongly for eternal condemnation on account of a single sin. God created Adam and Eve and placed them in a garden of delights wherein there was but one thing they were forbidden—to eat of the fruit of the tree of the knowledge of good and evil (Gen 2:16–17). Two related aspects of this command are salient: its lightness and its extraneity. Firstly, it was a light law, almost trivial in the bare fact of it.[27] It would have been no great difficulty to avoid this one fruit with so many other tree-fruits available to the first couple (not to mention other pleasures). As Stephen Charnock states, God "had allowed [Adam] a multitude of other fruits in the garden, and given him liberty enough to satisfy his curiosity in all except this only. Could there be anything more obliging to man, to let God have his reserve of that one tree?"[28] Secondly, this law, albeit consistent with God's will

---

[23] Golding, "Making Sense of Hell," 156.

[24] Golding, "Making Sense of Hell," 156.

[25] Golding, "Making Sense of Hell," 157.

[26] Given the darkening of the hearts of unbelievers brought about by sin, "intuitive" answers to scriptural problems may not be possible without the Spirit (1 Cor 2:14).

[27] This doesn't negate the conclusion, from at least the time of Tertullian, that all sins were comprehended in the first. Tertullian, *An Answer to the Jews* 2.

[28] Stephen Charnock, "A Discourse upon the Holiness of God," in *The Complete Works of Stephen Charnock*, ed. James Nichol (Edinburgh: James Nisbet, 1864), 2:202.

and character, was extraneous to the law as expressed in the Ten Commandments and the natural law written upon Adam's conscience. Turretin categorizes it as a "special" or "positive" law. [29] Apart from the specific and verbal revelation of God's will in the matter of this particular fruit, there was no stipulation to not eat from this or any other tree.

In spite of these minimizing aspects of the first law, the results of the fall were catastrophic. [30] The death promised by God comprehended not only physical death to the body, but eternal separation and divine punishment. And these effects accrued not only to Adam, but to all his offspring after him—"one trespass led to condemnation for all men" (Rom 5:18)—damning the whole race. Indeed, the entire creation was subjected to ruin, and currently waits with groaning until the beginning of eternity and the restoration of all things in the last Adam (Rom 8:20–22). Upon the scales of divine justice, the weight of this one piece of forbidden fruit was immeasurable and eternal.

2.2. Capital Punishment Would Be Preferred

Luke 17:1–2 provides a second proof for the justice of eternal punishment for a single sin. Jesus tells his disciples, "Temptations to sin are sure to come, but woe to the one through whom they come! It would be better for him if a millstone were hung around his neck and he were cast into the sea than that he should cause one of these little ones to sin." In Christ's warning there is a three-part comparison of evils: the evil of physical death by being cast into the water with a great weight, the evil of causing a child to sin, and the inferred evil of a fate worse than the described physical death. [31] This last ambiguity is given greater specificity in the parallel passage of Matthew 18:7–9 in which this worse fate is being thrown into "the hell of fire." Taking both passages together, Christ's conclusion is that the evil of causing a child to sin cannot be fairly compared to, or restituted by, the evil of capital punishment. It can only be fittingly punished by the evil of eternal damnation.

Two aspects of Christ's warning punctuate the severity of even a single, small sin. The first is that the offender does not sin himself, he "merely" causes another to be tempted and thereby sin. Secondly, the one who sins (with its inferred resulting punishment) is the "least" human being—a child. [32] An appeal could be made here to the ultimate and ontological equality of all human beings, but the interests of the Lord at this point lie in a different direction. Economically and functionally speaking, children are the least valuable human beings and so this minimizing aspect of the temptation/sin greatly emphasizes its heinousness that it should be punished in such a way that makes a physical death pale in comparison.

2.3. Against You Only Have I Sinned

Our third passage is taken from David's life, who is characterized in the Scriptures as a man after God's own heart (1 Sam 13:14). This positive portrayal is marred by several episodes in his life, most

---

[29] Francis Turretin, *Institutes of Elenctic Theology*, ed. James T. Dennison Jr. and George Musgrave Giger (Phillipsburg, NJ: P&R Publishing, 1997), 1:579.

[30] Not only in spite of these aspects, but also because of them, for the evil of this first sin is seen in Adam preferring the fruit to doing God's will.

[31] In the first and third examples I use "evil" in a technical, not a moral sense. See Aquinas, *On Evil*, ed. Brian Davies, trans. Richard Regan (Oxford, NY: Oxford University Press, 2003), 74–79 (Q1, Art. 4).

[32] The parallel passage in Matthew 18:5–6 is more explicit that the "little ones" are indeed children. However, it is possible that Jesus used this and similar expressions as a figure of speech for believers in some instances, an approach which may have been appropriated by John (Mark 10:24; 1 John 2:1).

notably his capital crimes against Bathsheba and Uriah, which I believe can be fairly characterized as rape and murder. Given the severity of these sins, David's cry to God in Psalm 51:4, "against you, you only, have I sinned," is staggering. On the face of it, it is a statement that is both irrational and preposterous.[33] Not only did he sin against Uriah and Bathsheba, he transgressed against them grievously. His statement can be explained however, by way of a comparative exaggeration, a rhetorical device used sometimes by Christ himself (Luke 14:26). As great as David's sins were against Uriah and Bathsheba, they fade into non-existence in comparison to their wrong against God.

While this third proof is perhaps less explicit than the first two, it is just as weighty. Measurement is not provided here by comparing "small" sins to their effects, whether directly as in the Fall, or indirectly as in Christ's warning in Luke 17, but by comparing the effects of "large" sins onto two groups/persons. The conclusion is as staggering as the original statement—the effects or results of the sin against God must be infinitely greater than the effects or results in the world of man.

This trio of passages demonstrate that the original (small) act of disobedience brought eternal ruin to the entire race, that sins against even the most insignificant individuals carry eternal retributive consequences, and that the greatest sins against man are comparatively inconsequential compared to their offense against God and that the punishment of those sins must therefore be equally infinitely distinguished.

3. Infinite Obligation in Anselm's Cur Deus Homo

Anselm's *Cur Deus Homo* contains one of the greatest proofs for the justice of an infinite punishment for a single sin. Sadly, its genius has been largely unrecognized by modern critics.[34] Annihilationists Clark Pinnock and Edward Fudge are among those who have argued that Anselm reasoned from his feudal context in which penalties for crimes varied based on the perceived honor of the offended party.[35] Gavin Ortlund, however, rightly states that Anselm's atonement theology is "richer and more nuanced than popularly portrayed, contains lasting insights that are not reducible to Anselm's feudal social context, and is untouched by the frequent charges of endorsing violence and being narrowly juridical."[36] The Archbishop of Canterbury does not argue based merely on an undefined construal of God's honor, but on the infinite obligation creatures have to God, a fact that helps to elucidate the logic of eternal punishment. Although a rational defense of hell may be possible without this honor-

---

[33] See D. A. Carson, "Sin's Contemporary Significance," in *Fallen: A Theology of Sin*, ed. Christopher W. Morgan and Robert A. Peterson (Wheaton, IL: Crossway, 2013), 24.

[34] Other critics who would fall into this category include Thomas Talbott, Marilyn McCord Adams, and Charles Kvanvig. For a more thoughtful critical view of Anselm's theory, see Charles Seymour, *A Theodicy of Hell* (Dordrecht: KluwerAcademic, 2000), 73.

[35] In addition to the error of this position, critics also haven't recognized that the historical record is not one-sided when it comes to punishment and honor concerning the classes. While there are plenty of example of peasants being punished quicker or more severely than a prince for the same crime, there are other instances in which those from a higher class had to pay *greater* fines or face greater punishment for criminal offences than the commoner. See Trevor Dean, *Crime in Medieval Europe* (Harlow: Pearson Education, 2001), 131–33; William Ian Miller, *Eye For An Eye* (New York: Cambridge University Press, 2006), 110–11.

[36] Gavin Ortlund, "On the Throwing of Rocks: An Objection to Hasty and Un-Careful Criticisms of Anselm's Doctrine of the Atonement," *Saint Anselm Journal* 8.2 (2013): 1–17.

obligation connection, the best theologians of hell, including Jonathan Edwards and L. B. Hartman, have argued similarly.[37]

In chapter 11 of *Cur Deus Homo*, Anselm defines sin as not paying the debt of obligation we have to God concerning his will. Any satisfaction for sin must therefore "pay back" the full debt in order to balance the divine scales of justice.[38] Prior to the marrow of his proof, Anselm explains that making satisfaction would involve paying back something not already owed to God and that recompense requires more than the value of the loss itself.[39] These are both basic elements of law and justice, and yet both requirements are impossibilities for creatures concerning their debts to God.

It is in chapter 21, however, that the devastating proof comes as Anselm not only states, but *measures* the debt and punishment of sin by means of a ratcheting series of comparisons between obligations. If justice is about balancing the scales, we can imagine Anselm placing a series of more weighty things in one of the pans to see whether or not they can bring the other pan of our obligation to God into equipoise. First, he states to his dialogue partner, Boso: "Suppose you were to find yourself in the presence of God and someone were to give you the command: 'Look in that direction.' And suppose that, on the contrary, God were to say: 'I am absolutely unwilling for you to look.' Ask yourself in your heart what there is, among all existing things, for the sake of which you ought to take that look in violation of God's will."[40] Here the Archbishop deliberately uses a very small sin in his first measurement, perhaps referencing the Fall, and Boso gives his answer: "I find nothing for the sake of which I ought to do this."[41] Place anything, or the command of anyone, on the other side of the scale, and even the smallest duty to God will tip the scales in his favor.

Anselm then adds to the hypothetical scale: "what if it were necessary either for the whole world and whatever is other than God to perish and be reduced to nothing or for you to do so small a thing which is contrary to the will of God?"[42] In other words, are all things *put together* enough to outweigh the smallest obligation we have to God?[43] To Anselm's challenge Boso answers, "I must admit that even for the sake of preserving the whole of creation, it is not the case that I ought to do something which is contrary to the will of God."[44] Having measured human obligation to God against any thing or person,

---

[37] Jonathan Edwards, "The Justice of God in the Damnation of Sinners," in *Hell and Future Punishment: Select Sermons of Jonathan Edwards* (Apollo, PA: Ichthus Publications, 2014); L. B. Hartman, *Divine Penology*, ed. Paul Dirks (New Westminster, BC: Decretum, 2021), 166.

[38] "No one who pays this debt sins; and everyone who does not pay it does sin. This is the justice-of-will, or uprightness-of-will, which makes men just, or upright, in heart (i.e., in will). This is the sole and complete honor which we owe to God and which God demands from us…. Whoever does not pay to God this honor due Him dishonors Him and removes from Him what belongs to Him; and this removal, or this dishonoring, constitutes a sin." Anselm, *Cur Deus Homo*, trans. Jasper Hopkins and Herbert Richardson (Minneapolis: Arthur J. Banning Press, 2000), 3.11. All subsequent quotations are from this translation.

[39] Anselm, *Cur Deus Homo* 3.11.

[40] Anselm, *Cur Deus Homo* 3.21.

[41] Anselm, *Cur Deus Homo* 3.21.

[42] Anselm, *Cur Deus Homo* 3.21.

[43] With this question, one is reminded of God's command to Abraham that he sacrifice his only son Isaac (Gen 22:2). To Abraham, Isaac was not merely the greatest thing—he was everything. He was the miracle son through whom all the promises of God would come to pass, even the blessing of the entire world.

[44] Anselm, *Cur Deus Homo* 3.21.

and against all things put together, he then invokes infinity: "What if there were more than one world, full of creatures, just as this world is?"[45] The answer? "If there were an infinitely multiple number of worlds and they too were exhibited to me, I would still give the same answer."[46] Anselm then arrives at his incisive conclusion: "You can do nothing more rightly. But if it were to happen that contrary to the will of God you were to take that look, consider as well what you would be able to render as payment for this sin."[47]

By a ratcheting measurement of man's obligation to God in even the slightest matter, Anselm demonstrates the infinite debt of our sin. The only just punishment is therefore also infinite—eternal. Hartman summarizes, "in the nature of things, the violation of law incurs a guilt equal to the measure of its obligation. This is also self-evident. The guilt of action consists in its being the violation of our obligation; therefore the guilt and the obligation must be mutual measurements of each other."[48] An eternal hell is just punishment for even a single sin due to man's infinite obligation to God in all things relative to his will. Although I have argued for the continuation of a particular kind of sin in hell, the question of whether or not the wicked continue to sin in hell, let alone increasingly and eternally, is immaterial to whether or not eternal punishment is warranted.

4. An Infinite God Upon the Cross

The infinite weight of a single sin also has significant implications for worship. The Lord Jesus stated of the love of the sinful woman at Simon's house, "Therefore I tell you, her sins, which are many, are forgiven—for she loved much. But he who is forgiven little, loves little" (Luke 7:47–48). The realization of the immeasurable debt of even our least transgressions, commends to us the atoning work of Christ all the more. Inadvertently, Golding's theory may suppress the worship of our Lord's mercy and grace towards his church as deservingly damnable sinners, apart from his intervention. Thomas Brooks states,

> Christ's outward and inward miseries, sorrows, and sufferings are not to be paralleled, and therefore Christians have the more cause to lose themselves in the contemplation of his matchless love. Oh, bless Christ! oh, kiss Christ! oh, embrace Christ! oh, welcome Christ! oh, cleave to Christ! oh, follow Christ! oh, walk with Christ! oh, long for Christ! who for your sakes hath undergone insupportable wrath and most hellish torments.[49]

At the cross Christ offered a ransom price beyond what any man could offer—"You were ransomed from the futile ways inherited from your forefathers, not with perishable things such as silver or gold, but with the precious blood of Christ, like that of a lamb without blemish or spot" (1 Pet 1:18–19). While it was Christ's humanity by which he died to offer payment, it was his divinity that supplied the infinite weight to balance the cosmic scales. Martin Luther writes, "We Christians should know that if God is not in the scale to give it weight, we, on our side, sink to the ground. I mean it this way: if it

---

[45] Anselm, *Cur Deus Homo* 3.21.

[46] Anselm, *Cur Deus Homo* 3.21.

[47] Anselm, *Cur Deus Homo* 3.21.

[48] Hartman, *Divine Penology*, 165.

[49] Thomas Brooks, "The Golden Key to Open Hidden Treasures," in *The Complete Works of Thomas Brooks*, ed. Alexander Balloch Grosart (London: James Nisbet, 1867), 5:141.

cannot be said that God died for us, but only a man, we are lost; but if God's death and a dead God lie in the balance, his side goes down and ours goes up like a light and empty scale."[50]

Golding agrees that this is the case, but then he adds to it his asymptotic theory in order to make the case for eternal punishment even more intuitive.[51] In adding, however, I fear he has subtracted. Unintentionally, his view subtly suppresses the heinousness of our sins, the deservedness of eternal wrath, and the surpassingly great work of Christ. The preacher can and ought to preach the torment of an eternal hell on account of sin—any sin—even a single, small sin. More than perhaps any other thing, this will cause the worshiper's questions concerning eternal punishment to be dispelled in the contemplation of the cost to Christ at the cross and his love for them in his ransom.

---

[50] Martin Luther, *Church and Ministry III*, ed. Jaroslav Jan Pelikan, Hilton C. Oswald, and Helmut T. Lehmann, Luther's Works 41 (Philadelphia: Fortress, 1999), 103–4.

[51] Golding, "Making Sense of Hell," 156.

Themelios 47.2 (2022): 348–65

Gender Dysphoria and the Body-Soul Relationship

— **Edmund Fong** —

Edmund Fong is a lecturer in systematic theology, hermeneutics, and Presbyterianism at Trinity Theological College, Singapore.

******

Abstract: After presenting the phenomenon of gender dysphoria as a state of consciousness experienced by the individual, I explore how the two major anthropological frameworks of materialism and substance dualism account for the conscious state of gender dysphoria. In particular, the article addresses the extent to which materialism and substance dualism support what I term a "created but misplaced being" scenario, where it is claimed that an individual could be created with an "inner" self gendered one way but placed in a body of a different biological sex. Three theological insights into gender dysphoria that follow from the findings of this exploration conclude the article.

******

Gaining prominence over the last decade or so has been transgenderism, with a particular focus on the phenomenon of gender dysphoria. Formerly defined as "gender identity disorder," the most recent edition of the *Diagnostic and Statistical Manual of Mental Disorders* (DSM-5) defines gender dysphoria as "incongruence between one's experienced/expressed gender and assigned gender" in conjunction with "clinically significant distress or impairment in social, occupational, or other important areas of functioning."[1] In other words, individuals with gender dysphoria often find themselves saying "I feel like …" and in stronger cases, "I *am* a woman trapped in a man's body," or vice versa.

Psychological, medical, biological, sociological, legal, and even political perspectives have been offered in the discussion of gender dysphoria.[2] Christian perspectives, especially those coming from ministerial practice or ethics, have also been represented. The contribution that this article brings to the table lies in its attempt to answer a specific theological question: where do we locate gender dysphoria within the larger ambit of theological anthropology, particularly the body-soul relationship? This is a neither trivial nor unimportant consideration, for it remains but a breath away from the individual experiencing gender dysphoria bringing a theological slant into his or her experience: "Could God have created me a woman but placed me in the wrong body as a man (and vice versa)?" So, even as Genesis

---

[1] American Psychiatric Association, "Gender Dysphoria," *Diagnostic and Statistical Manual of Mental Disorders*, 5th ed. (Arlington, VA: American Psychiatric Publishing, 2013), 452.

[2] For a resource summarizing the perspectives to its date of publication, see Ryan T. Anderson, *When Harry Became Sally: Responding to the Transgender Moment* (New York: Encounter, 2018).

1:27 tells us that "male and female [God] created them," could an individual with gender dysphoria fall under the curious scenario of what I term a "created but misplaced being"?

The consideration in this article proceeds via four main sections. With reference to philosopher John Searle, I begin by arguing how the phenomenon of gender dysphoria is fundamentally a conscious experience involving a unified self—an "I," so to speak. This forms an essential datum point that all views of the body-soul relationship must contend with in considering gender dysphoria. In the second section, I show how one of the major frameworks on the body-soul relationship, materialism or physicalism, accounts for gender dysphoria while remaining true to its commitments. The third section does the same, but with the other major framework: substance dualism. Both sections will pay particular attention to the "created but misplaced being" problem. Finally, I conclude with three implications our findings have for theological insights into the phenomenon of gender dysphoria.

1. The Conscious State of Gender Dysphoria

In arguing for how the notion of the "self" poses problems for neurobiology, philosopher John Searle presents three defining features of consciousness useful in helping us understand gender dysphoria as a state of consciousness.[3] First, conscious states are *qualitative* in that there is a certain undeniable qualitative feel that enables us to say we are in *this* conscious state rather than *that* (the example Searle provides is the qualitative difference between listening to Beethoven's Ninth Symphony and drinking cold beer). Contemporary literature on the topic of consciousness label this unique qualitative feel pertaining to a particular state of consciousness as "*quale*" (singular) or "*qualia*" (plural).[4] Second, conscious states require a subject for their very existence; there must be an "I," some subject that experiences the conscious state. Third, conscious states always come to us as part of *a unified conscious field*. Returning to Searle's example, we do not think of the individual having the experience of listening to music and the experience of drinking separately, but the drinking and listening come as part of one total conscious experience.[5] The three interrelated features lead Searle to affirm the problem of consciousness as "precisely the problem of qualitative, unified subjectivity," and the three features as really "different aspects of the one common essential trait of consciousness."[6]

The three features listed by Searle underscore the common points that all discussions on gender dysphoria relating to the body-soul relationship must attend to. Gender dysphoria is a conscious state that has its own *quale*, mainly identified as a sense of discordance; it is experienced by a distinct subject, and it comes as a unified field of consciousness—"I *feel* that *I* am of a gender that is different to my body's biological sex."

To these three points proposed by Searle we may add a fourth: the conscious state of gender dysphoria is causative in effect. It may result in an individual with this conscious state wanting to take definite actions that lead to physical events happening: "I feel that I am of a gender that is different to my body's biological sex, so I will pursue gender reassignment surgery." Of course, as Searle points out, in

---

[3] John R. Searle, "The Self as a Problem in Philosophy and Neurobiology," in *Philosophy in a New Century: Selected Essays* (Cambridge: Cambridge University Press, 2008), 137–51.

[4] Rocco J. Gennaro, "Introduction," in *The Routledge Handbook of Consciousness*, ed. Rocco Gennaro (New York: Routledge, 2018), 2–3.

[5] Searle, "Self as Problem," 141–42.

[6] Searle, "Self as Problem," 142.

normal non-pathological cases, the causation is not "automatic." The causes of one's action (in our case experiencing gender dysphoria) is never causally sufficient to determine the action (pursuing gender reassignment surgery). Instead, there is always a gap between the perceived causes and the action, and Searle refers to this gap as the freedom of the will.[7]

Notwithstanding the above, the core phenomenological datum point in relation to gender dysphoria is clearly stated: gender dysphoria is an *experienced qualitative and unified conscious state of the self with potential causative effects*. I will now turn to see how the major accounts of the body-soul relationship within theological anthropology accommodate this central datum point, paying particular attention to whether the different accounts of the body-soul relationship support the notion that we could actually be "created but misplaced beings" in relation to our sexuality.

2. Materialism and Gender Dysphoria

I begin with the first of the two broad positions adopted in body-soul relationship discussions: materialism. Materialism views the human being as an entirely physical entity; that is, we comprise no additional non-physical or spiritual substance. Consequently, materialists affirm that there is nothing required for having conscious mental states and properties (such as beliefs, desires, intentions, feelings, etc.) other than the occurrence of various types of biophysical and neural states and processes in the conscious individual's brain, body and perhaps the world around the individual. Materialism can be further broken down into "hard," "strong," or reductive materialism and "soft," "weak," or non-reductive materialism. Hard materialists either dismiss inner mental states or mental properties altogether (although this is an approach seldom taken) or, more commonly, maintain at best that mental properties are reducible to or explainable as biophysical and neural properties. Theological anthropologist Marc Cortez points out that few Christian thinkers would see themselves as hard materialists owing to the consensus that "*human persons have a real mental life that is important and efficacious*,"[8] preferring instead some version of soft materialism.

Soft materialists, in turn, can be divided into two kinds. While both kinds maintain—unlike hard materialists—that mental states and properties cannot be reduced to or explained away as biophysical base properties, the first type of soft materialists would conceive of all mental states and properties as *causally* reducible; that is, the causal powers of the biophysical base properties are able to completely account for all mental states and properties. Such is the view of Searle who goes by the label "biological naturalism" and maintains that "consciousness does not exist in a separate realm and it does not have any causal powers in addition to those of its neuronal base any more than [the characteristic of] solidity has any extra causal powers in addition to its molecular base."[9] Searle maintains that any form of causation that takes place is solely "bottom-up," "whereby the behavior of lower-level elements, presumably neurons and synapses, causes higher-level or system features of consciousness and intentionality."[10]

---

[7] Searle, "Self as Problem," 147.

[8] Marc Cortez, *Theological Anthropology: A Guide for the Perplexed* (London: Bloomsbury T&T Clark, 2010), 70 (emphasis original).

[9] Searle, "Why I Am Not a Property Dualist," in *Philosophy in a New Century: Selected Essays* (Cambridge: Cambridge University Press, 2008), 152–60, specifically 158.

[10] Searle, "Why I Am Not a Property Dualist," 152. Searle, in keeping to a "bottom up" causation only, has difficulty maintaining a genuine freedom in the gap between the perceived causes and the subsequent actions arising

Besides Searle, Nancey Murphy stands as another example of the first type of soft materialist. According to Murphy, nonreductive physicalism, especially what it has to inform us in terms of cognition and neurobiology, is able to lead us (humans) to a robust sense of moral responsibility.[11] To ward off the worry of neurobiological determinism (that is, "the case that all human thought and behavior are simply determined by the laws of neurobiology"),[12] Murphy allows for what she sees as "downward" or "top-down causation." In this type of causation, new emergent complex entities (the example Murphy provides is birds) are able to use lower-level causal forces (e.g., air pressure) in new ways to do new things (e.g., to fly). The key point to note is that downward causation, according to Murphy, "does not involve overriding lower-level laws, but rather *selection* among lower-level causal processes."[13] The end result is that "the whole person has downward causal effects on her own parts."[14] William Hasker (a substance dualist) and Kevin Corcoran (a constitutionalist) have responded by stating that Murphy's position is still ultimately causally reductionist.[15] The flaw comes from Murphy's insistence that all actions and interactions arising from entities in the natural world must consist entirely in the actions and interactions of the elementary parts that make up the entity, and that these actions and interactions must occur and be determined in accordance with the fundamental laws of physics. In other words, Murphy's notions of emergence and causality still operate within what Cortez calls the "causal completeness of the physical (CCP)" principle, where "every physical event that has a cause at t has a physical cause at t."[16] Murphy's refusal to allow for modifications in the physical laws according to which the elementary particles behave—modifications arising in turn from the emergence of a more complex organism larger than the sum of its parts—is what consigns her to a position of causal reductionism, despite her claims to the contrary.

The second type of soft materialist differs from the first in rejecting causal reductionism. Its proponents allow for mental states and properties—"wholly distinct mental phenomena," as termed by Timothy O'Connor—to emerge when physical elements are organized in the right sorts of ways in properly-functioning neurophysiological structures. These mental phenomena "in turn do fundamental causal work, affecting the very neural processes that sustain them."[17] Here, as Hasker puts it, is a form of "top-down causation" where "consciousness, which is a higher-order, emergent property, has effects on the micro-level, and causes the microelements to behave differently than would be predicted on the basis

---

from a state of consciousness, according to William Hasker, "Do My Quarks Enjoy Beethoven?" in *Neuroscience and the Soul: The Human Person in Philosophy, Science and Theology,* ed. Thomas Crisp, Steven Porter, and Gregg Elshof (Grand Rapids: Eerdmans, 2016), 20.

[11] Nancey Murphy, "Nonreductive Physicalism," in *In Search of the Soul: Four Views of the Mind-Body Problem,* eds. Joel Green and Stuart Palmer (Downers Grove, IL: InterVarsity Press, 2005), 115–38 (in particular 126).

[12] Murphy, "Nonreductive Physicalism," 132.

[13] Murphy, "Nonreductive Physicalism," 136 (emphasis original).

[14] Murphy, "Nonreductive Physicalism," 138.

[15] William Hasker, "An Emergent Dualist Response," in *In Search of the Soul: Four Views of the Mind-Body Problem,* eds. Joel Green and Stuart Palmer (Downers Grove, IL: InterVarsity Press, 2005), 144–45; Kevin Corcoran, "A Constitutional Response," in *In Search of the Soul: Four Views of the Mind-Body Problem,* eds. Joel Green and Stuart Palmer (Downers Grove, IL: InterVarsity Press, 2005), 148–49.

[16] Cortez, *Theological Anthropology,* 77.

[17] Timothy O'Connor, "Materially-Composed Persons and the Unity of Consciousness: A Reply to Hasker" in *Neuroscience and the Soul: The Human Person in Philosophy, Science and Theology,* ed. Thomas Crisp, Steven Porter, and Gregg Elshof (Grand Rapids: Eerdmans, 2016), 41.

of the physico-chemical laws alone."[18] The causal relationship between mental and physical properties in this case goes beyond the supervenience relations that mental properties have on their physical bases (Searle's view), or even emergent relations where the causal efficacy of the mental property or state is still limited by the CCP principle (Murphy's view), to a "stronger" emergent relation where the mental state or property exercises autonomous causal powers. Hasker terms this "the theory of emergent material persons (EMP)."[19] In my view, the EMP theory serves as the strongest possible specification of the notion of the "self" afforded to any materialist, positing a "self" that is constituted by, but not identical to, their physical bodies, while not positing that "self" as another immaterial substance basic to human ontology.

With the outline of materialism in place, I proceed to explore how materialism accounts for the core datum point established of conscious states in general and gender dysphoria in particular. When it comes to conscious states in general, it could *arguably* be said that both varieties of hard and soft materialism are able to satisfy the requirements of the first three aspects of the conscious state posited by Searle—the "qualitative, unified subjectivity" aspects—although hard materialists will generally adopt the strategy of reducing the particular *qualia* associated with a conscious state to their biophysical and neural bases. Furthermore, soft materialists who do not espouse epiphenomenalism (that is, the view that mental properties are real but causally irrelevant),[20] and who affirm some version of "top-down causation" would be able to affirm the fourth aspect that states of consciousness have potential causative effects.

However, I stated "arguably" because, as Hasker shows, the challenge for materialists lies in providing a robust account of "unified subjectivity"; in other words, the sense of unity associated with the "I" that is at the center of the conscious state. Hasker contends that "the self, the subject of experience, cannot be a complex physical object such as the human body or brain. Instead, it must be a *simple substance*, one that has no parts that are themselves substances, and which cannot be divided into parts."[21] This is an account that no materialist is able to provide, not even those who subscribe to the EMP theory, because the core tenet of materialism states that the human person is *just* materially composed of a multitude of parts—organs, cells, chemical compounds, and ultimately of elementary particles—and short of allowing the existence of another immaterial substance as an explanation, the "self" on materialism's terms is complex and cannot be a simple substance. Even should the materialist pinpoint the "unified subjectivity" down to the brain that "operates in a way that is *functionally simple* in undergoing the conscious experiences," Hasker questions the spatial location of this holistic and functionally simple aspect of the brain.[22] To this question, Hasker postulates that the best answer a materialist can give is to grant to the tiniest particle in a person's brain—the quark—the entirety of the person's conscious state. Yet, this answer stretches one's credulity to its very limits as there clearly cannot be any physical

---

[18] Hasker, "Do My Quarks?," 20

[19] Hasker, "Do My Quarks?," 25.

[20] Cortez, *Theological Anthropology*, 91.

[21] Hasker, "Do My Quarks?," 28 (emphasis original).

[22] Hasker, "Do My Quarks?," 34 (emphasis original). Goetz highlights that in brain science, this is known as the binding problem, where scientists or neurologists are interested in discovering where in the brain all the effects of diverse stimuli come together to create a single, unified first-person experience of an object. The binding problem remains an ongoing exercise in search for an answer. Stewart Goetz, "A Substance Dualist Response," in *In Search of the Soul: Four Views of the Mind-Body Problem*, eds. Joel Green and Stuart Palmer (Downers Grove, IL: InterVarsity Press, 2005), 140.

processes happening at the level of the quark itself that would correspond to the complexity of the conscious experience experienced by the self.[23] O'Connor has countered Hasker by stating that it is quite possible for the materialist subscribing to the EMP theory to assert that the conscious state is instantiated by the "self" as a whole, while not being instantiated by the self's basic parts. This is possible because O'Conner's sort of constituent ontology—"I am a unified, albeit composed individual"— allows for a "distinctive particularizing element, or substratum, to the human person that is wholly distinct from the substrata of the person's basic parts."[24] The debate continues, but enough has been said of the main challenge that materialists face in accounting for conscious states in general; that is, *where did the unified individual "self" come from*, and given their fundamental commitment that all human persons are materially composed, *where is this unified individual "self" to be located*? But turning aside from the finer intricacies of the debate, I believe that the materialist has sufficient explanatory power to account for the phenomenon of conscious states in general.

I turn now to explore how materialists might account for gender dysphoria. At the center of gender dysphoria is the unique *quale* of a discordant "gender identity," where the latter is defined as "someone's internal sense of being a man or a woman" to be differentiated from biological sex and gendered socializations.[25] While the distinction and differentiation is clear, the definition of gender identity is amorphous and subjective, depending largely on how one defines "internal." One thing is clear, however: gender identity presupposes the notion of an "inner" or "real" self who, in the case of gender dysphoria, is of a gender or sex different from what the body indicates. I suggest that it is precisely in addressing this "inner" self and its associated gender identity that the different and distinct ways in which materialism and substance dualism account for gender dysphoria can be clearly seen, and whether they are sufficient to face the theological challenge that comes from the charge of God having "created but misplaced my being" in the wrong body.

Based on the above discussion on materialism, I foresee two strategies open to the hard materialist (whom as we recall either dismisses mental properties altogether or reduces them explanation-wise to their biophysical properties).[26] The first strategy is for the hard materialist to appeal to Philosophical (or Logical) Behaviorism, a somewhat outdated theory that seeks to translate ordinary claims about mental states and properties into statements about *behavioral dispositions*. So in the case of gender dysphoria (and at the risk of gross over-simplification), "I feel that I am of a gender that is different to my biological sex," would be equivalent to "growing up, I preferred playing with doll houses and dress-ups rather than with toy guns and cowboy toy figurines," or "if offered, I would choose to undergo puberty blockers (for pre-pubescent individuals), hormonal therapy and eventually gender reassignment surgery." Behaviorism theories, in other words, tend to explain the "inner" self crucial to the notion of gender identity solely in terms of behavioral patterns. As detractors have highlighted, behaviorism's chief weakness is that it is virtually impossible to specify a subject's particular conscious state purely as behavioral dispositions,

---

[23] Hasker, "Do My Quarks?," 35–36.

[24] O'Connor, "Materially-Composed Persons," 45.

[25] Lucy Griffin, Katie Clyde, Richard Byng, and Susan Bewley, "Sex, Gender and Gender Identity: a Re-Evaluation of the Evidence," *BJPsych Bulletin* (2020): 1–9, https://doi.org/10.1192/bjb.2020.73. See American Psychological Association, "Answers to Your Questions About Transgender People, Gender Identity and Gender Expression," http://www.apa.org/topics/lgbt/transgender.pdf, which similarly affirms this distinction.

[26] Both strategies are gleaned from Janet Levin, "Materialism," in *The Routledge Handbook of Consciousness*, ed. Rocco Gennaro (New York: Routledge, 2018), 38–50.

either because one could have a certain conscious state without the relevant behavioral dispositions (and vice versa) or the disposition to behave in a certain manner already presupposes the presence of other more basic underlying mental conscious states.

This leads to the second strategy available for the hard materialist: Type-Identity Theory, which at its core contends that "for each type of mental state or process M, there is a type of brain state or process B, such that M is identical with B," or "*being a state of Type M* is just *being a state of Type B*."[27] The example provided is typically that of the mental property of pain being identical with the neural process of C-fiber stimulation happening in the brain. As some may have already intuitively noted, the success of type-identity theories depends largely on the ability to ascertain universal correlations between instances of different mental types (determined via introspective reporting of individuals in such mental states) and their relevant physical counterparts (determined via instruments such as brain scans). These universal correlations—otherwise termed Neuronal Correlate of Consciousness (NCC)[28]—will enable us to find out what is happening in the brain at the neurological level at a time when the subject is undergoing particular states of consciousness. From the NCCs established, the grand aim is to derive general theories or statements of the laws and principles concerning how a particular state of consciousness could operate causally in the life of the subject. Needless to say, difficulties arising from the manifold complexities and the overall ambitious nature of the project continue to plague type-identity explanations of gender dysphoria.[29] Furthermore, NCC approaches suffer from a basic methodological shortcoming. The process of establishing NCCs applied to particular states of consciousness (in this case, gender dysphoria) will only reveal the NCC for a particular *mode of consciousness* within an already pre-existing conscious field and fails to reveal how the brain as a whole produces consciousness in the first place.[30]

Because soft materialists are happy to affirm the distinct presence of mental thoughts and properties without explaining them away based on their biophysical bases, they are better primed than hard materialists to attest to the "inner self" and the *quale* of discordance the "inner self" experiences in a conscious state of gender dysphoria. But because of their basic commitment to the material composition of human persons, soft materialists can only appeal to biophysical approaches, especially those involving neurology, in explaining the causal links between certain biophysical states and the conscious state of gender dysphoria.

I have an important qualifier to state at this juncture. That is, what follows pertains not to gender identity problems that arise from intersex conditions or what is otherwise termed disorders of sex development (DSDs). These disorders, usually involving some form of hormonal or genetic maldevelopment, can on some occasions result in affected individuals experiencing gender dysphoria,

---

[27] Janet Levin, "Materialism," 41 (emphasis original).

[28] Searle, "Self as Problem," 143.

[29] An example of the difficulty can be seen in Stephen V. Gliske, "A new theory of gender dysphoria incorporating the distress, social behavioral, and body-ownership networks," *ENEURO* 6.6 (2019), https://doi.org/10.1523/ENEURO.0183-19.2019, where it is claimed that gender dysphoria is brought about by an alteration in how one's sense of gender is influenced by the reflexive behavioral responses associated with three neural networks. While promising, the article had to be subsequently retracted by the journal's editorial board in *ENEURO* 7.2 (2020), https://doi.org/10.1523/ENEURO.0149-20.2020, on the grounds of major flaws including a lack of supporting evidence in the literature.

[30] Searle, "Self as Problem," 144–45, highlights this larger problem.

but the numbers are low and it seems more the case that people with a DSD do not identify as transgender and most who do identify as transgender do not have a DSD.[31] My focus at this point is on the latter group: those who would claim that while their primary sex characteristics such as genitalia are developing normally, their secondary sex characteristics associated with the brain are developing along the lines of the opposite sex.[32]

This brings us to an explanation of gender dysphoria particularly appealing for the soft materialist: brain-sex theory. First mooted by Robert Sapolsky, the theory seeks a possible neurobiological explanation for cross-gender identification. Essentially, Sapolsky asserts that recent neuroimaging studies of the brains of transgender adults suggest that they have brain structures more like the gender they identify with than their biological sex. Based on this, Sapolsky concludes that there is a possibility of people being "born with bodies whose gender is different from what they actually are"; in other words, they have a female-type brain in a male body, or vice versa.[33]

Despite its relatively slender scientific basis, brain-sex theory has gone on to garner scientific and popular attention. Mayer and McHugh list a compilation of scientific studies that have sought to ascertain neurobiological causes such as brain structure or brain function differences between trans- and cisgender individuals as possible causes for gender dysphoria.[34] Their conclusions, however, are less optimistic, writing that "it remains unclear whether and to what extent neurobiological findings say anything meaningful about gender identity."[35] To Mayer and McHugh, what is actually needed to gain maximum profitability from such neurobiological investigations are "prospective longitudinal panel studies of a fixed set of individuals across the course of sexual development if not their lifespan." Such studies would involve the use of serial brain images at birth, in childhood, and at other developmental points. This would be the only way to ascertain fully whether certain brain features *caused* a trait or whether the particular brain feature noted is a *consequence* of the trait. If not, such studies, even if they were methodologically reliable, remain "insufficient to demonstrate that brain structure is a cause, rather than an effect, of the gender-identity behavior. They would likewise lack predictive power, the real challenge for any theory in science."[36] It should be noted that while some recent neurobiological studies conducted after Mayer and McHugh's report provide nascent promissory findings, they similarly affirm the need for more research before any definitive conclusions can be drawn.[37]

---

[31] Lawrence S. Mayer and Paul R. McHugh, "Sexuality and Gender: Findings from the Biological, Psychological, and Social Sciences," *New Atlantis* 50, Special Report (Fall 2016), part 3, https://www.thenewatlantis.com/publications/executive-summary-sexuality-and-gender; Anderson, *When Harry Became Sally*, ch. 4.

[32] Mayer and McHugh, "Sexuality and Gender," part 3. DSM-5, 457, continues to maintain a distinction between sexual dysphoria and an intersex condition.

[33] Robert Sapolsky, "Caught Between Male and Female," *Wall Street Journal*, 6 December 2013, quoted in Mayer and McHugh, "Sexuality and Gender," part 3.

[34] Mayer and McHugh, "Sexuality and Gender," part 3, under the subheading "Gender and Physiology."

[35] Mayer and McHugh, "Sexuality and Gender," part 3, under the subheading "Gender and Physiology."

[36] Mayer and McHugh, "Sexuality and Gender," part 3, under the subheading "Gender and Physiology."

[37] Jiska Ristori Carlotta Cocchetti, Alessia Romani, et al., "Brain Sex Differences Related to Gender Identity Development: Genes or Hormones?" *International Journal of Molecular Sciences* 21 (2020), https://doi.org/10.3390/ijms21062123; Ferdinand J. O. Boucher and Tudor I. Chinnah, "Gender Dysphoria: A Review Investigating the Relationship Between Genetic Influences and Brain Development," *Adolescent Health, Medicine and Therapeutics* 11 (2020), https://doi.org/10.2147/AHMT.S259168, and Alberto Frigerio, Lucia Ballerini and Maria

To sum up, materialism as a way of conceiving the body-soul relationship varies in its ability to account for the "qualitative, unified subjectivity" dimension of conscious states in general and the conscious state of gender dysphoria in particular, depending on which species of materialism one goes with. Hard materialists have a harder time (no pun intended!) affirming the "inner self" and the distinct *quale* of discordance experienced that forms the central feature of gender dysphoria. In fact, if they commit themselves fully to the tenets of hard materialism, there is no "inner self" and its associated *quale* of discordance to begin with, but only an "inner self" governed purely by behavioral patterns or neural networks and processes! This would consequently mean that there are virtually no grounds for the "created but misplaced being" problem to feature within a hard materialism, because the notion of an "inner" and "real" misgendered self remains vague and ill-defined under its terms.

Soft materialists, on the other hand, and especially those who subscribe to an "emergent material person" theory, are much better able to affirm the "inner self" and its associated *quale* of discordance. But because the soft materialist is still committed to the tenet of material composition of the human person, the utmost limit that the soft materialist can go is to allow for the elementary physical particles— the quarks, atoms, molecules, neurons, neural processes etc.—to interact in such a way that the distinct mental reality of the "inner self" emerges, all this time guaranteeing that this "self" is constituted by the body and its constituent parts rather than forming a whole new distinct immaterial substance altogether. The mental phenomenon of the "inner self" for the soft materialist is still inextricably linked to the body and its constituent parts. In cases where the primary sex characteristics such as genitalia are developing normally, the gender identity of this "inner self" should *by all accounts and in accordance with materialism's own commitments be the same as that of the biological sex identity of the body*. This in turn means that when it comes to the "created but misplaced being" problem, the most a soft materialist can ask is "could God have created me a woman but placed in me the brain of a man?" (or vice versa). Put differently, under a materialist framework, the "created but misplaced being" problem can at its very best and strongest form appear as an expression of brain-sex theory; even then, as we have seen, short of further research and scientific validation, it is highly unlikely and improbable that brain-sex theory serves as an explanation for gender dysphoria. In other words, there is very little basis within a consideration of materialism for one to lay claim to the charge that God created but misplaced my being in the wrong body, leading to my state of gender dysphoria.

3. Substance Dualism and Gender Dysphoria

I turn next to substance dualism. As the name implies, substance dualism maintains as its core commitment that there are two distinct mental and physical realms or substances: the soul/mind and the body. Both substances are fundamental and non-reducible to anything more basic, and can be conceived as capable of existing separately and of entering into causal relationships with each other. In particular, the soul under substance dualism is seen to possess a causal relation with its body such that it is able to act directly upon the body and be acted upon by the body.[38] Once the majority position held in the Christian tradition, the popularity of substance dualism as a way of explaining the ontology of the

---

Valdés Hernández, "Structural, Functional, and Metabolic Brain Differences as a Function of Gender Identity or Sexual Orientation: A Systematic Review of the Human Neuroimaging Literature," *Archives of Sexual Behavior* 50 (2021), https://doi.org/10.1007/s10508-021-02005-9.

[38] Cortez, *Theological Anthropology*, 83.

human person has waned in light of the rise of secular naturalism and its two closely related views of humanity: evolutionary humanism and secular humanism. The result is that fewer numbers continue to maintain, as Joshua Farris states, the traditional "belief in a soul created by some deity that places us in a unique relation to the rest of the world."[39]

Substance dualism, however, has not been totally replaced, and in fact could be said to be regaining lost ground especially in the philosophical and theological domains.[40] Philosophical arguments have been advanced that point to some form of substance dualism as the more appealing way of conceiving the ontology of human beings as compared to its rival framework, materialism. These philosophical arguments center on substance dualism being the more intuitive or "common sense" approach to how we conceive ourselves. As stated by philosopher Stewart Goetz: "One of the things that I, as an ordinary person, believe about myself is that I am a soul that is distinct from my physical (material) body."[41] In other words, philosophers like Goetz see an ordinary person's belief that he or she is a soul as an epistemologically basic belief that cannot be inferred or derived from any other more basic beliefs that this person might have. At the same time, Goetz contends that this basic belief that I am a soul finds sufficient epistemological warrant in just one's experience that consists of "my inner or introspective awareness of myself as a simple substance that exemplifies psychological properties."[42] Another philosophical argument arguing for the soul utilizes the notion of the unity of consciousness. As seen earlier, Hasker argues that it is only the simple immaterial substance of the soul that can vouchsafe the experience of the unity of consciousness—the "unified subjectivity"—crucial to any conscious state. The only other alternative available to the materialist would be to posit the idea that it is the smallest elementary particle—the quark—that carries the entirety of the person's conscious state; an idea that Hasker finds far-fetched.[43] The final philosophical argument is an argument from replacement that derives its strength from a thought-experiment. Alvin Plantinga argues that it is still possible to conceive oneself existing even if all our bodily parts—right down to the very cellular level consisting of every minute molecule, atom, and quark—were to be replaced at an imaginary lightning speed. The possibility of being able to still conceive my existence and more importantly the continuation of my personal identity under this situation translates to the possibility that I am not identical with the whole

---

[39] Joshua R. Farris, *An Introduction to Theological Anthropology* (Grand Rapids: Baker Academic, 2020), 25–26.

[40] In theology, Karl Barth could be held as one who maintained a form of substance dualism. See Marc Cortez, *Embodied Souls, Ensouled Bodies: An Exercise in Christological Anthropology and Its Significance for the Mind/Body Debate* (New York: T&T Clark, 2008). Another example would be Farris, *An Introduction to Theological Anthropology.*

[41] Stewart Goetz, "Substance Dualism," 33.

[42] Goetz, "Substance Dualism," 39. Goetz considers the counterargument that when the materialist carries out this similar introspection, he or she could very well reach the opposite basic belief that "one is one's physical body" (55). Goetz's response is to plunge deeper into the content of that introspective self-awareness and affirm that what I am aware is the fact that "I occupy that same space [that my physical body with its substantive parts occupy] in a different way by being present in my entirety at each point of the space that I occupy." That, Goetz affirms, is only achievable with the (simple) soul that is present in its entirety at each point in space where it experiences sensations (56). Hence, a stronger justification is provided for the substance dualist's basic belief than the materialist's. See Farris, *An Introduction to Theological Anthropology*, 20, where he maintains a similar common-sense argument for the soul.

[43] Hasker, "Do My Quarks?," 35–36.

of my body that I presently have or with the composition of my body. Instead, my identification lies with something deeper and immaterial: my soul.[44] Substance dualists contend that if any of the above three arguments work, we would have reasons to reject materialism in favor of the view that human persons are essentially a soul with a body.

We now engage with the specific issue of how substance dualism might account for conscious states in general and gender dysphoria in particular. An initial glance reveals that substance dualism has a smoother path than materialism in accounting for the "qualitative, unified subjectivity" aspect common to all conscious states and their potential causative effects. The very core tenet of substance dualism positing a separate immaterial simple substance known as the soul is what fulfils the key criteria required. Put differently, it is my soul that experiences the distinct *qualia* associated with the conscious state ("qualitative" aspect); my soul, being a simple immaterial substance, experiences the *qualia* in a unified manner and all at once ("unified" aspect); I identify myself with my soul rather than my body or any of my body parts ("subjectivity" aspect), and my soul, being a separate substance from my body, could potentially cause me or my body parts to behave in a certain manner ("potential causative effect").

When it comes to gender dysphoria, substance dualism via the positing of the soul is able to account for the "inner" or "real self" and the experience of gender identity discordance by pinpointing that "inner self" to reside in the soul. The substance dualist is able to say that one's "real self" is to be identified with one's soul, rather than with any "self" that might arise from the interaction or proper functioning of my body's constituent parts right down to the cellular level, which would still be materially composed on the final count. However, the move of locating the "inner" or "real self" to the soul sets the substance dualist to be wide open to the "created but misplaced being" problem: God created my soul as female, but I have been mistakenly placed in a male body (or vice versa). Leveled as a more serious charge: God created me to be in this state of gender dysphoria. What avenues are open to the substance dualist to counter this charge?[45]

Here is where it is beneficial to drill deeper into the different varieties of substance dualism. Two varieties of substance dualism—Emergent Dualism and Thomistic Dualism (or Hylomorphism)—hold the two components of soul and body in such a tight and interdependent relationship that any justification or basis for positing the idea of a soul mismatched with a wrongly sexed body is dematerialized. I begin with Emergent Dualism and turn to Hasker who could be said to be emergent dualism's foremost advocate.[46] Put simply, emergent dualism states that the soul (or mind) is an emergent entity or mental

---

[44] Alvin Plantinga, "Against Materialism," *Faith and Philosophy* 23.1 (2006): 3–32.

[45] At this juncture, I refer to Robert S. Smith, "Body, Soul and Gender Identity: Thinking Theologically About Human Constitution," *Eikon* 3.2 (2021): 27–37, https://cbmw.org/2021/11/21/body-soul-and-gender-identity-thinking-theologically-about-human-constitution/#_ftnref39; an article which complements this present piece. Smith similarly explores the extent to which human constitution or ontology supports what he calls "*spiritual gender identity theory*—i.e., the claim that a person can have the spirit or soul of one sex in the body of another" (28). This is similar to the "created but misplaced being" scenario which I am exploring. The key difference between the two articles, however, lies in the narrower focus of Smith's exploration. He focuses only on one version of substance dualism—"soft dualism" of a kind leaning towards Thomistic dualism—while my article explores the broad spectrum of views concerning human constitution, both of a materialist and substance dualist flavor. I would like to thank Brian Tabb (General Editor of *Themelios*) for alerting me to this article.

[46] William Hasker presents his views in his monograph *The Emergent Self* (Ithaca, NY: Cornell University Press, 1999). For a chapter-size summary of his view, see Hasker, "On Behalf of Emergent Dualism," in *In Search of the Soul: Four Views of the Mind-Body Problem*, eds. Joel Green and Stuart Palmer (Downers Grove, IL: Inter-

substance that *emerges* from a properly configured physical system, in this case the body with all the biological, chemical, and neural relationships and interactions. In this way, the emergence of mental properties and mental events, in fact, emergent novel causal powers, and—nay, can we even say more—a whole emergent "self" or person, is what emergent dualism shares with the "strongest" view of materialism, what we termed the theory of emergent material persons (EMP) earlier. The key difference between the two is that on emergent dualism's terms, once emerged, the soul or mind or mental state of the "self" *subsists as a distinct substance* that is *simple, immaterial,* and *ontologically distinct and separable from the body.* The "self" that emerges under the EMP theory, however, is still constituted by the body and its physical parts, hence complex, and certainly not another substance ontologically distinct and separable from the body.[47]

The important point to note that rules out the "created but misplaced being" scenario for emergent dualism is that the soul is not created "externally" outside of the body and then subsequently added or "plopped" into a body (a view Hasker labels as "creationism"); rather, the soul emerges "internally" from the physical, chemical, and neural operations in the created human body. The theist who subscribes to emergent dualism therefore sees the creation of one's human soul by the divine creator not as an act of creation *ex nihilo,* but a creation brought about through the natural process of the appropriate physical organization and function of the body and brain.[48] In situations where there is clearly no DSD at work, the body's biological sex would serve as the proximate cause for the "gender" of the soul and as Farris observes of such an outworking, "it is not clear what other cause would contribute to the emergence of a mismatching soul with body."[49] As with the case of our consideration of materialism, the best that a challenger could do is to point to brain-sex theory as a basis for the emergence of a wrongly gendered soul, but even then, as we have seen, the theory is still far from conclusive in serving as an explanation for gender dysphoria.

I move to the second variety of substance dualism that can fend off the challenges from the "created but misplaced being" problem: Thomistic Dualism (or Hylomorphism). As the name suggests, Thomistic dualism finds its influence in Aristotelian and Thomistic ontologies, which basically sees all material objects as composites comprising of first, matter, and second, a substantial form that determines the essential nature of the object at hand such that the material composite together counts as a member of the species to which it belongs.[50] As Thomist philosopher Eleonore Stump puts it, "Human beings, earthworms, daisies, rocking chairs, amethyst clumps, and bread dough share with all other material things the characteristic of having both matter and form."[51]

Varsity Press, 2005), 75–100; and Hasker, "Why Emergence?," in *The Ashgate Research Companion to Theological Anthropology,* eds. Joshua R. Farris and Charles Taliaferro (Burlington, VT: Ashgate, 2015), 151–61.

[47] Hasker, "Why Emergence?," 158–59.

[48] Hasker, "Why Emergence?," 153–55. Hasker contends that soul emergentism has the following advantages over soul creationism: 1) it provides a better account of the dependence of mind (or the soul) upon the body; 2) soul emergentism is less pressured than soul creationism to attribute divinely created souls to animals, and 3) soul emergentism coheres better with biological evolution than soul creationism.

[49] Farris, *An Introduction to Theological Anthropology,* 227.

[50] I am dependent on Eleanore Stump, "Non-Cartesian Substance Dualism and Materialism without Reduction," *Faith and Philosophy* 12 (1995): 505–31, for the description of Thomistic dualism.

[51] Stump, "Non-Cartesian Substance Dualism and Materialism without Reduction," 507.

Translated to the human being, Stump contends that the human soul is "the substantial form …
in virtue of which the matter informed by it … constitutes a living human body."[52] She adds further that
Aquinas takes the soul to be a particular, not a universal, such that the soul can be said to be that which
animates or actualizes a human body to not just be a human being, but *this* human being. The soul, on
Aquinas's terms, being a kind of form and an "essentially configurational state," is also immaterial, simple
(in relation to what it is), and located spatially in its entirety in each part of the body (in relation to the
wholeness of what it is).[53] Finally, Aquinas posits the idea that the soul is able to exist separated from the
body and engage in mental acts while in that state of separation. This is an idea that Stump admits may
be perplexing for some, given the question how there can exist "an essentially configurational state with
nothing that is configured" and furthermore, one that is able to engage in acts while separated from the
very body it is configuring. Stump's proposed solution is to adopt a broader view of what Aquinas has
in mind with the notion of form, and here, she brings in Aquinas's idea that it is possible for some forms
to be configured rather than to be configurers of things, given that "anything that has being—whether
that thing is material or immaterial—… will have configuration or form."[54] The human soul, on Aquinas's
terms as Stump posits, is just this amphibian of the metaphysical world: "Like the angels, the human
soul is itself configured; but like the forms of other material things, the human soul has the ability to
configure matter. The human soul, then, is a configured configurer."[55]

The above understanding of the human soul in its double aspect as a "configured configurer" is not
to be glossed over, for it is this central concept that enables Aquinas to accomplish three key things.
First, it enables him to hold out the continued existence of the soul separated from the body. Because
the soul is configured, it has being, and hence it can have an existence on its own, albeit not as a full
substance but as a "subsistent thing." Aquinas attributes any cognitive functions that the disembodied
soul can have to divine help.[56] Second, since the soul is itself an individual configured form (and Aquinas
holds that each soul is as it were handcrafted by God), the human soul makes matter be not just human
but also *this* human being with the full individuality of his or her personhood. This is a personal identity
that carries on after death in the separated soul.[57] Third, the double aspect of the human soul as a
"configured configurer" is what enables Aquinas to maintain that while each human soul is created
directly by God (the "configured" aspect), the soul is not created *before* the body and then infused into
an already existing body. Rather, as Stump states, "like the form of any material object, [the soul] exists
in the composite it configures and it comes into existence only with that composite, not before it."[58]
The soul is therefore created in the body, being produced simultaneously with human bodies at the
culmination of human generation (the "configurer" aspect).[59]

---

[52] Stump, "Non-Cartesian Substance Dualism and Materialism without Reduction," 508.

[53] Stump, "Non-Cartesian Substance Dualism and Materialism without Reduction," 512.

[54] Stump, "Non-Cartesian Substance Dualism and Materialism without Reduction," 513.

[55] Stump, "Non-Cartesian Substance Dualism and Materialism without Reduction," 514–15.

[56] Stump, "Non-Cartesian Substance Dualism and Materialism without Reduction," 517–19.

[57] Stump, "Non-Cartesian Substance Dualism and Materialism without Reduction," 516.

[58] Stump, "Non-Cartesian Substance Dualism and Materialism without Reduction," 516.

[59] Stump, "Non-Cartesian Substance Dualism and Materialism without Reduction," 515.

I am not expecting Thomistic dualism as a way of accounting for the body-soul relationship to satisfy everyone.[60] But taken on its terms, Thomistic dualism is able to defend itself against the charge of the "created but misplaced being" problem that substance dualism as a general framework might be open to. The understanding of the soul as the form or configurational state of the body has led some Thomistic dualists to maintain that while the immaterial soul by itself does not have a sex, the soul could be properly characterized as gendered on account of the fact that it serves as the vivifying or actualizing principle of an actually existing *sexed* human being.[61] And since the soul serves as the configurational state of this particular human body which is of a biological sex one way, on account of Thomistic dualism, it is virtually impossible for the soul to be gendered another way. Otherwise, how could a "male" human soul be the vivifying and animating principle for a "female" human body such that the soul-body unitive composite exists as a female human being (or vice versa)?[62] The plausibility of a wrongly gendered soul is also further removed when we consider Aquinas's contention that the soul, even though it is created by God, is not created before the body is, but at the same time that the soul configures the body that is identified with a particular biological sex.[63]

That leaves the last variety of substance dualism: Cartesian dualism, which is slightly more problematic. Cartesian dualism, especially in its stronger forms—what has been termed "pure-substance dualism"[64]— construes body and soul to be so fundamentally different that there is little interdependence between the two substances. On account of this version of Cartesian dualism, the soul is often seen as that which is real and the sole constituent of one's personal identity, including the continuance of personal identity upon death. The human body ends up being viewed as a nonpersonal instrument of the self. As Melissa Moschella highlights, "strong" Cartesian dualism could do damage in severing the link between sex (understood as biological identity) and gender (understood as a psychological identity). Because the soul alone is what constitutes the "real me" such that my biological sexual identity as a characteristic of my body is not definitive for the gender identity of the "real me," the door is opened

---

[60] The main difficulty for fully embracing Thomistic dualism comes from the ambiguous state of the human soul: is it a "substance" or not? Hasker, "On Behalf of Emergent Dualism," 94, sees that in positing the soul as "the form of the body," a pattern or structure of the body, and yet allowing the soul to continue subsisting and carrying out various mental activities in a disembodied state, "Thomistic dualism suffers from a fundamental incoherence." Hasker, *Emergent Self*, 167–70, presents two further problems that Thomistic dualism is not entirely able to shake off: the problem of mind-body interaction on Thomistic dualism's own terms and the problem of the souls of animals.

[61] Elliott L. Bedford and Jason T. Eberl, "Is the Soul Sexed? Anthropology, Transgenderism, and Disorders of Sex Development," *CHAUSA* (2016), https://tinyurl.com/35yc5hf7.

[62] Farris, *An Introduction to Theological Anthropology*, 226, states that for Thomistic dualism, "[p]ersons are matter-form composites, and persons are not, properly speaking, identical to their souls alone apart from the matter the soul informs."

[63] My conclusion regarding Thomistic dualism is similar to that of Smith, "Body, Soul and Gender Identity," 33–35. Smith highlights that although there is still some debate within Thomist scholarship, there is ample ground to read Aquinas as supporting the view that the soul takes its sex (or gender) from the body and not the other way around (34).

[64] Farris, *An Introduction to Theological Anthropology*, 65.

to the possibility that my soul could be created gendered one way but misplaced in a body of a different biological sex.[65]

Not all is lost for Cartesian dualists though. There is a way out of the conundrum and that is for Cartesian dualists to maintain that the soul is not gendered on its own in abstraction from a human body. On this view, even though the soul is seen as a substance fully in its own right in the sense of being a bearer of properties, "sex" or "gender" is *not held as an essential property of a human soul*, but an *accidental property held in conjunction with a human body of a certain biological sex*. This view derives its inspiration from the patristic theologian Gregory of Nyssa's understanding of sex and gender and its application to the human soul.[66] On this Nyssa-inspired model where the soul does not instantiate one's gender essentially but only derivatively as a common property it shares with the body, it is difficult to envisage a case of a soul gendered one way mismatched with the wrong body.[67] In other words, the (strong) Cartesian dualist in this case is at best able to assert that God created this human soul "female" because femaleness is a common property shared with the female body in which the soul coexists. The (strong) Cartesian dualist is not entitled to claim femaleness as an intrinsic and essential property of the created soul on its own. In fact, this is not a high price for strong Cartesian dualists to pay and it might be to their advantage. The idea of gender being an essential property of the human soul brings problems of its own. For one, if that were so, would the fact that God the Son assumed a human *male* soul in the incarnation show up the inadequacy of our Lord's redemption for human *female* souls? For the Lord would have at best assumed half a complete human soul—a male soul but not the female soul—since gender and sexuality is deemed an essential property of the soul under this way of thinking. The (strong) Cartesian dualist who subscribes to a Nyssa-inspired way of thinking about the human soul is free of this problem.

To summarize, while the "created but misplaced being" problem might initially seem to prove a challenge for substance dualism, a closer examination of the two varieties of emergent dualism and Thomistic dualism rule out the problem. For on account of these two types of substance dualism, the soul is inextricably linked to the body—emerging from the biophysical and neural operations of a body of a particular biological sex in emergent dualism, and acting as the form or configurational state of a body that is also of a particular biological sex in Thomistic dualism. Even with the third type of strong Cartesian dualism, the challenge can be mitigated by maintaining a Nyssa-inspired view of the human

---

[65] Melissa Moschella, "Sexual Identity, Gender, and Human Fulfillment: Analyzing the 'Middle Way' Between Liberal and Traditionalist Approaches," *Christian Bioethics* 25 (2019): 192–215, https://doi.org/10.1093/cb/cbz005.

[66] The traditional reading of the bishop's understanding on this matter is that sexuality and gender was added to humanity in view of the Fall, whereas the prelapsarian and eschatological state of humanity was intended to follow that of the angels in their asexuality. See, for example, Hans Boersma, "Putting on Clothes: Body, Sex, and Gender in Gregory of Nyssa," *CRUX* 54.2 (2018): 27–34, for this traditional reading of Nyssen. John Behr, "The Rational Animal: A Rereading of Gregory of Nyssa's *De hominis opificio*," *JECS* 7 (1999): 219–47, however, has proposed an alternative interpretation, suggesting that from the outset Nyssen conceived the existence of human beings as rational animals, embracing within their own being the two extremes of creation, namely, the asexual rational (which is in the image of God) and the irrational sexual (which humans share with the animals). Nyssen sees the human soul as the rational soul, and given that he associates gender and sexuality with the irrational, leads me to postulate that Gregory of Nyssa would not have seen gender and sexuality as essential properties held by the soul, even as he recognized the soul as a bearer of properties in its own right.

[67] Farris, *An Introduction to Theological Anthropology*, 226.

soul, where gender or sexuality is not counted as an essential property of the soul, but an accidental property held in common with the body in which the soul co-subsists.

Together with the findings that we uncovered from our exploration of materialism, one could safely assert that when it comes to gender dysphoria and the body-soul relationship, there is virtually no ontological space for the "created but misplaced being" scenario to happen, where God created the "real" me gendered one way but misplaced this "real" me in the wrong human body of a different biological sex. This is regardless of how the "real" me is conceived under the two main frameworks presented: according to brain-sex theory for materialism or the theory of a sexed soul for substance dualism.

4. Conclusion: Three Preliminary Theological Implications

Perhaps some might find the above exercise a tad too speculative in nature, but I am convinced that the exploration has its benefits for a theological consideration of gender dysphoria, and I offer three preliminary insights in closing.

First, in ruling out a "created but misplaced being" scenario, one concurrently rules out the origin or cause of gender dysphoria as being located in creation and pinpoints it instead to the fall. As this article has sought to prove, regardless of the body-soul framework one subscribes to—whether materialism or substance dualism—there is virtually no basis to lay claim to the charge that God created the "real" me gendered one way but mistakenly placed me in a body of a different biological sex. In other words, we can confidently assume that gender dysphoria as a phenomenon is not meant to be associated with any states of consciousness experienced by the human being *at the point of creation*; it is *not* a natural state of consciousness that God created us to experience. This in no way belittles the genuine sense of gender identity discordance that the gender dysphoric person struggles with, but it is to say that in the case of individuals with a clear-cut biological sex, the conscious state of gender dysphoria is a *psychological* phenomenon resulting from the fall, rather than a *physiological* (involving the proper functioning of the human body and brain) or *ethereal* (involving the human soul) phenomenon that finds its origin in creation.[68] Even when considered as a consequence of the Fall, I remain persuaded that gender dysphoria is to be "understood as a result of living in a fallen world, not a result of personal moral choice," as stated in a recent tract. As with those who suffer from mental health issues (e.g., depression or anxiety), "we do not discuss their emotional state as a moral choice, but a condition that manifests as a result of the fall. A person may make choices in response to the symptoms or an overall treatment approach which may have ethical or moral dimensions, but they did not choose their condition and they are not morally culpable for it."[69] Such an identification allows for the *quale* of gender identity discordance to

---

[68] Once again, the exploration of individuals with DSD or those born with intersex conditions experiencing gender dysphoria lies beyond the scope of this article and deserves a separate treatment. Even then, it can be preliminarily argued that any gender dysphoria associated with DSDs be seen as *physiological* effects of the Fall not intended at creation. As the paper "A Theology of Gender and Gender Identity," *Sydney Diocesan Doctrine Commission* (2017), https://www.sds.asn.au/diocesan-doctrine-commission-0, states, "The biblical account of creation thus indicates that God has created each human being as either male or female. We are given no encouragement to consider male and female as two extremes at either end of a broad continuum, or to consider those with an intersex condition as intended from the beginning as a third sex" (§3.2).

[69] "Transformed: A Brief Biblical and Pastoral Introduction to Understanding Transgender in a Changing Culture," *Evangelical Alliance* (2018), https://www.eauk.org/resources/what-we-offer/reports/transformed-understanding-transgender-in-a-changing-culture.

be conceived as a psychological misworking of the mind in terms of its thought processes and rightful identification of the states of consciousness the mind undergoes. As John Calvin highlighted, the fall has brought about a vitiation of every part of our human nature such that the supernatural gifts were withdrawn and the natural gifts corrupted in terms of soundness of mind and uprightness of heart being taken away.[70] In gender dysphoria, the thought processes and identification of conscious states which lead to one affirming his or her gender identity in a way that follows naturally from one's given biological sex have sadly been *disordered*, and once again, this is due to the fall rather than creation itself.

Second, I believe that the above exercise reinforces a central point in thinking after a theological-anthropological manner about gender: the need to retain some aspect of what has been termed "essentialism." While factoring in the role of cultural contexts and social constructs in shaping how we as a society understand our gender norms, expressions and roles, our gender identification cannot run away from being grounded in the biological givens of life.[71] The above exploration shows that all the body-soul relationship accounts featured locate the gender identity of the "inner" or "real" self as having some form of connection to one's biological sex, regardless of whether the idea of the "inner" self stands in need of further clarification and definition (on account of hard materialism), or the "inner" self is to be identified with the "emergent material person" (on account of soft materialism), or the human soul (on account of substance dualism). The necessity of some form of "essentialism" in turn establishes once again that gender dysphoria—especially in cases where there is no evidence of a DSD condition—is really to be seen as a psychological rather than a physiological or ethereal problem.

Third, the recognition of gender dysphoria as essentially a psychological issue resulting from the fall should provide guidance in our pastoral care and restraint in our psychological assessment and treatment of gender dysphoric individuals. At the very least, it should give pause before gender dysphoric clients or patients are hastily—in some cases, almost automatically—recommended gender-affirming therapies that usually culminate with gender reassignment surgeries.[72] Gender affirming therapies, insofar as they involve any form of medical interventions on a human body that is clearly identified as belonging to a certain biological sex, do irreversible violence to one's bodily integrity and directly harm one's capacity for marriage and reproduction. These actions thwart the very purpose of human flourishing that our bodies are biologically-sexed for and so should be regarded as morally wrong actions.[73] It is also questionable whether such medical measures, especially gender reassignment surgeries, achieve the alleviation of psychological distress they are purported to bring about.[74] Even if

---

[70] John Calvin, *Institutes of the Christian Religion*, ed. J. T. McNeill, trans. Ford Lewis Battles (Louisville: Westminster John Knox Press, 1960), 2.1.8 and 2.2.12.

[71] Cortez, *Theological Anthropology*, 55.

[72] Gender-affirming therapies typically consist of a set of stages beginning with social transitioning, puberty blockers (especially if the gender dysphoric individual is still a child), hormonal treatments, and finally, gender reassignment surgeries.

[73] Moschella, "Sexual Identity, Gender, and Human Fulfillment," 200–201.

[74] See, for example, Cecilia Dhejne, Paul Lichtenstein, Marcus Boman, Anna L. V. Johansson, Niklas Lång-ström, and Mikael Landén, "Long-Term Follow-Up of Transsexual Persons Undergoing Sex Reassignment Surgery: Cohort Study in Sweden," *PLoS One* 6.2 (2011), http://www.ncbi.nlm.nih.gov/pmc/articles/PMC3043071; Richard Bränström and John E. Pachankis, "Reduction in Mental Health Treatment Utilization Among Transgender Individuals After Gender-Affirming Surgeries: A Total Population Study," *American Journal of Psychiatry* 177 (2020): 727–34, https://doi.org/10.1176/appi.ajp.2019.19010080; and "Correction to Bränström and Pachankis," *American Journal of Psychiatry* 177 (2020): 765, https://doi.org/10.1176/appi.ajp.2020.1778correction.

they do appear to do so, the findings uncovered in this article reveal that the procedures' "success" in relieving psychological distress would ultimately be premised on a falsehood: on all accounts of the body-soul relationship outlined above, the true gender identity of the "inner" or "real" self is inextricably bound to the biological sex of the human body in which this "self" is located, and *not the other way round*. In the case of one whose biological sex is unambiguous, gender dysphoria involves a psychological pathology where created reality is misperceived. The feeling of being a man trapped in a woman's body (or vice versa) might well be the genuine subjective feeling of the gender dysphoric individual, but it is not an objective fact. The question remains: in this situation, does it make more sense to change the body to match the mind (changing objective reality to match subjective misperception), or to change the mind to match the body (changing subjective misperception to fit with objective reality)?[75]

---

[75] See Griffin, Clyde, Byng, and Bewley, "Sex, Gender and Gender Identity," where, coming from a purely psychiatric perspective, the authors issue a stirring call in the name of good psychiatry and medicine to give pause to simply going with medical/surgical transitioning procedures as a way of treating gender dysphoria. Their conclusion is worth quoting substantially (p. 9):

> Language that confuses or conflates sex and gender identity, while appearing inclusive, might have the unintended consequence of closing down the means to understand complexity and respond appropriately to patients' emotional and material reality.... Viewing transgender as a fixed or stable entity, rather than a state of mind with multiple causative factors, closes down opportunities for doctors and patients to explore the meaning of any discomfort ... [especially] when multiple medical interventions are required on an otherwise healthy body or doctors are expected to deny the concept of sex or the sexed body.... It is confusing to liken open-minded working with young patients as they figure out who they are to conversion therapy. Holding an empathic neutral middle ground, which might or might not include medical transition, should not be equated with this. Psychiatrists need to feel empowered to explore the meaning of identity with their patients, treat coexisting mental illness and employ a trauma-informed model of care when appropriate.

It is hoped that my article provides a theological/philosophical basis to these findings that have otherwise come from a psychiatric perspective.

Church-State Relations: Lessons from China

— Luke Wesley —

Luke Wesley is a pen-name used to safeguard the identity of the author. The author is a missionary who has lived and served in China for most of the past three decades.

****

Abstract: This article delineates various biblical principles that circumscribe the church's relationship to the state. In addition to more general principles, these include the recognition that the mission of the organized church is distinct from that of individual Christians, that political institutions tend to become anti-Christ and oppressive, and that our context will determine the extent to which the church can exercise its prophetic voice. In view of these principles and on the basis of his experience in China, the author highlights five theological truths that will inevitably be challenged by totalitarian governments. Our faithfulness or lack thereof will hinge on our response to these challenges.

****

Normally, my wife and I live in China, and life in the U.S. appears to us to be a distant reality. Yet, as a result of the COVID pandemic, we have spent the past two years in the U.S. While this has been a challenging time in some respects, it also has been a fruitful period, filled with unexpected opportunities. For me, one such opportunity has been the ability to experience and witness a chaotic and disturbing period of North American history, and to reflect on these events in light of God's word and our twenty-eight years of experience in China.

Let me begin by pointing out the obvious. North America (I think here primarily of the U.S. and Canada) is rapidly moving toward a more authoritarian, totalitarian form of governance. This trend undoubtedly has been accelerated by the COVID pandemic, but the more recent expansion of governmental power and the resulting loss of personal freedom in the region appears to be more than a temporary phenomenon, a small blip on the political horizon. The normalization of "soft totalitarianism," which demands conformity to and acceptance of a state-sponsored ideology, suggests that Christians and the church in North America may be headed for difficult times. Since Christians in China have lived in a totalitarian state from Chairman Mao's rise to power in 1949 to the present, it is not unreasonable to assume they might have something to teach us in this regard. The incredible growth of the church in China during these past 70 years also calls us to listen attentively. I begin, however, by articulating three general principles, drawn from the New Testament, that will guide our discussion. I then seek to push the discussion beyond generalities by examining how we might apply these principles to specific groups, contexts, and situations. Finally, based on my experience in China over the past three decades, I would like to outline five key theological issues with which Christians living in a hostile, totalitarian environment must inevitably grapple.

1. General Principles

Not long ago I was privileged to celebrate China's National Day (October 1) in China. This important day, which that year (2019) commemorated the 70th anniversary of the founding of the People's Republic of China, was marked by impressive parades, huge beautifully choreographed performances, and powerful displays of military might. My perspective was a bit different from most there in China and from those in other countries. I watched the military parade, a display of awesome power, in the home of Chinese friends. Their two sons were required to watch the televised parade and they had to display proof of this fact in the form of photos sent to their teachers at the local elementary school. Virtually all of the television channels in China showed the parade and the subsequent, massive and meticulously planned celebrations in Tiananmen Square. After watching the awe-inspiring parade, I walked with my friends from their small apartment to a place of worship.

The worship service began with prayer and praise. The 30-plus Chinese believers who had gathered represented six different people groups. They sang with great emotion one of my favorite Chinese songs, *"Zhi Dao Zhu Ye Su Zai Lai de Shi Hou"* (直到主耶稣再来的时候, "Until the Lord Jesus Comes Again"). A key line goes, "until the Lord Jesus returns I will travel the road of service, I will bear my cross." The song continues, "when I complete the journey of service, I will see the Lord's glory, the glory of the Lord Jesus Christ … you are the Lord and Savior of all the earth."

As we sang this song I couldn't help but compare the two, vastly different scenes: the military parade and the scene of worship. The contrast might be made whether in China, the U.S., or any other country of the world. On the one hand, a dazzling display of human power and military hardware. On the other, a song extolling the power and glory of God, revealed in the love of a crucified and risen Lord. Both scenes, one might argue, issue a call for commitment. I am very thankful that the Lord enabled me to worship together with this dedicated group; for, as we sang songs of worship to Jesus, we declared that our primary allegiance is "to him who sits on the throne and to the Lamb" (Rev 5:13).

In the section that follows I want to look more specifically at the relationship between the church and the state—not just in China, but anywhere in the world.[1] The key texts we will consider are Romans 13:1–7, Acts 4:18–20 (cf. 5:27–32), and Revelation 13. In these texts we are confronted with three important truths: government is God's gift to us, there are limits to government's authority, and our primary allegiance is to Christ.

1.1. Government as God's Gift (Rom 13:1–7)

Let everyone be subject to the governing authorities, for there is no authority except that which God has established. The authorities that exist have been established by God. Consequently, whoever rebels against the authority is rebelling against what God has instituted, and those who do so will bring judgment on themselves. (Rom 13:1–2)

---

[1] I wish to acknowledge my indebtedness to R. C. Sproul for his helpful book, *What is the Relationship between Church and State?* (North Mankato, MN: Reformation Trust, 2014), which was a source of inspiration for this section.

In this passage we see that government is God's gift to us. Rulers, "governing authorities," are established by God. Indeed, Paul continues, "For the one in authority is God's servant for your good. But if you do wrong, be afraid, for rulers do not bear the sword for no reason. They are God's servants, agents of wrath to bring punishment on the wrongdoer. Therefore, it is necessary to submit to the authorities" (Rom 13:4–5).

Paul makes it clear that the state has a clear and important purpose. It has been given the responsibility of protecting its citizens, their rights and property (Rom 13:3–4). This role is fulfilled by establishing laws and enforcing them. The state, then, is God's gift. The state is thus called to restrain evil and thereby bring order to society. When they achieve this end, governments and their leaders the world over act as "God's servants" and are worthy of our respect and honor (Rom 13:5–7).

When I think of the poverty, hardships, and chaos of pre-1949 China, I am reminded that there is much to be thankful for in the very imperfect, but at times, extraordinary achievements that have taken place as a result of efforts orchestrated by the government of modern China. In fact, I have often thought that just as Christ came in the "fullness of time" (Gal 4:4), to a world that benefited from: the *Pax Romana*, the peace provided by Roman rule; an excellent system of roads that enabled travel; and a common commercial language (Greek) that facilitated communication; so also, in today's China the church has unprecedented opportunities due to these same strengths—relative peace, efficient modes of travel, and a common language—to proclaim the gospel and establish churches.

1.2. Limitations of the Government's Authority (Rom 13:3–4; Rev 13:5–10)

Since all governments are established by God, they are also thus *accountable* to him. God is the ultimate authority, not human leaders or governments. This means that the authority of all rulers, all governments, is provisional and limited. The proper role of government, which is foundational for Paul's words in Romans 13:1–7, is to protect citizens and their property by restraining evil (cf. 13:3–4).

Problems arise when governmental leaders deny God's authority and seek to become *the ultimate authority*. When rulers embrace this kind of idolatry and self-worship, serious problems ensue. In Revelation, with his graphic description of the beast from the sea, John highlights the demonic nature that this kind of government can in the present and will at the end of time take (cf. 2 Thess 2:1–12). John writes, "The beast was given a mouth to utter proud words and blasphemies and to exercise its authority for forty-two months. It opened its mouth to blaspheme God, and to slander his name and his dwelling place and those who live in heaven.... This calls for patient endurance and faithfulness on the part of God's people" (Rev 13:5–6, 10).

The way to avoid this kind of tyranny is to recognize that the church and the state represent two different spheres of God-given authority.[2] They each have separate and unique callings. The government,

---

[2] The Reformed tradition speaks of different "spheres," while the Lutheran tradition speaks of two distinct kingdoms (gospel and law). Although both traditions thus recognize this basic truth, their different language has led to different emphases. Lutherans have been less willing to relate the gospel to the political sphere. Robert Benne notes, "While Luther tended to emphasize the distinctions between the two kingdoms, Lutheran jurists tended to emphasize their cooperation." The Reformed position sees the gospel impacting the state in an indirect way. James K. A. Smith describes the Reformed perspective in this way: "As spheres, the church as institute is distinct from the state, but the church *as organism* is called to be faithfully present—and a reforming influence—in *every* sphere, including the state." Quotes from Robert Benne, "The Lutheran (Paradoxical) View," and James K. A. Smith, "The Reformed (Transformist) View," in *Five Views on the Church and Politics*, ed. Amy E. Black (Grand Rapids: Zondervan, 2015), 64, 155, respectively.

as we have noted, is called to restrain evil by establishing and enforcing laws. The government is called "to take up the sword" and exercise authority to achieve this end.[3] By way of contrast, the church has a different calling. The church is called to worship God, edify and encourage believers, and witness to unbelievers (Acts 13:1–3). To use John Nugent's helpful phrase, we are to "embrace, display, and proclaim" the kingdom of God.[4]

History shows that when the state attempts to assume the church's role or the church attempts to usurp the divinely ordained function of the state, trouble is inevitable. The state cannot minister the gospel and the church cannot wield the sword. God has not called and equipped either of these *institutions* to perform these functions. Rather, each of these institutions has a specific call and purpose: the state wields the sword; the church possesses the keys to the kingdom.[5]

A related and important observation is that the early church never forced people to become Christians. Paul writes, "we make it our goal to please [the Lord].... For we must all appear before the judgment seat of Christ.... Since, then, we know what it is to fear the Lord, we try to *persuade* men" (2 Cor 5:9–11). We seek to persuade, warn, and plead (cf. Acts 2:40), but never use physical force to compel. When the church has forgotten its true calling and sought to use physical force to extend the kingdom of God, the result has been disastrous (e.g., some of the crusades of the Middle Ages).

History also tells us that the state is often tempted to view itself rather than God as the ultimate authority. When it does so, it seeks to deny the church its legitimate role to embrace, display, and proclaim the kingdom of God. The actions of the emperor Domitian in the late first century are described well with John's depiction of the beast from the sea, who will "utter proud words and blasphemies" and seek to receive worship and exercise absolute control and authority (Rev 13:5, 7–8, 14–17). Domitian loved to be called "our master and god" and could not tolerate allegiance to the true God, for this diminished his power.[6] Since Domitian, countless rulers have followed in his footsteps and sought to exalt themselves over God. These rulers persecute the church and ultimately seek to destroy or control it. This leads us to our final point.

1.3. Primary Allegiance to Christ (Acts 4:18–20; Rev 13:9–10)

In the face of tyrannical despots who demand ultimate allegiance, John's message to the church is clear. We cannot bow down to these kinds of idolatrous demands; rather, we must stand firm and remain committed to true worship. We must worship Christ, who is the "King of kings and Lord of lords" (Rev 19:16), for "Salvation belongs to our God, who sits on the throne, and to the Lamb" (Rev 7:10).

We must never forget that the role and the authority of the state is limited and comes from God. So, when the state seeks to take the place of God or his church, we cannot obey. This calls for wisdom and "patient endurance" (Rev 1:9; 13:10; 14:12). In Revelation, a phrase that we hear repeatedly is the phrase "patience endurance" (ὑπομονή: 1:9; 2:2, 3, 19; 3:10; 13:10; 14:12). With this phrase (cf. Rev 13:9–10) John declares that we will be victorious, not by overcoming in human terms with brute force, but through faithful witness even unto death.

---

[3] The KJV of Romans 13:4 reads, "...for he beareth not the sword in vain."

[4] John C. Nugent, *Endangered Gospel: How Fixing the World is Killing the Church* (Eugene, OR: Cascade, 2016), 171.

[5] Sproul, *Church and State*, 19.

[6] Suetonius, *Domitian* 13.2 (*dominus et deus noster*), noted by Brian J. Tabb, "Wisdom and Hope in Difficult Days: Reading Revelation in 2022," *Themelios* 47 (2022): 10 n. 43.

The early church provides a wonderful model of courageous resistance. In their first encounter with persecution, Peter and John boldly reject the command of the leaders of their day, "not to speak or teach at all in the name of Jesus." Peter and John reply, "judge for yourselves whether it is right in God's sight to obey you rather than God. For we cannot help speaking about what we have seen and heard" (Acts 4:18–20).

I often emphasize to my Chinese friends: *I am a Christian first*, and then every other identity marker follows and pales into insignificance by comparison (e.g., a St. Louis Cardinal baseball fan, an American citizen, etc.). My faith in Christ is what defines me. So, I have a closer sense of connection with my Chinese Christian friends than I do with non-Christians, including those who were raised in the same culture and nation. Paul puts it well: in Christ we are now fellow citizens and members of the same family (Eph 2:18–22).

I do believe that we can and should love our homeland. I am also convinced that by courageously serving Christ in our respective countries, we will become a great blessing to these nations. Indeed, the greatest gift we can give our homeland is to display and proclaim the good news of the kingdom of God. As we serve God, he will help us bless the country of our birth. But we must always remember that first and foremost, we are citizens of God's kingdom. When we do this, we will bless our country as no one else can.

2. Beyond Generalities

The general principles noted above, while offering important boundaries, must be applied to the complex and varied situations that we as Christians living in the inter-advent period face. With this task in mind, I want to press beyond the general principles outlined above by offering a few guidelines that might help us apply these basic principles to our daily lives.

How we understand the mission of the church significantly shapes how we approach the question of the church's relationship to the state. If we view the mission of the church in broad terms, encompassing the total transformation of human society and all of God's creation, then we see the church's relationship with the state as necessarily a vital and close one, involving both prophetic and collaborative dimensions.[7] If the church's mission is ultimately to transform every aspect of society, then by definition the church must be politically engaged and relate in meaningful ways to the state.

However, a number of recent works by evangelical scholars have challenged this broad understanding of the mission of the church.[8] In various ways, each of these works argues that the mission of the church should be understood more narrowly as centering on the proclamation of the gospel and

---

[7] For this perspective see N. T. Wright, *Surprised by Hope: Rethinking Heaven, the Resurrection, and the Mission of the Church* (New York: HarperOne, 2008), 133–34, 189–289; Chris Wright, "Participatory Mission: The Mission of God's People Revealed in the Whole Bible Story," in *Four Views on the Church's Mission*, ed. Jason S. Sexton, Counterpoints (Grand Rapids: Zondervan, 2017), 63–91; Amos Yong, *Mission After Pentecost: The Witness of the Spirit from Genesis to Revelation* (Grand Rapids: Baker Academic, 2019), passim. Cf. Robert Menzies, "A Tale of Two Stories: Amos Yong's Mission After Pentecost and T'ien Ju-K'ang's Peaks of Faith," *Themelios* 46 (2021): 391–401.

[8] See Nugent, *Endangered Gospel*; Jonathan Leeman, "Soteriological Mission: Focusing in on the Mission of Redemption," in *Four Views on the Church's Mission*, ed. Jason S. Sexton, Counterpoints (Grand Rapids: Zondervan, 2017), 17–45; Kevin DeYoung and Greg Gilbert, *What is the Mission of the Church? Making Sense of Social Justice, Shalom, and the Great Commission* (Wheaton, IL: Crossway, 2011); and Jerry M. Ireland, *The Missionary*

making disciples (Matt 28:18–20; Luke 24:46–48; Acts 1:8). Space does not permit me to engage in this important discussion in depth, but for the purposes of this paper it will suffice to note that our vision of the church's mission largely determines our perspective on church-state relations. I shall examine the church-state relationship from the perspective of a narrow understanding of the church's mission and describe the important implications that follow.

2.1. Responsibilities: Gathered Church or Individual Christians?

In his illuminating essay, Jonathan Leeman helpfully distinguishes between the mission of the church and the mission of individual Christians. Leeman declares that we must "keep these two missions or jobs distinct," and then insists that "the church-as-organized-collective and church-as-its-individual-members" must each do their "God-assigned jobs."[9] The former is focused more narrowly on proclamation and making disciples (Matt 28:18–20; Luke 24:46–48; Acts 1:8), the latter includes the broader responsibility of every Christian to live as followers of Christ in their individual callings and with their unique giftings.[10]

Individual Christians face many questions as they seek to relate to the state: How do I vote? Shall I work for a political party? Shall I run for public office? Shall I obey the laws of the state? However, it should be recognized that the relationship between the organic church (individual believers) and the state is quite different from that of the organized church and the state. The organized church has a specific and narrow mission; the organic church, by virtue of the unique calling and giftings of each individual, has a much broader one. The organized church is called to help its members think and act in uniquely Christian ways through teaching God's word and the process of discipleship, but it is not called to "wield the sword" by determining the many and varied political decisions that shape the larger (generally, non-Christian) society. Individual Christians, when possible, appropriate, and in accordance with their unique God-given calling and gifts, may participate in the governing process. As members of the body of Christ we are called "to do good" to all (1 Thess 5:15; 1 Pet 4:19) and thus to exert a positive influence in society through political engagement when possible. Nevertheless, the organized church is not called or equipped to transform the world through political activism nor should it seek to encroach on the state's God-given role of maintaining order in society. As John Nugent aptly states, "The church's goal is not to transform the world but to live together as a transformed world, and to invite the nations in word and deed to the Transformer."[11]

Contemporary calls for the church to work for "social justice" by linking arms with diverse political forces in order to take command of the apparatus of the state are, from the narrow mission perspective, misguided. This relatively apolitical understanding of the church's mission, which views the mission of the organized church as distinct from that of the state, has the advantage of enabling the church to feature a message that centers on the word of God and that thus serves to unite the community of faith. The further the church moves into the realm of political or social action, the less it is able to speak with clarity about its suggested course of action. Should Christians support a welfare state as a compassionate choice for the poor? Or should they encourage less government intervention so that individuals and

---

Spirit: Evangelism and Social Action in Pentecostal Missiology, American Society of Missiology 61 (Maryknoll, NY: Orbis, 2021).

[9] Leeman, "Soteriological Mission," 44.

[10] Leeman, "Soteriological Mission," 44.

[11] Nugent, *Endangered Gospel*, 192, 194.

churches have more freedom and resources to minister to them? These are the kind of questions that individual Christians must consider. However, because these questions are not directly dealt with in the Scriptures, they normally generate conflicting responses. Evangelical Christians have, for the most part, avoided theological reflection and philosophical speculation that takes the church away from its apostolic foundations and its central truths.[12] They show little interest in political theology. Some see this as a weakness, but I think history has shown that it is a great strength.[13]

If the mission of the organized church is distinct from the state, it should also be acknowledged that the fruit of any political engagement on the part of Christians, individual or corporate, will also always be provisional and limited in nature. This leads to our next point.

2.2. The Church's Prophetic Voice: Its Nature and Limitations

If, as we have suggested, our ecclesiology dramatically impacts how we view church-state relations, so also does our eschatology. Indeed, our vision of the future shapes how we view our present lives and mission. Evangelicals rightly proclaim that our vision of the future centers on "the blessed hope," the return of Jesus. This hope informs our understanding of the nature of our mission. While we believe that we are called and empowered to display and proclaim his kingdom in the present, we have no illusions about how this glorious kingdom will be realized fully in the future.[14] The promises of God concerning an eternal kingdom of righteousness will not find fulfillment in the gradual transformation of society through political activism. In Revelation John describes in unequivocal terms the fallen, demonic nature of the social and political structures of the world in his day and ours (the inter-advent period). Although, as we noted, his cry—"Come out of her, my people, so that you will not share in her sins" (Rev 18:4)—needs to be tempered and placed alongside other biblical themes (Rom 13:1–5), its relevance and challenge for us should not be minimized.[15] It encourages evangelicals to steer clear of the siren calls of Protestant liberals to embrace uncritically political movements for "social justice" and link arms together with non-Christian activists promoting them. John Nugent's warning in this regard is apropos:

---

[12] A central part of the problem here is that for Christians most political decisions require both an understanding of biblical teaching and an analysis of contemporary culture. While we may agree on the former, the latter often proves to be a source of contention. I was reminded of this fact as I considered recent public statements of a friend. Although our theological perspectives are quite similar, our analysis of contemporary culture is very different. So, our political views clash at numerous points.

[13] Zhao Wenjuan, in her illuminating article, "Being a Protestant Church in Contemporary Mainland China: An Examination of Protestant Church-State Relationships," *Asian Journal of Theology* 33 (2019): 1–31, describes how the government-recognized TSPM churches, the conservative house churches, and the radical house churches (a recent, largely Reformed group of churches that arose in the 1990s among Chinese intellectuals) relate to the state. The author argues that whereas the TSPM churches and the radical house church movement have lost sight of the church's unique mission by either conforming to the state (TSPM) or seeking to subvert it by transforming Chinese society around democratic ideals (radical house churches), the conservative house churches have remained faithful to the counter-cultural ecclesiology advocated by Paul and reflected in the early church. Through their apolitical stance, the conservative house churches have formed distinct communities marked by unique intimacy and solidarity. Zhao concludes, the Chinese Protestant conservative house church's "historical and current strategy is by no means a 'withdrawal' from society, but, rather, a faithful witness to Jesus Christ" (p. 30).

[14] Robert Menzies, *The End of History: Pentecostals and a Fresh Approach to the Apocalypse* (Springfield, MO: ACPT Press, 2022), 125–47.

[15] Brian Tabb also highlights the contemporary relevance of this text from Revelation in "Wisdom and Hope in Difficult Days," 13.

> It is not of the kingdom if it does not participate in the Spirit's work of *forming*
> communities that embrace, display, and proclaim God's kingdom, and *scattering* them
> through the world as witnesses to God's accomplished work through Christ. It may be
> good work and well worth our time, but it's not our vocation.[16]

Evangelicals have for good reason placed a priority on the proclamation of the gospel, the formation of disciples, and the establishment of churches. We do strive to practice social justice, but generally do so *within* the community of faith,[17] for how can communities reflect the life of God's kingdom without a focus on the King? It is only in communities that listen to the voice of the Spirit and worship Jesus that we can truly prepare for the end of history, the return of the Lord of lords.

While we have reason for "sober optimism" with respect to our mission of proclaiming the gospel and making disciples (Rev 11:1–13), we must resist visions of the future that are overly optimistic and largely uncritical with regards to the state, political involvement, and related movements. These utopian dreams fail to give sufficient attention to the demonic nature of many of the social and political movements of our day (cf. Rev 18:4). N. T. Wright, for example, chides evangelicals for our quietism (i.e., our lack of political involvement). I found his criticism—we are too supportive of the political status quo—particularly ironic, coming as it does from a leader in the Church of England.[18] I would suggest that "sober optimism" must acknowledge that, along with our call to engage in kingdom work in the present, the final days of history will also be marked by growing apostasy, persecution, and demonic political power. This should make us suspicious of placing too much confidence in political activism and what it might achieve.[19] The alternative is not escapism and defeatism—not allowing "evil to proceed unchecked"[20]—but rather, to embrace with abandonment the unique call and mission of the church.

The recognition that we cannot bring God's kingdom—we simply bear witness to the King, who will consummate his reign when he returns—and that the political institutions of the inter-advent age are flawed, tend to become anti-Christ and oppressive, and will spiral downward (or are already there)

---

[16] Nugent, *Endangered Gospel*, 171 (italics original).

[17] Graham H. Twelftree, *People of the Spirit: Exploring Luke's View of the Church* (Grand Rapids: Baker Academic, 2009), 203. Twelftree concludes, "Social action, in terms of caring for the physical needs of the outsider, plays no part in Luke's view of mission" (p. 203). On the priority of proclamation over social action in Luke's view of mission, see also Robert Menzies, "Complete Evangelism: A Review Essay," *Journal of Pentecostal Theology* 13 (1998): 133–42.

[18] N. T. Wright, *Surprised by Hope*, 264–71. State churches have not had a good track record. For example, Eric Metaxas notes how the Nazis attempted to and often succeeded in co-opting the church in Germany. He writes, "Bonhoeffer knew that something of this unwillingness [of pastors] to speak out with boldness had to do with money. The state provided financial security for the pastors of Germany" (Metaxas, *Bonhoeffer: Pastor, Martyr, Prophet, Spy* [Nashville: Thomas Nelson, 2010], 282).

[19] Ben Witherington III, *Revelation*, New Cambridge Bible Commentary (Cambridge: Cambridge University Press, 2003), 258: "John is clearly an apocalyptic thinker and, as such, would see most modern theodicies as incredibly naïve, not taking into account the depth of human and supernatural evil."

[20] Wright decries the "radical distortion of Christian hope" that combines it "with a quietism that leaves the world as it is and thus allows evil to proceed unchecked." He suggests that "the church must learn the arts of collaboration without compromise.... There are good things going on in the wider world, and we must join in while always remaining on the lookout for the point where we will be asked to do something that goes against the grain of the gospel" (Wright, *Surprised by Hope*, 269). For a response to Wright, see Menzies, *The End of History*, 142–47.

shortly before the end (2 Thess 2:1–12) limits our expectations concerning government's potential for good. At its best, the state can serve to restrain evil and bring a reasonable degree of stability and order. Yet, history teaches that all too often the state will become a malignant, idolatrous force. This is why discernment is required.

As Christians consider how the church should relate to the state, we must be sensitive to and understand our specific context. Sweeping generalizations at this point are not very helpful. The central question Christians in a given location and specific time must ask is: Does the state acknowledge the church and allow it to pursue its sacred mission? If this is the case, then the opportunity exists for the church to relate to the state without significant conflict. We can then give "to Caesar what is Caesar's,"[21] while we pursue our calling to embrace, display, and proclaim the kingdom. However, if the state is unwilling to recognize God's ultimate authority and seeks to usurp the church's unique role, then conflict (i.e., non-violent resistance by defying the state's mandates) is inevitable.[22]

A second and related question is this: Does the state allow for and acknowledge the church's prophetic voice? If this is the case, then the opportunity exists for the church to speak truth—God's truth—to power. Indeed, the church has a responsibility to address moral issues confronting a society that are clearly articulated in God's word (e.g., the sanctity of human life and the evil of abortion). As with Esther, opportunity entails responsibility. Some use the term "moral proximity" to speak of the heightened responsibility one has to those who are within one's direct sphere of influence. The closer the relationship, the greater the responsibility. Should we not, then, also speak of the principle of "moral opportunity" with reference to the responsibilities that come with unique opportunity? When possible, the church should exercise its prophetic voice by rebuking sinful and destructive acts and laws perpetrated by the state. When the church is allowed to function in this type of prophetic role, it can truly become a blessing to the larger society and nation.

However, we must acknowledge that the church is rarely accorded the privilege of exercising its prophetic voice. Prophets did not fare well in ancient Israel (Acts 7:52). They don't do much better today. As the situation in China today illustrates so well, generally the state brooks no rivals. It is uninterested in hearing dissenting voices, especially voices with a divine mandate. In these contexts, it is not possible for the church to speak truth to power.

It is important at this point to define what we mean when we speak of the church's prophetic voice. If we follow the New Testament definition, and particularly the early church's understanding of this concept as recorded in the book of Acts, we will define the term as bold, Spirit-inspired witness for Jesus (Luke 24:46–49; Acts 1:8).[23] Typically, however, Protestant churches understand "the church's prophetic voice" to refer to the church's role of serving as the moral compass or conscience of the state and society. Mainline pulpits often thunder with the message, "let justice roll on like a river, righteousness like a never-failing stream!" (Amos 5:24). Unfortunately, as Nugent so powerfully argues, the message of the prophets is all too often misapplied.[24] The prophets spoke first and foremost to Israel, the people of God;

---

[21] Matt 22:21; Mark 12:17; Luke 20:25.

[22] This does not mean that the church and individual Christians must openly, publicly defy the state. In China, the house church, which has little or no political power, has (for the most part) quietly and clandestinely pursued its mission. Thus, the house church movement in China is an "underground" movement. House churches generally do not register with the government or seek the government's approval.

[23] Robert P. Menzies, "The Spirit in Luke-Acts: Empowering Prophetic Witness," *Pneuma* 43 (2021): 409–41.

[24] Nugent, *Endangered Gospel*, 56–58.

not to the surrounding nations. So, if the church is called to serve as a conscience, it is the conscience of the people of God rather than the nation as a whole.

In this biblical sense of the term, the church is *always* called to bear prophetic witness. It must bear bold witness to the gospel and demonstrate its truth through the godly quality of its worship and community life. This counter-cultural lifestyle, along with its prophetic voice (proclaiming the gospel), represent a significant challenge to every totalitarian state.

Nevertheless, as we have noted, in some settings the church may have the opportunity to speak openly and publicly to the moral issues of the day. I would suggest that in North America, unlike China, the church still has an opportunity to exercise its prophetic voice in this larger sense. Yes, the church must also be a counter-cultural community, a *polis* or *ecclesia* that represents God and proclaims his reign in Christ. But when possible, it must also denounce the idolatrous pretensions of a government intent on usurping the church's authority and role. We must not bow down to the gods of the state religion, but rather expose them for the idols that they are. Whether it be the state's attempt to redefine God-given gender roles or its modernized version of child sacrifice, the church *must speak while it still can*. Responsibility comes with opportunity.

The church, if it is able to speak to the state and the larger society, must do so carefully. This "carefully" might be defined in two ways: first, church leaders should only speak to those political/moral issues where a clear biblical response is affirmed by a strong consensus of evangelical Christians (and particularly Christians within their particular church body); and secondly, wisdom calls for discernment of one's specific context and the suitability of issuing a public statement. As I have stated, not all contexts are alike. The situation of house churches in contemporary China is considerably different from that of the state church in Hitler's Germany. One has no possibility of turning the wheels of power; the other is already an integral part of the ship's means of propulsion. The "just war" theory might be helpful here. Just as Christian participation in a "just war" was limited to wars in which one has a reasonable chance of success, so also the church's political assertions, its prophetic voice (in this larger sense), should not be offered as "pearls" to an unhearing herd of swine (Matt 7:6). As a wonderful Chinese proverb puts it, this is like "playing the piano for cows" (对牛弹琴, *dui niu tan qin*).[25]

In short, if political speech on the part of Christian leaders is to be meaningful, it must be addressed to specific issues in particular contexts. Typically, broad generalities or tropes are not helpful since they lack specificity and fail to take into consideration the distinctive elements of particular contexts. For this reason, discussion of political issues is often most constructive when it is undertaken among Christians *within* their specific communities of faith. These discussions may or may not reveal a strong consensus

---

[25] While I admire the courage of Wang Yi and the other Chinese pastors who issued *A Joint Statement by Pastors: A Declaration for the Sake of the Christian Faith* (issued and signed by 116 Chinese Christians on August 30, 2018 and, by mid-November, signed by 458 prominent house church pastors), I question whether the *public* nature of this statement, openly addressed to Chinese governmental leaders, was prudent. Pastor Wang Yi was arrested on December 9, 2018 and remains in a Chinese prison. For more on this statement, see part 3 below. Some in the Reformed tradition (such as Pastor Wang Yi), with its emphasis on the church's calling to proclaim God's word, feel compelled to speak to the political powers whatever the setting (so, even in contemporary China). I feel this view does not adequately recognize the church's primary calling (to proclaim the gospel and make disciples) and fails to distinguish between the different responsibilities the church has to those *within* the body of Christ (to teach and practice kingdom living) and to those *without* (to proclaim the gospel). The church is not responsible for bad government or for fixing it. Its responsibility to serve as the conscience of the state is contingent on its opportunity for influence, whether direct or indirect, within the various political settings in which it exists.

and, depending on the results, could lead to specific action, whether it be a public statement, passive non-resistance, or even peaceful demonstration.

2.3. Resistance: Appropriate Means

When the state acts as Satan's servant, how should we respond? This is a difficult question and it has been answered in various ways by Christians and church groups through the ages. Certainly, John the Revelator calls Christians to resist. His sobering exhortation calls for passive, non-violent resistance. Paul's words in Romans 8:18 offer strong motivation for this kind of patient endurance: "our present sufferings are not worth comparing with the glory that will be revealed in us." We need to view our lives and situations from an eternal perspective. Only then are we able to act in a righteous and just manner.

However, the question must be asked, in our differing contexts, how shall we appropriate the teaching of the New Testament on this matter? Here, I believe the distinction between the role of the organized church and the organic church is again helpful. The organized church can *never* use force to achieve its divinely mandated purpose. The power of the gathered church is not of this world. Yet, individual Christians, as Bonhoeffer saw so clearly, may be forced to take sides. Their Christian consciences, informed by the Holy Spirit, may require them to take up arms. Whether it be at Lexington and Concord or Bull Run, historically many Christians have made that difficult decision to bear arms. When they do so, they act as citizens of earthly, fallen kingdoms; but they also do so as citizens of God's eternal kingdom.[26] There is perhaps no more dramatic illustration of the "already present/not yet" tension that marks our present existence than this. But who is able to say that this option is not open to Christians who have one foot in God's eternal kingdom and one foot in this present evil age? "Not all evil can be avoided … to let violence and aggression go unchecked does not eliminate the evil, nor does it leave me unimplicated if I could do something about it."[27]

I do believe that, while the possibility of individual Christians bearing arms both in war and revolution cannot be discounted on principle (of course, some will disagree), several considerations call us to examine the possibility of participating in such extreme measures (i.e., violence) with the utmost care and only after fervent prayer and much soul-searching reflection.

First, we have already noted the provisional and limited nature of all earthly governments and political movements. Our ultimate hope is not found in political redemption but in divine intervention. Our ultimate allegiance can never be granted to fellow human beings or institutions of their creation.[28] These theological convictions should chasten us when we are tempted to throw our lot in with those who advocate war or revolution. The horrors of slavery and the Holocaust remind us that evil must be restrained, but the bloody extremes of the French revolution also serve as a cautionary warning.[29] Even when the cause appears just, we must be mindful of the character of the group with which we align.

---

[26] This is why the Anabaptist tradition rejects the use of violence. Yet most Christians have determined that pacifism does not flow from a careful and nuanced reading of the Scriptures, nor does it adequately account for our responsibility to restrain evil.

[27] Arthur F. Holmes, "The Just War," in *War: Four Christian Views*, ed. Robert G. Clouse (Downers Grove, IL: InterVarsity Press, 1981), 118.

[28] C. S. Lewis creatively makes this point in *The Screwtape Letters*, reprint ed. (New York: HarperOne, 1996), 31–35 (ch. 7).

[29] James K. A. Smith, "The Reformed (Transformist) View," 160.

Second, an honest appraisal of our limited ability to understand the complex realities of our world should also encourage us to exercise extreme caution concerning decisions that might lead to violence. No doubt many felt that the Czar's cavalier attitude towards the plight of the peasants justified violent revolution in Russia. But could they envision the suffering that Stalin's totalitarian regime would bring? Humility should bring anyone contemplating violence, whether in war or revolution, to their knees.

Third, the problems associated with the application of the "just war" theory to our contemporary setting, particularly if revolution is in view, also call for pause. Arthur F. Holmes's seven-point summary and discussion of the just war theory—just cause, just intention, last resort, formal declaration, limited objectives, proportional means, and noncombative immunity[30]—highlights that the theory's intent is "to place severe limits on war that would prevent its lapsing into barbarism."[31] He also acknowledges that the "theory insists that *private individuals have no right to use force.*"[32] This does not necessarily exclude all forms of violent rebellion. For example, although Calvin confines the use of the sword to civil authorities, he does recognize that in extreme cases rebellion may be necessary. Holmes summarizes Calvin's position in this way:

> As for rebellion, a tyrant may not be forcibly deposed unless the just rule of law no longer exists; in such an extreme, authority reverts to the people, who may then form a new government which accordingly has the right to use force against the tyrant. But private individuals per se in a civil society may not fight.[33]

Nevertheless, the way the just war theory limits the use of force to civil authority suggests that the participation of Christians in rebellion or revolt should be limited to the most extreme cases.

3. Lessons from China

On the basis of my experience in China over the past 30 years, I want to highlight five theological truths that inevitably emerge as crucial "battle ground" issues for Christians living in a hostile, totalitarian environment. These truths will be challenged by totalitarian governments and our faithfulness or lack thereof will hinge on our response to these challenges.

3.1. The Head of the Church

Jesus Christ is the head of the church, not any government or human authority. The Chinese Communist Party (CCP) has consistently sought to assert its authority over the church since the formation of the "new China" in 1949. I vividly remember a dialogue I had some years ago with a Chinese government official. When he asked, "Are you here to propagate religion?" I responded, "I am a Christian. If people ask about my faith or express interest, I will tell them about Jesus." He shouted his response: "You will obey Chinese law."

Here you have it: Who is in charge: Jesus or the state? Christians are ultimately accountable to a higher power (Acts 5:29). This is one of the reasons why state churches have had such a checkered past throughout the history of the church. The Barmen declaration (1934) was a call to resist the theological

---

[30] Holmes, "The Just War," 120–21.

[31] Holmes, "The Just War," 121.

[32] Holmes, "The Just War," 120 (italics original).

[33] Holmes, "The Just War," 130.

claims of the Nazi state. More recently, Chinese "house church" leaders have issued their own kind of Barmen declaration, *A Joint Statement by Pastors: A Declaration for the Sake of the Christian Faith*. The initial statement, released on August 30, 2018, was signed by 116 Chinese church leaders, including the main author of the statement, Early Rain Covenant Church (Chengdu, Sichuan) Pastor Wang Yi. By November 17, 2018 (the 11th edition), 458 prominent Chinese house church pastors, including one of my close friends, had signed the document. Pastor Wang Yi was arrested on December 9, 2018 and remains in a Chinese prison. In this statement Chinese believers boldly declare, "we believe…that all true churches in China…must proclaim Christ as the sole head of the church." Many of those who signed this statement have been imprisoned and countless more interrogated and harassed by the Chinese police. But, as the statement declares, "Christian churches in China are eager and determined to walk the path of the cross of Christ and are more than willing to imitate the older generation of saints who suffered and were martyred for their faith."[34] Are we willing to do likewise?

3.2. The Nature of the Church

The church, by its very nature, is a global, trans-national community. It cannot be reduced to any single socio-economic class, ethnic group, or nationality; rather, it includes all people who are willing to repent and follow Jesus as Savior and Lord (Acts 2:38–39). Totalitarian governments often try to limit the church to a select group for their own purposes. Hitler's regime in Germany tried to limit the church to ethnic Germans alone. Bonhoeffer and the confessing church saw through this: they saw that it was not a question of whether they should meet separately (e.g., from Jewish Christians), it was a question of whether they would truly be the church!

So also, in today's China, the CCP attempts to limit the church in China solely to Chinese nationals. Recent regulations severely restricting the role of foreigners in the life of the church are nothing more than a thinly disguised attempt to isolate Chinese believers from the larger body of Christ. The notion that the church in China should only have Chinese characteristics and exist exclusively for the Chinese, devoid of any external influence, is profoundly unbiblical (Eph 2:11–12).[35] The attempt to isolate the Chinese church is actually part of the state's larger goal of molding it into an image of its own creation. In China, the CCP has announced its intention to create a "Sinicized Christianity." One aspect of the CCP's new "Sinicization of Christianity" policy is the prohibition of children from attending services in the government-recognized (TSPM) churches. This attempt to limit further the church's reach reveals the state's true motivation.

Yet, as history has shown, the efforts of the CCP to "chain" the gospel will fail (2 Tim 2:9). I will not soon forget a beautiful "house church" worship service in a forest of Southwest China. An evangelist from the Miao tribe shared his testimony with a group of largely university-educated Han Chinese. He began by noting that the Miao are generally looked down upon by other groups in China, especially the dominant Han majority. He said that normally there would be no opportunity for him to speak to a group of largely Han, educated city-dwellers like the present group. However, he declared, "Our faith in Christ has changed all of that. In Christ, we are all one family." In that setting, marked by the Spirit's presence, this Miao brother felt at ease, a member of the family of God!

---

[34] The full text of the "Joint Statement" can be viewed at <u>https://chinadeclaration.com/en/</u>.

[35] Jackson Wu, "'Sinicized Christianity' is Not Christianity," *Patheos*, 20 March 2019, <u>https://www.patheos.com/blogs/jacksonwu/2019/03/20/sinicized-christianity-is-not-christianity/</u>.

How will Christians in North America respond to the demands of an increasingly repressive government that seeks to reshape the church into its own image? How will American Christians react to attempts to divide us along socio-economic, racial, ideological, or nationalistic lines? Will we quietly acquiesce and accept a church that is not really whole?

3.3. The Message of the Church

The gospel of Jesus Christ is not a political ideology or an agenda for social justice. It is the message of how we might be reconciled to God and to one another through repentance and faith in Jesus Christ.[36] At the heart of the gospel is the declaration that Jesus is the risen Lord and Savior of the world. There is only one Lord and one Savior (Acts 2:36; 4:12). This is a message that cannot be co-opted by any political movement or governmental body.

Yet totalitarian governments try to do this very thing. The Sinicization of Christianity, declares the CCP's 5–year plan, "must be guided by the core values of socialism." Since atheism is a core value of the CCP's version of socialism, there is a glaring contradiction here. Equally startling are the CCP's attempts to minimize access to and the influence of the Bible. So, the official 5–year plan flatly states, "Contents of the Bible that are compatible with the core values of socialism should be deeply researched in order to write books that are popular and easy-to-understand." At the same time, in early 2018 the CCP banned major retailers from selling the Bible.[37] It is evident that the CCP wants to co-opt the church and it knows that if it is to be successful in this task, it must alter its message. The message that centers on Jesus, the risen Lord, challenges the CCP's ultimate authority.

Thankfully, the Chinese church has a rich heritage of ministers who have been willing to sacrifice everything for the sake of the gospel. From Wang Mingdao (arrested in 1955) to Wang Yi (arrested in 2018), countless Chinese ministers have not succumbed to intimidation and pressure. They have remained firm in their call and mandate to "preach the word" (2 Tim. 4:2), irrespective of the cost.

I pray that North American Christians, strengthened by the Holy Spirit, will exhibit similar courage in the face of opposition and the threat of persecution. May we too preach the word boldly (Acts 4:31). As one Chinese friend put it, "In the good times, we should be careful. But when we encounter persecution, we must be fearless."

3.4. The Power of the Church

The power of the church is not found in worldly might or the power of this world (Eph 6:12; 2 Cor 10:4). As the Psalmist beautifully states, "Some trust in chariots and some in horses, but we trust in the name of the Lord our God" (Ps 20:7). The Chinese church has, in a remarkable way, exemplified this declaration of faith. In the 2018 *Declaration for the Sake of the Christian Faith*, Chinese believers declare, "We are willing and obligated under any circumstance to face all government persecution, misunderstanding, and violence with peace, patience, and compassion. For when churches refuse to obey evil laws, it does not stem from any political agenda; it does not stem from resentment or hostility;

---

[36] For a thoughtful, evangelical perspective on the gospel and the church's mission, see Brian J. Tabb, *After Emmaus: How the Church Fulfills the Mission of Christ* (Wheaton, IL: Crossway, 2021). Tabb demonstrates that Jesus's words in Luke 24:46–47 serve as an interpretative lens for understanding the Messiah and his mission in Luke-Acts.

[37] Wu, "'Sinicized Christianity' is Not Christianity." Both quotations in this paragraph are from this source.

it stems only from the demands of the gospel and from a love for Chinese society." This is the way of the crucified Savior. Is there anything more powerful?

3.5. The Mission of the Church

The mission of the church, described so beautifully in Acts 13:1–3, involves three elements: the worship of God (v. 2); the edification of the saints (cf. prophets and teachers, v. 1); and the proclamation of the gospel to the lost (vv. 2–3). Totalitarian governments inevitably try to hinder the church from fulfilling this mission, particularly its mission to bear bold witness for Christ "to the ends of the earth" (Acts 1:8). The single greatest difference between the "house churches" and the government-recognized churches of China is found right here. How do they respond to the CCP's attempt to restrict their engagement in the mission of God?

The house churches, in the face of every conceivable barrier, have attempted to proclaim the gospel and plant churches, not only in every province, town, and village in China, but even beyond China's borders in the regions beyond. This vision to bridge every conceivable barrier in order to take the gospel to the lost is what animates "the back to Jerusalem" movement, a movement dedicated to evangelizing the predominately Muslim nations that lie between China and Jerusalem.

By way of contrast, I have yet to see TSPM leaders at a high level openly talk about engaging in missions; that is, their responsibility to take the gospel to unreached people groups of other cultures and nations. I have heard, however, many stories of how TSPM pastors who are too active or aggressive in reaching out to other communities are reprimanded and punished. One friend's vehicle was confiscated because he strayed beyond the state-established boundaries in order to reach the lost. Can a church that does not view missions (proclaiming the gospel to those culturally distant who are not Christians, especially those who have not heard) as a central part of its purpose really be considered the church? Does it have a future?

How will the church in American respond when we find that our efforts to engage in cross-cultural missions are ridiculed and impeded by the state and related institutions? Will we have the courage to resist the lies of a secular society that already decries missionary service as a form of racism and a vestige of a colonial past?

4. Conclusion

I have argued that, in addition to several general principles—the state is a gift, but has a limited sphere of authority; the church also has a specific calling and mission; ultimate allegiance must always be given to God in Christ—there are also additional theological themes that circumscribe the church's relationship to the state. First, the mission of the organized church should be distinguished from the larger responsibilities of individual Christians. Although the gathered church should seek to teach believers as a matter of discipleship what it means to live as Christians in society (and therefore address from a biblical perspective a wide range of contemporary issues), it should only speak publicly on those moral/political matters that it can address with clarity from the Scriptures.

Secondly, the recognition that we cannot bring God's kingdom and that the political institutions of the inter-advent age tend to become anti-Christ and oppressive will limit our expectations concerning government's potential for good. This recognition should serve as a warning for Christians not to place too much hope in political movements. Our primary identity must be firmly rooted in Christ and his call on our lives. It goes without saying that this warning is especially relevant for revolutionary movements that espouse violence.

Thirdly, I have highlighted the fact that our context will determine the extent to which the church can and should exercise its prophetic voice. While the church must *always* bear witness to the gospel, I have argued that the church should not feel compelled to function as the conscience of the state when its voice is not recognized. The Reformers (e.g., Luther and Calvin) addressed a society shaped largely by the Christian tradition and their perspectives assumed this unique setting. Although the Anabaptists were severely persecuted, their perspective was also significantly influenced by their experience within Christendom. Today, large numbers—perhaps the majority—of Christians live in societies that are hostile to the church, both organized and organic. This calls us to prayerfully reflect on the specific contexts in which we live and to discern the unique opportunities and challenges that come with them.

Finally, I have noted that North America is rapidly shifting from a post-Christian society to an anti-Christian society. A totalitarian state seems to be emerging, one that with growing intensity demands total allegiance. Christians in North America thus have much to learn from our brothers and sisters in China. The experience of the Chinese church highlights five theological truths that will inevitably be challenged by totalitarian governments. These truths include: the church's head (Christ); its nature (a trans-national community); its message ("repentance and forgiveness of sins…in [Christ's] name," cf. Luke 24:47); its power (not of this world; cf. Acts 1:8); and its mission (bear witness "to all nations," Luke 24:47–48). Each of these truths and the imperatives that flow from them will be challenged by totalitarian regimes. Our faithfulness or lack thereof will hinge on our response to these challenges.

Book Reviews

— OLD TESTAMENT —

— NEW TESTAMENT —

— HISTORY AND HISTORICAL THEOLOGY —

— SYSTEMATIC THEOLOGY —

— ETHICS AND PASTORALIA —

— MISSION AND CULTURE —

— OLD TESTAMENT —

Daniel I. Block. _Covenant: The Framework of God's Grand Plan of Redemption._ Grand Rapids: Baker Academic, 2021. xxiii + 680 pp. £39.99/$54.99.

Daniel I. Block is Gunther H. Knoedler Professor Emeritus of Old Testament at Wheaton College in Wheaton, Illinois. He is the author of _For the Glory of God: Recovering a Biblical Theology of Worship_ (Grand Rapids: Baker Academic, 2014) and commentaries on Deuteronomy, Judges, Ruth, and Ezekiel. In this work, Block has given us a monumental demonstration of his Christotelic reading of the "First Testament," his preferred designation for the Hebrew Scriptures (p. xvi). Block's Christotelic approach is an attempt to read OT texts in the integrity of the original author's intended meaning, in their place within God's redemptive work that climaxes in Christ, rather than reading Christ back into every OT text. Block affirms Jesus as "the heart and goal (_telos_) of all revelation," but argues that "it is not the starting point of interpretation for any text" (p. 10). He calls us to go back to where the original authors stood, and look forward to Christ. He calls this "reading the text from the inside out" (p. 186). In his words, "I seek to read the New Testament in light of the antecedent texts, rather than the reverse, which often yields forced and unnatural readings of earlier texts" (p. 9). He describes this volume as "a 'Here I stand' sort of statement" (p. 7). He does not engage with alternate views, which gives the reader a clean and undistracted opportunity to listen.

Block calls for the rehabilitation of the First Testament. He observes that "for many evangelicals, the First Testament is at worst the problem that the New Testament supposedly fixes and at best a dead book that we would do well to bury ceremoniously in a genizah" (p. 9). While he recognizes that there are "parity covenants, between parties of equal social status," he argues that "all covenants involving God are fundamentally monergistic suzerain-vassal pacts" (pp. 1–2). He rejects the classification of covenants as irrevocable (Abrahamic and Davidic covenants) and revocable (Israelite/Sinai covenant), arguing that they all involve divine irrevocability and the vassal's options of fidelity or infidelity (along with the appropriate covenant consequences). Regardless of the vassal's choices, God's covenants "remained in force in perpetuity" (p. 3).

Block abandons the categories of conditional/unconditional covenants. Instead, he distinguishes missional/communal/ecclesial covenants (the Cosmic and Israelite) from administrative covenants (Adamic, Davidic, and Levitical). The former focus on "the health of the group (communal) and God's mandate for them (hence missional)" (p. 4). The missional covenants address the triangular relationships between God, the earth, and living things. These relationships were inverted in Genesis 3:1–6:8 (pp. 32–33). They were restored in microcosm between YHWH, the people of Israel, and the land of Canaan (p. 41). Administrative covenants operate within missional covenants to appoint "individuals and their descendants to promote the smooth operation of these broader covenants" (p. 4).

Block argues that we need to think in terms of "covenance" rather than individual covenants (p. 4). Covenance focuses on the overall mode of God's relating to his creation and his people. He sees God's plan of redemption as playing out in five acts: (1) creation, (2) rebellion, (3) God's grace through history leading up to (4) the work of Jesus, and (5) the recreation of the new heaven and the new earth

(p. 14). Block sees no place for covenance prior to Genesis 3, "because these relationships were natural" (p. 24). He states that "by definition, a covenant formally establishes a relationship that does not exist naturally or re-establishes a relationship that has disintegrated" (p. 40). Therefore, he does not engage with historic debates in reformed theology concerning a covenant of works or covenant of grace (see WCF 7.2–6). Nevertheless, his concept of covenance is in accord with WCF 7.1.

In part 1, Block takes us through the Cosmic and Adamic Covenants. He locates the Cosmic Covenant in Genesis 8:21–9:17, noting that "YHWH specifically identifies the earth as his covenant partner in 9:13" (p. 39). Note that this is not "the Noachian covenant"; rather, "Noah was the agent through whom God established his covenant with the cosmos" (p. 40). In chapter 2 Block addresses the contentious question of the Adamic covenant. Allowing that Genesis 6:18 could mean the confirmation of a covenant previously made, he concedes, "If we must have a pre-existent covenant … God probably made it with Adam and Eve as they were leaving the garden of Eden (Gen 3:23–24), rather than at the time of their creation (chapters 1–2)" (p. 46). He identifies God's covenant with Noah and his sons (Gen 9:9) as the Adamic covenant (pp. 61–65).

In part 2, Block guides us through the four stages of the Israelite Covenant: (1) the Abrahamic Covenant, (2) the Covenant at Sinai, (3) the renewal on the Plains of Moab, and (4) the New Covenant. Through detailed exegesis, Block points out the unity of all four stages as the progressive development of the one covenant, which in turn builds on the Cosmic and Adamic. In this section, Block highlights the integrity of his Christotelic reading.

In chapter 8 (looking at Deuteronomy), Block reminds us that "this book portrays Moses not as a legislator but as a pastor-teacher (Eph 4:11)" (p. 245). The law was God's gift to a people redeemed (p. 262). He challenges the assumption that YHWH's commands could not be kept: "If the Israelites failed in their performance, it was not the fault of the law" (p. 265). He concludes this discussion with the observation that "the Pentateuch provides no evidence that First Testament believers expected a future Messiah to take the punishment for their sins and die in their place.… The association of a messianic figure with sacrifice and substitutionary death occurs for the first time in Isaiah 52:13–53:12" (p. 272). Block affirms that "when God observed faith demonstrated in a pure life and rituals performed as he instructed, he applied to that person the forgiveness made possible through the blood of Christ.… But now we have reached far beyond the data available in the First Testament" (p. 272).

In chapter 9, Block argues that it is better to think of the New Covenant as "a renewed covenant" (p. 286). He finds that none of the features set out in Jeremiah 31:27–40 is new except for the promise that all Israel would be saved (v. 34; p. 285).

In part 3, Block traces references and allusions to the Davidic Covenant through the rest of the OT. He observes, "Many of these are commonly identified as messianic texts, but the notion of a single eschatological anointed Davidide is not evident in all of them" (p. 331). In part 4, Block works his way through the NT looking at how it builds on each of the covenants and stages that he identified in the First Testament. He notes the way the NT writers conflate the various covenants into one covenantal process such that the whole is fulfilled in Christ. "Because the New Testament identifies Jesus with YHWH … Jesus's teachings build on his previous revelation as YHWH in the First Testament" (p. 600). He concludes by reminding the reader, "The divine drama of redemption did not end with the close of the New Testament: Act 5 is still to come" (p. 621).

Throughout this work, Block throws up gem after gem, inviting us to rethink and investigate familiar texts without domesticating them to later constructions. A Christotelic reading invites imagination and speculation, but rigorous controls are needed. Used in combination with the Christocentric approach, each may provide some mutual control. With respect to Genesis 3:15, Block does not want to read Jesus directly back into this text. He asserts that "a collective understanding is preferable" (p. 304). Further, "the prediction concerning the woman's seed says nothing about the extraordinarily significant role the new/second Adam would play as head of a new humanity" (p. 424; see also pp. 35, 55).

Block has filled this volume with seeds for further reflection and investigation. He writes as a scholar inviting discussion. Scholars focused on the structure of covenant treaties or theologians engaged in the historical debates of covenant theology will find here a fresh set of eyes. Future research in biblical theology and exegesis will need to engage with this volume.

David R. Jackson
Werrington, New South Wales, Australia

Gregg Davidson and Kenneth J. Turner. *The Manifold Beauty of Genesis One: A Multi-Layered Approach*. Grand Rapids: Kregel Academic, 2021. 210 pp. £18.23/$22.99.

Davidson and Turner invite the readers to come out of the "fortified theological trenches" that they have constructed to defend their unidimensional, dogmatic views regarding the interpretation of Genesis 1. This invitation is offered on the premise that Genesis 1, like the rest of Scripture, ought to be read from the perspective that the Creator God who inspired the Bible could very well have incorporated multiple layers of complementary truth into this ancient text.

In the introduction, the authors set forth their task, state their hermeneutical presuppositions and biblical convictions, then address most of the probable questions and objections to their proposal for reading Genesis 1. In chapter 2, they discuss the peculiarities and inconsistencies included in Jesus's genealogies in Matthew 1 and Luke 3 to demonstrate that the biblical text may "freely employ literary devices and accommodation or challenge cultural norms in ways that may run counter to modern literary expectations" (pp. 21–22). They then highlight how literary devices and accommodation in Genesis 1—namely, the twofold separation of light from darkness, the "separation of light from the absence of light," the evenings and mornings of the first three days before the creation of the sun, and the repeated occurrence of the number seven (or factors of seven)—betray an "underlying richness to the text" (pp. 23–24).

The greater part of the book is devoted to a careful explanation of the commonly proposed frameworks that are proffered for interpreting Genesis 1. While the individual discussions are not exhaustive, the main points are explained fairly and clearly. Chapters 3–9 introduce and review the following interpretive grids: Song, Analogy, Polemic, Covenant, Temple, Calendar, and Land. Unlike the Counterpoints series (published by Zondervan Academic), these chapters do not attempt to compare and critique each view in light of the others. Rather, the authors argue that these frameworks are complementary "layers" that not only draw out meaning on their own but also overlap with one another to reveal deeper significance from the text of Genesis 1. While these dynamics are not highlighted in every chapter, Davidson and Turner do suggest some creative interplays between the layers that underscore their argument that these interpretive grids are not mutually exclusive. Each chapter concludes with a section called "Challenges and Responses." Herein the authors address questions and objections that might be raised as to the legitimacy of the interpretive methodology of each layer that is presented.

The concluding chapter offers "short summaries of the main points or themes of each layer before addressing lingering questions readers may have" (p. 167). Reviewing each layer in sequence, the authors also highlight a characteristic aspect of God's nature that is illumined by that layer—Song portrays God as artist, Analogy depicts God as farmer, Polemic affirms God as "I Am," Covenant represents God as suzerain, Temple speaks of God as presence, Calendar reminds us that the Creator is the God of Sabbath, and Land establishes an eschatological hope of God as Redeemer. After each summary, there is a single paragraph that delineates how that layer points to aspects of the person and work of Christ.

Given that the book is co-authored by a professor of geology (Davidson) and a professor of Old Testament (Turner), one may have anticipated that the book would either offer a scientific commentary on Genesis 1 with biblical supporting arguments or offer a commentary on Genesis 1 with scientific evidence to support the biblical interpretation. Such works are often used to defend a favored interpretation of Genesis 1 and thereby define the limits of orthodoxy which tends to fracture the Christian community. However, the authors' intention in writing this book is to turn our internecine diatribes into dialogue.

A fundamental conviction that informs this work is that the contemporary reader should "understand the [biblical] text through the eyes of the original audience" (p. 7). As the authors discuss each of the layers that are commonly proposed as interpretive grids for understanding Genesis 1, they explain how each layer would have been perceived by the ancient Near Eastern audience. This opens vistas for understanding that many contemporary readers miss when they read the opening chapter of the Bible from a literalist point of view or through the lens of a single layer.

This monograph is informative, accessible, and largely free of technical jargon or highly complex arguments. In almost every chapter, the authors provide numerous tables that visually distill the information that is presented. Occasional illustrations elucidate specific points, and strategic text box inserts supplement the content for the reader. This book would be suitable for any interested reader who desires to understand the message of the first chapter of the Bible. Each chapter of the book includes discussion questions that facilitate deeper learning or could provide the structure for a meaningful conversation with others in a study group—possibly in a Christian school Bible class, a church-based "book club," or in a college classroom.

Steven W. Guest
Baptist Theological College Cebu Graduate School of Theology
Cebu, Philippines

James M. Hamilton Jr. *Typology–Understanding the Bible's Promise-Shaped Patterns: How Old Testament Expectations are Fulfilled in Christ*. Grand Rapids: Zondervan Academic, 2022. 432 pp. £30.00/$39.99.

In recent decades, with the rise of assessments such as the Enneagram or the Myers-Briggs Type Indicator, the word "typology" has been a bit of a buzzword pertaining to methods of measuring or categorizing personality traits. It is not this form of typology that James Hamilton, professor of biblical theology at the Southern Baptist Theological Seminary and senior pastor at Kentwood Baptist Church in Louisville, has in mind in this book. Hamilton suggests the Greek word τύπος, from which the English ideas of "type" and "typology" are derived, indicates an "impression" of consciousness that informs how a person interprets further information. Rather than the form of typology lauded in popular culture, Hamilton defines typology in biblical studies as "God-ordained, author-intended historical correspondence and escalation in significance between people, events, and institutions across the Bible's redemptive-historical story" (p. 26). The study of typology "amounts to active reflection on one passage in light of others" (p. 8). It is the process of reading Scripture in the broader context of the biblical canon to see how certain words, phrases, themes, ideas, or symbols find their fulfillment as the writings progressively reveal God's message to the world.

Hamilton explains that there are two types of biblical typology: "micro-level" and "macro-level." "Micro-level" biblical typology is "the quotation of lines, the reuse of key terms, the repetitions in sequences of events, and the similarities in covenantal and salvation-historical import we find when we focus in on particular texts" and "macro-level" is "wide-angle literary structures" (p. 3). Micro and macro-level indicators work together to communicate the meaning an author intends to convey through their writing (p. 332). Micro-level typology encompasses most of the book, being considered in detail throughout chapters 1–10, while macro-level typology takes a minor role examined only in the final chapter (ch. 11). Hamilton looks at micro-level typology pertaining to people (Adam, priests, prophets, kings, and "the Righteous Sufferer"), events (creation and exodus), and institutions (the "Leviticult" and marriage), arguing that God's promises recorded in Scripture informed how the biblical authors wrote and, thus, why the biblical authors intended to communicate these types in their writings. He furthers this argument in the final chapter by demonstrating how parallelism and, specifically, chiasms, serve the same function at the macro-level.

Hamilton does a thorough job examining micro-level typology in *Typology*. He examines micro-level typology from a variety of angles, making clear cases in each example for how the biblical authors intentionally reused certain types to illustrate a greater purpose to be revealed in Christ. One area that could have used more attention in *Typology* is macro-level typology. While Hamilton addressed macro-level typology, he devoted only the final chapter to it. His discussion of macro-level typology amounts primarily to a discussion on the nature and role of chiasmic structure in biblical writing, which is helpful but brief. Greater attention could be given to explaining and illustrating the inner workings of macro-level typology to the extent micro-level typology was addressed. As it is, his relative inattention to macro-level typology weakens his argument that micro-level and macro-level typology work hand-in-hand.

A key issue in the study of typology addressed by Hamilton is the concept of authorial intent. An important question that underlies the study of typology is, *did the biblical authors believe they were writing to their immediate audience or contributing toward a larger corpus as they were carried along by the Holy Spirit?* To address this question, Hamilton writes, "The most important criterion for determining what a text means is determining the intent of its human author" (p. 18). Hamilton further argues that, because the Bible is inspired by the Holy Spirit, the intent of the human authors of Scripture are in alignment with the intent of the Divine Author. Since God inspired both the earlier and later books of Scripture he serves as the unifier of thought and idea across Scripture as written by the human authors and, thus, the dichotomous relationship between the original audience and later audiences of Scripture can coexist under the banner of divine authorial intent (p. 28). Hamilton believes that Genesis 3:15 is the key to understanding both typology and authorial intent because it anticipates the types that come later in Scripture to which the human authors of later biblical books contribute under the guidance of God's Spirit. To best determine what the human author intended, Hamilton states that the historical-grammatical method should be the standard in the study of typology, which he employs throughout *Typology*.

The key phrase for Hamilton is "promise-shaped typology," which he says "attempts to capture what happens when God makes a promise that results in those who know him interpreting the world in the terms and categories either communicated in the promise or assumed by it" (p. 4). These promises, revealed in Scripture, have "been pressed into the consciousness of those who believe [them], and that impress results in reality being interpreted in light of God's word" (p. 15–16). Hamilton believes that by better understanding the typological promises made in Scripture people may better come to understand reality as God intends, which should inform a person's belief and practice.

Typology is a helpful work in the field of biblical theology that is scholarly, accessible, and bridges the gap between intermediate and advanced students of Scripture. Hamilton helps the concept of biblical typology come to life in a way that is spiritually encouraging and academically compelling. This book is well-suited for biblical-theological scholars interested in biblical theology and typology, pastors or other ministry workers responsible for regular preaching and/or teaching responsibilities, or serious students of Scripture interested in deeper study of the Bible's weave of interconnectedness. This would make for an ideal textbook in a biblical theology or survey course at the Bible college or seminary level and an excellent resource to keep on the bookshelf of any student or teacher of the Bible. *Typology* would make a worthy addition to the resource list of anyone desiring to see how many big, confusing, or seemingly unrelated concepts within the Bible interconnect to reveal a grandiose masterpiece woven by God through inspired human authors to impact students of his Word with a clearer and sweeter picture of reality that will deeply impact their knowledge of the things of God.

Andrew McIntyre
Sweet Home Community Chapel
Sweet Home, Oregon, USA

Editor's Note: See also the review below by Ross D. Harmon.

Christophe Nihan and Julia Rhyder, eds. *Text and Ritual in the Pentateuch: A Systematic and Comparative Approach*. University Park: Eisenbrauns, 2021. xii + 336 pp. £104.62/$129.95.

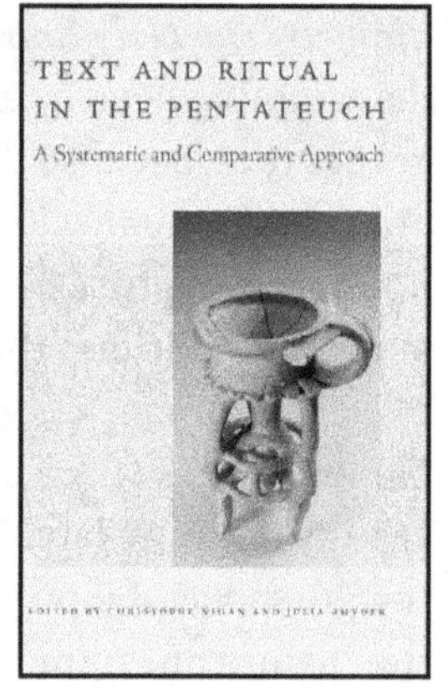

Recent years have seen an increased focus on biblical ritual texts. This is due, in part, to the advent of ritual studies as a discrete discipline in the 1970s and 1980s. One of the key questions to emerge is how interpreters ought to construe the relationship between ritual text and ritual practice. James Watts's observation has, for many, become axiomatic: "texts are not rituals and rituals are not texts" (*Ritual and Rhetoric in Leviticus: From Sacrifice to Scripture* [Cambridge: Cambridge University Press, 2007], 29 [emphasis removed]). Within this conception, ritual texts are not straightforwardly prescriptive or descriptive. Instead, as literary entities, ritual texts encode persuasive ends. The resulting relationship between text and practice is correspondingly multifaceted and non-linear. The thirteen essays in *Text and Ritual in the Pentateuch*, edited by Christophe Nihan (University of Münster) and Julia Rhyder (Harvard University), are a timely engagement with this complex field. The approach taken is explicitly comparative: to situate ancient Israel/early Judaism alongside other ritual cultures of the Mediterranean and West Asian worlds with the aim of opening new perspectives on ritual and ritual texts in the Hebrew Bible (p. 1).

The introduction by Christophe Nihan states the assumed position of contributors: "the performance of a ritual and its textual representation are not one and the same thing" (p. 2). This, in turn, raises two crucial questions that the volume explores: (1) how close are ritual texts to performance? and (2) what is the function of textualized ritual? (p. 3). Readers are encouraged to not only consider *what* ritual texts say but also *how* they were used in relation to ritual performance (p. 6). Nihan helpfully distills four implications this volume has for future scholarship: demonstrating the relevance of comparative approaches, the need for more complex models, the importance of material culture, and the integration of biblical and early Jewish ritual studies (pp. 22–27).

Five essays examine the relationship between ritual and text in Egyptian (Giuseppina Lenzo), Greek (Dominique Jaillard), Neo-Assyrian (Lionel Marti), Syrian (Patrick Michel), and Hittite (Yitzhaq Feder) contexts. The insights into cognate fields are invaluable for students and researchers working with biblical texts and are indicative of the potential of this kind of dialogue. Feder, for example, isolates five functions of Hittite ritual texts: (1) memorization to aid ritual performance; (2) preservation of tradition; (3) enactment of authority; (4) production of new rituals; and (5) regulation of legitimate practice (pp. 134–41). He notes points of substantial overlap with biblical texts (albeit also acknowledging divergence). Feder concludes, "the recent explosion of research into the textualization of Hittite ritual offers fascinating prospects for understanding the formation of the Priestly source" (p. 145). However, at this point, methodology becomes crucial. How and to what degree comparative insights should shape understanding of the Old Testament remains the central, and debated, question.

Further essays elucidate ritual in ancient Israel. Rüdiger Schmitt surveys material evidence from pre- and post-exilic Judah to ascertain the degree to which cultic, especially pagan, practices changed (pp. 151–71). Based on the ongoing use of figurines in the Persian period, Schmitt concludes that there is little evidence for a strongly centralized cult in this era (p. 166). James Watts provides a useful survey of ritual theory and its proponents (pp. 173–79) before turning to Leviticus 12 to test his thesis that interpreting a ritual text does not interpret the meaning of the ritual. In line with his wider program to read Leviticus as supporting Aaronide hegemony, Watts argues that Leviticus 12 is best understood as a "payment schedule" written to emphasize priestly dues (p. 181). In an intriguing essay, Christian Frevel argues that the function of ritual textualization in Numbers is, somewhat paradoxically, to enable variance, with biblical texts intentionally forming only a framework for ritual practice (p. 208). Hence, against an understood background of Late Persian "Judaisms" (pp. 206–7), biblical ritual texts preserve tradition while also legitimating diversity (p. 209). Jeremy Smoak's excellent speech-act analysis of the Aaronic blessing in Numbers 6:22–27 finds that priestly annunciation of these words performs YHWH's act of speaking blessing, thereby authorizing the priests as divine messengers (pp. 224–25). Dorothea Erbele-Küster posits that Leviticus 12–15 "do[es] not support any conclusions about real-world cultic-ritual praxis" (p. 252). Instead, the legislation becomes a means of producing gendered bodies through discourse.

The remaining three chapters explore the reception of ritual texts. Julia Rhyder examines Ezra-Nehemiah and Chronicles to ascertain why ritual practice differs from the Torah that is so highly esteemed in each work (pp. 255–79), Daniel Falk turns to the Dead Sea Scrolls (280–311), and William Gilders analyses the use of Leviticus 16 in Mishnah Yoma, Tosefta Kippurim, and Sifra Aḥare Mot (pp. 312–25).

Text and Ritual in the Pentateuch is an eclectic collection. This is not a fault of the volume; rather, it simply reflects the diversity of approaches and presuppositions inherent to Old Testament and ANE studies. Accordingly, different views are articulated regarding how best to interpret ritual texts. The essays by Watts and Frevel are a case in point. Whereas Watts views the skeletal nature of Leviticus 12 as a tell-tale indicator that persuasion is focused on legitimizing priestly prebends, Frevel understands ritual lacunae as a deliberate device whereby variant groups could claim Torah conformity. Hence, readers hoping for any kind of neat resolution to the hermeneutics of ritual texts will be disappointed. Those, on the other hand, who are seeking a robust induction into a complex but nonetheless vital discussion will find themselves well-served.

G. Geoffrey Harper
Sydney Missionary & Bible College
Croydon, New South Wales, Australia

Iain Provan. *Seeking What Is Right: The Old Testament and the Good Life*. Waco, TX: Baylor University Press, 2020. xii + 500 pp. £45.50/$54.99.

This volume guides the audience to read the Bible deeply and accurately so that they can live a good life according to it. The book consists of three parts addressing issues concerning the "good life" as found in history and Scripture and several appendixes that provide resources for further study. Each chapter concludes with discussion questions to internalize the information and consider ways to live it out.

Part 1: Foundations includes three chapters. Chapter 1 introduces the concepts of the "good life" considering God's character and his creation design as presented in Scripture and several historical documents. Chapter 2 examines what is meant by "Scripture" and ways people read it, especially the OT. Provan

avers that both Testaments have authority over Christian life and demonstrate that being "good" means to imitate God in character and behavior (p. 27). Chapter 3 tells the story of the Bible from Creation to Revelation, focusing on the place of Israel and its Torah and the church and the NT in God's relationship with his people (p. 43).

Part 2: Explorations investigates how Christians throughout history have understood the "good life" by reading or misreading the biblical narrative and how contemporary Christians should wrestle with ethical questions while searching and interpreting the Scriptures. Chapters 4 to 6 examine the claims of early ecclesiastical leaders and imperial rulers to establish a Christian kingdom and accomplish "a task of Christian salvation" by means of state policy, law, and violence. Provan believes that idealizing pagan kings/rulers as biblical heroes and their kingdoms as "a little short of the kingdom of God on earth" has resulted in misinterpretation and misappropriation of godly rule and Christians' engagement with political powers (pp. 57–59), bringing about "apocalyptic purification theology" which sanctioned the Crusades (p. 98) and widened the gap between Christians and pagans, Jews, and Muslims.

Chapters 7 to 9 examine the church's attempts to establish a godly society in post-Reformation Europe which regulated one's sexual and marital life, employed capital punishment to subvert any opposition to Christian rule, and justified the violence of expansionist wars. Provan's study of Scripture demonstrates that the church's misreading of the OT passages on personal life, executions, and just war resulted in the unjust overreach of the church into the lives of both believers and unbelievers, causing pain and mistrust of Christianity. Provan believes that post-Pentecostal believers are called to a life of peacemaking and non-violence (p. 157) and the laws of Leviticus 18 on sexual relationships (p. 123) and Leviticus 20 on capital punishment do not apply to them (p. 138).

Chapters 10 to 12 investigate the overlapping of civil and ecclesiastical polities which shaped the order of society in the New World and Europe, particularly as they pertained to the matters of Sabbath observance, governance, and the institution of slavery. Having examined different types of government and their treatment of the people and the biblical story, Provan concludes that no government is best suited for Christians as they are called to seek the kingdom of God and obey their civil governments as long as seeking the good life allows it (p. 200). This makes overzealous observance of the Sabbath or imposition and support of slavery unacceptable Christian practices.

Chapters 13 to 15 discuss wrongful Christian practices by focusing on the vocation and rights of women, Christians' views of Jews and Palestinians, and creation care. Provan finds no basis in Scripture to see women as lesser humans subordinate to men (p. 241) and identifies the historical treatment of women as "a shameful legacy" which robs the contemporary church of any credibility (p. 243). The historical misreading of the Bible concerning the restoration of Israel in the Holy Land has caused Christians to support the Israelis over against the Palestinians instead of loving both groups and being their image of God-bearing neighbors (p. 262). Additionally, a misunderstanding of what "dominion" over creation means has led to misuse of nature instead of co-laboring with God in his garden (p. 283).

Part 3: Conclusions invites readers to use a consistent approach to interpreting various ethical issues through the lens of Scripture to enable them to live good lives in counter-cultural or counter-endorsing ways (p. 289). Chapter 16 offers a recap of the biblical story and ways of understanding the role of the church in the world. Chapter 17 presents the author's treatment of biblical ethics of creation care, abortion, suicide, and euthanasia. Chapter 18 discusses the very complex issue of gender identity. Chapter 19 portrays the dangerous landscape of the exile in which Christians find themselves now when they choose to oppose the state's polity which goes against the biblical teachings, especially regarding sexual orientation and gender identity. Chapter 20 invites the reader to develop authentic Christian ethics deeply rooted in the story of God and his character to demonstrate to the post-Christian world what a good and godly life is and why it is important to embrace it rather than settling into the dominant culture (pp. 379–80).

This volume addresses several important issues which historically the church has failed to engage with from the perspective of biblical ethics. The book sheds light on the implications of misreading and misinterpreting Scripture. The author dedicates a lot of thought to the church-state relationship from the first to the eighteenth century. It would have been beneficial if he had discussed the contemporary situation between the two entities. In addition, one wonders why, having embraced 2 Timothy 3:15 as the guiding principle for viewing the Bible, the author still chooses to see some of the OT teaching as not applicable to Christians. It would have been helpful if Provan had identified contextual ways of reading these laws in a new reality rather than dismissing them.

Nevertheless, this book is a valuable addition to the field of Christian ethics and a source of enriching discussions on the "good life."

Larisa Levicheva
Wesley Seminary, Indiana Wesleyan University
Marion, Indiana, USA

Jason A. Staples. *The Idea of Israel in Second Temple Judaism: A New Theory of People, Exile, and Israelite Identity*. Cambridge: Cambridge University Press, 2021. xxiii + 426 pp. £29.99/$39.99.

How would a first-century Jew think of herself? What terms would she use to describe her national, cultural, and social identities? A bulk of scholars have maintained that she would call herself an Israelite among those who share her identity. They argue that Israelite is an insider term. Those who were not Israelites would call her a Jew—an outsider term. She may appropriate the term Jew when in dialogue with outsiders or diaspora Jews that had accommodated on this term.

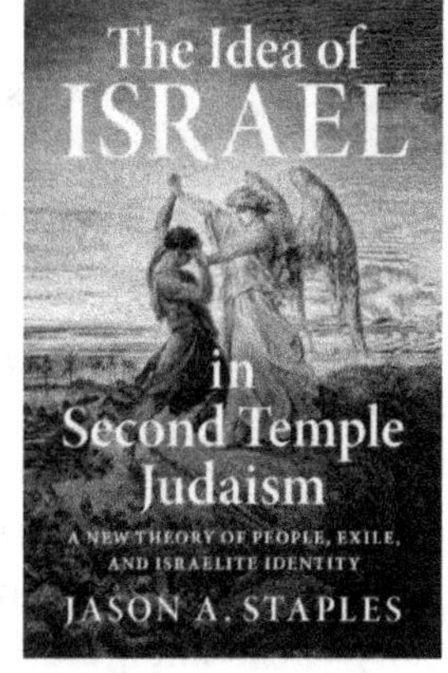

Jason Staples argues persuasively against this understanding of the terms. For Staples, Second Temple texts use *Ioudaios* (Jew) to refer to "a person descended from the southern kingdom of Judah or otherwise incorporated into that ethno-religious group" (p. 52). Israelite refers to a broader category including not only those descended from Judah, but the entire twelve-tribe people of Israel. Israel most frequently refers to either the ancient kingdom of Israel or a future, eschatological restoration of the twelve tribes of Israel. Staples divides his argument into three parts.

In part 1, Staples shows the history of the insider/outsider paradigm for understanding the terms Israelite and Jew. He shows that the paradigm arose from sociological concerns of nationalistic Germany in the early twentieth century and not from the Second Temple period sources. He also discusses the relationship of Samaritans to Jews, showing that Second Temple period sources refer to the Samaritans as non-Jews, yet of Israelite heritage. They remain Israelites, but not Jews.

In part 2, Staples shows that narrative, prophetic, and post-exilic canonical texts all present a rather consistent restoration eschatology. The Pentateuch, Former Prophets, and Chronicles all argue that

Israel was, is not, but will be again. The prophets declare a future, restored Israel alongside a restored Judah. Post-exilic texts look at the return to Yehud as incomplete and ultimately failed. Those who returned are not a restored Israel and Judah but Persian "slaves" (Neh 9:36) in the land of ancient Israel. Across these diverse texts, Israel refers to either the northern tribes, the ancient covenantal people, or a future restored people.

In part 3, Staples addresses a wide-ranging group of Second Temple period sources—from the Old Greek to Josephus, Philo, the Dead Sea Scrolls, and even Second Temple period apocalyptic literature. He argues persuasively against those who claim some of these texts contain a diaspora-positive theology. He shows that they continue to assert the restoration theology of both earlier non-canonical and canonical sources.

Though technically the final chapter of part 3, chapter 12 serves as a summary and conclusion to the entire work. Staples concludes that across the wide array of literature assessed, "the *partitive* relationship between Israel and Judah established in biblical literature persisted ... 'Jew' continues to refer to a subset of Israel" (p. 340, emphasis original). He concludes, "Jews in this period did not anticipate merely a *Jewish* restoration but a full restoration of *all Israel*" (p. 341, emphasis original). With helpful charts, he shows how a Second Temple period Jew would consider the relationship between the terms Israelite, Jew, and Hebrew. He notes that the New Testament is itself Second Temple period literature and suggests that we reassess terms like "kingdom of God" in light of Israelite restoration theology and reconsider passages like Romans 11:26—"all Israel will be saved."

The book presents massive and wide-ranging research. Staples easily moves from discussions of Chronicles to Josephus to 2 Baruch. The footnotes are voluminous and helpful. Despite the occasional mistake, such as the misattribution of a quote by Franz Rendtorff to Rolf Rendtorff (p. 186), the book has been well edited. The immense bibliography of 56 pages will profit readers and scholars interested in further work on this topic.

For a book so well researched and presented, there are a few areas for improvement. First, in discussions of diaspora theology, the book would have profited by greater interaction with the Joseph narrative in Genesis—a text ripe with questions of cultural identity. Occasional mention of the Joseph narrative appears, but greater interaction could have strengthened Staples's arguments even more. Second, although the initial thesis set out to distinguish Israelite, *Ioudaios*, and Hebrew, the latter term often appears extrinsic to the book's argument. As Meir Sternberg has shown (*Hebrews Between Cultures* [Bloomington: Indiana University Press, 1999]), evolving Hebrew identity plays a significant role in Israelite and Jewish thought. Finally, the reader longs for more interaction with the New Testament and early Christian literature. The final pages leave the reader hoping for direct interaction with the New Testament, which one hopes Staples will present in a future monograph.

The Idea of Israel is an excellent resource—even if readers may disagree with a conclusion or presupposition here or there. Although technical, the book remains readable and engaging. Students of biblical theology will profit from the implications for understanding Israel in both the Old and New Testament—especially in relation to Israel, the church, and their relationship. Pastors will profit from consulting the book when preaching from texts as diverse as the Major and Minor Prophets, Ezra-Nehemiah, Esther, Ephesians 2–3, and Romans 9–11.

G. Kyle Essary
Malaysia Baptist Theological Seminary
Kuala Lumpur, Selangor, Malaysia

— NEW TESTAMENT —

Channing L. Crisler. *Echoes of Lament and the Christology of Luke*. NTM 39. Sheffield: Sheffield Phoenix Press, 2020. xviii + 335 pp. £69.99/$97.00.

Channing Crisler, associate professor of New Testament at Anderson University in South Carolina, offers the reader this intriguing exploration of lament in the Third Gospel. His thesis is that "the metaleptic interplay between Lukan laments and their echoes of OT laments generate two highly suggestive Christological points of resonance that reach their hermeneutical climax in the crucifixion scene" (p. 3). These two Christological points are that (1) Jesus, in Luke, answers laments as only "Yhwh can" thus pointing to his share "in the divine identity" and (2) "the Lukan Jesus is presented as the 'ideal righteous lamenter'" (p. 3).

In the introduction, metalepsis is defined as a form of intertextuality which sees connections between a pre-text and a text on the word and/or conceptual level (cf. Richard B. Hays, *Echoes of Scripture in the Letters of Paul* [New Haven: Yale University Press, 1989]). The pre-text refers in this case to the Old Testament and the text to Luke's gospel. After distinguishing his approach slightly from Hays—notably in his use of "echo" to designate all Lukan uses of the OT rather than distinguishing them into categories such as "citation, allusion, or echo proper" (p. 7)—he lists seven criteria that an OT "pre-text must meet most, though not all [of]" in order to qualify as an echo. These include "volume," i.e., "at least three semantic or syntactical points of contact," and "recurrence," i.e., whether "the pre-text" is echoed "elsewhere in Luke-Acts" (p. 10). Beyond this, Crisler posits a category of "Lukan lament," which, for him, is the text to the corresponding pre-text. He lists four criteria for discerning Lukan lament: (1) an "episode" in which a person is afflicted in some way; (2) the presence of a "cry for deliverance" from said affliction; (3) "answer" to "the cry of distress"; and (4) "some indication of a shift from lament to praise" (p. 12).

Drawing from the work of Richard Bauckham, he describes "'Christological' points of resonance" (p. 3), namely, laments *to* Jesus, laments *by* Jesus and laments both *to* and *by* Jesus at the scene of the crucifixion. In the first chapter, Crisler surveys Lukan lament in the history of interpretation, focusing on Christology, intertextuality and prayer in Lukan scholarship. He builds on prior scholarship with his recognition that Jesus "models, teaches, and participates in lament" (p. 49) and in his agreement with Hays's and Henrichs-Tarasenkova's use of the idea of divine identity Christology to explain Luke's use of the OT, adding to the former's work by provided further synthesis as he seeks to more fully incorporate lament and the crucifixion scene (p. 42).

Chapter 2 walks the reader through lament in the OT. Here, Crisler defines lamenters as "afflicted individuals and entire communities," with this affliction stemming from "political enemies, disease, death, evil, guilt for sin, and even God himself" (p. 85). Chapter 3 discusses lament in the second temple era. While lament as such was overshadowed by petitionary prayer, he sees fragments of lament in these petitions. Yet, while Second Temple era prayers bolster his overall discussion, he states that Lukan laments are closer to pre-exilic laments than they are to post-exilic petitionary prayers, as the latter lack the lamenter's protest to God and the "claim that God's reputation is in jeopardy" if the prayer goes unanswered (p. 93).

In chapters 4–6, Crisler walks through Luke to demonstrate his thesis. Each passage he treats in these chapters is treated with methodological rigor, consisting of four consistent components: (1) literary context of the passage; (2) echoes of OT passage(s); (3) Lukan lament in the text; and (4) Christological resonances. Four areas are covered in the fourth chapter: (1) laments for forgiveness (e.g., Luke 5:4–11); (2) deliverance from disease (e.g., Luke 17:12–19); (3) from death (e.g., Luke 7:1–10); and (4) from evil (e.g., Luke 8:22–25). Three categories are explored in chapter five: (1) "Jesus' laments over Jerusalem" (e.g., Luke 13:34–35); (2) "Jesus' teaching on lament" (e.g., Luke 18:1–8); and (3) "Jesus' laments over his impending death" (i.e., Luke 22:39–46) (p. 195). Chapter 6 explores lament both *to* and *by* Jesus at his crucifixion scene. Regarding the former, Crisler discusses Luke 23:39–43; regarding the latter, he discusses Luke 23:44–48. The chapter concludes with a demonstration that "the crucifixion scene evokes previous Lukan laments and how these laments, both previous laments and laments at the crucifixion, are mutually interpretative of one another" (p. 240). The final chapter gives attention to the implications of this study's findings for Luke's narrative structure, our understanding of Acts, Christology in Luke-Acts and early Christianity as well as "larger discussions within the Christian tradition" (p. 275).

There a number of strengths that characterize this work. It is methodologically rigorous. Crisler builds on and advances previous scholarship on Luke, lament, and Christology in the NT by combining all three and demonstrating that lament does in fact provide more avenues for understanding Luke's Gospel. This is a study that will be consulted for years to come by students of intertextuality, Christology, lament, and the Gospel of Luke. The only possible weakness is that he provides a maximalist interpretation of lament echoes in a way that may not be persuasive to all. However, taking each text as part of a cumulative case, we would argue that his thesis is clearly and powerfully demonstrated.

Thomas Haviland-Pabst
One Family Ministries
Asheville, North Carolina, USA

Michael Graves. *How Scripture Interprets Scripture: What Biblical Writers Can Teach Us about Reading the Bible*. Grand Rapids: Baker Academic, 2021. ix + 230 pp. £17.93/$24.99.

Interpreting the Bible is no straightforward task. Interpretation mostly happens unselfconsciously in personal and liturgical reading, but as the continuing hermeneutical conversation suggests, the church is still trying to articulate what how the Bible should best be interpreted.

Michael Graves seeks to shed light on biblical interpretation by examining how the Bible interprets itself. In his words, he sets out to "illustrate and explain what we can learn about biblical interpretation by paying attention to how Scripture interprets Scripture" (p. 1). In one sense, Graves follows previous work done in the more historical vein of biblical scholarship, such as Michael Fishbane's study of "inner-Biblical interpretation" (*Biblical Interpretation in Ancient Israel* [Oxford: Oxford University Press, 1985]), which set out how 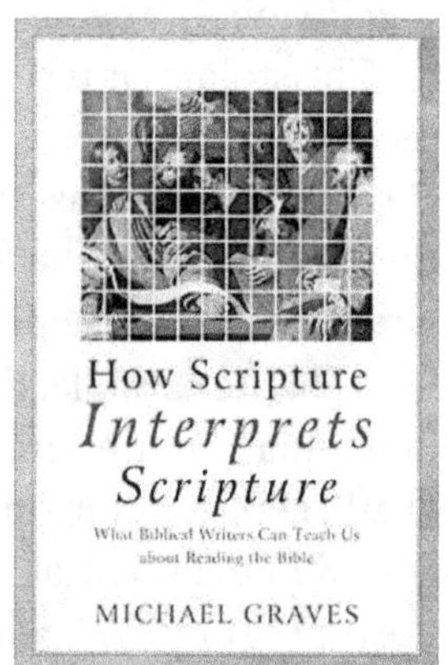 biblical authors interpreted earlier biblical texts. In another sense, Graves seeks to go a step further. To borrow a phrase from Kevin Vanhoozer, he apprentices himself to Scripture by observing the biblical authors and then extending their interpretive practice into his own constructive theological reading.

Each chapter seeks to make sense of a particular issue as it develops across the canon: corporate and individual responsibility; insiders and outsiders; marriage, polygamy, and divorce; sacrificial offerings; and the afterlife. The issues are well-chosen—this is a strength of the book. They are significant topics in the New and Old Testaments, they exhibit a variety of biblical voices, and there is interpretative controversy surrounding each. I found the discussions about marriage and the afterlife especially stimulating. In each chapter, Graves makes a series of interpretive moves. First, he summarizes key texts relating to the topic. Next, he looks in more detail at passages where biblical texts are picked up and reinterpreted by other biblical texts. Finally, in light of the exegetical work, he "pulls it all together" by setting out how the issue is best understood in a contemporary Christian frame of reference.

Another strength of the book is its attention to the biblical text, with a healthy mixture of brevity and depth. Graves maps the biblical landscape by traversing many of the relevant texts, but then homes in on the most significant texts for closer analysis. I also appreciated the way Graves seeks to understand the variety of biblical texts in a coherent way. Rather than simply harmonizing them, Graves locates the different passages in their historical and theological contexts and shows how once they are put into the different contexts they cohere with each other. As one example, in the chapter on marriage and divorce, Graves positions the permissive text of Deuteronomy 24:1–4 in the context of protecting women from existing divorce practices (pp. 91–92). He then understands Jesus's teaching on divorce not as an overturning of Deuteronomy 24:1–4, but as an interpretation in light of the wider context of the purpose of marriage in Genesis 2 (pp. 104–6). Together, these texts teach that marriage should be for life, divorce should be avoided, and vulnerable women should be protected (p. 112).

I offer two points of critique. The first is that the book seems to be less about inner-biblical interpretation and more about thematic biblical-theological interpretation. By thematic biblical-theological interpretation, I mean that Graves mostly sets out different biblical texts on a topic, understands those texts in their original and salvation-historical contexts, and then constructively reads them together in light of the life and teaching of Jesus Christ. Of course, there is nothing wrong with this. It is simply that the title and the stated purpose are different from what the book mostly does. Graves does explore some cases of inner-biblical interpretation, and the final chapter draws together hermeneutical lessons from these cases. However, I wished that this chapter was far more developed, given the purpose of the book.

The second point of critique is that when Graves pulls things together, his conclusions sometimes leave problematic texts behind with insufficient argument. In his chapter on corporate and individual responsibility, he wrestles with corporate punishment texts such as Exodus 34:6–7. He briefly discusses transgenerational punishment in the killing of firstborn on Exodus 12, and only quickly suggests that this is a case of hyperbole for the purpose of teaching about justice (p. 42). Similarly, in his chapter on sacrifice, he asserts that texts that criticise sacrifice are cases of "rhetorical exaggeration," and does no more to argue his point (e.g., pp. 128, 130). Given that one of Graves's stated aims is to illustrate how various biblical texts can be understood coherently, the book would be stronger if he spent more time probing these texts or arguing his case on the basis of genre or literary theory.

Overall, Michael Graves has produced a stimulating book that explores thought-provoking topics from inner-biblical and biblical-theological interpretive perspectives. It both clarifies these controversial topics and contributes to the discussion of interpreting the Scriptures.

Timothy R. Escott
St Mark's Anglican Church
Darling Point, New South Wales, Australia

James M. Hamilton Jr. *Typology—Understanding the Bible's Promise-Shaped Patterns: How Old Testament Expectations are Fulfilled in Christ*. Grand Rapids: Zondervan Academic, 2022. 432 pp. £30.00/$39.99.

James Hamilton Jr. is professor of biblical theology at The Southern Baptist Theological Seminary. Additionally, he serves as senior pastor at Kenwood Baptist Church. Hamilton is a prolific writer whose recent publications include *Psalms* (Bellingham, WA: Lexham, 2021) and *Work and Our Labor in the Lord* (Wheaton, IL: Crossway, 2017).

Typology seeks to illustrate that "God's promises shaped the way the biblical authors perceived, understood, and wrote" (p. 4). Hamilton uses the phrase "promise-shaped typology" to frame how God's promises cause His people to reorient their worldview, including their communication (p. 4). The book is divided into three parts: (1) Persons, (2) Events, and (3) Institutions.

Before part 1, Hamilton provides a helpful introduction, defining typology and discussing the method. Specifically, he seeks to show how "micro-level indicators," that is, "the quotation of lines, the reuse of key terms, the repetitions in sequences of events, and the similarities in covenantal and salvation-historical import" (p. 3), may establish authorial intent (p. 1). Hamilton identifies "promise-shaped patterns" from the "micro-level indicators" (pp. 3–5). According to Hamilton, the biblical authors intentionally include the patterns to be used as types, but the writers may not have known "the significance of the pattern and/or how the promise would be fulfilled" (pp. 4–5).

Hamilton fittingly begins the first section, "Persons," with Moses's account of Adam (ch. 2), suggesting that "Adam is the prototypical man" or archetype (pp. 35–36). Therefore, ectypal figures in Scripture following Adam create an Adamic pattern that culminates in "the antitypical fulfillment" in Jesus Christ (p. 36). Subsequent chapters in part one cover priests (ch. 3), prophets (ch. 4), kings (ch. 5), and the righteous sufferer (ch. 6). Part 1 covers approximately half of the book, while parts 2 and 3 are shorter because some information about events and institutions was necessary to mention alongside the persons. Part 2 focuses on event types: creation and exodus (p. 221). Hamilton chooses these events because they provide a paradigm of God's salvific plan (p. 221). In part 3, Hamilton examines how the institutions of marriage and the "Leviticult" function as types, writing "The goal [of part 3] is to explore and exposit the ways that certain institutions create and/or contribute to patterns that typify the way that God delivers his people, forges relationships (i.e., covenants) with them, and continues in ongoing intimacy between himself and his beloved" (p. 285).

Typology is an accessible resource that covers select types and their function across Scripture, showing how "God's promises shaped the way the biblical authors perceived, understood, and wrote"

(p. 4). The book is accessible to seminary students and pastors because it is well organized and provides visual aids. Bearing in mind the complexity of typology, Hamilton has done an exceptional job presenting his argument. This, in part, occurs as Hamilton begins with "micro-level" patterns that allow the reader to start small and build or pyramid to more complex patterns. Moreover, the material reflects the canonical order of the western Bible (i.e., beginning with Genesis/Adam and moving to the New Testament/Jesus). Also helpful are the visual aids, which include side-by-side English and Hebrew translations, charts to display similarities between Bible passages, and diagrams.

The two critiques that I offer focus on (1) the slightly confusing presentation of typological connections when considering the whole Bible, and (2) the brevity with which Hamilton discusses the term "metaphor." First, the typological connections between Moses/Joshua, Elijah/Elisha, and John the Baptist/Jesus are difficult to understand when assessed as a group. Hamilton presents the "Moses-Joshua and Elijah-Elisha" typological connection between the succession of individuals (p. 131). He also highlights the similar succession-type links of Elijah/Elisha to John the Baptist/Jesus (p. 271). Yet, in the next paragraph, Hamilton discusses the typological connection between Moses and Jesus (p. 272). A careful reader will question how the succession narrative connects Moses/Elijah/John the Baptist and Joshua/Elisha/Jesus, while typology also relates Moses/Jesus. The book does not explain to the reader how to understand Moses serving as a type for both John the Baptist and Jesus. At the micro-level and within each chapter, the typological connections appear clear, yet when viewing the type connections at the macro-level, it is less clear how typology functions.

Second, considering the importance of "metaphor" in typology, the book insufficiently covers it, creating two problems. One, Hamilton does not define or provide instruction on how to identify a metaphor (p. 15). Thus, either capable or not, readers are burdened to supply the information. Two, the presentation of Hamilton's linguistic approach, i.e., "micro-level indicators," to identify typology may imply it dissolves the previous problems inherently found in studying typology and metaphors in literature. Yet, Hamilton's method still relies on an Aristotelian approach to metaphors, while not eliminating its associated limitations. It would have been beneficial to discuss "metaphor" further and engage with modern metaphor theory (e.g., conceptual metaphor theory).

Typology is a well-written resource defining and illustrating typology in Scripture. Hamilton's work is commendable and recommended to seminary students and pastors. Yet, readers should be aware that Hamilton's method does not completely relieve the problems associated with the linguistic analysis of metaphors and typology.

Ross D. Harmon
Midwestern Baptist Theological Seminary
Kansas City, Missouri, USA

Editor's Note: See also the review above by Andrew McIntyre.

Georges Massinelli. *For Your Sake He Became Poor: Ideology and Practice of Gift Exchange Between Early Christian Groups*. BZNW 251. Berlin: de Gruyter, 2021. xi + 420 pp. £94.00/$118.99.

In the published form of his doctoral dissertation from the University of Notre Dame, Georges Massinelli has written a remarkable new study on the charitable practices of the early church. As the subtitle of the book suggests, the overall contribution is a new frame through which to view early Christian charity, the theological and sociological motivations that lay behind it, as well as its place amongst other types of gift-giving practices. His contribution is a welcome one.

The crux of Massinelli's argument is a new proposal for understanding the Jerusalem collection and its place in the first few centuries of Christianity, namely that instead of patronage, the Jerusalem Collection should be understood as an early example of intergroup support in the beginning of Christianity. In chapter one, Massinelli lays the groundwork for what is to follow. First, he reviews what he calls "an emerging tendency" (p. 18) to interpret Paul's collection in light of ancient patronage, which is based on the assumption that benefaction underlies "all extramercantile economic interactions" (p. 18). In the main, this tendency understands Paul to be erecting an anti-patronage system among early Christians, free from reciprocity and power dynamics, as "an intentionally subversive activity that was meant to radically change the social relations of Christians among themselves and with the wider world" (p. 21). Massinelli demurs and offers instead a multifaceted approach to ancient exchange based on John Davis's idea of a "'repertoire' of exchanges" (pp. 34–35). According to Davis's idea, cultures possess a variety of different types of exchange that should not be reduced. This theoretical approach allows Massinelli to plot out the diversity of exchanges in antiquity and simultaneously argue for a cluster of exchanges in the collection itself. Whereas the dominant scholarly approach reads the collection through the lens of patronage, Massinelli argues "that Paul drew not on a single but on several social conventions of gift exchange, which, along with typical Greco-Roman forms of exchange, included one practice from Jewish tradition (almsgiving) and a specifically Christian *exemplum* (Christ's self-giving)" (p. 39).

Chapters 2 and 3 are concerned primarily with sketching out the repertoire of exchange in Greco-Roman culture as well as Judaism. In chapter 2, Massinelli gives a detailed description of patronage and benefaction. While much of what Massinelli covers in this chapter will be review for those familiar with the conversation, he presents the material clearly in such a way that even those unfamiliar with patronage will find it informative and elucidating. His primary concern is to highlight "what the sources reveal about the exploitative dimensions" of patronage and benefaction, not only in Greco-Roman culture, but also in the Jewish communities (p. 46). Having worked through patronage, Massinelli then looks at ancient sources to summarize a variety of different types of exchange in chapter three. Attending to the "full complexity and heterogeneity of gift exchange within the world of nascent Christianity" (p. 112), he places the different types of exchange in two general groups: reciprocal exchange, gifts that are "upheld by virtue of the norm of reciprocity" (p. 113), and non-reciprocal exchange, gifts that escaped such norms p. 135). Massinelli's helpful survey demonstrates quite clearly that exchange was not a single model in antiquity but was both multilayered and multifacted, adaptable to several different situations. Boundaries were not clear cut but were "easily permeable and subject to manipulation" (p. 172).

The next two chapters contain the bulk of Massinelli's exegetical work of 2 Corinthians 8–9, which is nothing short of exemplary. The basic claim of chapter 4 is that the primary concerns of the Corinthian church with Paul's collection request were two: "the fear of impoverishment … and a mistrust of Paul's leadership" (p. 222). This is directly contrary to those who see the collection in terms of patronage, in which issues of "status hierarchy and obligation" are the primary concerns (p. 223). Hierarchy and obligation appear, but not necessarily in positive terms. In terms of hierarchy, Massinelli argues that the Corinthian church is acting like a client, afraid of exploitation, rather than as a patron giving benefits (p. 197). Therefore, when Paul does bring up issues of hierarchy, he does so in order to stress equality, rather than subservience or superiority (2 Cor 8:13–15). And Paul is insistent that giving should be done, not out of obligation but out of liberal generosity (2 Cor 8:3, 12; 9:7). And he does this not because of any perceived obligation to Jerusalem, but, as Massinelli suggests, because of a perceived obligation to Paul, displaying Paul's aversion to heavy-handed leadership and a concern for the liberty of early Christian groups.

Having placed the concerns of impoverishment and leadership in the background, Massinelli then analyzes Paul's language of the collection to determine what types of exchange can be identified in it, or the repertoire of exchange. The most important term for Paul is simply χάρις, "gift." Here Massinelli provides a rich and persuasive reading of the collection texts that show Paul's concern is not sociological, but theological: "Despite the material exchange that takes place between them, the language of χάρις fails to put Corinth and Jerusalem in relation directly with one another. They apparently interact only with God" (p. 230).

The final chapter places the Jerusalem collection in the context of early Christian intergroup support. Each instance of support shares four main features that unify them: similar patterns of collection and distribution, given because of persecution and imprisonment, the support spans the ancient world, and each gift, overseen by a bishop or leader, contributed to the prominence of certain churches and church authorities (pp. 280–81). Here Massinelli provides a great service by showing clearly how the Jerusalem collection fits within the broader stream of intergroup support. What Paul did was not unique to early church but was apparently the first of several similar collections.

In terms of style alone, *For Your Sake He Became Poor* is a salutary example of how academic writing should be done. This may be the most well-written dissertation that I have read. The subject matter is dense, but Massinelli's style is lucid and exact. He lays out his arguments clearly and accessibly so that even a non-specialist can follow along, summarizing and synthesizing mountains of data in ways that are both manageable and yet also substantive.

Of the voluminous literature on the Jerusalem Collection and early Christian ideologies on gift-giving, Massinelli's contribution stands out as an important volume. Previous scholarship is summarized adeptly and the argument, brilliantly simple, ably adds to the discussions on how Christians supported one another, and why. There is plenty here to chew on and consider as it relates to Pauline theology. Perhaps the chief takeaway, though, is the helpful pushback to the current obsession with patronage and benefaction in Paul. As Massinelli shows, ancient gift-giving was not nearly so monochromatic, and Paul's thought is much more complex than a simple identification will allow. Such an approach may provide nuance to the recent work of Barclay and others.

J. Brittain Brewer
Calvin Theological Seminary
Grand Rapids, Michigan, USA

Greg Stanton. *Unity and Disunity in Greek and Christian Thought under the Roman Peace*. STAC 125. Tübingen: Mohr Siebeck, 2021. xii + 360 pp. £105.29/$125.00.

After various contributions to Greek, Roman, and New Testament studies, Greg Stanton, adjunct associate professor at the University of New England in Australia, is offering the reader his first full length monograph. His main intent with this volume is to "explore what Greeks under Roman control thought about unity at several levels" (p. v) while also giving attention to "Christian writers of the first two centuries" (p. 34).

The several levels of unity create the outline of the book. Chapter 1 sets the stage with a survey of modern approaches to unity and by situating his study in the era of the *pax Romana* (i.e., Roman peace), which he designates from "27 B.C.E." to "197 C.E." (p. 240). In chapters 2–6, he discusses the concept of unity in Greek thought. Chapter 2 gives attention to unity in Greek cities; chapter 3 explores the unity of the Roman empire; chapter 4 surveys views of the unity of humankind; the fifth chapter analyzes the unity that exists between God/gods, humans and the universe; and the sixth chapter explores the unity of the universe. He focuses in depth on five Greco-Roman authors: (1) Epictetus; (2) Dion of Prousa (or Dio Chrysostom); (3) Plutarch; (4) Aelius Aristides; and (5) Marcus Aurelius. In addition to these five, he gives attention to "the Hermetic corpus" (p. 35) and the Pseudo-Aristotle work *On the Universe.*

The seventh and eight chapters explore early Christian views of unity, comparing these views to the broader discussion of unity found in the previous chapters. He gives attention to the New Testament, the Apostolic Fathers (e.g., 1–2 Clement; Shepherd of Hermas) and the Apologists (e.g., Justin Martyr, Tatian). The ninth chapter concludes the book by summarizing his findings.

Some highlights will suffice to give the reader a sense of the book's content. In the second chapter, Stanton argues that discussion of human relationships centered around two opposite poles, namely, "harmony" (*homonoia*) and "factional conflict" (*stasis*) (p. 44). Remarkably, *statis* was held in such contempt that war was preferred to it and tyranny was deemed more moderate than it. *Stasis*, Stanton states, "can be called the chief of humiliations and disasters"(!) (p. 51). Morever, Stanton finds the Greek authors he treats as being either too idealistic in their promotion of unity and harmony or disingenuous. In the third chapter, Stanton asks how "Greek intellectuals" conceived of the Roman empire. He concludes that views ranged from full acceptance of Rome as uniting "the whole of the inhabited world" to reluctant admission that "there were peoples beyond the Roman frontier" (p. 90). Yet all agreed that the peace achieved by the empire was commendable.

In the fifth chapter, Stanton argues against the notion of some scholars that monotheism existed "among non-Christian authors" (p. 125), stating that there was "a tendency to assert … [a] harmony or unity," even though "such an assertion went beyond the author's beliefs" (p. 128). Thus, apparent monotheistic statements were in fact the promotion of one specific deity while retaining polytheism. Moreover, god(s) were frequently identified with the universe, which, Stanton asserts, is "explained by … the desire to … have one concept of unity overlapping with another" (p. 146). Regarding the unity of the universe, he argues that belief "in the harmony of the universe" (p. 172) was widespread and often connected to "harmony in human affairs" (p. 173).

Turning to Christian views of unity, Stanton suggests that the NT contains both expressions of unity (e.g., the body metaphor in Ephesians) and disunity (e.g., 3 John; Jude). The author sees the NT as setting the pattern for approaches to unity and handling of disunity among the writings of the Apostolic Fathers and Apologists, describing the handling of disunity in the NT and subsequent writings as "ruthless" (pp. 194–95). Additionally, he sees the advice given by Christian writers to avoid envy and dissension in order to promote unity as parallel to similar advice offered by Greek writers. Whereas he discerns significant overlap regarding church unity between the NT and subsequent Christians, Stanton argues that the NT is not the source of adherence to the unity of humankind nor of the harmony of the universe by some patristic writers. Rather, it reflects a shared heritage with "educated members of the Roman empire" (p. 224).

One criticism mars an otherwise strong work. Stanton's caricature of the New Testament approach to disunity as "ruthless" with very little discussion lacks the kind of careful reading one would expect. Moreover, one wishes he had discussed Romans 5 in more depth in his explication of Christian views of the unity of humankind. Nevertheless, Stanton has provided much food for thought regarding approaches to unity in the first two centuries of the common era. As his nearly fifty-page bibliography demonstrates, he is deeply conversant with both primary and secondary literature on the topic and yet he conveys his findings in just over 250 pages—a remarkable feat indeed.

This book will benefit several different audiences. For students and scholars of the NT, he places NT statements on unity and disunity in their broader Greek cultural context; for classicists and patristics students, he provides a thorough discussion of key approaches to unity and disunity in Greek thought as well as how generations of Christians after the NT received the ideas of the NT and the wider cultural heritage that they shared.

Thomas Haviland-Pabst
One Family Ministries
Asheville, North Carolina, USA

Jarvis J. Williams. *Redemptive Kingdom Diversity: A Biblical Theology of the People of God*. Grand Rapids: Baker Academic, 2021. xiii + 189 pp. £17.99/$24.99

In *Redemptive Kingdom Diversity*, Jarvis Williams states that his purpose is "to provide an introductory biblical and theological survey of God's multiethnic and cosmic redemptive kingdom vision for the diverse people of God scattered throughout the world and for the cosmos … to help God's ethnically diverse people live faithfully together in obedience to him and to his redemptive kingdom vision as they proclaim God's redemptive acts in Christ, love none another and live as bright lights in a dark world … (and) to motivate the ethnically diverse people of God to live in intentional pursuit of God's vision for redemptive kingdom diversity" (pp. 7–8).

Most of the book focuses on tracing the theme of the people of God in the Old (chs. 1–2) and New Testaments (chs. 3–5). After a brief synthesis of his findings in chapter 6, Williams offers "some practical applications to demonstrate a few specific ways the people of God can pursue redemptive kingdom diversity in Christ in the everyday rhythms of life in a racialized society and in an ethnically diverse world" (p. 152). These practical applications address several important issues such as racism, classism, multiethnic churches, and love for one another. Williams argues that the "new chosen multiethnic community in Christ should obey the gospel, be opposed to racism, and be in pursuit of Spirit-empowered love for one another" (p. 151). Addressing matters of racial injustice should be part of the church's mission (p. 154) to love God and neighbor (p. 171).

Two strengths stand out in this book. First, Williams surveys the theme of the people of God in every major section of the Bible. Williams is clear at several points in the book that he is not aiming at a detailed or comprehensive treatment of each section but at highlighting/discussing selected themes as they relate to the people of God (e.g., pp. 74, 106). In doing so, Williams argues that the Old Testament anticipated the redemption of an ethnically diverse community marked by characteristics such as Torah obedience, concern for justice, and love for neighbor (p. 148). Secondly, as an African American New Testament scholar, Williams brings awareness and understanding of issues of race and ethnicity (especially in the US context) to this biblical theological study. In the introduction, he explains how he is using terms such as race, ethnicity, and "whiteness" (p. 3–6) and helpfully suggests a number of resources for further study in this area. It is, however in his final chapter ("The People of God and Orthopraxy") that his belief that Christians must "be rigorous exegetes of both the Bible and our own social locations" (p. 155) is most clearly displayed. His socially located perspectives especially in this chapter, helpfully move us beyond many other biblical-theological treatments of the people of God.

However, while Williams does engage with each major section of the Bible, readers will notice the lack of commentary on passages that are often discussed in relation to race and ethnicity in the Bible (e.g., Gen 9:18–27, the so-called "curse of Ham"; Num 12:1 and Moses's marriage to a Cushite, etc.). Brief commentary or some development on the contribution of such passages would further enrich and strengthen his biblical presentation, application, and thesis in ways that go beyond general comments about the people of God that can be gleaned from other resources. Interaction with other related publications on biblical theology would also have strengthened the overall thesis and situated the book in the context of these other contributions. For example, the biblical-theological treatment of race/ethnicity by J. Daniel Hays's (*From Every People and Nation: A Biblical Theology of Race* [Downers Grove, IL: InterVarsity Press. 2003]) does attempt to address passages such as Genesis 9:18–27 (and others) but it is not mentioned or interacted with, even though Williams refers readers to other works on biblical theology (p. 7). Moreover, while Williams uses the language of the church's mission at various points (pp. 154, 171, 175, 183), popular biblical theological works on the church's mission such as Christopher Wright's (*The Mission of God's People: A Biblical Theology of the Church's Mission* [Grand Rapids: Zondervan, 2010]) and Michael Goheen's (*Light to the Nations: The Missional Church and the Biblical Story* [Grand Rapids: Baker Academic, 2011]) are not mentioned or interacted with even though they would further support the missional direction of Williams's thesis.

In spite of these critical reflections, *Redemptive Kingdom Diversity* is a helpful introduction to the biblical theology of the people of God, drawing attention to a very important theme that is neglected by many other biblical theologies of the people of God. In this way, it makes an important contribution to our understanding of the people of God for "churches, Christian colleges, universities, seminaries, and for any person or any other organization with ears to hear" (pp. 4–5)

David H. F. Ng
Melbourne School of Theology
Wantirna, Victoria, Australia

— HISTORY AND HISTORICAL THEOLOGY —

J. Cameron Fraser. *Missionary Baptism & Evangelical Unity: An Historical, Theological, Pastoral Inquiry*. Eugene, OR: Wipf & Stock, 2021. xx + 94 pp. £13.00/$17.00.

When a book on baptism has two forewords, one by a Baptist and one by a Paedobaptist, it probably merits some attention. When the same book has commendations by Clair Davis, John Frame, Liam Goligher, David Feddes and Kenneth Stewart, the interest levels are raised further. When that same book offers the hope of evangelical union, it becomes almost irresistible!

J. Cameron Fraser was raised in a conservative Presbyterian denomination in Scotland but has spent most of his ministry among Dutch Reformed Christians in Canada. The purpose of this book is to examine the doctrine and practice of baptism with a view to seeking evangelical unity, despite varying practices. He does this by focusing on the "household baptisms" of the New Testament, which he calls "missionary baptism." He argues that, in most Paedobaptist churches, the normal practice is infant baptism and that this has somewhat skewed their understanding of baptism. In missionary situations, on the other hand, where the majority of baptisms are of converts and their families, a somewhat different understanding of baptism develops. Similarly, in most western countries, individualism has caused churches to view baptism in a particular way, whereas in cultures where family and tribe are held to be more important than individuals, a different view of baptism often persists.

Fraser wants to argue that, if the missionary baptism position were to be held, then baptism would be seen in its true light. In such a scenario, adult baptism would be the norm and infant baptism would be seen in that light. To support this case theologically, Fraser looks to the Scottish 19th-century theologian William Cunningham. Fraser notes that Cunningham's view of baptism stands in opposition to that of his friend and contemporary, Charles Hodge, who believed in presumptive election. It also stands in opposition to the view made famous by the Dutch theologian Abraham Kuyper, who believed in presumptive regeneration. Fraser sums up Cunningham's position: "He believed that the biblical and confessional model was of adult (or believers') baptism and that infant baptism, while defensible in its own right, was a modification of adult baptism" (p. 19). Fraser demonstrates that Cunningham was supported in this position by his colleague James Bannerman and by the later Principal of the Free Church College, John MacLeod. Cunningham went so far as to argue that, when the Westminster Divines wrote about baptism, it was adult baptism they had in mind.

Fraser is honest enough to present the case against Cunningham's view of baptism (and particularly his view of the Westminster Divines), as argued by a formidable group of scholars: John Murray, Sinclair Ferguson, Bob Letham, Tony Lane, and David Wright. Despite this, Fraser continues to maintain that, at its heart, Cunningham's view presents a strong basis for a new consideration of baptism. Rejecting the views of Hodge and Kuyper, Fraser presents his thesis in this way: "This study argues instead that a view closer to Cunningham's will help clear up misunderstandings between fellow-believers, and further, that a dual practice of infant baptism and baby dedication will promote the unity of Christ's church" (p. 41).

The remainder of the book consists of a defence of this thesis and a consideration of related issues, highlighting both individuals who have written on the subject and also the practice of the CRC church. There is a particular emphasis on covenant children and the contrasting (but yet similar) ways in which these children are treated in Reformed Presbyterian and Reformed Baptist churches.

It is a very short book, less than 100 pages, but what shines through is a passionate desire for evangelical Christians to be united and for a consensus (or accommodation) to be reached on the matter of baptism, so as to allow that greater unity which he seeks. Whatever your view of baptism and whether or not you are persuaded by the argument, this is a book worth reading.

A. T. B. McGowan
Rutherford Centre for Reformed Theology
Dingwall, Scotland, UK

Bruce Gordon. _Zwingli: God's Armed Prophet_. New Haven: Yale University Press, 2021. 376 pp. £25.00/$32.50.

Since the early Victorian period, evangelical Protestant readers have given the lion's share of their interest in Reformation-era figures to two men: Martin Luther (1486–1546) and John Calvin (1509–1564). There was no necessity requiring this focus; in the preceding age of Enlightenment neither had been well-remembered. But the Romantic-era decision having been made that Luther and Calvin (and not their contemporaries) would be highlighted as representatives of the age of Reformation, there followed the flood of translated treatises, commentaries, and expositions which are still with us (frequently as reprints of Victorian editions). Not so for their sixteenth century contemporaries, who were largely left in oblivion. Today, the very abundance of this Luther-Calvin material from the 1800s appears to buttress the impression of their original 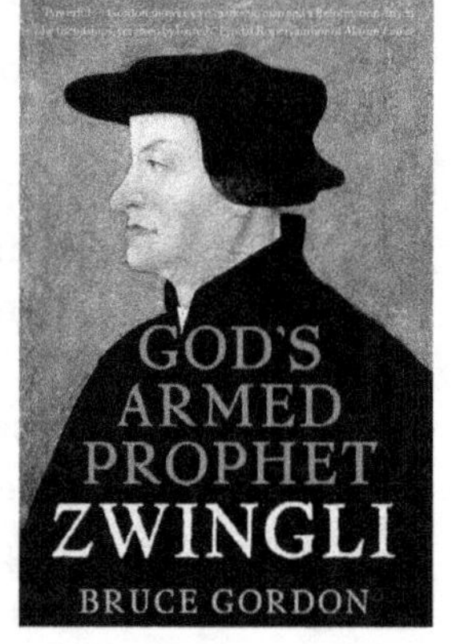dominance. In fact, the prevalence of this literature largely reflects choices made for us by the Victorians. Accordingly, Zwingli (the subject of this biography) had no English-language biographer before 1901 and his major writings were not made available in modern English until that author, S. M. Jackson, produced three translated volumes of Zwingli's writings (1912–1929). Other such Reformation "greats" have waited still longer.

Bruce Gordon, who has already established his reputation in this field with writings on the Swiss Reformation (2002), John Calvin (2009), and Calvin's _Institutes_ (2016), provides the reader with many good reasons to re-assess this "conventional wisdom" about who were the influencers and who were the influenced in the sixteenth century. Zwingli married his Anna before Luther married Katie (1524 versus 1525) (p. 69). The complete Bible, freshly translated at Zurich, was available in Swiss German by 1530; Luther's complete German Bible did not appear until 1534 (p. 240). If we know that John Calvin prefaced his original _Institutes_ of 1536 with an appeal to France's monarch, Francis I, we ought also to know that this strategy had been relied upon by Zwingli, in his dedication of his *Commentary on True and False Religion* to Francis in the spring of 1525 (pp. 148–49). The ultimately counter-productive *placards* (poster-like assaults on the Roman mass) which infuriated the authorities of Paris and other French cities in the autumn of 1534 (giving Calvin reason to flee to Basel), were the product of a Swiss Protestantism which had already been fueled by Zwingli. The very canton of Bern with whose assistance Geneva threw off the jurisdiction of its Catholic prince-bishop in 1535, was a Bern which had earlier been influenced by Zwingli and Zurich to embrace the Reformation. The neglect of Zwingli has thus been unjustified.

For such reasons as these, Gordon makes a powerful case for naming Zwingli as "the originator of what became the Reformed tradition" (pp. 92, 275). No first-generation Protestant reformer stood closer to Erasmus; they only finally parted company over Zwingli's insistence on the perspicuity of Scripture (pp. 81–82). Zwingli was an accomplished musician as well as composer of music (p. 110). We can trace to him the simplification of the church year with an honored place kept only for the Lord's Day, Christmas, and Easter (p. 135). He displaced the medieval Catholic notion that once-yearly participation in Holy Communion was sufficient; at Zurich there would now be four observances of the Lord's Supper per year, in which worshippers would be expected to participate—rather than observe (p. 139). Zwingli was the first Reformer to give extensive thought to the parallels between the Passover meal and the Supper, between OT circumcision and Christian baptism (pp. 140, 170). The 120 priests of Zurich at the time of Reform were gradually re-oriented to a sturdier biblical faith by the ongoing weekday "prophezei," in which sound biblical interpretation was modeled (pp. 142–45). Both Geneva and the English Puritans took pages from this Zurich manual and made this practice their own. But there must be more to it than this, or we would have long been united in our praises of Zwingli.

Therefore, Gordon must be frank in acknowledging that though musically-gifted, Zwingli eschewed reliance on music, religious art and church furnishing. He favored the "piety of the mind" (p. 36); *that* was what was supremely important. These views once inculcated moved the Zurich council to ordain the removal of all such distractions (including organs) from the city's churches; this was not left to mobs. Having rallied those who would eventually lean to Anabaptism by his early learned advancing of reform, he would later reverse himself and consent to their exile or execution (p. 271). Supremely, Zwingli—dying on the battlefield in 1531—was the man who was "a casualty of his own willingness to use force to religious ends" (p. 232). He was also no friend of ecumenical Protestant reform, if that cooperation meant conniving at theological unity with Luther and his followers. His angular writings and behavior in the lead-up to the important Marburg Colloquy of 1529 (in which he was supported by Oecolampadius of Basel) ensured not only the failure of that attempt at Protestant unity, but also brought nearer the political isolation of Zurich in the face of the Swiss Catholic hostility which led to that city's defeat and Zwingli's death.

In sum, Gordon has made a very effective case that we have seriously underestimated the impact of Zwingli and the Zurich Reformation. While the power of its example was felt most in Basel, St. Gallen, Schaffhausen, and Bern (which eventually followed Zurich in siding with Reform), we need to be aware that this movement also made waves farther afield in the south German lands of Constance, Augsburg and Regensburg. It was also Zwingli's teaching (in print) that encouraged the friends of reform in France in the 1520s, when Lefevre d'Etaples was at his most active (p. 151). The reviewer looked for but did not find corresponding attention paid to the legacy of Zwingli and Zurich manifested in the English Reformation. The writings of Zwingli and his Basel counterpart, Oecolampadius, on the Lord's Supper were being taken note of by Catholic authorities in England in the 1520s. Early Protestants such as John Hooper (1495–1554) had read Zwingli in England; he subsequently dwelt in Zurich for a time before returning home under Edward VI. The same was true of early Scottish reformer, George Wishart (1513–1546), who found refuge in Zurich soon after Zwingli's death; he later mentored John Knox. The era of Marian persecution (1553–1558) exposed a larger swath of English Protestants to Zurich under Heinrich Bullinger, Zwingli's successor. The distinctive notes of the Puritans were not simply home-grown.

The reader should not neglect Gordon's timely concluding chapter, "Legacies," and concluding "Afterword" in which he reflects on how the character and career of Zwingli have been variously appraised since his death, right up to and including the 2019 feature film produced by Stephen Haupt (p. 296). By reflecting on Gordon's distillation of past interpretations of Zwingli, evangelical Protestant readers will be reminded of the fact that we, also, have our favored perspectives on the leading characters of that age. If anything, we are likely to have absorbed guarded views of Zwingli—views attributable to Calvin, who we are predisposed to echo.

Zwingli: God's Armed Prophet is both a timely and an important book. The perspective provided by Gordon, the historian, is very sure-footed. At the same time, those concerned to better understand the development of Zwingli's theology will still benefit by W. Peter Stephen's *The Theology of Zwingli* (Oxford: Oxford University Press, 1986).

Kenneth J. Stewart
Covenant College
Lookout Mountain, Georgia, USA

Bradley G. Green. *Augustine of Hippo: His Life and Impact*. The Early Church Fathers. Fearn, Scotland: Christian Focus, 2020. 224 pp. £8.99/$12.99.

Bradley Green, professor of theological studies at Union University, gives evangelical readers an approachable introduction to the life and thought of Augustine. *Augustine of Hippo: His Life and Impact* is another great entry in the Early Church Fathers series, edited by Michael A. G. Haykin and Shawn J. Wilhite and published by Christian Focus. The series aims to provide modern evangelical readers with portraits of early Christian thinkers for the purpose of appreciating their work and connecting the past with modern day Christian thought. This particular entry on Augustine accomplishes that goal. Part biography, part theological essay, and part guidebook, Green's work provides evangelical readers with a go-to source to understand Augustine's profundity and place in the tradition of Christian thought. In under 200 pages, Green manages a feat of brevity while maintaining integrity and thoughtfulness. As far  as introductory texts on the life and thought of Augustine, this will be a go-to source for years to come.

In chapter 1, a brief biography of Augustine is presented, drawn primarily from *Confessions*. This establishes the ground for doctrinal explorations in Augustine, from the doctrine of God (ch. 2) to creation (ch. 3), to Augustine's understanding of original sin and its effects on humanity (ch. 4). Green provides an overview of Augustine's discussion on nature and grace in light of the Pelagian controversy (ch. 5), as well as his doctrine of the church in light of the Donatist controversy (ch. 6). The final chapters of the work cover Augustine on epistemology and learning (ch. 7), Augustine's public theology (chapter 8), and the relationship of Augustine to Protestant theology (ch. 9). Readers are given a select bibliography of primary and secondary sources to enhance their study of Augustine.

Green treats readers with easy-to-read chapters on the significant movements of Augustine's thought in light of various doctrinal controversies of his time. He avoids the temptation of painting Augustine as a mere controversialist. Rather, his theology is brought forth not only in light of controversy but is also nurtured by Scripture and in service to the church. A beautiful example of this is Green's reflection on sin and the need for grace in Augustine's theology: "For Augustine, knowing what we ought to do is not enough. We must also *delight* in doing what we ought to do" (p. 85, emphasis original).

Green helps readers appreciate the nuance of Augustine's thought without unduly placing Augustine on a pedestal. This is represented in Green's final chapter on Augustine and Protestants, wherein he gives a threefold grid for how evangelicals can appreciate and appropriate Augustine's thought. This situates the work for a primarily evangelical audience, which is a strength rather than weakness. Green is not afraid to show the pitfalls of Augustine's thought. For example, Augustine's sacramental theology, particularly his view of baptism, would be an impossible pill for evangelical Christians to swallow. Augustine's view of the visible church in concert with the sacraments administered by its clergy is foundational for Roman Catholic ecclesiology. Not so much for evangelicals. It was this view of the church, in it is evolved late medieval form, that gave rise to the Protestant Reformation. Augustine's advocation of force against Donatists, likewise, should be irksome for evangelical readers, and Green does well to highlight the complicated nature of Augustine's thought on this subject. Green highlights where Augustine's theology serves as foundational for evangelical theology, namely his doctrine of God, his understanding of nature and grace, his epistemology, and his reflection on the earthly pilgrimage of the church, set forth namely in his *City of God.*

Augustine of Hippo: His Life and Impact should be commended to anyone who wishes to understand the legacy of Augustine's thought. Its short-form nature, Green's ability to cut to the marrow of the topic, and the presentation of Augustine's ideas in readable fashion make it the ideal text for readers new to Augustine. Missing in the work is some reflection on Augustine as pastor as well as his contributions to Christian spirituality. While Green does prompt readers to explore these topics in the secondary literature, such discussion may have enhanced the volume and contributed to a facet of Augustine's legacy in need of continued recovery and reflection. Despite this small critique, Green should be commended for producing such a helpful work for new readers of Augustine. Green's text should find itself in courses introducing the life and thought of Augustine, as well as courses on patristic thought and theology in general. It's approachable for students of all ages, and its particular attention to Protestants make it ideal for such audiences.

Coleman M. Ford
Texas Baptist College
Fort Worth, Texas, USA

Stephen Hampton. *Grace and Conformity: The Reformed Conformist Tradition and the Early Stuart Church of England*. Oxford Theology and Religion Monographs. Oxford: Oxford University Press, 2021. 412 pp. £64.00/99.00

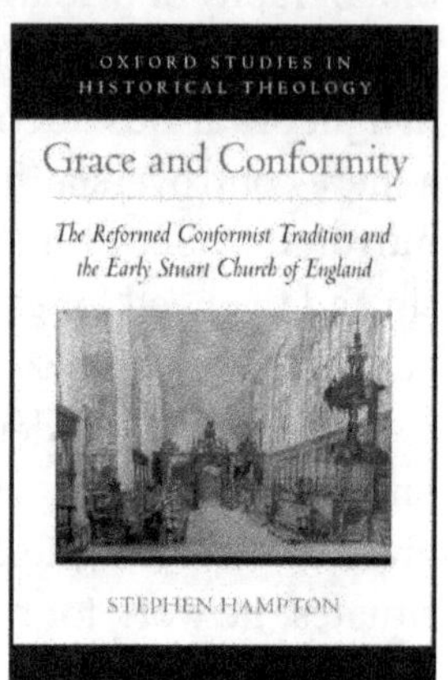

Scholarly study of early modern English theological and ecclesiastical identities has progressed enormously in recent decades with new terms such as "moderate puritan" and "avant-garde conformist" becoming part of a growing historical vocabulary that facilitates more nuanced discussions of the complex and overlapping array of positions evident in the period. Hampton's study represents a significant contribution to this historical conversation by identifying a distinct and significant early-Stuart theological and ecclesiastical identity, namely "Reformed Conformism." This party was "neither Puritans nor Laudian" (p. 24) in that it held Reformed theological convictions with respect to the doctrines of grace yet combined them with what might be described as "high church" ecclesiology. That is, they not only rejected the Presbyterian (Puritan) critique of established English ecclesiastical polity and liturgy, but they also moved beyond moderate Puritanism's merely reluctant acceptance of this ecclesiastical status quo, making selective use of late-Elizabethan avant-garde conformist thought (esp. Richard Hooker) to argue that England's approach to such "things indifferent" (*adiaphora*) had positive spiritual value. Here was a group of decidedly Reformed clergy who championed episcopal polity, established liturgy, and ceremonial piety (along with a positive disposition toward church aesthetics and sacred space) whilst championing the same account of the doctrines of the grace that historians typically associate with Puritanism. With respect to ecclesiology, whereas Puritans made the church center on preaching and Laudians made it center on liturgical prayer, Reformed Conformists envisaged a church that emphasized both.

Hampton's study focuses on ten figures representing the Reformed conformist position, namely John Prideaux (1578–1650), Joseph Hall (1574–1656), Daniel Featley (1582–1645), Thomas Morton (1564–1659), Samuel Ward (1572–1643), George Downame (c.1566–1634), John Davenant (1572–1641), George Carleton (1559–1628), John Williams (1582–1650), and Richard Holdsworth (1590–1649). The breadth of Hampton's selection of representative figures, as well as their evident collaboration, justifies the contention that they represent a broad position that can neither be accommodated to the typical Puritan-Laudian options nor marginalized as idiosyncratic. Indeed, Hampton demonstrates that Reformed Conformists were central players in the key religious disputes of the early-Stuart period.

Chapters 1 to 5 highlight the Reformed Conformist commitment to the Reformed doctrines of grace as well as their prominence in the promulgation and defence of these doctrines. Chapter 1 examines John Prideaux's Act Lectures at Oxford University (1616–1624) as representative of Reformed conformist thought on grace. There, Prideaux offered nuanced Reformed accounts of the absoluteness of God's decree of reprobation, effectual grace, conversion, justification, assurance, and perseverance of the saints, whilst emphasizing that the church was where the means of grace were to be found. Chapter 2 focuses on the English delegation to the Synod of Dort (1618–1619) which initially consisted entirely of Reformed Conformists (Carleton, Hall, Davenant, and Ward). This group exhibited some theological diversity of views, for example regarding the extent of the atonement, yet foregrounded that the atonement was intended for the elect. Chapter 3 examines the responses of Prideaux, Featley, Ward, Carleton, and Hall to the notoriously "Arminian" tracts of Richard Montagu which challenged the Reformed doctrines of grace. Here Reformed Conformists took the lead in demonstrating that the Church of England held to Reformed theology. Chapters 4–5 highlight Reformed Conformist teaching on grace in the aftermath of the 1626 Proclamation which sought to end these disputes on grace, but which was also used to silence Reformed views. Hampton highlights the efforts of Ward and Davenant to ensure that the Reformed doctrines of grace and of justification continued to be propounded in Cambridge University and in publications flowing from her printing press.

Chapters 6 to 8 turn to the ecclesiological aspect of Reformed Reformist identity, and particularly its opposition to Laudian innovations. Chapter 6 discusses Reformed Conformist opposition to Laudian eucharistic innovations which sought to rehabilitate language of "altar" and "sacrifice." Williams and Morton took the lead in demonstrating that these practices represented a decisive departure from the teaching of the English confession. Chapter 7 examines Reformed Conformism's distinct commitment to episcopacy as the divinely ordained form of church government, arguing that the practice was grounded in Apostolic succession. Here, Reformed Conformists took a critical stance toward other national Reformed churches, asserting that other ecclesiastical polities diverged from God's ordinance. Finally, chapter 8 describes the Reformed Conformist defense of the English liturgy, including its liturgical calendar of festivals and saint's days, as giving positive expression and support to decidedly Reformed piety. Much that is distinctive of the Reformed Conformist position is summed up by their representation of the Church of England at the Synod of Dordt, where they not only concurred with the assembly's condemnation of Arminianism but took the opportunity to argue that episcopacy was God's ordinance and that all Reformed churches had freedom to institute whatever religious ceremonies they believed would edify their populace.

Hampton's study will likely establish itself as a standard work in a growing body of literature which recognizes the continuity of a distinctly Reformed Anglican tradition through the seventeenth and eighteenth centuries. (Hampton's earlier study, *Anti-Arminians: The Anglican Reformed Tradition from Charles II to George I* [Oxford: Oxford University Press, 2008], ought to be consulted for the later end of this period). It notably makes the argument of a range of Latin language and manuscript sources available to a wider audience. Students of Reformed historical theology cannot afford to ignore this work. It will likewise be of particular interest to modern Anglicans who seek to benefit from the Reformed theological riches of their own tradition, and access to rich historical examples of reflection on how Anglicanism's distinct churchmanship may stand in positive relation to matters of Reformed theology and piety.

Hampton highlights that his study could be expanded to consider other figures, including James Ussher and Robert Sanderson. It could also be supplemented with respect to the formative influences upon this group of theologians. This reader, for example, detected more of the influence of William Perkins upon the thought of various of these figures than Hampton's study indicates. It is also regrettable that the present work was released contemporaneously with Michael Lynch's focused study, *John Davenant's Hypothetical Universalism: A Defense of Catholic and Reformed Orthodoxy* (Oxford: Oxford University Press, 2021). Lynch's work might have enriched and clarified Hampton's discussion of that theme in Davenant (cf. pp. 99–106). Nevertheless, Hampton's wide-ranging study convincingly establishes Reformed Conformism as a distinct and highly significant early-Stuart party and offers the reader a compelling entry-point into their thought.

Matthew Payne
University of Sydney
Sydney, New South Wales, Australia

Daryl R. Ireland. *John Song: Modern Chinese Christianity and the Making of a New Man*. Studies in World Christianity. Waco, TX: Baylor University Press, 2020. xix + 248 pp. £45.50/$49.95.

John Song (alternatively, John Sung; pinyin, Sòng Shàngjié; 宋尚节) was arguably China's "premier revivalist" during the first half of the twentieth century, calling millions of Chinese to new life in Jesus Christ (p. 4). Around 10% of all Chinese Protestants in Asia made a profession to follow Jesus Christ at his meetings during the second quarter of the twentieth century (p. 10, 82). The typical accounting of Song's life—both in academic literature and in hagiography—generally progresses as follows: John Sung went to Union Theological Seminary where he encountered theological liberalism. Sung became convinced of liberalism. Eventually, after an emotional, psychological, and spiritual crisis, Sung rejected theological liberalism, burned his theology books as "books of the demons," and confronted Harry Emerson Fosdick (Lian Xi, *Redeemed by Fire* [New Haven, CT: Yale University Press, 2010], 141).

Through meticulous archival work and access to newly available primary sources, Ireland successfully challenges and corrects this traditional narrative of Song's life. Ireland relies upon thousands of pages of journals from Song coupled with archival material to paint a more accurate story. In chapter 1, Ireland shows the depth of Song's mental breakdown and the fact that Song likely did not experience an evangelical conversion in the United States. Further, Ireland argues that Song practiced a mystical non-Protestant spirituality with Mary during his breakdown (pp. 19–27). Finally, Ireland suggests that Song did not reject Union Seminary's liberal theology while in the States since he expressed his joy at the prospect of returning to Union Theological Seminary after recovering his health (p. 30). This reconfiguration of Song's biography is the most significant achievement of Ireland's book.

In chapter 2, Ireland shows how Song rewrote his conversion story upon returning to China. Song sought to position himself in light of the broader fundamentalist-modernist controversies, which had reached Chinese Christianity (pp. 38–41). In chapters 2 through 7, Ireland uses the motif of moving from old to new as the foundation for Song's life and ministry. Ireland ties this movement from old to new with a deep reading of contemporary Chinese history, focusing particularly on the May 4th movement of 1919 and its quest for a new China. In chapter 2, Ireland shows how Song recast his spiritual autobiography as a movement from old to new, even though Song had an ostensibly pious youth (p. 44). However, Ireland is right to identify how Song seems keen to paint a particular conversion story that highlights some facts and sidelines others.

In chapter 3, Ireland traces Song's involvement with the Bethel Band as they traveled across parts of China and held revival meetings. Through Bethel, Song's prominence grew considerably (pp. 71–72). Ireland chronicles the dramatic and emotional nature of Song's preaching (p. 75). Song also emphasized moral rigor and the high standards of God's law (p. 76). Interestingly, Song's travels made a marked impact on Bible sales in the regions Song visited (p. 69), though many people who responded to Song's revival invitation did so for the tenth or twentieth time (p. 83).

In chapter 4, Ireland elucidates the urban context in which Song ministered, especially in Tianjin. Ireland argues that Song tried to identify with the precarious lives of his hearers (p. 106). Similarly, in chapter 5, Song outlines the predominant demographic of Song's auditors, namely the *xiaoshimin* or petty underclass (p. 114). Ireland provides a detailed and rich contextual picture of the Chinese culture into which Song preached. In chapter 6, Ireland outlines Song's influence in Singapore (and broader Southeast Asia) as well as the prominent role that women played in Song's ministry. Ireland successfully shows how Song tailored some of his work to either accentuate or attenuate the role of women depending upon his audience and context (p. 149).

In chapter 7, Ireland elucidates Song's public healing ministry, likening it to Chinese shamanic practices (p. 180). This comparison is somewhat overdone as the predominant soil for Song's healing practices likely lies not in Chinese shaman but in the burgeoning Christian faith-healing practices seen in different parts of China and the world—practices Song experienced both in China and in the United States. In the conclusion, Ireland argues that four "features of modern Chinese Christianity"— charismatic figures, faith healing, evangelism, and urbanization—"were first hammered into place" in Song's ministry (p. 206). Ireland likely overstates his case here, but the connection between Song and contemporary Chinese Christianity is still well-taken.

One brief methodological critique is in order. On a handful of occasions, Ireland focuses on sociological explanations to the exclusion of theological ones. For example, Ireland explains Song's insistence that his auditors renounce adultery not on theological grounds but on socio-cultural grounds. Ireland sees that "renouncing such [immoral] behavior was to re-enshrine rural codes of sexual conduct" (p. 132). Other scholars, such as Phillip Koo in his 2018 dissertation on Song's preaching, offer a more holistic account of Song's motivations in moral preaching. Other similar examples exist in Ireland's book where Ireland largely misses theological motivations and convictions. This reviewer is reminded of Edmund Morgan's recollection of the famed Harvard historian Perry Miller, who despite his atheism, insisted that the self-stated theological motivations of subjects must be taken as seriously socio-political motivations.

Nonetheless, Ireland's book is a must-read for any serious student of Chinese Christianity. As Ireland provides rich social and historical context in each chapter, the book is accessible not only to academics but also to interested laypeople. The book is also well written, accessible, and enjoyable to read. Ireland's extensive use of archival materials and primary sources to correct the story of John Song is a triumphal achievement.

Eric Beach
University of Oxford
Oxford, England, UK

Donald M. Lewis. *A Short History of Christian Zionism: From the Reformation to the Twenty-First Century*. Downers Grove, IL: IVP Academic, 2021. x + 373 pp. £28.59/$36.00.

Christian Zionism represents an important movement that is often closely identified with theologically and politically conservative evangelicals, especially (but by no means exclusively) in the USA. Theologians debate the relationship between Israel and the church, the nature of the land promises in the Old Testament, evangelistic initiatives directed toward Jews, and how all these issues and more intersect with eschatology. While Christian Zionism is often associated with dispensationalism, recent years have witnessed the advent of a New Christian Zionism that has attracted scholars who do not identify with classical or even progressive dispensationalism.

Christian Zionism has also attracted significant attention from historians, who have explored the origins of the movement, discussed the role Christian Zionism plays within American evangelicalism, and attempted to discern its relationship to the Religious Right. Regent College historian Donald Lewis, a distinguished scholar of global evangelicalism, is keenly interested in all these questions. He previously published *The Origins of Christian Zionism: Lord Shaftesbury and Evangelical Support for a Jewish Homeland* (Cambridge: Cambridge University Press, 2009). In his newest book, *A Short History of Christian Zionism: From the Reformation to the Twenty-First Century*, Lewis attempts to bring together the best insights of recent scholarship in a coherent narrative. The results are impressive, offering a helpful introduction to a movement that continues to evolve in response to both theological trends and geopolitical developments.

The first five chapters of Lewis's survey address what might be called proto-Zionist tendencies among some of the early church fathers, Reformation theologians, English and American Puritans, and German-pietists. He shows that Christian thinkers debated how the Jews and their land fit within God's purposes long before the advent of dispensationalism. Many theologians believed that there would be a mass conversion of the Jews to faith in Jesus and some advocated a restoration to their ancestral lands in Palestine. This is noteworthy because many scholars identify Christian Zionism and dispensationalism as nearly synonymous. Lewis shows that the roots run much deeper in Christian history.

The middle chapters turn to Christian Zionism in Great Britain and the USA between the nineteenth century and the creation of the modern state of Israel in 1948. Much of this material will be familiar for scholars of Christian Zionism: Jewish-Christian alliances, the idea that God blesses nations that support the Jews, the prophecy conference movements in the English-speaking world, the Balfour Declaration, the English protectorate period in Palestine, Harry Truman's unexpected support for the creation of Israel, etc. But Lewis also unearths additional insights less widely known.

For example, Lewis makes a helpful distinction between restorationism, the idea that the Jews would be restored to the land because of God's promises, and dispensationalism, which is a particular form of Christian Zionism. He argues that historicist premillennialists were often just as inclined to restorationism as dispensational premillennialists. He shows how a number of the English diplomats who first allied themselves with Jewish Zionists hailed from evangelical backgrounds sympathetic to restorationism. He highlights continuities and discontinuities between John Nelson Darby's dispensationalist views of the Jews and those of later dispensationalists such as William Blackstone, demonstrating there was never such a thing as *the* dispensational understanding of when Jews would experience mass conversion and be restored to the land, and of how those events relate to the rapture and millennium. He notes that some evangelical supporters of Zionism ironically became less committed to Jewish evangelism, focusing on their role in fulfilling prophecies about the land and leaving the converting up to God at some point in the future.

The final chapters bring the narrative from 1948 to the present day, including helpful discussions of major Christian Zionist organizations and trends within the movement. Dispensationalists and other non-dispensational Christian Zionists, such as the mainline theologian Reinhold Niebuhr, became key advocates of the nation of Israel and at times influenced US foreign policy in the early years of US-Israeli relations. A growing number of American Christians began to make pilgrimages to Israel. Support for Israel became a key plank of the Religious Right, influencing Republicans and even some Democrats. Evangelicals debated whether and how much to focus attention on evangelizing individual Jews. At times there have been tensions between evangelical support for Jews as a chosen people and moderately antisemitic views of Jewish influence on American culture, even among such notable figures as Billy Graham. Similar to how Russian and later Communist oppression of Jews influenced an earlier generation, the threat of radical Islamic regimes to Israel has motivated contemporary Christian Zionists.

Lewis's survey of recent theological trajectories within Christian Zionism is insightful. Increasingly, Christian Zionism has come to be less identified with dispensationalism and more closely tied to the prosperity gospel promoted in some Pentecostal and charismatic circles. This prosperity-oriented Christian Zionism has been exported more widely to believers in the majority world and exerted considerable influence on the Trump Administration through some of the President's key advisors. Lewis also suggests the New Christian Zionism is new only in the sense that it is not classical dispensationalism. The loose-knit coalition includes some progressive dispensationalists, some non-dispensational restorationists, Jewish converts to Christianity, and even some Niebuhrian Christian realists. As helpful as these discussions are, one topic that seems curiously underdeveloped in Lewis's study is messianic Judaism. While he touches on the topic here and there, much more could be said about the place of this tradition within the wider orbit of Christian Zionism.

Lewis has provided an excellent introduction to the history of Christian Zionism and an important contribution to the scholarly literature. He writes from an evangelical perspective, so his treatment of the topic is empathetic, though not always sympathetic. He understands that Christian Zionism is a modern expression of an ancient belief, deftly navigates nuances within theological traditions like dispensationalism, and helpfully demonstrates how theology, politics, and foreign affairs intersect in recent developments within Christian Zionism. Indeed, Lewis's most important contribution is in making clear that there is no such thing as a normative Christian Zionism, but rather different Christian *Zionisms* that have similar aims, but often for different reasons based on a variety of presuppositions both theological and non-theological. Moving forward, *A Short History of Christian Zionism* should be the go-to introduction to the subject and a springboard to more narrow studies within the field. Highly recommended.

Nathan A. Finn
North Greenville University
Tigerville, South Carolina, USA

— SYSTEMATIC THEOLOGY —

Matthew Aaron Bennett. *The Quran and the Christian: An In-Depth Look into the Book of Islam for Followers of Jesus*. Grand Rapids: Kregel Academic, 2022. 251 pp. £16.28/$19.99.

Christians and Muslims, if grouped together, comprise the majority of the global population. Approximately 55% of the world's inhabitants belong to one of these two great faiths, which, not surprisingly, are missionary religions. Endless interfaith possibilities and permutations exist in the areas of theology, missiology, and geo-politics.

How should a believer of one religion understand the holy book of another? The orthodox Islamic doctrine of *Tahrif* claims that the Bible has been corrupted. On the other hand, how should Bible-believing Christians view the Qur'an? And should these views be held internally, or could they be articulated publicly among Muslim friends and neighbors?

Matthew Bennett provides a great service in responding to these challenges with *The Qur'an and the Christian*. Bennett articulates his plan to address the Qur'an: "In this book I intend to walk the line between presenting my understanding of my Muslim friends and their beliefs in ways that they would recognize as accurate while also being clear to demonstrate where their claims and beliefs diverge from biblical teaching" (p. 9). In that same paragraph, Bennett states his opening position that salvation is in Jesus Christ alone.

This positive beginning manifests in a well-ordered exploration of the Qur'an. The book is organized into three parts: (1) The Qur'an as Revelation, (2) The Qur'an as a Text, and (3) The Qur'an and the Christian. Considering the wide variety of topics, Bennett hones his treatment into a concise 250 pages.

Compared to the Bible, the Qur'an generally lacks narrative statements. Further, the Qur'an does not present itself in chronological order. In fact, the earlier material comes at the end of the book. For these reasons, readers of the Qur'an may find their experience perplexing. And for these reasons, Bennett renders a useful service to interested Christians.

The study of Christianity and Islam produces significant thematic overlap and shared terms and names, such as Abraham, Jesus, the Virgin Mary, John the Baptist, and the Day of Judgment. Comparative religious studies tend to emphasize either theological convergence or theological divergence. Bennett provides clarity to this subject as he concludes, "the teaching of the Qur'an cannot be reconciled with the biblical Gospel without doing violence to both" (p. 13). Such an assessment is frank and fair; orthodox Muslims would agree with Bennett here, and conservative Christians should as well. In another place, Bennett notes that the Qur'an presents a mosaic of biblical references and personalities, but that it is a "subversive mosaic" (p. 140) which undermines the biblical metanarrative. Throughout the book, Bennett maintains a charitable tone, without backing away from his missional emphasis.

Bennett frequently provides the Arabic words which English Qur'anic translations are based upon. This proves helpful, not so much because of the Islamic doctrine that the Qur'an is untranslatable and must be read in Arabic, but because some Muslim translators have at times massaged their translations to render them more appealing to Western readers. Thus, for a project such as Bennett's, it would be expected and required to both provide and explain the Arabic source words under study. Bennett does not clearly state which English translation of the Qur'an he is quoting, though he frequently cites notes from A. J. Droge's *The Qur'an: A New Annotated Translation* (Bristol, CT: Equinox, 2015). Throughout this work, Bennett exhibits a clear mastery of his subject, excellent interaction with Muslim and non-Muslim commentators, and reliable interpretations for his Christian audience.

Qur'anic studies, as a subsection of studies on the origins of Islam, have experienced a seismic shift in recent decades. Bennett wisely engages with the revisionist thoughts of John Wansbrough, who notably suggested the early Islamic history is unreliable, as well as Mark Durie's more recent *The Qur'an and Its Biblical Reflexes* (Lanham, MD: Lexington). One recent contribution to this emerging field not mentioned by Bennett is Daniel Brubaker's *Corrections in Early Qur'ān Manuscripts* (Lovettsville: Think and Tell, 2019). Brubaker's research into the Qur'anic manuscripts contradicts the standard Islamic narrative by contending that the Qur'an was continually edited over centuries until it arrived at its modern format. One other area which Bennett does not explore is the "Qur'an as Poetry," which explains much of its allure for Muslims.

Bennett's finest work appears in the concluding section of the book. Therein, he evaluates one of the thorniest issues in modern missiology—the intentional utilization of the Qur'an in Christian witness. With poignant reasoning, Bennett explains why trendy missiological initiatives, such as "The Camel Method," "Muslim-idiom Bible translations," and "insider movements" tend to do more harm than good in presenting the Gospel to Muslim peoples. Bennett concludes regarding these new Western missional experiments:

> They all include an optimistic view of the Qur'an as a natural tie-in to the biblical testimony. As the previous chapters have demonstrated, however, the Qur'an's history, internal claims, and traditional interpretations fight against such a positive view of its message. As it has been received throughout the last 1,400 years, most Muslims view the Qur'an as a corrective of the biblical material rather than a supplement to it. (p. 226)

Bennett's assessment is spot on, and he is fast becoming a leading, trusted source of information related to Islam and Muslims. Christians who appreciate a theologically robust read will find *The Qur'an and the Christian* well worth their while.

Fred Farrokh
Evangelical Theological College
Tirana, Albania

Paul D. Molnar. *Freedom, Necessity, and the Knowledge of God: In Conversation with Karl Barth and Thomas F. Torrance*. New York: Bloomsbury T&T Clark, 2022. xiv + 354 pp. £33.99/$46.95.

The offerings of modern theology are at the same time various and controversial. They are various in that the lines of inquiry are ever expanding as our world is becoming increasingly self-identified and self-orientated to its own pluralism. They are controversial in so far as modern theology has distanced itself from classic Christian theology, even, at times, repudiating its very essence. With this book, Paul Molnar, a Catholic theologian and professor of systematic theology of St. John's University in New York, offers a foray into modern theology, placing it in conversation with the theology of Karl Barth and T. F. Torrance and demonstrating both the underlying similarities that exist between the various modern theological offerings and the tragic turn away from what is incontestably the heart of Christianity, namely, Christ.

The book is divided into eight chapters. Chapter 1 analyzes whether God's act of creation is a necessary act. He gives special attention to Bruce McCormack's formulation that God's election for us constitutes the Trinity and provides a trenchant reading of Brandon Gallagher's monograph *Freedom and Necessity in Modern Trinitarian Theology* (Oxford: Oxford University Press, 2016). Molnar argues that the fundamental problem with Gallagher's work is that he "attempts to apply what he calls (F3), a third type of freedom to God" which "creates a situation in which one could conceptualize the relations between God and us as relations of mutual conditioning" (p. 34). Rightly, Molnar, with Barth and Torrance, rebuts Gallagher, arguing that God is not bound by any necessity to either create or redeemed sinners. Rather, his love is free and thus arising from spontaneously.

With the second chapter, Molnar places Barth in conversation with Roman Catholic theologians Karl Rahner, Walter Kasper, and Elizabeth Johnson. Here, Molnar is seeking to discern "whether or not the real problem dividing Roman Catholic and Reformed theologians is the *analogia entis* [analogy of being]" (p. 59). Intriguingly, he answers in the affirmative that despite the gains of post-Vatican II with its return to Scripture and Christ as center of theology, the *analogia entis* remains in Catholic theology. Rather, with Barth, Molnar asserts that Jesus must be "the *first* and *final* Word in theological and ethical reflection" (p. 60, emphasis original).

Chapter 3, on natural theology, explores the deficiencies of one of Molnar's theological heroes: T. F. Torrance. Molnar concludes that while Torrance's proposed "new" natural theology is unhelpful, it is ultimately, albeit inconsistently, dictated by his larger Christocentric theological convictions. Chapter 4 contrasts Karl Rahner's and T. F. Torrance's understanding of a non-conceptual knowledge of God, arguing that Torrance's assertion that one only knows God "through God" (p. 158) shuts the door to the subjectivism that Rahner's understanding of epistemology allows.

In the fifth chapter, Molnar focuses on Rosario Rodriguez's defense of liberation theology. Molnar argues that, although "the struggle for liberation" is important, "Christ the Liberator" must be the starting point for the Christian faith in order to avoid "the danger of self-justification" (p. 164). Chapter 6 combats the tendency of feminist theology to revise language of God since traditional language promotes the maleness of God over against the feminine by arguing that "the revelation of God alone in his Son Jesus Christ" must inform our experiences, not the other way around.

Chapters 7 and 8 deal with universalism and pluralism, respectively. The former focuses on David Bentley Hart's defense of universalism, arguing that by making it a theological necessity rather than a hope, Hart undermines God's own freedom. The latter combats that notion that the three monotheistic faiths—Islam, Judaism, and Christianity—are in essence the same by clearly arguing that the Christian faith is not a bare monotheism but a triune one. Helpfully, Molnar suggests that what unites these three faiths is not monotheism but rather their invitation of the adherents of each to believe the gospel of Jesus Christ.

Molnar's treatment of modern theology uncovers a unifying thread: a bent toward experience and the subject and therefore a rejection of the centrality of Christ and the triunity of God. As such, his work is a welcome contribution to and engagement with modern theology as Molnar, with force and conviction, pulls the reader back to the revelation of God the Father in his Son through the Holy Spirit.

For those less acquainted with Barth and T. F. Torrance, Molnar demonstrates how their insights reflect a broader Reformed emphasis in *solus Christus* (not the mention the other four *solas*) and as such, in the hands of Molnar, they provide a model for how orthodox Protestantism ought to engage with the theological deficiencies of our time. Students and scholars of classic Reformed theology will not agree with all his conclusions, such as his assertion, with T. F. Torrance, that so-called "limited atonement" is a Latin heresy. Some readers may find Molnar repetitive at points and grow apprehensive of the long footnotes that permeate the book. Nevertheless, Molnar's deep engagement with modern theology as well as the theology of T. F. Torrance and Barth, combined with clear writing and conviction, makes this a worthwhile read for anyone interested in modern theology and the corrective thereof offered by a capable theologian.

Thomas Haviland-Pabst
One Family Ministries
Asheville, North Carolina, USA

James K. A. Smith. *The Nicene Option: An Incarnational Phenomenology*. Waco, TX: Baylor University Press, 2021. xi + 238 pp. £31.50/$39.99.

James K. A. Smith is an Augustinian philosopher-theologian and is also one of the voices of Radical Orthodoxy. Amos Yong considers him as "one of the most promising young theologians on the horizon today" (In "Radically Orthodox, Reformed, and Pentecostal: Rethinking the Intersection of Post/Modernity and the Religions in Conversation with James K. A. Smith," *Journal of Pentecostal Theology* 15 [2007]: 236).

Though this book is purely academic and loaded with philosophical-technical jargon, understanding the book's structure can serve as an aid. The first half of the book functions as a "methodology" of Smith in explicating continental philosophies and phenomenology to the philosophy of religion. In the second part, readers are invited to journey with different philosophers, including Jean-Luc Marion, Jacques Derrida, and Immanuel Kant.

In the first half of the volume, Smith discusses the development of continental philosophy and the "methodological method" of this discipline. This section explains that the philosophy of religion is not about abstract ideas but rather a philosophical reflection on the practices or liturgies embedded in religion. This is a common argument in his Cultural Liturgies trilogy (published by Baker Academic) and *You Are What You Love: The Spiritual Power of Habit* (Grand Rapids: Brazos, 2016). Perhaps one main difference in this book is that he operates based on the central affirmation of the Nicene Creed (325 AD), which he calls the logic of incarnation in contrast with the logic of determination. The former appreciates our finitude and particularity while the latter sees our imperfections and limitations as violence. One can understand this more in chapter 4.

To understand the background, Smith argues that there is a lacuna in the contemporary philosophy of religion because of the grip of Cartesian thought. Human beings are assumed as "thinking things"; hence, the focus is on ideas or propositions (what we believe), discounting the importance of liturgy, worship, and practices (what we do) in the formation of a Christian and manifestation of religious beliefs. Following his Cultural Liturgies series, he uses liturgy as a source to present a philosophy of religion that differs greatly from the cognitive phenomenon. Smith argues that "religion takes practice," and he emphasizes the appreciation of the centrality of liturgy, whether in Christian worship or the "secular." For him, even non-religious people have liturgies of their own; thus, they remain religious and believers—so to speak. Throughout the book, I observe the repetitive argument by Smith that religion is not just an intellectual phenomenon or "heady" affair. Moreover, modernity's assumption concerning the neutrality of the secular is false since every standpoint has its tradition and biases.

In the second part, Smith expounds on Derrida's "logic of determination." Instead of seeing finitude, interpretation, and embodiment as violence, Smith argues for an alternative rooted in the councils of Nicaea and Chalcedon that affirmed the divinity and humanity of Christ. That affirmation shows the importance of finitude, particularity, and embodiment. The rest of the second part discusses Derrida's proposal of religion without content (dogma) or a "contentless religion" that focuses on justice (pp. 97, 105). Such kind of religion assumes a quasi-eschatology or a "hope that has no hope" (p. 127). Smith concludes that such a vision is a false hope for it lacks ground and object. For example, Derrida's proposal of justice is detached from any embodied particularities. Smith categorizes such quasi-eschatology as "excarnation"—a pure ideal of justice that devalues "embodied particularity" (pp. 5, 6). In short, Derrida fails to present the content of what he is hoping for. In chapter 7, Smith proposes an alternative which is the Christian eschatology as the only hope in post-modernity.

In sum, Smith argues that religion is embodied, not just a composition of ideas. Second, humans by nature are desiring beings or creatures of love. Third, human reason is inadequate to sustain a moral being. Therefore, ethics is not just about decision-making based on reason but more on where the desire or love is aimed at.

The latest work is an impressive display of Smith's understanding of philosophy and engagement with Derrida. This book serves as an extended footnote and a deeper reflection of Smith's earlier work. Readers would do well to acquaint themselves with his Cultural Liturgies volumes to grasp *The Nicene Option* better.

The Nicene Option is heavy reading, but since most of the contents are published articles originally, readers do not need to read the entire book in one sitting. Reading the volume chapter by chapter over a few days or weeks does not make the readers forget the overall theme as long as they are aware of the two contrasting nomenclatures: the logic of the incarnation and the logic of determination. In layman's explanation, Smith contends that we should see our finitude, particularity, imperfection, and materiality as gifts. That argument differs from Platonist and Cartesian dualistic approach to reality which sees our limitation and finitude as problematic.

Francis Jr. S. Samdao
Philippine Baptist Theological Seminary
Baguio City, Philippines

— ETHICS AND PASTORALIA —

Herman Bavinck. *Reformed Ethics, Volume 2: The Duties of the Christian Life*. Edited by John Bolt. Grand Rapids: Baker Academic, 2021. 544 pp. £39.99/$59.99.

A Bavinck craze is upon us. Significant works by Herman Bavinck are popping up with surprising frequency as some of his works are discovered and others are translated into English for the first time. *Reformed Ethics, Volume 2*, is one of the newly discovered volumes. After more than one hundred years it has recently reached the hands of readers, many of whom are only slightly less excited than those standing in line to watch a superhero movie on opening night. Bavinck readers are slightly less likely to wear costumes. John Bolt and his team of translators have delivered an excellent product again, following up on the earlier translations of *Reformed Dogmatics* and the first of three volumes in the *Reformed Ethics* set.

The story of the manuscript of *Reformed Ethics* is the stuff academics dream about. A handwritten document buried in the archives of a library came to light as the result of diligent research. In this case, the discovery was amplified because modern technology enables scanning, photographing, and rapid transmission of images so that the work of deciphering Bavinck's handwriting could turn into the translation project that has become the volume just released by Baker Academic. *Reformed Ethics* required a bit more work than a straight translation because, as the editor notes in the preface to *Volume 1*, the original text was a set of notes, rather than a finished work. The work that is *Reformed Ethics* is a reconstruction of Bavinck's material in Bavinck's style by those deeply engaged in representing him faithfully, even when they dislike his biases. The most significant flaw of *Volume 2* is that the history of the text is not reiterated for those who lack access to the previous volume. It is a story worth retelling, though no doubt there are good reasons for not repeating it.

The whole of Bavinck's ethics is an exploration of what it looks like to love God and live a holy life in every stage of existence. *Reformed Ethics, Volume 2*, deals with the duties of humanity after conversion. Those familiar with the sub-discipline of Reformed ethics will find a familiar approach to moral thinking that builds on the positive and negative implications of the Ten Commandments. Readers careful in their reading will see how Bavinck keeps Law and Gospel together throughout to make a coherent, grace-filled portrait of the Christian life.

This volume is divided into nine chapters, which move from an overview of duties through duties toward God, those toward ourselves, and finally those toward our neighbors. The chapter numbering continues from the first volume, so chapters 13 and 14 frame the concept of duty against the philosophical and theological history within and without Christianity, arguing that in practice there are no morally neutral actions, and wrestling with the possibility of conflict among duties. In chapter 15, Bavinck shifts to duties toward God, focusing on fulfilling the First and Second Commandments. Then in the sixteenth and seventeenth chapters, the Third and Fourth Commandments are discussed respectively. Bavinck's take on the Sabbath is strict by contemporary standards, but he warns against avoiding legalism.

Chapter 18 marks a shift toward the discussion of duties toward ourselves. Bavinck's emphasis is on self-preservation that is balanced by self-denial to prevent selfishness; the body is good and must be cared for. The nineteenth chapter moves on toward concern for caring for the body specifically. Here the need for nutrition and a discussion of alcohol are prominently featured. Chapter 20 deals with the duties toward the soul, which include the prohibition of self-harm, including suicide, the need for chastity, and concern for the development of character. In these chapters it is easy to imagine Bavinck standing before a hall of exhausted, hungry students urging them to take better care of themselves. In the twenty-first chapter, the emphasis is on love of neighbor. Here Bavinck includes discussion of such matters as respect for the dead, passing on a legacy of faith, and the effect of proximity on moral claims.

The recurring feature of all of Bavinck's ethical discussions is detailed research and careful reasoning through a Scripture-saturated world and life view. In his discussion of the ethics of opium, for example, Bavinck uses specific, current data for imports and exports to prove his point. Where appropriate he researches Buddhism and Hinduism as alternative perspectives, even when those views were a tiny minority of his likely audience. Given research methods when *Reformed Ethics* was composed, long before the convenience of internet search engines, Bavinck demonstrates a doggedness in research and a concern for accuracy.

The translators are to be commended for a thorough and helpful result, although the text of *Volume 2*, for obvious reasons, more closely resembles a reconstructed set of notes with more lists and less prose in comparison to *Volume 1*. The précis at the beginning of each chapter greatly benefits those encountering the material for the first time or seeking to remember the gist of Bavinck's argument.

Reformed Ethics is a treasure, even for those who are only marginally interested in the ongoing renaissance of Dutch Reformed theology. These volumes have been sitting as a sort of time-capsule of orthodox moral reasoning, coming now as an antidote to the influences of modernity that threaten to drown out any other sensibilities. Bavinck is distinctly anti-modern while engaging thoroughly with modernity, which enriches his careful, principled approach and helps it transcend its own era. Of course, the fact that twenty-first century scholars are translating this earlier volume make it seem more relevant to our own era than a similar English language volume by one of Bavinck's contemporaries. However, the value goes beyond the words chosen to the content itself.

Andrew J. Spencer
CrossPointe Church
Monroe, Michigan, USA

Jacob Alan Cook. *Worldview Theory, Whiteness, and the Future of Evangelical Faith*. Lanham, MD: Lexington Books, 2021. 344 pp. £92.00/$120.00.

Last fall, Professor David Gushee wrote an article praising various scholars engaged in the "intellectual deconstruction of … 'evangelicalism'" ("The Deconstruction of American Evangelicalism," *Baptist News Global*, 11 October 2021, (https://tinyurl.com/4uz2az7m). Many people would recognize the books he cited: Kristin Kobes Du Mez's *Jesus and John Wayne* (New York: Liveright, 2020), Beth Allison Barr's *The Making of Biblical Womanhood* (Grand Rapids Brazos, 2021), Jemar Tisby's *The Color of Compromise (Grand Rapids: Zondervan, 2019)*, and Andrew Whitehead and Samuel Perry's *Taking America Back for God* (New York: Oxford University Press, 2020). All these works were read widely in evangelical circles and received coverage from media outlets like *NPR*, the *New York Times*, and the *Washington Post*. However, one book on Gushee's list is less well-known, presumably because it isn't written for a popular audience. That book is Jacob Allan Cook's *Worldview Theory, Whiteness, and the Future of the Evangelical Faith*.

An ambitious and scholarly volume, packed with endnotes and drawing on psychology, theology, and critical theory, *Worldview Theory* is not an easy read. Cook structures his work around three influential evangelical theologians: Abraham Kuyper (former prime minister of the Netherlands), Harold Ockenga (founder of Fuller Theological Seminary), and Richard Mouw (former president of Fuller). All three men deployed the concept of *worldview* in their work to make sense of the Christian life and to guide Christian socio-political engagement. In the final chapter, Dietrich Bonhoeffer is presented as a foil to these figures, since Cook sees his work as offering an alternative to the "world-viewing impulse" so deeply engrained within modern evangelicalism.

It's challenging to summarize a work as dense as *Worldview Theory* but Gushee's three-page foreword does an admirable job. Here is its opening paragraph:

> It is a time of profound deconstruction of white American evangelical Christianity. The illusions and delusions, the prejudices and harms of a religious group with whom many of us once identified are currently being unveiled, attacked, and abandoned. Where #exvangelicals have not given up entirely on faith, seedlings of postevangelical Christian discipleship are being planted. (p. vii)

Gushee goes on to say that the idea of a "Christian worldview," which challenges Christian laypeople and scholars to run "all fields of human inquiry … through biblical categories," has dominated evangelicalism for decades (p. vii). However, Gushee now believes (as Cook goes on to argue) that "the 'world-viewing' project needs to be deconstructed both as a way of thinking about knowledge and as a paradigm for forming Christian disciples" (p. viii). According to Cook, "world-viewing" was "tainted by European white supremacism from the beginning" and was "deployed as part of the European colonial project" and so "has always dripped with cultural chauvinism" (p. viii). While evangelicals assumed that their worldview was drawn from Scripture, it was "very, very often" the case that "white/straight/ Protestant/evangelical world-viewers simply imported their social location and its blind spots into 'The Christian Worldview,' with effects sometimes just irritating and sometimes truly disastrous" (p. viii). Thus, the aim of Cook's work is not to *reform* our understanding of the "Christian world-view" but to *reject* it in favor of "interpersonal knowing, based on relationship with God and people" (p. ix).

Cook identifies at least three problems with "the world-viewing impulse," by which he means our desire to understand the world in terms of a "[lean] structure of principles that make sense of the whole, including oneself and God" (p. 13).

First, Cook believes that the "world-viewing" impulse is fundamentally the same temptation faced by Adam and Eve in the Garden of Eden, the desire to "become like God." Cook argues that world-viewing abandons "a social way of being and 'knowing' God and one another" (p. 267) in favor of seeking to know good and evil "'on the basis of an idea, a principle, or some prior knowledge about God'" (p. 266, citing Bonhoeffer's *Creation and Fall*). He similarly writes, "World-viewing does not flow from the reversal of our cognitive rebellion; rather, it *is* the cognitive structure of that very rebellion once we have abandoned our limit as creatures within the created world" (p. 291, emphasis added). World-viewing presents itself as a pious enterprise, which seeks to understand God, the universe, and our place in it in terms of universal, abstract propositions when, in reality, world-viewing is an impious rejection of our creatureliness, an attempt to sit on God's throne and see the world from his divine perspective.

Second, Cook believes that world-viewing simplifies people, alienating *us* from *them* and even us from *ourselves*: "the conceptual form [of 'world-view'] inaccurately represents and sinfully mishandles everyone it imagines while providing exhilarating psychological motivation for the powerful world-viewer to press on" (p. 29). To claim that one person has a "Christian worldview" while another has a "Marxist worldview" or a "Buddhist worldview" is to flatten, and even do violence to, the complexity of every individual. Moreover, world-viewing obscures the ways in which our own identities are multivalent rather than singular. Claiming to have a single, salient "Christian identity" and a comprehensive, coherent "Christian worldview" makes us arrogant: "Misplacing the concreteness of a confessed unity in one's prototypic self-concept offers us too much confidence in our inner unity and leaves us less open to the ways the world, others, and even ourselves do not conform to our neat ideals; in fact, it can even motivate us to avoid acknowledging this sometimes painful reality" (p. 87). This is particularly true of those with a "privileged, normative status (e.g., as a white heterosexual male American)" (p. 86) to the extent that "the unquestioned structural integrity of one's consciousness—conceived under a single salient identity (e.g., evangelical)—in many white persons is, in itself, a kind of social-psychological pathology" (p. 98).

Third, what theologians and apologists tout as "*the* Christian worldview" is actually a product of their social location. Their "Christian worldview" is an amalgamation of their political beliefs, personal prejudices, and social assumptions all passed off as the clear teaching of Scripture. According to Cook, this tendency is evident in Kuyper: "What appeared to [Kuyper] as a rationally consistent, Bible-extending theory of everything actually held together in nineteenth-century colonial race-logic, and his reading of Scripture undergirded his racism and cultural imperialism" (p. 57). It is evident in Ockenga: "Ockenga and company were, in fact, playing identity politics *as evangelicals* [so] their agenda was also influenced by their whiteness, US patriotism, Republican partisanship, sexuality, and so on—the stuff of their Christian tribalism" (p. 141). It is evident in Mouw, who "[carried] the marks of whiteness" in his "approach to resolving the tensions around same-sex marriage" (p. 232). The problem is not that these particular theologians deployed the concept of "world-view" incorrectly. Rather, the very concept of a Christian worldview itself is flawed because it is predicated on an omni-competent world-viewer who will pass off his limited, biased, socially-conditioned perceptions as divine truth.

Of particular concern to Cook is the way that "the Christian world-view" is a product of "whiteness." Cook cautions us that "whiteness" is "not exactly about ethnicity or specifically about skin color" (p. 13).

Rather, it "means involvement in the ubiquitous, transparent norms of reality. It means feeling right, feeling like a well-meaning person" (p. 13). Elsewhere, "whiteness is one prevailing head of an enduring, hydra-like problem generated atop humankind's deep insecurity following the first humans' alienation from the garden and its God" (p. 14). Whiteness is "about the ability to disappear into one's perspective; to claim a cool, rational blandness; to assume self-normativity while only superficially registering the world's contestation" (pp. 182–83). It "appeals to common sense, neutral Christian orthodoxy, and the uninterpreted meaning of Scripture" (p. 183). Crucially, "whiteness" has so thoroughly suffused our culture (and the world via colonialism) that even non-white-skinned people can participate in "whiteness": "Throughout his writings, [Black evangelical Bill Pannell] describes how he began to discover within his own patterns of thought signs that whiteness had colonized his mind" (p. 157). Whiteness, like sin, is ubiquitous and, like sin, it must be exposed and expunged wherever it is encountered.

Like many of the other books in the *evangelical deconstruction* genre, *Worldview Theory* suffers from a serious under-engagement (one might even say non-engagement) with Scripture. Cook's most lengthy discussion of the actual text of Scripture comes via Bonhoeffer's decidedly non-exegetical reading of Genesis 3. Otherwise, Cook's analysis is almost entirely psychological, sociological, or historical in nature. Even when he interfaces with theology, he rarely makes more than general references to "communion with God" (p. 93) or our "creaturely limit" (p. 278). This is a serious short-coming given Scripture's repeated injunctions for us to "be transformed in the renewing of [our] minds" (Rom 12:2), to "love God with all [our] mind" (Matt 22:37), and to "take captive every thought to make it obedient to Christ" (2 Cor 10:5). One might certainly argue that none of these verses is enjoining us to adopt a singular, coherent *Christian worldview*. But, of course, that is the kind of exegetical argument that needs to be *made* not merely *assumed.*

Second, one of Cook's fundamental arguments against "world-viewing"—namely, that it necessitates a hubristic attempt to "see the whole world" from God's perspective—seems fundamentally wrong. One need not see the whole world or arrogantly imagine that one sees the whole world in order to affirm truths about the whole world. For example, it would be arrogant for my 12-year-old to attempt to make pronouncements about how to drive a car. However, if I told my 12-year-old "The emergency brake is on the left. Make sure not to touch it" and instructed him to inform his siblings, then it would not be arrogant for him to believe me and obey me. In the same way, human beings do not need to assume we have a God's-eye view of reality in order to trust what God has told us about reality. We do not need to know all things exhaustively to know some things truly. Therefore, the argument that human beings have arrogated to themselves knowledge that belongs only to God is predicated on the (false) assumption that God has not communicated certain universal truths to us in the Bible. Moreover, Scripture never suggests that there is a strict dichotomy between knowing God relationally and knowing propositional truths about God. On the contrary, it is in part through knowing propositional truths about God that we come to know God better relationally.

Third, there is certainly a danger that we can "overelaborate" the Christian worldview. Kuyper seems to have fallen into this error, by seeing all kinds of political, economic, and cultural beliefs as necessary and obvious elements of "the Christian worldview." However, some minimal Christian worldview seems not only possible but necessary. For example, the Nicene Creed affirms that the universe was created by the triune God of the Bible, that Jesus came to die for us, and that he will one day return to judge humanity. This is a particular way of viewing the world that offers particular answers to basic questions about reality. These answers differ markedly from the answers that would be provided by a Marxist, a

Muslim, or a Buddhist. I don't see how we can avoid calling this minimal set of affirmations a *worldview*, even if it is not detailed. Moreover, Cook alludes to the fact that when theologians like Ockenga and Mouw described the *Christian worldview* they did indeed refer to this kind of *thin* framework shared by all Christians which could then be elaborated or filled in by various *thick* Christian traditions. So even if we fully agree with Cook's criticism of Kuyper's overreach, it by no means follows that we must jettison the very concept of a worldview.

Fourth, Cook's criticisms of "world-viewing" can be applied just as well to any kind of systematic theology and to any universal theological claim, including his own thesis about the sinfulness of world-viewing. Thus, if his criticisms were valid, we'd have to jettison far more than "world-view theory." Cook admits as much towards the end of his book where makes statements like the following:

> Life with God in Christ is not about humans grasping and fulfilling God's lawlike will as uncovered and organized into a comprehensive (abstract) life-system, but about humans living as creatures before the person of God, within their creaturely limit. (p. 279)

> The chief problem plaguing God's people is not unrighteousness owing to their inability to fulfill the Law (as revealed by its so-called elenctic purpose in Calvinist theology), but the intermittence of their openness to the law's Lord while enslaved to its letters. (p. 281)

> Bonhoeffer resists the objectification of God in any sense, including the frequent appeal of some evangelicals to Scripture's verbal inspiration. Scripture as an epistemological resource in the way that modern philosophy has taught us to hold it must be sacrificed to God in faith that it will be given to us, as a way of knowing, as the (sub)text of a conversation between God and humankind. (p. 281)

These conclusions seem inescapable entailments of Cook's reasoning. If we balk at the notion of even a minimalistic Christian worldview we certainly can't accept the minutiae of the Athanasian Creed or the Westminster Confession of Faith.

Finally, much could be said about Cook's understanding of *whiteness*, which tracks with the usage of Willie James Jennings and a variety of critical social theorists like Peggy McIntosh, Zeus Leonardo, and Barbara Applebaum. No doubt, people within the majority "white" culture are more prone to certain blind spots, just as those in minority cultures are more prone to other blind spots. But the term *whiteness* tends to function as a catch-all phrase to describe whatever critical social theorists want to impugn (e.g., objectivity, neutrality, hegemonic power, universality, self-normativity, individualism), even when those attributes are embraced by "non-white" individuals and cultures. Moreover, historically and globally, it's highly questionable whether the purported negative elements of *whiteness* bear any unique relationship to Anglo-Europeans, since (for example) most cultures see themselves as the norm against which other cultures are measured. Lastly, the supposed transparency (i.e., invisibility) of *whiteness* is a convenient defense against any critique; those who question the presence of *whiteness* merely demonstrate its insidious nature and their own captivity to its power. This is a classic, manipulative kafkatrap which forces the listener to either *admit* their colonization by whiteness or to *demonstrate* their colonization by whiteness by *denying* their colonization by whiteness.

Given its academic style and dense content, it is unlikely that *Worldview Theory* will have a significant impact among non-scholars. Its main relevance to pastors is to demonstrate how far-reaching the aims of some scholars within the *evangelical deconstruction* project are. Cook is not merely trying to strip twenty-first century American evangelicalism of its cultural accretions. His aim is to use critical social analysis to reframe the entire theological enterprise. What will be left of historic Christian belief when these deconstructive methods have been allowed to fully run their course is anyone's guess.

Neil Shenvi
The Summit Church
Durham, North Carolina, USA

Chuck DeGroat. *When Narcissism Comes to Church: Healing Your Community from Emotional and Spiritual Abuse*. Downers Grove, IL: InterVarsity Press, 2020. 192 pp. £14.99/$24.00.

Occasionally, a book is published that is "for such a time as this." This often happens when a crisis or something about the current cultural moment invites deep reflection on a particular topic. In this moment, Chuck DeGroat has written a manifesto for our age: *When Narcissism Comes to Church: Healing Your Community from Emotional and Spiritual Abuse.* In this important work, DeGroat provides a lucid and sobering tale of what happens when narcissism invades communities of faith. Written both from personal experience and academic research, this work is one that faith leaders would do well to consult as the world faces a crisis of narcissistic leadership, both inside and outside the church.

The problem with labels is that they often get thrown around haphazardly. Such is the case with the key term in the book's title: narcissism. In fact, DeGroat notes that the use of the term greatly increased "during the 2016 election cycle, when Donald J. Trump found himself in the crosshairs of both amateur and professional diagnosticians" (p. 3). This work, though terse, explores what narcissism is, how it is manifesting in our current cultural moment, and a way forward for both narcissistic systems and leaders. DeGroat approaches the subject with both honesty and compassion: honesty in that he does not shy away from raw descriptions of narcissistic tendencies found in some individuals; compassion in that behind every narcissist is a heart full of shame, fear, and isolation.

In chapter 1, DeGroat argues that narcissistic tendencies show up in churches because many ordinary Christians and pastors live deceitfully by hiding behind a spiritual mask, which is important because "hiddenness is the breeding ground for narcissism" (p. 16). In particular, Christian ministry can be a magnet for narcissistic personalities, for "who else would want to speak on behalf of God every week?" (p. 19). Driven out of insecurity and anxiety, pastors of both large and small churches, begin to see themselves not as humble shepherds of God's people, but of God's human agent of proclamation. In chapter 2, DeGroat invites us into the ongoing conversation between psychologists and clinicians who are attempting to decipher the criteria for narcissistic tendencies. Many symptoms, coming from the DSM-V, would not be unfamiliar to many Westerners: grandiosity, attention seeking, and impairment of empathy and intimacy. Though the DSM-V is helpful, DeGroat argues that narcissism "exists along a spectrum from healthy to toxic" (p. 36). In chapter 3, and in a unique way, DeGroat introduces the "nine faces of narcissism," which are the specific ways narcissism manifests in each of the Enneagram types.

In chapter 4, DeGroat brings the conversation from the clinical perspective to the *ekklesia*, as he discusses two words that seem totally incongruent: *narcissistic pastor*. Expounding Ezekiel 34:1–4, DeGroat argues that narcissistic pastors are those that fundamentally profit from the sheep rather than serve the sheep. This chapter includes a detailed list of the ways that narcissism manifests itself in the life of a pastor. For those who have sat under narcissistic and authoritative leadership, this list of behaviors will not be unfamiliar. In chapter 5, DeGroat explores the inner world of the narcissist's operating system. What drives a pastor towards narcissistic behaviors? DeGroat's answer is summarized in two words: rage and shame. In chapters 6 and 7, DeGroat then helps us to see the problem of narcissistic systems that enable certain pastors to flourish and the problem of gaslighting within these systems. Lastly, chapters 8 and 9 focus on the way forward for healing, both personally and corporately—for those that have been hurt, for the narcissist, and for churches.

As I mentioned earlier, this is a book written for our times. While narcissistic leaders have been around since Genesis 3, one wonders if DeGroat's book would have been as popular one hundred years ago. This speaks to both the necessity of DeGroat's work and the contextual nature of it. This book gives language to many of the abusive, domineering, and narcissistic traits we have seen displayed in the public square of late. As you read this work, you get the sense that you are speaking to a chaplain in the Army who has felt the devastating effects of war both on himself and the soldiers he has served. DeGroat does not write as a pontificating philosopher but as someone who has had close contact with narcissistic pastors, both personally and clinically.

The strength of DeGroat's work is the compassion that pervades the book. When considering the nature of the work, I presumed I would meet a man who has a lot of judgment against narcissistic pastors; what I found was the exact opposite. DeGroat exudes both compassion and curiosity as he longs to discover why people lash out in narcissistic tendencies. Written with severe honesty, you can tell that DeGroat has sat with dozens of men and women, inviting them to discover God's grace afresh, even when they are stuck in their narcissistic sin patterns. DeGroat's posture is a welcome dose of kindness in a world full of outrage.

While not a problem for me personally, for Christians who are cautious about integrating secular counseling theories and psychological insights with biblical teaching, this book may leave some perturbed. As licensed therapist, who holds a PhD in psychology, DeGroat has no qualms about integrating non-Christians sources into his approach, while filtering everything through a biblical and theological worldview. However, in my view, he not only successfully "spoils the Egyptians" but ensures that psychology is interpreted in the light of Scripture, rather than the other way around.

This is a timely book for our generation of Christians struggling with the influx of narcissistic pastors. Young pastors, who may be overly influenced by megachurches and social media trends, would be wise to heed the wisdom of this book. For as an even wiser author has written, "Pride goes before destruction and a haughty spirit before a fall" (Prov 16:18).

Dustin Hunt
Coram Deo
Las Cruces, New Mexico, USA

Gloria Furman with Jesse Scheumann. *Labor with Hope: Gospel Meditations on Pregnancy, Childbirth, and Motherhood*. Wheaton, IL: Crossway, 2019. 151 pp. £14.99/$19.99.

I remember sitting in birth class with my husband and the midwife telling us birth pains were an evolutionary adaptation to encourage ancient pregnant women to seek caves to shelter in to give birth. To be honest, I'm not sure even the midwife was convinced. Thankfully, *Labor with Hope* shows that the Scriptures contain much richer insights and more helpful truths concerning not just labor, but pregnancy and motherhood as well.

As the subtitle promises, *Labor with Hope* is a series of "gospel meditations on pregnancy, childbirth and motherhood." The chapters are brief (generally 4–5 pages) but theologically rich and pastorally warm.

Furman's goal is to lead the reader to worship (p. 19)—to see how "every aspect of birth and motherhood serves to fuel our worship of Jesus … birth is not about us, but about God" (p. 65). The reader is invited to see that "our birth pain is like God's, not the other way around" (p. 92); "our childbirth and fertility is not about us, but about God" (p. 128) and that "God has designed every detail of your child's life to direct you (and them) to worship him" (p. 133). Again and again, the reader is drawn into a God-centered view of what is so often a human-centered topic.

The explicit target audience is women who are expecting (either biologically or through adoption). However, if mindful of this focus, it would also be of encouragement to parents and interested Christians more broadly. Furman has written in partnership with Jesse Scheumann, drawing on his thesis on birth pains in the Bible. This partnership is evident particularly in some of the earlier chapters. Nevertheless, rather than moving topic by topic through subjects which we may deem relevant, the meditations move "passage by passage," jumping back and forth through a whole range of bible passages which mention either physical, spiritual or metaphorical labor or childbirth. *Labor with Hope* is not seeking to give a systematic overview of all that could be said on these issues. Rather it uses each passage as a launchpad to consider how the physical realities of birth point to eternal truths.

At times the choice of passages can feel unexpected. On reflection, this is actually one of the strengths of the book. By allowing the content to be so explicitly Scripture-driven, it means that the book is plush with unexpected theological insights which can really turn on its head what we think labor is about. It is refreshing to read a book on this important topic that is more theological than anecdotal, challenging but still warm. Highlights include the realization that birth pains are frequently used in the Old Testament as a metaphor describing God's judgment (e.g., p. 47) and the implications this has for passages like Matthew 24:8 and Romans 8:22. Furman also provides a helpful consideration of 1 Timothy 2:15 ("saved through childbearing") (ch. 20) and a courageous and compassionate reflection on abortion (ch. 8).

Another strength of *Labor with Hope* is the series of pastoral appeals peppered through the chapters. Furman is winsome and strong in her encouragements to reconfigure our approach to birth and motherhood. I particularly appreciated her gospel clarity on the purpose of having children (ch. 2), her acknowledgment of the pain in parenting (ch. 5), her encouragement to keep up the struggle of raising spiritual disciples (ch. 12), her rebuke of the "mommy martyr complex" (ch. 13), and her challenge to boast in the cross (ch. 17).

In terms of weaknesses, I felt the absence of a chapter on infertility and/or miscarriage. While these struggles are touched upon at various points in the book, their prevalence in life (and in the Scriptures) perhaps provided an avenue along which *Labor with Hope* could be of even more benefit to readers.

There are also a couple of points when perhaps the reader is led too quickly from Scripture to theological conclusions. For example, in chapter 7, I wanted to see more of the workings which linked the depiction of God as our rock in Moses's song in Deuteronomy 32:18 with the incident at the rock at Meribah in Exodus 17:1–7, a link which Furman reiterates in chapters 8 and 10 (see pp. 60, 70). The conclusion she draws is that "there at the rock of Meribah, Yahweh gave birth to his people" (p. 60). Yet even in light of 1 Corinthians 10:1–4, I'm hesitant to see such a strong prefiguring of Christ's penal substitutionary atonement in the words "I will stand there before you by the rock at Horeb. Strike the rock, and water will come out of it for the people to drink" (Exod 17:6). I celebrate how richly the Scriptures find their resounding "yes" in Christ and his cross, yet perhaps we see the anguish of God's birthing of his people (so helpfully highlighted by Furman), not so much in one incident at Meribah, but in the entire Exodus narrative, including his ongoing faithfulness to a persistently unfaithful people. Having said this, I'm mindful that these are gospel meditations, part of the joy of which is bouncing along with the author's reflections.

Labor with Hope may be a book of devotions specifically for women, but in a world which is increasingly confused about what it means to be a woman, that is more significant than we may think. By focusing on the uniquely *womanly* topics of pregnancy, childbirth, and motherhood it sheds light on biblical themes which many may have overlooked, and it invites women to explore their God-given identity by reorientating the very personal experience of birth in a radically Christocentric direction. What a blessing that is!

Annabel Nixey
Crossroads Christian Church
Canberra, Australian Capital Territory, Australia

Elizabeth Hernandez. *Christ and the Marginalized: Bringing Refuge to the Broken*. Eugene, OR: Wipf and Stock, 2022. xviii + 179 pp. £19.00/$25.00.

Elizabeth Hernandez urges that Christian counseling services are a way of urban mission and ministry. The founder and former director of The Place of Refuge, a counseling service in Philadelphia's inner city, Hernandez explains her three decades of work with mainly Puerto Rican women and men. Her counseling agency contextualized Christian counseling using secular resources and accreditation. The book is to equip local church members to counsel, to encourage traumatized inner city Christian believers and others.

Hernandez, a second-generation *puertoricana*, realized how restorative evangelical ministry can be after connecting with a Puerto Rican church in the Bronx in her teen years. She says the key to effective counseling is to understand the personal and social context of the sufferers. Appreciating Puerto Rican marginalization and the continuing influence of their home culture is essential to ministry. In Philadelphia as in the Bronx, structural racism brings severe personal problems (p. 13). History illuminates the Puerto

Rican context. American interactions with the Caribbean island after the Spanish-American War of 1898 revolutionized its governance, religion, language, and authority, encouraging an individualistic identity over a communal one. After Puerto Ricans began to migrate to the mainland after the 1950s, American racism and resistance to assimilation on both sides left them as an underclass (p. 21). As a result of their marginalization, Puerto Ricans have startlingly lower rates of achievement than those of the majority culture. But knowing their story brings empathy. Hernandez tells of a counselor and army veteran whose PTSD was triggered by inner-city experiences. Hyperarousal elicited his anger, but learning something of Puerto Rican history freed him, giving him compassion for those he served.

Hernandez says that many inner-city Hispanics come to counseling with a spirit crushed from a history of suffering. The physical community with littered sidewalks reflects Puerto Ricans who "internalize their subordination through lack of care for the environment or community" (p. 22). Philadelphia police call the area "the Badlands." But Hernandez urges that these are "not lazy people," though "stereotypes of laziness, entitlement, poor character, and so forth" represent a challenge (p. xii). These are mostly American citizens or people who aspire to citizenship. They persist through great suffering. Their community has strengths and challenges (p. xiii).

In Hernandez's early counseling in Philadelphia, she found that most Hispanic clients experienced a strictly clinical approach as incomprehensible. "It has been difficult for me to implement existing counseling psychology while treating psychological symptoms, since my training reflected the norms of middle-class whites" (p. 159). Hispanic clients desired Spanish language sessions, less formality, and professional but warm interaction. Since low-income minority populations in an inner-city setting are traumatized—especially women (p. 96)—her counseling model has five foci: trauma treatment, cross-cultural competency, advocacy, lay counseling, and faith-based intervention.

Gender is a significant ministry issue here. Hispanic women's identity is centered on relationship with family; no category exists for a woman on her own (p. 17). Male *machismo* sponsors a corresponding female *marianismo* under the influence of Catholicism, an identity in considerable tension with an imperative for sexual attractiveness. The result is a madonna/whore dichotomy with clear potential for a madonna/victim (p. 20). Some Hispanic women adopt *hembrismo* in reaction, a strong female identity suited to work settings but creating tension in home settings. Christian counseling can help relieve those tensions by lifting up the biblical vision of women's image-bearing dignity.

Hernandez's experience and analysis leads her to prioritize ministry by local churches. The Bronx church gave Puerto Ricans an awareness that they are "made in the image of an awesome and holy God," "regardless of how secular American culture systematically diminished us as a people" (p. 23). Hernandez saw the sanctification of her culture in the church (p. 9). A case study of one counselee introduces readers to a victim of poverty, physical and sexual abuse, at points a prostitute and drug abuser. But "Maria" experienced conversion, and her "healing will come out of holy relationships, rooted in the sacredness of the gospel … modeling that we can create a space for her of safety and trust" (p. 168). In Hernandez's lens, the greatest assets Puerto Rican communities possess are their religious leaders.

The Refuge counseling model relies on parallel perspectives rather than an integrated model. Chapter 2 lays out the theological schema of creation, fall and redemption to accent the "irreplaceable" role of suffering as witness to Christ by God's people in local communities. But the theology is not connected in chapter 3, where neuroscience is said to reveal trauma's effect on the brain. Hernandez uses models of trauma recovery from Sanctuary and Bruce Perry. Though she calls for an integration of scientific findings with biblical faith, she takes the empirical data at face value. She does not question the assumptions that generate the data or interrogate the relation of brain to mind. However, trauma research functions at least to sensitize counselors to the effects of long-term suffering on counselees.

Chapter 4 tells how the Place of Refuge saw its lay counseling model diffused to government and other organizations. The model developed from work with interns, community presentations, and church workshops. Modules came to include training on listening, trauma, suicide prevention and intervention, cross cultural competency, bereavement, and others—now eight modules for lay counselors. In keeping with the emphasis on the local church as healer, a lay counseling outreach should not create human dependency but created dependency and the thirst for God. Chapter 5 details how churches and agencies are using the Refuge model.

Hernandez's big contribution is a theology of hope in conditions of suffering that may not get much better, but under which one can live with dignity—if the suffering of Christ is the pattern. Those who are convinced that holistic caregiving means joining the fight against socio-economic conditions, including endemic racism, will struggle with the message of this book. But Hernandez has a big God and a sober view of the human situation in which sin persists and redemption is a present reality. For her, recovering from trauma can be much helped when the sufferer gets an idea that God can work through evil for good (p. 152). Historically, the belief that God in Christ is with them in suffering did not disable but empower marginalized communities to fight for justice; the confidence gave them agency. Hernandez's approach does not exclude activism. But in an activist era where many deeply desire structural change, the suffering and victory of God are a counter-cultural message. Hernandez is either preaching irresponsible quietism or equipping others to pass out cups of water so God's people go the distance in truly hard places. For Hernandez, Christian counseling gives heart to hard-pressed inner-city folk. It is a vital element of urban mission.

Ted Newell
Crandall University
Moncton, New Brunswick, Canada

Christopher Landau. *A Theology of Disagreement: New Testament Ethics for Ecclesial Conflicts*. London: SCM, 2021. xxv + 214 pp. £30.00/$42.00.

As anyone who has been part of Christian communities for an extended period will know, conflict among Christians is disturbingly prevalent, causing both damage to those in the church and missional ineffectiveness. As observed in this book, this is at odds with the desire of the church's founder, Jesus Christ, who stated "By this everyone will know that you are my disciples, if you love one another" (John 13:35). While there are numerous books on conflict resolution, there are surprisingly few that seek to develop a comprehensive theology for how Christians should approach disagreements. Christopher Landau (Chaplain at Oxford and former BBC world service religious affairs correspondent) has therefore undertaken an important task in aiming to "establish how New Testament texts might inform a theological ethic of disagreement" (p. viii). In his introduction, Landau explains that he has deliberately addressed disagreements rather than conflicts, noting that while disagreements often descend into conflicts, change at this earlier

stage "might reduce the scale and frequency of damaging disputes and conflicts" (p. xvi). Landau also states his intent to engage with Richard Hays's approach to drawing ethical principles from Scripture in *The Moral Vision of the New Testament* (New York: HarperCollins, 1996). Landau splits the remainder of his book into three parts.

In part 1 ("Disagreement in the New Testament"), Landau systematically works through many passages relevant to disagreement among Christians in the Synoptic Gospels (ch. 1), John's Gospel (ch. 2), Acts (ch. 3), the Pauline epistles (ch. 4) and other New Testament texts (ch. 5). He considers passages that give direct instructions on how to approach disagreements, but also deals with other related issues, observing, for example, the centrality of Christian unity and love in John's Gospel (p. 25), and the importance of godly speech (pp. 63–64, 86–91). He also examines narrative examples of disagreements but is attentive to context to avoid misinterpretation. Part 1 is rich and nuanced with many helpful observations.

In part 2 ("Disagreeing Christianly: Constructing a New Testament Ethic of Disagreement"), Landau aims to develop an overarching theology of how Christians should approach disagreements, flowing from his New Testament observations (p. 105). In chapter 6, he begins by examining the methodology of Hays (and others) for developing ethical principles from the New Testament. (I note in passing that while reflection upon the most faithful means of synthesizing and applying Scripture is certainly important in developing biblical ethics, such an extended discussion seems somewhat tangential to the topic of Christian disagreements.) Landau then helpfully justifies his own approach of using Jesus's "double love command" in Matthew 22:36–40 as an interpretive framework (pp. 117–20).

In chapter 7, Landau returns to the New Testament texts. He notes, in opposition to Hays, the importance of examining apparent contradictions rather than ignoring the more marginal texts (p. 125). He then discusses four instances of apparent contradiction in the New Testament witness of how to approach disagreements and interprets them using Jesus's double love command. These include: how Jesus's varied responses to those challenging him can be unified in his underlying aim to reveal the nature of his kingdom (pp. 126–27); how instructions to either face disagreement or avoid it may be appropriate depending on what is most loving (pp. 127–29); how the church may sometimes seek to mediate reconciliation or exclude individuals, again based on what is required in love (p. 129); and how different styles of speaking to opponents, such as listening or rebuking, can also be applied in light of what is most loving in each situation (pp. 130–31). After a further reflection on Hays's hermeneutic, Landau summarizes the core of his proposed theology of disagreement with the following four New Testament principles:

> Let your speech always be gracious, seasoned with salt, so that you may know how you ought to answer everyone. (Col 4:6)
>
> Pursue godly speech, inspired by the Spirit. (Matt 10:19–20; Luke 12:12; Acts 4:31)
>
> If it is possible, so far as it depends on you, live peaceably with all. (Rom 12:18)
>
> Cultivate the fruit of the Spirit. (Gal 5.22–23). (p. 135)

This list is particularly beneficial in aiding Christians to examine the way they seek to navigate disagreements. At the same time, given the wealth of observations Landau makes in his first section, he could have drawn out some further principles—for example, including the importance of involving others in the church when disagreements are unable to be resolved.

In part 3 ("Ecclesiological Implications of a Theology of Disagreement"), Landau seeks to discuss some ways his "emerging theology of disagreement" could be applied to the church (p. 139). In chapter 8, he argues that the way the church disagrees publicly can undermine the church's witness (p. 141). This is true in principle; however, the areas Landau chooses to examine are controversial. He considers both the debate over how the Anglican Church should respond to homosexuality (p. 142) and the disagreements between Roman Catholic and Protestant Christians (p. 153) to be examples of Christians failing to be united. Landau does acknowledge that there might necessarily be division in the church where there is "teaching that marks a departure from orthodox Christianity" (p. 147). However, he doesn't clearly define orthodox Christianity or explain his position in these situations, and although he states that adjudicating on these issues is not the goal of his work (p. 145), this allows space for understanding him to mean that compromise is expected of Christians in areas where there should not be compromise.

In chapter 9, Landau highlights the importance of seeking the cultivation of the fruit of the Spirit in our lives (p. 163) to facilitate loving disagreements, and rightly suggests that, when facing disagreement, "if both parties take seriously the mutual presence of the Spirit, that theological reality must surely have a bearing on the ethical approach to disagreement that follows" (p. 169).

Finally, in chapter 10, Landau helpfully examines the potential for liturgy to reinforce ethical principles. He acknowledges that liturgy may produce "mere imitation" in some (p. 178) but suggests that if individuals "come before God in worship, open to the possibility of divine inspiration" (p. 178), liturgy and other forms of worship can produce transformation. He then gives the example of exchange of "the Peace" in the Anglican Eucharist service and notes its potential to express peace towards others flowing from the peace individuals have with God (pp. 183–84).

Overall, Landau's work is important and timely and will assist both Christians and churches in developing a theological basis for how to approach disagreements. His thorough and nuanced engagement with Scripture is a particular highlight. Although some sections of the book require discernment (if not disagreement!), *A Theology of Disagreement* is a challenging and thought provoking read, and given the endemic nature of Christian disagreement this book is likely to be helpful for all Christians, whether in vocational ministry or not.

Emma Bott
Grace Evangelical Church Newcastle
Newcastle, New South Wales, Australia

Jonathan Leeman and Andy Naselli. *How Can I Love Church Members with Different Politics?* Church Questions. Wheaton, IL: Crossway, 2020. 63 pp. £3.99/$4.99.

There is a detail hidden in the title of this short book that is key to its wisdom: it is a book about loving *church members*. It's not a book about bringing civility back to politics, nor about how Christians should engage in political vocations, even less is it an argument for a set of political doctrines that Christians should embrace. At heart this book applies the theology of church membership associated with 9Marks to a specific threat to church unity. It isn't a stretch to see it as an appendix to Mark Dever and Jamie Dunlop's *The Compelling Community* (Wheaton, IL: Crossway, 2015). The focus is fellowship not political philosophy and this makes for a disarmingly simple and yet very helpful resource for churches.

There is a sense in which this framing of the problem of political disagreement is politically naive: the authors do not engage with questions about why contemporary political disagreement is particularly fraught, nor with the broader range of psychological and social forces that sort us into political tribes and make it hard to change our minds. We need thoughtful discussions of these questions, but what the authors have given us is more important. Political disagreement among fellow Christians is a problem that rests on foundations in theological anthropology: creation, fall, redemption, the human task of discernment, and believers' obligation to maintain the unity of the Spirit. This theological ballast is often invisible—the bulk of the berg is below the waterline—but it means that anyone who is committed to those truths will find the logic compelling and the solutions not bound to one historical moment. A church member will feel the weight and find wisdom. That's the book's genius and limitation.

The bulk of the book is structured around six recommendations. The first two recommendations invite us to correctly frame the relationship between church members and note the implications for political disagreements. We need to adjust our expectation that church members will all think the same about political matters and that any disagreements in this arena fundamentally threaten our unity. Rather, God designed his churches to be "gatherings of his followers from every tribe and tongue and nation. Your church and ours are communities of former enemies learning to love one another. They are communities of political rivals working together" (pp. 27–28).

Recognizing "what a church is" requires us to see that our diversity—whether in ethnicity, gender, age, or even political affiliation—can bear witness to the reconciling power of the gospel.

> There's been nothing like the church in the history of the world. Every other nation has been united either by powerful men with swords or by family relations, including ancient Israel. Yet now a new nation exists, held together by neither sword nor family but only by Word and Spirit. (p. 28)
>
> You show up at the church's gathering on Sunday knowing your job is to beat those swords into plowshares. (p. 29)

As Christians enact love across boundaries—including those of political affiliation—the church gathering becomes a powerful witness to the peace that Christ has won for us. Love in the midst of this diversity is "gospel-revealing" (to borrow a phrase from Dever). So we lean into the challenge of loving those who might politically offend us because together with them we might become not merely witnesses to our theory of justice but to the Lord. This is the wonderful performance art of the church, the theater of divine glory, in which the manifold wisdom of God is being declared to the cosmos.

It's possible to overplay the loving-across-diversity theme such that there are no matters on which Christians must share a common judgment. Consequently, the authors correctly maintain that loyalty to Christ and the faith that flows from hearing the gospel results in a definite core of Christian doctrine which must be maintained as the basis of church unity. This requires us to make a distinction between "whole church issues"—"the things that we as a church agree a Christian must believe or practice" (p. 30)—and those which belong to the domain of Christian freedom. The latter half of the book is devoted to the thorny business of helping us distinguish between which issues belong to which category. The primary tool for doing this is the distinction between "straight-line judgments [in which there] is a simple straight line between a theological or ethical principle found in the Bible and a political conviction" (p. 40) and "jagged line judgments" in which a biblical principle will require a number of extra-biblical supporting premises or judgments about states of affairs in the world before it yields a political conviction. There is a helpful discussion of how to keep *calibrating* your conscience" (p. 48, emphasis original) in matters of Christian freedom and a stirring reminder to keep focused on what is most important: true justice will come when Jesus brings his kingdom to consummation, so keep making disciples.

It is saddening but self-evident that we need good pastoral wisdom in this area. Even in Australia where I write—which has one of the world's most blessedly boring polities—divisions within churches over the legitimacy of COVID-19 vaccination requirements and extended social isolation rules have been disastrous. Churches and families have split. This has been especially the case in smaller rural communities which we already struggle to resource with gospel ministers. Pastors who are barely coping with the anxiety of shepherding their people through the change and uncertainty of the pandemic are broken by the vitriol from congregants who oppose a decision they've taken about how quickly (or not) to relax mask-wearing or resume in-person gatherings. I can only imagine and pray for those pastoring churches through the febrile heat of American politics.

We need to know how to love church members with different politics. We need to be theologically pastored through these strained relationships. We do, however, also need theological wisdom that moves us to action outside the relationships we have with each other in church. There is a world of difficult issues of justice that Christians must engage with as soon as they leave the church building. As much as the distinction between "straight-line" and "jagged-line" political judgments is true and necessary, it inevitably succumbs to the reality that every specific course of action in the political sphere involves some degree of jagged-line judgment. Therefore, one of the potential dangers of a book like this is that pastors may feel that having said something like this, they have said enough. That will not always be the case. Regardless, beginning with these foundations will be more fruitful than any amount of punditry about the fragmentation of mass media or some other bête noire of contemporary political polarization theorists. For Christians "working for justice, loving the justified" (p. 55) is something which flows out of the new political reality we confess when we pray "your kingdom come" (Matt 6:10) and is nourished as we proclaim and embody these gospel truths to one another.

Daniel Anderson
Lachlan Macquarie Institute
Murrumbateman, New South Wales, Australia.

J. I. Packer. *Pointing to the Pasturelands: Reflections on Evangelicalism, Doctrine, & Culture*. Bellingham, WA: Lexham, 2021. 295pp. $24.99.

I now know the perfect gift for Christian friends in need of cheer as much as challenge. It's this very lovely collection of J. I. Packer's writings, originally composed for *Christianity Today* and now compiled by Lexham Press.

There are twenty-seven mini "Columns" on topics as wide-ranging as jazz and humor and cake and detective novels. But then there are very personal columns on temptation and impatience and criticism and church envy. Plus, there are also thoughts on George Whitefield and C. S. Lewis and John Calvin and his friend, David Jenkins.

Here is Packer on reading detective novels. Should he "repent of time wasted in … light reading? Not necessarily. If overloaded academic and literary people never read for relaxation their brains will break" (p. 7). And on being tempted to buy a book called *The Amazing Book of the Packers in Canada*, "I shall pass up 'The Amazing Book of the Packers' and continue concentrating on the amazing grace of God. The wedding garment will do more for me than the Packer coat of arms" (p. 14).

Packer reflects on his own writing gift, his job as a "plumber and sewage" man (theologian), his hope of heaven and how he would like to be remembered—as a man who "pointed to the pasturelands" (p. 62). Hence the book's title. "I hope to be remembered as a voice (like John the Baptist, crying in the wilderness) encouraging people to think, rather than as a personality whose felt status and charisma stopped them thinking" (pp. 61–62).

After the "Columns" come the "Articles." These range from four to fifteen pages each in length. It's here that Packer comes out swinging on issues like sickness and pleasure and citizenship and the charismatic movement. He is generous to the latter—"when God has brought new life to so many along charismatic channels, it would be perverse conceit on the part of noncharismatics to be unwilling to look and learn" (p. 108)—but not to the World Council of Churches—"the debacle of the WCC" (p. 172). He is defensive of his position on his support for "Evangelicals and Catholics Together"—"ECT is not at all a sell-out of Protestantism, but is in fact a well-judged, timely call to a mode of grassroots action that is significant for furthering the Kingdom of God" (p. 198)—and superb on why he "walked" from his Westminster denomination in Vancouver. The pressure from the bishop to bless same-sex unions opened "a Grand Canyon-wide difference about the nature of the Bible and the way it conveys God's message to modern readers.… [O]ur task is to stand fast, watch, pray, and fight for better things: for the true authority of the Bible, for the 'true truth' of the gospel, and for the salvation of gay people for whom we care" (pp. 234, 238–39).

Packer neatly contrasts and draws lessons from various twosomes, like Whitefield and Spurgeon, Lloyd-Jones and F. F. Bruce, Oswald Chambers and C. S. Lewis. There are *insight gems* as he compares these great men: "Spurgeon's tincture of country-boy truculence and his obtrusive melancholy streak put him behind Whitefield" (p. 16). On Lloyd-Jones and Bruce he writes: "to Lloyd-Jones, Bruce seemed not to be serious about theological truth, while to Bruce, Lloyd-Jones's antithetical definiteness seemed to set restrictions on academic endeavor.… One can see why they found it hard to tune in to each other. But it was a pity they did, since both were such precious gifts to the modern church" (p. 76).

In other chapters, Packer reflects helpfully (from a distance) on "The British Scene" (ch. 28), why traffic flows from Protestantism to Catholicism (and vice versa) (ch. 36) and how we should be thinking of God himself (ch. 34).

His brilliant way with words is a pleasure and a joy. "Christianity is a religion of revelation received; all other faiths are religions of revelation denied" (p. 100). Trials are "therapeutic workouts, planned by a heavenly trainer" (p. 9).

The third section of the book contains thirteen answers to "Questions" on issues like Satan and prayer and sin and Scripture. A fine epilogue from Mark A. Noll closes the book.

Christianity Today and Lexham Press are to be thanked for making these treasures available in one small volume. Discovering that Ecclesiastes is Packer's favorite biblical book (ch. 46—a very moving chapter), why humor saves us from playing God (ch. 18), what bungee-jumping taught him about the Christian church (ch. 23), and how he felt growing up as an "isolated oddity" (p. 242)—all this and more is contained in these pages.

If it sounds as if Packer writes much about himself, it can honestly be said that in each chapter he is subtly or strongly pushing the reader towards Christ in whom are all the riches of the kingdom.

I had the privilege of meeting J. I. Packer a number of times. The last time, he was walking with great difficulty on a terrible hip. But the thing I remember was the joy rising up from his life. This book will do your head good, but it will do your joy good too.

Simon Manchester
All Saints Woollahra
Woollahra, New South Wales, Australia

Bridget Eileen Rivera. *Heavy Burdens: Seven Ways LGBTQ Christians Experience Harm in the Church*. Grand Rapids: Brazos, 2021. 240 pp. £13.99/$19.99.

In one sense, Bridget Eileen Rivera's *Heavy Burdens* is exactly what its subtitle claims: an exploration of *Seven Ways LGBTQ Christians Experience Harm in the Church*. But in another sense, this book seeks to do much more. Put simply, *Heavy Burdens* endeavors to present a new paradigm for the church's theological reflection upon and ethical response to the important but also contentious issues of sexuality and gender.

Several internal and external factors make this a difficult book to review. To use the author's preferred language, this is a book about the experience of gay, lesbian, bisexual, and transgender American Christians. I, however, am a female, never-married, opposite-sex attracted, Australian Christian. Such contextual distinctions have significant implications for the reader. Another complicating factor lies in the amount of ground Rivera attempts to cover. Her explorations—ranging from Ancient Roman cultural mores to Freudian sexual theory, from evolutionary insect biology to present-day queer theory—demonstrate that she is very well-read. However, the overcrowding of her argument left me with the sense of constantly rushing from one significant matter to the next, with little opportunity to absorb, discern and question along the way. As a result of these and other complexities, this review will provide some commentary on the book's main rhetorical strengths and weaknesses, while primarily focusing on the author's essential methodological—and indeed, theological—moves.

As a theologian and Christian historian with particular interests in the fields of singleness, sexuality, and anthropology, I found Rivera's historical analysis of the Reformation's legacy on these matters to be especially masterful. She expertly recounts how the "reformers introduced new assumptions to the Christian imagination—sex and sexuality as integral to human identity; celibacy as unnatural; marriage as a human right; pursuit of marriage for romantic love" (pp. 32–33). In doing so, she skillfully demonstrates the extent to which contemporary Protestantism's questionable preoccupation with these things is equally the result of our theological inheritance as it is of a pervasive secular influence.

Another of the book's strengths lies in the power of its many personal testimonies, narratives and anecdotes. Rivera is eminently successful in persuading the reader to a much deeper understanding of the trauma, distress, isolation, and grief that have come to bear unfairly upon many same-sex attracted and gender dysphoric Christians. I found myself gasping in horror, shock, and outrage on multiple occasions. Many of the stories brought me deep sadness, sorrow, and despair. *Heavy Burdens* rightly confronts the reader with the failure of God's people to have consistently and comprehensively loved many of our brothers and sisters in Christ. It compels the contemporary Christian to reckon with our past, seek forgiveness in the present, and commit to change in our future.

And yet, it is also at this precise point that one of the book's chief weaknesses is exposed. The rhetorical usefulness of personal narrative lies in its profoundly persuasive and emotive pull. However, there is a flip side to this stylistic device—namely, the temptation for an author to absolutize specific personal stories for the sake of their argument. Unfortunately, this is an enticement that Rivera regularly proves herself unable or unwilling to resist. Such a conclusion is evidenced not only by the stories she includes but also by those she excludes. A particularly illustrative example of this is found in her recounting of two pastors' heinous responses to the 2016 Pulse nightclub massacre, both of which are cited as proof that "the gay folk devil remains a compelling and powerful illusion in the imagination of Christians today" (p. 82). While such a conclusion is undoubtedly justified by the imagination of those two particular men, what of all the other Christians who lamented, cried, prayed, and mourned over that evil and its horror? Why are their stories rendered invisible in Rivera's retelling? On what basis are these men and women guilty of perpetuating the gay folk devil delusion and perhaps even of contributing to "the context in which LGBTQ people simply cannot access life-giving Christianity" (p. 192)?

At other points, the author unhelpfully distorts or conflates concepts. For instance, Rivera eagerly expands the definition of gender essentialism from the fundamental conviction that men and women are biologically different, into the systematic "dehumanizing" of people based on their gender—e.g., essentialism says that women can't be good at math (p. 150). Concrete examples from specific American evangelical contexts are frequently depicted as being obviously representative of the Western church, Western evangelicalism, or Western Christianity as a whole. Other inconsistencies and imprecisions occur in discussions about sexual pathology, desire, orientation and identity, and discourse on transgender and intersex experiences.

However, it is essential to realize that the author's trend towards ambiguity and absolutizing is neither accidental nor the result of poor argumentation. Instead, it is necessary to the book's foundational methodological move—namely, an intentional trajectory away from assumed clarity about sexuality and gender and towards embracing confusion and mystery in these matters. This is perhaps the key to understanding the argument of *Heavy Burdens*. And yet it is also easily missed within the dynamic environment of the book's storytelling. As such, it requires both attentive reading and careful analysis.

In chapter 4, we are introduced to Camilla, a woman who has never experienced any sexual attraction (and who therefore identifies as asexual) but whose "relationship to herself [is] as a lesbian" (p. 55). Rivera seeks to dispel any potential confusion amongst readers concerning Camilla's self-identification. She contends that being gay or lesbian "might describe sexual attraction but not necessarily (asexual people like Camilla can be just as gay as RuPaul)" (p. 60). This curious negation of same-sex sexual attraction as an essential component of "being gay" strikes me as a distinctively recent (Christian?) redefinition of the concept itself. Prominent secular gay rights figures such as Andrew Sullivan would seemingly critique Rivera's conclusion, speaking as they do of "gay men [being] defined by our attraction to our own biological sex" ("The Nature of Sex," *Intelligencer*, 1 February 2019, https://tinyurl.com/y3c8bzk3).

Nevertheless, Rivera is confident that to be gay (or lesbian) does not *necessarily* entail the experience of sexual attraction to one's own sex but describes a "broader relational experience … that impacts everything about how any person relates to the world" (p. 60). In this sense, being gay "evades reductionism" (p. 60) and is well encapsulated by the term "queer." Queer people are those who provocatively and confoundingly "reimagine things in ways that straight and cisgender people can't" (p. 61).

This is where Rivera's move from clarity to confusion comes into starkest relief. In broader secular discourse, to be queer means to be human in a way that intentionally defies definition. However, in the theological discourse of this book, being queer means to be a self-determining human being. This is aptly demonstrated through Rivera's assertion that the only way we can know the *who* of someone's identity is by talking to that human person (p. 156). Or, to use a more specific example, it is demonstrated in "believing a person when they tell us their gender instead of assuming that you or I or a microscope in a lab know better" (p. 201).

The importance of this assertion is crucial for understanding the methodological and, indeed, the theological argument of *Heavy Burdens*. What it means for someone to have been made in the image of God is seen to be primarily grounded in that person's unique understanding of their individual humanity, rather than in God's natural or special revelation about our shared humanity. In this sense, the individual becomes their own authoritative theological anthropologist. Determining what it means to be human is no longer a collective endeavor, belonging to the entire ecclesial community and undertaken in the context of our corporate relationship with God. Instead, it becomes a private endeavor, belonging to the individual and lying beyond the reaches of external analysis and appraisal. According to Rivera, what it means to be human defies shared theological clarity and instead embraces mystery.

This leads her to posit a two-fold hamartiological genus: namely, that there are sins of violence and sins of conscience (p. 173). The former sins (such as murder, rape, abuse, etc.) are easily recognizable and rightly condemned by all. There is a legitimate and standard "right" way to think about these sins. However, Rivera's sins of conscience relate to an individual's unique sense of how to embody their own humanity within a discretely personal relationship with God. As such, there can be no common objective "right-thinking" about these things. They are "inherently messy and confusing" (p. 173).

Furthermore, because sins of conscience are profoundly personal and private, they are not open to being scrutinized by other people. This leads Rivera to position grappling with godliness in areas of sexuality and gender as something individuals need to work out for themselves "regardless of the convictions that others might have about the same questions in their own lives" (p. 188). Otherwise put, we should "worry about the sin in our own lives, instead of trying to condemn others for the sins that look 'clear' to us" (p. 170).

So it is that *Heavy Burdens* concludes by envisaging a future "better way" in which all Christians might be able to stand united, even as they believe very different things about gender, sexuality, sin, and sanctification. This better way entails theological anthropology and its ethical application to be a singly personal task rather than a publicly joint endeavor. It requires giving those who identify as LGBTQ exclusive space to work out their own answers on their own terms, rather than insisting that they "need to get gender and sexuality 'right' in order to win God's love" (p. 164). It means ensuring our theological and ethical convictions are a "yardstick for ourselves, not others" (p. 194). To explain the practical force of this, Rivera uses a personal example relating to her own singleness and celibacy:

> For myself, as I've journeyed with Jesus, I've found a traditional approach to sexual ethics to be compelling and am celibate as a result. In addition … I've also found celibacy to be life-giving. That doesn't give me the right to legislate my journey upon the rest of the church … [Why] should my *own* pursuit of holiness take *other* people captive? (p. 195, emphasis original)

At the beginning of this review, I contended that *Heavy Burdens* offers a new paradigm of theological and ethical reflection about the crucial contemporary matters of sexuality and gender. We have seen that the proposed paradigm removes complex consideration about same-sex attraction and gender dysphoria from the common life and mind of the whole body of Christ and instead sequesters it as the privilege and responsibility of those Christians who describe themselves as queer. Unfortunately, such a paradigm is grounded in deeply flawed ecclesiological, anthropological, hamartiological and hermeneutical principles.

Rivera's paradigm also has implications for the integrity of her own argument. In one and the same paragraph, she explains how her approach requires Christians to "embrace that process [of conversation and examination] *together* for the sake of a healthier church" (emphasis added) while simultaneously insisting that we put "in check this *fallen human tendency* to scrutinize" others (p. 138, emphasis added). Given that the critical argument of her book—that the church has unfairly and unlovingly burdened "LGBTQ Christians"—is wholly reliant upon *her* entirely appropriate scrutiny of others' actions and behaviors, it is difficult to see how her methodology is not either internally inconsistent or self-selectively applicable.

Heavy Burdens is an important book. It is important because it powerfully compels Christians to reckon with any sinful attitudes and actions towards LGBTQ people, humbly seek forgiveness, and prayerfully commit to enacting loving change. However, it is also important because it discloses the increasingly powerful gravitational trajectory of contemporary theological and ethical reflection about sexuality and gender away from the common life of the body of Christ and towards the subjectivity of the individual. This too is a very heavy, long enduring, and deeply destructive burden for *any and all* of us to bear.

Danielle Treweek
St Stephen's Anglican Church
Newtown, New South Wales, Australia

— MISSION AND CULTURE —

Elliot Clark. *Mission Affirmed: Recovering the Missionary Motivation of Paul*. Wheaton, IL: Crossway, 2022. 235 pp. £14.50/$19.99.

Jesus's final earthly instructions to his disciples issue a clarion call to "make disciples of all nations" (Matt 28:19). These instructions—particularly the bit about "all nations"—have launched the church into the global task of disciple-making. The church has come to often refer to this task as "missions." Throughout church history, one encounters a hodgepodge of success (i.e., the Moravians) and failures (i.e., the Crusades) in global disciple-making efforts. On the whole, however, research by groups such as the Joshua Project shed light on the enduring advance of the gospel. Despite marked difficulties in penetrating certain blocks of the remaining unreached (most notably in India and some Muslim contexts), mission efforts continue to adjust to geographic, linguistic, religious, and socio-political obstacles in an effort to close the gap on what remains of the task.

Elliot Clark's book, *Mission Affirmed*, not only affirms the biblical foundations for global missions, but also encourages readers to model contemporary missions efforts after the approach of the first missionary: Paul the apostle. For some readers, the idea that Paul should serve as a model missionary might seem too obvious to warrant a new book. Regrettably, from Clark's perspective, much contemporary missiology has challenged the assumption that Paul can teach us about contemporary missions (p. 227). It is this disregard for Paul's approach that has prompted Clark to pen this challenge to those contemporary critics of Paul as a model missionary. He states,

> My concern, and one reason for writing this book, is that we're living at a time in global missions today in which the gospel and faithful ministry are threatened by the tyranny of the urgent. We're driven by a vision of "Mission Accomplished." To that end, we've often sacrificed the important for the immediate, the best for the most pressing. Over the past few decades, as our focus has been on reaching the unreached and finishing the task, we've increasingly prioritized rapid reproduction, with a programmatic and results-driven focus that looks more like Western capitalism and business franchising than genuine Christlike servanthood and faithful stewardship. (p. 23)

For Clark, in contrast to the driving force of pursuing "mission accomplished," the apostle Paul strove for something else—the affirmation of God. Clark argues that the prospect of divine evaluation (and hoped-for commendation) animated Paul's preaching (1 Corinthians 9:27) and also motivated his missionary endeavors (1 Cor 3:5–8; p. 27) In contrast with Paul's theocentric concerns, contemporary missionary methods seem to prioritize anthropocentric concerns, valuing rapid multiplication through the use of almost any means.

Throughout *Mission Affirmed*, Clark calls his readers to assume Paul's missionary objective for themselves: pursuing the commendation of the Father (p. 151). Clark contends that it is only the divine assessment, "well done good and faithful servant" (Matt 25:23), which provides sufficient grounding for the task. Contrary to popular methods focused on speed, a faithful missionary cannot merely chase numbers regardless of the cost (p. 153).

In presenting Paul as an exemplary missionary model, Clark builds much of his argument from his study of 1 and 2 Corinthians. His summary of Paul's methods is drawn from examples he detects within these letters and it is supplemented throughout with excerpts from missions history. Clark's critique of contemporary missionary methods presents episodes taken from Paul's missionary journeys as a foil to help the reader understand that the differences in approaches are not simply misreadings of a particular context. Nor are these differences merely a result of accessing and applying modern social theory to missiology. Rather, some of the methods represent a departure from Paul's example and perhaps—even more seriously—from essential biblical doctrine itself.

The strengths of Clark's focused exegetical work in the letters to the Corinthians could, perhaps, also be seen as a weakness. Though he makes a serious case for Paul as the prototypical missionary from these two letters, his argument could have been strengthened if he would have extended his analysis to other New Testament writings and apostolic examples. Observing the ministries of Peter and Barnabas, for instance, certainly could have reinforced Clark's critique of contemporary mission methodology.

Additionally, though Clark notes that the book assumes that the Pauline approach is worth emulating, he does not take the time to make the case for why the Pauline approach is still valid today. For readers who cut their missiological teeth on Hesselgrave and MacGavran, Winter and Peters, this might not be problematic as Clark would be preaching to the choir. But for the generation of missionaries whose mission theory is expressed in CPM and DMM approaches, the need for a Pauline apologetic cannot be overlooked.

In sum, Clark has done the Church in the West a favor by shining a bright light on contemporary mission practice which at times has adopted both means and ends which value rapid advance and task-oriented completion over and against a Pauline example. His work issues a needed reminder that we must put pursuit of the affirmation of God ahead of all other motives—even in missions and among the perishing. As the Church continues its efforts to see the Gospel penetrate yet further into the many as-yet unreached domains, she would do well to heed the advice that Clark offers here.

Richard Kronk
Toccoa Falls College
Toccoa Falls, Georgia, USA

Warrick Farah, ed. _Motus Dei: The Movement of God to Disciple the Nations._ Littleton, CO. William Carey, 2021. xvii + 352 pp. $26.99.

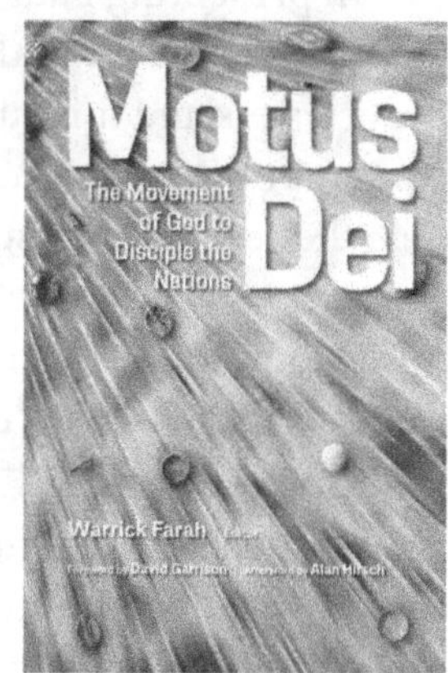

Motus Dei: The Movement of God to Disciple the Nations studies the phenomenon of global Christian movements through the insights of thirty authors whose diverse experiences and areas of expertise contribute to its content. The book describes the phenomenon of movement as when "more than a thousand individuals have chosen to become followers of Jesus Christ or more than a hundred churches have been planted in the third generation" (p. 297). The concepts of rapid multiplication, indigenous house churches, and transformation are also commonly included in the understanding of movement (p. xiii). The book asserts that movements need to be studied in order to elicit common factors contributing to global movements and to consider how to more effectively facilitate them (p. xv).

Motus Dei is organized into five parts that examine movements from different angles. Part 1—"The Big Picture of Movements"—provides an overview. Part 2—"Missional Theology of Movements"—examines the biblical and theological basis for movement methodology. Part 3—"Movement Dynamics"—includes various topics such as ethnic worship in movements, social media as a spiritual interest filtering tool, and diaspora populations as both an opportunity and challenge for movements. Part 4—"Case Studies"—presents contemporary insights into the growth and challenges of movements in four locations provided by teams of local leaders and outside authors. The final section, part 5—"Movement Leadership and Next Steps," offers practical advice to those seeking to facilitate movements or lead workers toward a movement mentality.

Motus Dei has several strengths and some weaknesses. One strength is that the book deliberately addresses criticisms of movement thinking and methodology rather than sidestepping the critiques that have been levied against it. Common objections to movements are reviewed by David Coles in chapter 3 and are addressed less directly by other authors.

A second strength is the wide range of topics presented in the book. Of particular importance is the section on theology, which helps to undergird the understanding of movements and to address some criticisms. Craig Ott offers a balanced investigation of the growth of the church in the book of Acts. The selected case studies present grass-roots information about current movement dynamics and practices. And the chapter by Pam Arlund and Regina Foard outlines an important but often-ignored topic: the role of women in building movements. These various topics contribute to a robust presentation of contemporary movements.

Third, the variety of authors is a strength of _Motus Dei_. The book includes contributions from both scholars and practitioners. In addition, since movements are occurring primarily in the Global South, the intentional inclusion of many non-Western authors adds strength to its exploration. The various authors write from different perspectives that serve to complement and temper one another. One key example of this can be seen in the way that the book defines movements as exhibiting rapid growth (p. xiii), while the authors also wisely caution that "rapid growth is not a goal," that movement principles do not guarantee quick success (p. 40), and that patience is needed in ministry (p. 225). Though _Motus Dei_ endorses movement methodologies, the authors recognize that it is God—not humans—who determines if a movement happens (pp. 40–41, 104). This helps address criticism that simply following movement principles will produce movements.

One weakness of the book is that authors at times overstate their case for movements. For example, in describing house church networks, David Lim writes, "These contextualized, holistic, and transformational simple churches are truly indigenous: self-governing, self-supporting, self-propagating, and self-theologizing. They are planting [house churches] that can be copied by future generations of Christ-followers, so they intentionally avoid denominational churches and missions, which have too often been uncontextualized and have almost always produced marginalized Christ-followers separated from their communities" (p. 89). This quote demonstrates the tendency to praise house churches while criticizing and avoiding traditional churches. Other contributors to the volume echo Lim's suspicions regarding conventional churches and traditional multiplication methodologies (e.g., p. 236). Yet members of the body of Christ are to value each other despite differences. Lim's chapter does not encourage readers to acknowledge the gospel-reality of unity between traditional churches and house churches. Fortunately, other authors do recognize the validity of God's historical work outside of movement methodologies (e.g., pp. 284–85). Richard Grady, for instance, highlights the need to improve relationships between "longer established churches and emerging kingdom movements" (p. 334).

A second weakness is the absence of clear definitions of key terms. The concept of "church," though discussed in the book, should be more clearly defined. Since the definition of a local church is important in understanding, identifying, and counting movements, it is helpful to include an example of how a movement determines when a Bible study becomes a local church. Grady identifies the need for a "more nuanced understanding" of terms such as "church," "discipleship," and "conversion" (p. 335). Specific definitions are not offered, however.

Although the financial aspect of movements is referred to briefly in the book (e.g., pp. 27, 240), this topic requires more attention and precision. Another topic which greatly influences movements and deserves further discussion is the manner in which individuals are discipled, trained, and equipped. Due to the prominent roles that Discovery Bible Studies and mentoring play in laying the foundation for movement growth, one would hope to find a more robust discussion about how these methods facilitate discipleship, leadership training, and multiplication.

Although *Motus Dei* has weaknesses, it accomplishes its purpose of providing diverse research to further the global conversation on Christian movements. As such, *Motus Dei* is beneficial for those currently involved in movements as well as those desiring to understand more.

Thomas W. Seckler
Liberty University
Lynchburg, Virginia, USA

Matthew Kaemingk, ed. _Reformed Public Theology: A Global Vision for Life in the World_. Grand Rapids: Baker Academic, 2021. xii + 336 pp. £21.99/$29.99.

In _Reformed Public Theology_, Matthew Kaemingk brings together global voices from the Reformed theological tradition to consider how the distinctives of the Reformed tradition impact the way Christians think, speak, and live in the public square today. The volume is dedicated to Richard Mouw whose thinking and influence is evident throughout the work. In fact, Kaemingk did his doctoral work under Mouw and he frames the entire volume within Mouw's idea of searching for a "holy worldliness" (p. xii).

Kaemingk introduces the book by outlining the contours of public theology as a discipline. He also clarifies the common intention of the various authors: to demonstrate ways that the Reformed tradition is particularly well-suited to making a contribution to the discipline of public theology (pp. 14–18). The book is divided into six sections. It begins with several chapters addressing public culture, then focuses on economics, justice, aesthetics, and education, and terminates with considerations of public worship.

Rubén Rodríguez exemplifies the strengths of the volume by beginning the "Public Culture" section with a chapter that demonstrates the Reformed heritage to be defined by migrants in order to argue for the importance of the voices of migrant peoples today. Relatedly, this section contains James Eglinton's discussion of lingual diversity, Nico Vorster's juxtaposition of African decolonization writings and Reformed theology. The section also includes fascinating personal and theological reflections of a healthcare worker, Margriet van der Kooi, and a pastor, Cornelis van der Kooi, as they worked in the midst of the euthanasia openly endorsed in the Netherlands. The final essay in the section is its strongest. N. Gray Sutanto reflects on the Indonesian policy of _Pancasila_—a policy meant to protect religious pluralism. Drawing on Kuyper's concept of "sphere sovereignty," Sutanto exposes this policy's limits and abuses, and he also addresses inappropriate Christian responses under the policy.

Katherine Alsdorf's chapter opens the "Public Markets" section of the book by arguing argument that the gospel should have a disruptive and transformative impact on New York City's industries. Lucas Freire follows with a Kuyperian response to Brazil's regulation-heavy market policies. Agnes Chiu concludes the section by making the case from the Reformed tradition's upholding of human dignity for labor unions to uphold and fight for labor rights in China.

The "Public Justice" section begins with an overview of Reformed political ideologies written by Bruce Riley Ashford and Dennis Greeson. The section then moves on to the more specific applications in Romel Begares's treatment of nationalism and violence in the Philippines and Stephanie Summers who appeals for justice in the institutions, practices, and politics in the United States. Of note is Summers's concept of cobelligerency. Though advocating side-by-side with LBGTQ activists might appear initially scandalous to many Christians, Summers appeals to the unifying effect of common grace, while maintain distinctive differences, to provide a powerful ground for Christians to listen and work humbly with non-Christian neighbors for the common good when their goals align.

The "Public Aesthetics" section provides insight into Reformed theology's interaction with the arts. Makoto Fujimura's chapter powerfully blends his personal narrative as an artist with scriptural engagement in the book of Isaiah to produce insight into the materials, influences, and styles that define his art. James K. A. Smith draws from the well of common grace, in the world and writing, to highlight the power and beauty of well-crafted words. Robert S. Covolo retrieves Calvin, Kuyper, and Dooyeweerd to think through how fashion can be a means to push against the cultural zeitgeist and market forces while working creatively in the world as God intended. Eric O. Jacobsen pulls the reader into his expertise to demonstrate how urban planning can both serve to glory in man's idolatry or glory in God through the promotion of human flourishing by seeking the common, cultural, and civic goods.

In the section devoted to the "Public Academy," Bethany Jenkins offers first-hand perspective on the opportunities and difficulties facing people of faith on secular college campuses. Nicholas Wolterstorff follows with a reflection on the academy itself and how the Reformed tradition's promotion of diverse worldviews allows for better scholarship. Finally, Jeff Liou offers a street-level perspective on how Christians interact charitably in affirmation, critique, and correction on Critical Race Theory.

The volume's final section provides the powerful conclusion towards which it has been driving: "Public Worship." Such a conclusion reinforces the Reformed impulse that "the walls between the sanctuary and the street should be made increasingly porous" (p. 18). This section features chapters that treat the sacraments, corporate prayer, and public piety as means by which the people of God carry their public burdens into the sanctuary and lay them on the altar. It is in worship that the displaced finds a home, trauma finds divine concern, the marginalized find belonging, and reality finds clarity.

While the book exhibits significant strengths, the contributors regrettably seem to draw from a limited portion of the "treasured texts" of Reformed tradition (p. 13). Though the authors themselves represent a global diversity of voices, they almost uniformly seem to refer to the same sources found in Calvin, Kuyper, and Mouw. The limited pool of sources leads to a sense of redundancy from chapter to chapter. Admittedly, Kuyper's concepts of sphere sovereignty and antithesis are foundational and therefore unavoidable within the Reformed engagement with the public square. Still, the reader is left to wonder how the broader Reformed tradition—especially the tradition between Calvin and Kuyper— might speak into the problems of the world today.

In the end, however, the book succeeds in what it sets out to do: *Reformed Public Theology* offers robust conversations at the intersection of Reformed Theology and public life (p. 2). The diverse contexts represented by the global voices and concerns of the authors call the reader to humbly sit and listen, while lifting their eyes to see all that God is doing throughout the world through his people. The Reformed tradition truly does have much to offer the Christian who seeks to faithfully and fruitfully engage within the global public square.

Skyler Flowers
Grace Bible Church
Oxford, Mississippi, USA

Brian J. Tabb. *After Emmaus: How the Church Fulfills the Mission of Christ*. Wheaton, IL: Crossway, 2021. 272 pp. £17.50/$24.99.

If you ask missiologists how they teach missions from the Bible, you may get different answers. In seminary, my missiology professor taught us missions using only two passages. Christians make disciples (Matt 28:18–20) so that the end will come (Matt 24:14). Some of my missionary friends approach every verse of the Bible with a "missional hermeneutic" that sees missions everywhere. Others see missions as everything that God intends to do through his people to make himself known—from evangelism to creation care. Still others argue that missions is just about gospel proclamation in the Holy Spirit and to the end of seeing churches established among all nations. The key question is one of approach: how do we constrain ourselves as we read about mission in the Bible so that we rightly handle God's Word?

In *After Emmaus*, Brian Tabb argues that a proper hermeneutical lens for missions is given by Christ himself in Luke 24. Tabb ably demonstrates that Christ traced the relationship between his work, the work of his disciples, and the testimony of the Scriptures in order to provide the church a proper framework for interpreting the Bible both Christologically and missiologically (p. 12).

Tabb begins by examining Luke 24, where Christ emphasized that his suffering, resurrection, and the mission to the nations all follow the script of the Scriptures (p. 23). Notably, only two of these three events had been fulfilled when Christ was speaking. Thus, Christ both reviewed what had happened and previewed what was to come (p. 23).

Drawing on OT quotations and allusions in the NT, Tabb covers how the following are foretold in the Scriptures:

- The substitutionary death of Jesus from the New Testament's use of Isaiah and Psalms 31 and 118.
- The victorious resurrection of Jesus from Exodus, Psalms 2 and 110, Jonah, and Hosea.
- And the ongoing proclamation of Christ's work by his witnesses to the nations from Isaiah and Ezekiel.

In reviewing how these events are foretold, Tabb says Jesus clarified the Scriptures for his disciples and, further, granted them understanding so that they could teach the Bible as he did.

To support this claim, Tabb shows that the apostles used many of the same OT passages in much the same way that Jesus did. Even Paul and Barnabas—absent during the events of Luke 24—learned to let OT prophecies guide their ministry activity (Acts 13:46–47). Additionally, during Paul's defense of the gospel before King Agrippa, he closely followed the same outline Jesus had used (compare Luke 24:44–47 with Acts 26:22–23). Tabb then shows how material in Matthew, John, Romans, and 1 Peter mirrors the emphases of Christ's discourse in Luke 24. Matthew, for instance, shows how Jesus fulfills Isaiah's prophecies that the Messiah would heal and offer hope for the Gentiles (p 177). Therefore, Tabb says, "The church today should adopt the same hermeneutical lens in our Bible reading, for it grounds our gospel message and galvanizes us to participate in Christ's global work" (p 12).

These points lead Tabb to three conclusions. First, like Christ, the church should teach mission from the OT. Second, like Christ, the church should emphasize that the central task of the church is the verbal proclamation of the gospel and making disciples of all nations, resisting attempts to broaden the idea of mission to include everything Christians do in the world. Finally, the church should speak about Christ with courage and clarity, understanding that the disciples of the suffering servant will suffer hardship as they proclaim him among the nations.

After Emmaus is a valuable resource for pastors and missiologists. Tabb invites the reader to join him on a fascinating journey as he plumbs the rich depths of the NT's use of the OT. Overall, his reasoning and handling of Scripture are sound. Tabb has demonstrated that, indeed, there is a proper missiological lens and that lens is provided by our Lord himself.

Moreover, Tabb contributes to the current discussion of mission by demonstrating a vital biblical link between Christology and missiology. Missiologists may find Tabb's use of pronouns with mission a bit confusing (variously "the mission," "Christ's mission," "their mission," or "his people's mission"); however, by linking Christology and missiology he underscores that "Christ's own mission is the basis for his people's mission" (p. 34) and ensures missiology remains subservient to Christ. This link has important implications for missions beyond hermeneutics.

As one point of critique, Tabb would do well to include attention to the NT teaching on union with Christ. While the book focuses on Jesus's Emmaus road conversation as the framework for Christ-centered missions theology, the outworking of missions implications of union with Christ would greatly enhance his arguments in *After Emmaus*. The connection between Christology and missiology is best explained by this vital union between Christ and His people. Our living Savior continues to provide his people power for mission through their union with him. Jesus promises to be *with his people* while they are on mission (Matt 28:20); he chastises Saul for persecuting *him* (Acts 9:4); Tabb does well to show how the OT promises about Christ are appropriated by the apostles as *their own* marching orders for mission (Acts 13:47); and he demonstrates how *Christ* proclaims light to the Gentiles after his resurrection (Acts 26:23). These passages all have greater implications when we understand that Christ lives in us and we in him (Gal 2:20). After all, we struggle with all his energy that he powerfully works *within us* (Col 1:29). According to the Bible, power and motivation for mission are personal and relational, centered on Christ himself who now lives in his people (Gal 2:20).

Indeed, one might find fertile ground for building upon the missiological implications of union with Christ in order to extend Tabb's insights in *After Emmaus* even further. Reading Scripture with Christ and being united with him may reveal the most compelling reason for Christians to participate in Christ's global work: we go to the ends of the earth because our Savior is still fulfilling the Scriptures today—he is proclaiming repentance and forgiveness of sins in his name to all nations—through his church who lives in union with him by the Spirit!

Scott A. Logsdon
McLean Bible Church
Vienna, Virginia, USA